Children's Peer Relations:
Issues in Assessment and Intervention

Children's Peer Relations: Issues in Assessment and Intervention

Edited by
Barry H. Schneider
Kenneth H. Rubin
Jane E. Ledingham

With a Foreword by Willard W. Hartup

Springer-Verlag
New York Berlin Heidelberg Tokyo

Barry H. Schneider
Child Study Center
School of Psychology
University of Ottawa
Ottawa, Ontario
Canada K1N 6N5

Kenneth H. Rubin
Department of Psychology
University of Waterloo
Waterloo, Ontario
Canada N2L 3G1

Jane E. Ledingham
Child Study Center
School of Psychology
University of Ottawa
Ottawa, Ontario
Canada K1N 6N5

With 12 Figures

Library of Congress Cataloging in Publication Data
Main entry under title:
Children's peer relations: Issues in intervention and assessment
  Bibliography p.
  Includes Index.
  1. Social interaction in children.   2. Social skills
in children.   3. Social desirability in children.
I. Schneider, Barry H.   II. Rubin, Kenneth H.
III. Ledingham, Jane E.
BF273.S6C46   1985   155.4'18   85-12660

Typeset by Publishers Service, Bozeman, Montana.
Printed and bound by R.R. Donnelley & Sons, Harrisonburg, Virginia
Printed in the United States of America

9 8 7 6 5 4 3 2 1

ISBN 0-387-96163-1 Springer-Verlag New York Berlin Heidelberg Tokyo
ISBN 3-540-96163-1 Springer-Verlag Berlin Heidelberg New York Tokyo

To Selma, David, Margo, Joshua, Amy, Betty, and Bob

Foreword

Willard W. Hartup

This volume amounts to an anniversary collection: It was 50 years ago that Lois Jack (1934) published the findings from what most investigators consider to be the first intervention study in this area. The experiment (later replicated and extended by Marjorie Page, 1936, and Gertrude Chittenden, 1942) concerned ascendant behavior in preschool children, which was defined to include: (a) The pursuit of one's own purposes against interference and (b) directing the behavior of others. Individual differences in ascendance were assumed to have some stability across time and, hence, to be important in personality development. But ascendance variations were also viewed as a function of the immediate situation. Among the conditions assumed to determine ascendance were "the individual's status in the group as expressed in others' attitudes toward him, his conception of these attitudes, and his previously formed social habits" (Jack, 1934, p. 10). Dr. Jack's main interest was to show that nonascendant children, identified on the basis of observations in the laboratory with another child, were different from their more ascendant companions in one important respect: They lacked self-confidence. And, having demonstrated that, Dr. Jack devised a procedure for teaching the knowledge and skill to nonascendant children that the play materials required. She guessed, correctly, that this training would bring about an increase in the ascendance scores of these children.

Certain themes from this investigation remain contemporary and recur in the current volume. First, Dr. Jack assumed that ascendant behavior (independence in securing play materials, asserting property rights, successful direction of the behavior of others, and successful modeling) has some adaptive significance. The monograph does not include an extensive discussion on this point but the assumption is there nevertheless. Second, it was assumed that ascendance has some stability across time, although the notion of "generalized personality trait" was firmly rejected by Dr. Jack as a theoretical model for preschool personality development. Third, self-confidence was identified as a component of ascendance. Fourth, success experiences, deriving from skilled use of relevant play materials, were believed to be the underpinnings of self-confidence. Fifth, it was thought that a programmed series, not unlike "coaching," would increase the child's skills and self-confidence. Sixth, the hypothesis was advanced that increases in self-confidence will be reflected in increases in ascendance.

No guesses were made in this investigation about the long-term implications of nonascendance in preschool children; only "stability over a short period of time" was assumed. Moreover, no hypotheses were advanced concerning the long-term implications of the intervention. Finally, there is no way to know whether the author would have expected similar results were the study to have been done with school-aged children instead of preschoolers. But the six assumptions/hypotheses/ findings mentioned above continue to concern investigators as evidenced by the essays to be found in this volume.

The 50 years between the publication of this work on ascendant children and the appearance of the current volume was not marked by a steadily accumulating literature. Interest in peer relations and their significance in child development virtually vanished after the publication of Chittenden's (1942) study in which she devised some ingenious ways for *reducing* ascendance in preschool-aged children. World War II greatly reduced the production of new studies throughout child psychology, but the postwar investigators who were interested in socialization turned to the neo-Freudian and social learning theories that emphasized parent-child relations as the wellsprings of social competence in the child. Numerous important studies appeared, culminating in the work that is the most widely cited today: Diana Baumrind's (1967; 1971) studies indicating that "authoritative" child rearing is the best context for the development of social competence among children in Western culture. During this time, the only major contributions to an improved understanding of child-child relations dealt with group formation and functioning (Sherif, Harvey, White, Hood, & Sherif, 1961; Lippitt, Polansky, & Rosen, 1952). Almost 30 years elapsed without a major substantive investigation concerning variations in peer relations, their predictive significance, and the desirability of intervention in certain cases.

Nevertheless, there were some important stirrings of interest in these questions toward the end of the 1950s. These produced some improvements in sociometric assessment and it seems to me now that the work of Mary Northway, Norman Gronlund, Helen Marshall, and Boyd McCandless should be recognized as important antecedents of the current activity in this area. Not only was measurement improved, but those of us working somewhat later were able to demonstrate more clearly than earlier investigators that these assessments have a certain validity. Nowadays, this earlier work seems crude and undifferentiated. The restricted choices required by the picture sociometric (McCandless & Marshall, 1957) have been replaced with more sophisticated ratings and nominations procedures and the once-dramatic discovery that we could differentiate "popular" from "rejected" four-year-olds has been replaced with the important discoveries of "neglected" and "controversial" children. But one of the notable themes in the current collection is that even these categories have their limitations in identifying children at risk in social development.

Activity in this research area was sporadic until a decade later when three types of investigations began to suggest that child-child relations may be more important in childhood socialization than had been realized. First, Gerald Patterson, myself, and others conducted a series of process-oriented studies outlining the various mechanisms through which children socialize one another. Second, Edward Mueller, Carol Eckerman, and others found infants and toddlers to be more sophisticated in relations with other children than had been appreciated previously. Third, Merrill Roff and Emery Cowen published results from two longitudinal studies demonstrating that difficulties in peer relations among school-aged children were predictive of serious difficulties in later development (see Hartup, 1983, for relevant references). But it remained for investigators working within the last decade to extend this work significantly into the areas of clinical assessment and intervention. And it is the thoughts and findings resulting from this effort that are summarized in this book.

Here are the things that readers should look for: First, the authors have engaged in stocktaking. For example, how well has sociometric status worked as an index of social competence? How well have the interventions worked? Have some worked better than others? Are operant procedures more or less effective than cognitive procedures? Are the results more promising with children of certain ages than others? Do classroom interventions generalize to other settings? What populations are best served by which interventions? There is considerable merit to this collection as a summary of the existing literature.

Second, the authors raise a variety of new issues—in some instances, issues that have been inherited from earlier investigators. For example, most of the contributors are no longer content to assume that frequency of social contacts or general sociometric indices provide sufficiently differentiated diagnostic measures. Too much heterogeneity is encompassed by even the most finely calibrated assessment schemes of this sort and too little is revealed about the processes underlying these classifications. "Nonascendance" and "social withdrawal" are questioned increasingly as diagnostic categories and it has also become necessary to distinguish between assertive and aggressive children in identifying those who are at risk in social development. In short, these essays provide a stimulating and differentiated "new look" at the assessment of social competence in children.

Third, the investigators have challenged certain basic assumptions: Do children with poor peer relations, in fact, lack social skills? As it turns out, the answer depends on the context in which peer relations are measured and the social skills in question. One cannot select relevant social skills without considering the situation in which the child's behavior is assessed. Certain general elements in effective peer interaction have been documented (e.g., entry skills) and individual assessments of these skills have been validated. Strong interest is also expressed in the child's acquisition and utilization of social information and their role in social adaptation. But Dr. Jack's assertions seem to have contained considerable wisdom; assessment and intervention need to be both individualized and contextually relevant in order to be most effective.

Fourth, the "self-system" emerges as a key construct in these essays. No one, 10 years ago, gave much attention to self-knowledge or self-evaluation in measuring the child's social competence. But essays in this book provide impressive evidence that the development of the self constitutes a central orientation in personality development. Isolate children turn out not to be disliked or socially incompetent so much as negative about their own competence; lonely children are especially likely to view social failures as internally rather than externally caused; and patterns of acceptance and rejection among school-aged children can be mapped onto characteristic causal attributions. Increasingly, then, the evidence suggests that both peer assessment and intervention efforts need to be anchored phenomenologically.

Fifth, this volume contains some hints about things to come. Recognition is given, for example, to the observation that friendships may differentiate troubled and nontroubled children. To date, investigators have been more concerned with friendliness than with friendships in their assessment and intervention studies. Yet friendships are the contexts within which social skills are acquired, are important cognitive and emotional resources, and serve as templates for the child's construction of notions about intimacy and commitment—notions that have important implications for future relationships. Close relationships, and their importance in childhood socialization, have received too little attention in the social skills literature. Fortunately, that situation seems to be coming to an end.

Sixth, assessment and intervention work seems to have acquired a more developmental orientation. Curiously, neither age differences nor developmental change have received much attention in this area. Developmental demands have not routinely been used as criteria in assessing children's social skills, the more widely used theoretical models (e.g., instrumental conditioning, information processing) have not been utilized developmentally, and intervention strategies have not been tested with children of different ages. This state of affairs has been lamentable, not only because good outcome studies are lacking but because developmental considerations would seem essential to effective assessment and intervention work with children. This situation is changing: This volume contains important longitudinal data on social isolation in early and middle childhood as well as several interesting cross-sectional studies.

Thus, in this volume, the reader will encounter old wine in new bottles— with the flavor much improved. New vintages are also well represented in the collection. And, finally, there is some indication that next year's harvest will be a good one.

References

Baumrind, D. (1967). Child care practices anteceding 3 patterns of preschool behavior. *Genetic Psychology Monographs*, *75*, 43–88.

Baumrind, D. (1971). Current patterns of parental authority. *Developmental Psychology Monograph*, *4*(1, Part 2).

Chittenden, G. E. (1942). An experimental study in measuring and modifying assertive behavior in young children. *Monographs of the Society for Research in Child Development*, *7* (*1*, Serial No. 31).

Hartup, W. W. (1983). Peer relations. In P. H. Mussen (Series Ed.), E. M. Hetherington (Vol. Ed.), *Handbook of child psychology*, Vol. 4, *Socialization, personality, and social development* (pp. 103–196). New York: Wiley.

Jack, L. (1934). An experimental study of ascendant behavior in preschool children. *University of Iowa Studies in Child Welfare*, *9*, No. 3, 7–65.

Lippitt, R., Polansky, N., & Rosen, S. (1952). The dynamics of power: A field study of social influence in groups of children. *Human Relations*, *5*, 37–64.

McCandless, B. R., & Marshall, H. R. (1957). A picture sociometric technique for preschool children and its relation to teacher judgments of friendship. *Child Development*, *28*, 421–425.

Page, M. L. (1936). The modification of ascendant behavior in preschool children. *University of Iowa Studies in Child Welfare*, *12*, Whole No. 3.

Sherif, M., Harvey, O. J., White, B. J., Hood, W. R., & Sherif, C. W. (1961). *Inter-group conflict and cooperation: The Robbers Cave experiment*. Norman, OK: University of Oklahoma Press.

Preface

Social skills have been seen as the nexus between the individual and the environment (Phillips, 1978), the tools used to initiate and sustain the peer relations that are a vital part of our psychological well-being. Over the years, research has left little doubt as to the significance of social competence for general adaptation. Clinicians and educators have become increasingly and appropriately concerned about the welfare of children deficient in social skills. However, the clinical application of research findings has proven difficult because of the sheer number of studies done and because of the lack of integration in the area. While many methods to assess children's social functioning have been proposed, few attempts have been made to explore the comparative value and consequences of each approach. Evaluations of intervention efforts have used vastly dissimilar methodologies developed to determine the attainment of related but unidentical outcomes. The bottom line is that to discern clearly how helpful we can be to the socially unskilled child is not an easy enterprise, though a degree of optimism does not seem unwarranted.

The resurgence of interest in the area of children's peer relations has inspired a myriad of basic and applied investigations conducted by scholars of various disciplines and theoretical persuasions. Their labors have greatly expanded knowledge of children's social behavior and multiplied the ways in which it can be conceptualized. While the importance of these contributions should not be minimized, it is premature to presume that we have resolved all of the ambiguities that impede diagnostic and intervention endeavors. We maintain, furthermore, that prevailing procedures in the assessment and training of children's social skills have not fully capitalized on the current data base. From this perspective, it is not surprising that social skills training is not always successful. Indeed, the degree of success it has achieved could even be considered paradoxical.

The purpose of this volume is to strengthen the ligament that connects social skills assessment and training to the emerging psychology of children's social behavior. The chapters are organized around four major issues: what elements should be included in social skills training, how should we assess the components, who should receive social skills training, and what are the optimal procedures for carrying out such training.

In Part I, Dodge (Chapter 1), Hops and Finch (Chapter 2), and Furman and Robbins (Chapter 3) discuss the factors that describe the construct of social competence. Dodge presents a model of the components of social interaction that suggests that children's social difficulties can arise from a variety of factors, including cognitive behavioral, situational, and transactional variables. Hops and Finch indicate that phenomena such as motor and language development and parent-child relations make essential contributions to social competence. These writers present a striking argument that social skills researchers have previously ignored these developmental factors and have focused their concern instead on the child's display of problematic social behaviors. Hops and Finch, as well as Furman and Robbins, suggest that this singular focus has oversimplified the construct of social competence. Furman and Robbins point to the importance of studying different kinds of social relationships within and beyond the realm of peer relations.

In Part II, Krasnor (Chapter 4), Hymel and Franke (Chapter 5), Sobol and Earn (Chapter 6), and Ledingham and Younger (Chapter 7) present data relevant to the assessment of social behavior. Krasnor presents an observational taxonomy for the assessment of children's goals, strategies, and successes in interactive situations. Hymel and Franke underline the importance of self-ratings of social competence and delineate the social-rational correlates of children's loneliness and social anxiety. Sobol and Earn indicate that the child's own perception of the social world may be a significant determinant of his or her relationships and skills. Ledingham and Younger explore the importance of rater characteristics and the social-interactional context for the identification and assessment of children's social skills.

Chapters by Rubin (Chapter 8), Coie (Chapter 9), and Asher (Chapter 10) address the selection of suitable target groups for intervention in Part III. Rubin reviews the literature concerning social withdrawal in childhood and suggests areas that may prove particularly problematic for withdrawn children. Coie makes an important distinction between sociometrically neglected and rejected children. He suggests that these two groups of children, previously both labeled "unpopular," are not at equal risk in the development of later problems. Moreover, he describes the behavioral characteristics that distinguish these two groups. Asher expands on Coie's presentation and delineates the sociometric model of risk. In his model, targets for change derived from sociometric assessment constitute the core of social skills interventions.

In Part IV, Schneider and Byrne (Chapter 11), Strain (Chapter 12), Argyle (Chapter 13), Weissberg (Chapter 14), and Ladd (Chapter 15) report on the content and implementation of social skills training programs and their outcome. Schneider and Byrne present the results of a meta-analysis of the effects of social skills training in terms of training technique, outcome measure, therapist and child characteristics, and duration of training. Strain outlines a model of peer-guided intervention and indicates how it was derived from a more general model for generating social skills interventions. Argyle proposes a model for developing social skills with adolescents that is the product of a long career of clinical practice and theory building. Weissberg identifies several controversies relevant to the content of social skills training and provides some nuts-and-bolts suggestions for service delivery. In the final chapter, Ladd reviews the assumptions which underlie social skills intervention.

Interwoven in counterpoint to these major themes run several additional threads that constitute an important part of the pattern in the fabric of current social skills research. The status of social-cognitive research is reviewed by Dodge, Hymel and Franke, Krasnor, and Sobol and Earn. The significance for social adjustment of relationships with others in addition to peers is discussed by Furman, Ledingham and Younger, and Argyle. The importance of establishing ecologically valid assessments and treatments is underlined by Krasnor, Sobol and Earn, Strain, and Weissberg. Rubin, as well as Sobol and Earn, comment on the significance of age-appropriate norms, while Hops and Finch, Hymel and Franke, and Schneider and Byrne present evidence for sex differences. The impact of situational variability is discussed by Dodge, Krasnor, and Argyle. Overall, this collection mirrors the increasingly fine-grained approach taken by researchers in the field as they seek to specify and assess target samples in a more multidimensional fashion and to provide greater individualization of intervention programs.

The editors thank their families, research staff, and secretaries for their support and patience during the preparation of this volume. Thanks are also due to participants in the June 1984 conference held in Ottawa that contemplated the future of research in this area, where many of the ideas expressed here were first exchanged, and to those who helped with the administrative aspects of that conference and this volume, especially Lois Langevin and Yves Barbeau. Appreciation is also extended to the Social Science and Humanities Research Council of Canada and the Laidlow Foundation for their support of the conference.

It is our hope that this volume will enable social skills educators, therapists, and researchers to better fulfill their mandate in enhancing children's peer relations.

Reference

Phillips, E. L. (1978). *The social skills basis of psychopathology.* New York: Grune & Stratton.

Barry H. Schneider
Kenneth H. Rubin
Jane E. Ledingham

Contents

Contributors

Michael Argyle
  Acting Head, Department of Experimental Psychology, University of Oxford, Oxford, England OX1 3UD

Steven R. Asher
  College of Education, Bureau of Educational Research, University of Illinois at Urbana-Champaign, Champaign, Illinois 61820, USA

Barbara M. Byrne
  Child Study Center, School of Psychology, University of Ottawa, Ottawa, Canada K1N 6N5

John D. Coie
  Department of Psychology, Duke University, Durham, North Carolina 27708, USA

Kenneth A. Dodge
  Department of Psychology, Indiana University, Bloomington, Indiana 47405, USA

Brian M. Earn
  Department of Psychology, University of Guelph, Guelph, Ontario, Canada N1G 2W1

Melissa Finch
  Oregon Research Institute, Eugene, Oregon 97401, USA

Sylvia Franke
  2300 Children's Plaza, Chicago, Illinois 60614, USA

Wyndol Furman
  Department of Psychology, Child Study Center, University of Denver, University Park, Denver, Colorado 80208-0297, USA

Willard W. Hartup
  Institute of Child Development, University of Minnesota, Minneapolis, Minnesota 55455, USA

Hyman Hops
Research Director, Oregon Research Institute, Eugene, Oregon 97401, USA

Shelley Hymel
Department of Psychology, University of Waterloo, Waterloo, Ontario, Canada
N2L 3GL

Gary W. Ladd
Department of Child Development and Family Studies, Purdue University,
West Lafayette, Indiana 47907, USA

Jane E. Ledingham
Child Study Center, School of Psychology, University of Ottawa, Ottawa,
Canada K1N 6N5

Philip Robbins
Department of Psychology, Child Study Center, University of Denver, University Park, Denver, Colorado 80208-0297, USA

Linda Rose-Krasnor
Child Studies Program, Brock University, St. Catherines, Ontario, Canada
L2S 3A1

Kenneth H. Rubin
Department of Psychology, University of Waterloo, Waterloo, Ontario, Canada
N2L 3G1

Barry H. Schneider
Child Study Center, School of Psychology, University of Ottawa, Ottawa,
Ontario, Canada K1N 6N5

Michael P. Sobol
Department of Psychology, University of Guelph, Guelph, Ontario, Canada
N1G 2W1

Phillip S. Strain
Early Childhood Research Institute, University of Pittsburgh, Pittsburgh,
Pennsylvania 15260, USA

Roger P. Weissberg
Department of Psychology, Yale University, New Haven, Connecticut
06520-7447, USA

Alastair J. Younger
Child Study Center, School of Psychology, University of Ottawa, Ottawa,
Canada K1N 6N5

PART I

Delineating the Realm of Social Competence

Facets of Social Interaction and the Assessment of Social Competence in Children

Kenneth A. Dodge

The number of definitions of social competence in the developmental literature today approaches the number of investigators in the field. Certainly, most definitions have in common several features, such as a child's response to an environmental stimulus and an emphasis on social effectiveness. These definitions, however, have emphasized different facets or aspects of social interaction. One theorist may emphasize specific behaviors, such as assertion (Bornstein, Bellack, & Hersen, 1977) and frequency of interaction (Furman, Rahe, & Hartup, 1979), whereas another theorist may emphasize a child's self-concept (Harter, 1982), and still another may emphasize cognitive skills (Gottman, Gonso, & Rasmussen, 1975). These differences are not trivial, for they lead researchers to measure competence in highly divergent ways, and they lead clinicians to intervene with divergent goals in mind. While theorists could debate which of each of these approaches "truly" constitutes a study of social competence, it is probably more fruitful to recognize that each of these facets represents a component of social interaction and that each facet is relevant to understanding competence. How these components are relevant must be articulated. What is needed at this time is a scheme or model of the various components of social interaction, which could lead to hypotheses concerning the manner in which various aspects of social interaction are related to each other.

The goal of this chapter is to describe such a scheme. This scheme includes five major aspects of social interaction, and it covers most of what psychologists study under the rubric of social competence. The components of social interaction will be described, as will empirical research relating one component to another. This research will lead to the conclusion that there are many different ways in which a child can be socially incompetent. It will be argued that comprehensive assessments of children in clinical settings, therefore, should take into account each of these five aspects. Finally, the relevance of these assessments for interventions with socially incompetent children will be articulated.

Scheme for Conceptualizing Social Interaction

A scheme depicting five components of social interaction is found in Figure 1.1. This scheme owes its origins to the work of Flavell (1974), McFall (1982), Goldfried and d'Zurilla (1969), Spivack and Shure (1974), and many other social

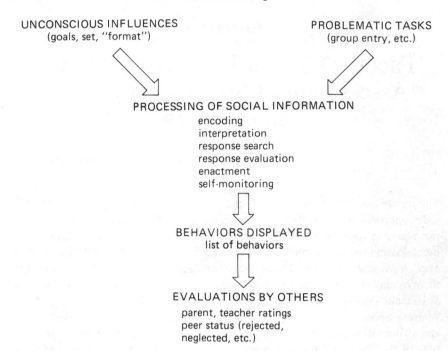

FIGURE 1.1. Assessing social competence.

theorists. (The cornerstone of this scheme is the notion that social behavior can ✳
be conceptualized as occurring in response to specific tasks. These tasks are alter-
nately known as stimuli, settings, situations, contexts, and domains.) These tasks
are highly complex, in that they consist of an enormous amount of information,
but they are also coherent. They comprise the first facet of social interaction.
(This scheme is formulated as a description of what happens in response to the
presentation of a social task) It is proposed that the child comes to this task with
a set of prior experiences which help the child cope with the complexity of the
task. These past experiences influence a child's response to the present task by
forming a filter through which the child can process information about the task.
The filter constitutes the second component of social interaction and consists of
all that the child brings to the social setting. It may consist of a "set" to perceive
the world in a particular way, a set of goals for social interaction, a transitory
mood, or the child's self-concept. We will call these features "unconscious
influences" for want of a better term. The action of the filter is to influence how
the child processes the social cues present in the situation. This processing,
which comprises the third aspect of social interaction, is hypothesized to occur
in sequential steps. These steps include the encoding of social cues, the mental
representation and interpretation of those cues, a search for possible behavioral
responses to the cues, an evaluation of the responses including the selection of an
optimal response, and the enactment of the chosen response. The outcome of this
processing is a behavioral response to the social task, which comprises the fourth

fourth component of social interaction. This behavioral response is then viewed and evaluated by others in the environment. These others often form some judgment of the child's level of social competence or form some opinion of the child's behavior. These judgments comprise the fifth aspect of social interaction.

While this structural model describes the individual in a social situation, at first glance it does not appear to describe the transaction between the child and another individual. However, when one recognizes that the "other" is also involved in a social task and is presented with social cues (some of which are the first child's behavior), then the other becomes a processor of social information as well. The transactional aspects of the scheme are clear when it is noted that the "other" who is making a judgment about the first child's behavior is subject to the same processes as the first child.

An example may help clarify the features of this scheme. Imagine that Rebecca, a 6-year-old girl, is at the playground. She notes that several peers are jumping rope. The peers who are at play constitute a social setting for Rebecca and may represent a task for her if she wishes to join in their play. This task has, in fact, been studied extensively, and has been labeled *peer group entry* (Putallaz & Gottman, 1981), *assimilation* (Phillips, Shenker, & Ravitz, 1951), and *access* (Corsaro, 1981). Rebecca comes to this task with a set of experiences (the unconscious influences) that shapes how she will understand and view this task. She may like to jump rope and may be skilled at it, or she may remember that once before when she tried to jump rope she fell and peers laughed at her. The range of possible prior experiences, of course, is great. They form a filter for Rebecca that helps shape how she will respond in this particular instance. Her actual response occurs as a function of how she processes the present task information. She encodes the cues, including the peers' smiles and laughter, and represents the task mentally as, say, a chance to become included. She mentally accesses several possible behavioral responses, including a greeting to the peers and a request to play. She evaluates these responses as "too dangerous," that is, too likely to be met with rebuff; she decides instead on a response of moving closer to the physical proximity of the peer group with a forlorn, pleading look on her face, hoping to be invited to play. She enacts this behavioral response. A peer named Sara sees Rebecca and now becomes involved in the transaction as well. Rebecca's cues constitute a situation for Sara. Sara's task may be to remain accepted by the peer group and to respond to Rebecca. Her prior experiences and her insecurity about her own role in the group shape her processing of Rebecca's cues. She sees Rebecca's approach, perceives it as a threat, and judges Rebecca to be an unworthy (incompetent) play partner. She accesses and enacts a response of ridicule of Rebecca's facial expression. This transaction could continue, as Sara's ridiculing becomes a set of cues for Rebecca. Of course, this transaction occurs in real time, and the sequence of events is so fast that compartmentalization of these events into the structural components of Figure 1.1 may seem forced. Still, this scheme offers a way of bringing order to the complete events of this transaction.

By imposing this structure on social interaction, we are also able to classify and bring order to the large body of research on children's social competence. Most researchers define competence in terms of one or more of these five aspects of social interaction, and most empirical studies are an examination of the relation between one aspect and another. Most clinicians have a goal (at least an implicit one) of changing the incompetent child's functioning in one or more of these aspects. The scheme may be useful, therefore, to both researchers and clinicians. Each of the aspects will now be reviewed in more detail, as a way of demonstrating these points.

Judgments of Social Competence

Perhaps the most common form of assessment of children's social competence is to rely on judgments by others about a child's behavioral performance. This aspect of the social interaction scheme therefore seems to be an appropriate point to begin a discussion of assessments. Judgments are commonly used to identify an incompetent child. A parent, teacher, or school counselor may observe a child's behavior and judge that the child is socially deviant, deficient, or in some other way incompetent. This also occurs at the time of a referral to a mental health center for social behavior problems. These judgments are often made systematically, through standardized forms such as the Kohn Social Competence Scale (Kohn & Rosman, 1972), the Health Resources Inventory (Gesten, 1976), and the Achenbach Child Behavior Checklist—Social Competence Scale (Achenbach & Edelbrock, 1981). Each of these scales consists of items on which the adult is asked to make an evaluative judgment about the child's behavior.

This approach to assessment is also reflected in the use of peer sociometric techniques, in which the peer group evaluates the behavior of a child. Peers are asked to rate the degree to which they like or dislike a child (Asher, Singleton, Tinsley, & Hymel, 1979), to nominate others for specific social roles (Bower, 1969; Pekarik, Prinz, Liebert, Weinraub, & Neale, 1976), or to evaluate a child's competence at a specific task, such as peer group entry (Dodge, in press). For both adult and peer raters, the evaluation could be a judgment of general competence or judgments of competence in particular domains.

These judgments are useful because they identify specific socially incompetent children for later assessment and intervention. Putallaz and Gottman (1981) have labeled sociometric judgments an "indicator variable" because they indicate a problem, but they do not explain the nature of the problem. The judgments by peers also have been found to be a relatively powerful predictor of later maladjustment in adolescence and early adulthood (Cowen, Pederson, Babigian, Izzo, & Trost, 1972; Kupersmidt, 1983; Roff, Sells, & Golden, 1972). For these reasons, peer judgments have been used more frequently than other aspects of social competence assessment (those in the scheme of Figure 1.1) to identify children who are incompetent and at risk for later social maladjustment. As a parenthetical point, while the predictive validity of peer judgments should not be minimized, the predictive powers of other aspects of social competence (social cognitive skill deficits, behavioral assessments, deficient self-esteem, etc.) have not yet been evaluated. Longitudinal studies of these factors have begun only recently (Rubin & Krasnor, in press; Rubin, Chapter 8 this volume).

In spite of the utility of judgments by peers, there are many problems with the use of these measures. As already noted, ratings give little information about the nature and sources of a child's incompetence. While a good deal of research has been devoted to a search for "the" major correlates of sociometric judgments (Asher & Hymel, 1981), the outcome of that research is simply that the problems of incompetent children are heterogeneous. Peer judgments alone have identified three distinct groups of incompetent children; socially rejected (not liked and highly disliked by peers), neglected (not liked but not disliked either), and controversial (highly liked by some and highly disliked by others) groups (Coie, Dodge, & Coppotelli, 1982). These groups differ from each other in other aspects of social interaction (including rates of aggressive behaviors, Dodge, 1983; social cognitive skill deficits, Dodge, Murphy, & Buchsbaum, 1984; and self-concept and loneliness, Asher & Wheeler, 1985), but they also display within group heterogeneity. To understand the nature and source of a child's difficulties (in any of these three groups), we must conduct further individual assessments of that child.

Another problem with relying on judgments by others is that sometimes we fail to get a consensus on evaluations, such as when adults and peers disagree about a child. Even within the peer group, there may be a high variance in evaluative judgments. This is especially true during the early adolescent years. Worse yet, in some circumstances, raters have been found to be systematically biased in their evaluations and perceptions of others. For example, Dodge (1980; Dodge & Frame, 1982) has found that once a boy is labeled as rejected or aggressive, peers become four to ten times more likely to attribute hostile intentions to his subsequent behavior. Peers also selectively attend to and recall the deviant behaviors of this boy to the neglect of his benign and prosocial behaviors. Peers also systematically maltreat this child once they identify him as a "problem." It must be remembered that the child is interacting in a social system in which the judges of his or her behavior are also participants in the system. The judges may be biased and inaccurate in their evaluations and may promote deviant behaviors by a child. The point here is that the judges are not merely objective external evaluators but are part of the transaction. Their judgments may not only reflect aspects of the child's behavior but may have an impact on that behavior as well.

This brief discussion of peer judgments of a child leads us to conclude that the relation between ratings by peers and other aspects of the child's social functioning (behavior, processing of information, self-esteem) is less than perfect. Still, because of the face validity of judgments and the longitudinal predictive power of these measures, most research on children's social competence has involved this aspect of the social transactional process. Observational research has focused on the behavioral correlates of judgments (Asher & Hymel, 1981), and studies of social information processing (Rubin & Krasnor, in press) have emphasized the relation between these factors and ratings of social competence by others. In fact, the goal of many preventive intervention efforts has been to change peer ratings of a child. Clinicians have tried to accomplish this change by changing other aspects of the child's functioning, including social behaviors (Oden & Asher, 1977) and cognitive skills (Ladd, 1981). Most interventions have ignored the possibility of changing peers' ratings directly. Only recent efforts by Bierman and Furman (1984) have explicitly included the peer group as a focus of intervention, but even this study focused primarily on changing the problem child.

Social Behaviors

The problems associated with relying on ratings have led some researchers, especially behaviorists, to define social competence by the occurrence, sequencing, or quality of specific behaviors. Presumably, the judgmental aspects are minimized when competent behaviors are operationalized and recorded by trained observers. Researchers have been broad in their operationalizations, referring to aggressive behaviors as incompetent and prosocial behaviors as competent, but also they have been quite specific, including behaviors such as "eye contact" (Beck, Forehand, Neeper, & Baskin, 1982) and "refusal assertiveness" (Bornstein, Bellack, & Hersen, 1977) as competent.

One obvious problem with this approach is that the researcher's values often determine which behaviors come to be labeled as competent. The anthropologist Ogbu (1981) notes the cultural biases in defining competent behaviors, and concludes that "competence is increasingly being used to distinguish people who possess certain attributes associated with a white middle-class type of success in school and society" (pp. 413-414). For example, early scales of social competence, such as those by Phillips (1953) and Whittman (1941) declare homosexual behavior to be unequivocally incompetent. Zigler and Trickett (1979) pointed out the problem in this declaration and called it a "value-laden bias." Ironically, they went on to declare teenage pregnancy and dropping out of school as socially incompetent social behaviors. While there might well be consensus that these behaviors constitute social problems, the irony is that Zigler and Trickett came to their declarations in the same manner that Phillips and Whittman had, namely, intuitive judgment or a value-laden bias.

A similar problem has occurred among developmental researchers who have declared a low rate of social interaction to be inherently problematic (or incompetent) among children. These researchers have identified incompetent children on the basis of either low rates on an absolute level (such as Walker, Hops, Greenwood, & Todd, 1979) or low rates relative to the rates by the peer group (such as Furman et al., 1979).

Several interventions have been designed to increase a child's rate of social interaction (e.g., Furman et al., 1979; O'Connor, 1969), often with some success. The arbitrariness of these interventions has been pointed out by Asher, Markell, and Hymel (1981), who noted that "the use of total interaction rate as a measure of identifying children as withdrawn and at risk in their peer relations is not empirically based" (p. 1243). They concluded that these interventions, and likewise the definition of social incompetence as involving a low rate of interaction, are unwarranted.

For some behaviors, such as autistic stereotypy and destructive aggression, maladaptiveness may be readily apparent, and little empirical justification may be required to declare them as incompetent. For other behaviors, this maladaptiveness may not be so readily apparent. One reasonable research path is to study the correlates and outcomes of specific behaviors, and to declare as incompetent those behaviors that indicate a degree of risk for later maladaptation. In fact, Putallaz and Gottman (1983) have defined social incompetence as those behaviors that place a child at risk. Not surprisingly, aggressive behavior toward peers during the early elementary school years has been found to be the strongest predictor of later deviant and maladaptive outcomes (Lefkowitz, Eron, Walder, & Huesmann, 1977; Robins, 1966). Similarly, Rubin (Chapter 8 this volume) has studied the consequences of social withdrawal (similar to a low rate of interaction, but defined specifically by inappropriate solitary behavior frequencies) and has found that those children who are continuously withdrawn over several years may constitute a group at risk for internalizing problems.

Another approach to solving the value-laden bias in definitions of socially incompetent behaviors has been to select children who have been declared by a consensus of judgments to be socially incompetent and to observe their behavior, relative to the behavior of children judged to be socially competent. In this way, researchers are declaring what competent children do to be engaged in socially competent behavior. This is the basis of many studies of the behavioral correlates of sociometric status. A number of these studies, such as the ones by Dodge, Coie, and Brakke (1982) and Hartup, Glazer, and Charlesworth (1967), have shown that socially competent (popular) children display positively reinforcing behaviors and high frequencies of cooperative play, relative to socially incompetent (rejected) children. On the other hand, the incompetent group displays high frequencies of negative reinforcements, physical and verbal aggression, and deviant social approaches. Several researchers (Coie & Kupersmidt, 1983; Dodge, 1983; Putallaz, 1983) have noted recently that defining social competence by the behavioral correlates of peers' judgments is problematic because the behavioral patterns may sometimes represent the consequences of peers' judgments, rather than the bases for those judgments. These researchers have solved this problem by observing children during their initial encounters with peers and by noting the behavioral antecedents of peer judgments. Coie and Kupersmidt (1983) and Dodge (1983) created play groups of four to eight previously unacquainted children and observed the emergence of sociometric status over time. They then assessed the specific behaviors that temporally preceded the acquisition of status. The results of these studies are generally consistent with the behavioral correlate studies in pointing toward interpersonal aggression, contentious statements, and inappropriate solitary behaviors (such as daydreaming, norm violating, etc.) as antecedents of judgments of incompetence by peers.

In spite of the existence of behavioral differences between groups judged as competent or incompetent, Asher (1983) pointed out that the magnitude of group differences in most of these studies is relatively small. Another way of stating this conclusion is that the relation between specific behavior displays and general judgments by others is weak. Perhaps one reason for these perplexing findings is that researchers have not paid sufficient attention to the possibility that topographically similar behaviors (such as initiating play with peers) may have different meanings in different situations and at different times. Dodge et al. (1982), for example, found that at the playground popular children display more social initiations than do socially rejected children, whereas the reverse is true in the classroom. In other words, this behavior may be favorably received in one setting but not in another.

Because of the arbitrariness of deciding which specific behaviors are called competent and because of the obvious importance of setting factors in the meaning of specific behaviors, some researchers have chosen to select a situation or a social task and to develop an empirical means of identifying which behaviors lead to success and thus are clearly competent *in that setting*. In a situation in which the goal or task is clear (such as a peer group setting in which the goal is to initiate play with peers), socially competent behaviors can be defined as those behaviors that increase the probability of favorable outcomes. Socially competent behaviors, therefore, may be defined empirically within a specified setting.

Putallaz (1983; Putallaz & Gottman, 1981) has followed this path in a series of elegant studies of children's behavior during a peer group entry situation. She selected this situation because, logically, it appeared that a child must successfully initiate play in order to develop more complex and sustained peer relationships. Also, this situation is a commonly occurring one and is one that has been studied extensively in the past (Corsaro, 1981; Phillips, Shenker, & Ravitz, 1951). Her procedure was quite simple. It consisted of asking two children (called hosts) to play a word-naming game with each other. After a short period of time, a third child (the subject) was instructed to enter the hosts' room and to initiate play with them. She videorecorded the subject's behavior and the hosts' responses. Because the task was controlled experimentally and the goal for the subject was clear (to be accepted into the game by the hosts), Putallaz could define social competence as behaviors that have a high probability of leading to a successful outcome. She found that behavior patterns involving attention to the group's frame of reference (such as statements about the game) had a high probability of leading to success, whereas egocentric, self-focused behaviors had a relatively high probability of leading to failure. The former could therefore be called socially competent behaviors in this setting.

Dodge, Schlundt, Schocken, and Delugach (1983) extended the study of peer group entry behavior to the natural setting. They noted the occurrence of each entry episode during children's free play, and coded the *tactics* used by children to gain access to a peer group, as well as the peer responses to these tactics. Their findings supported those of Putallaz, in that group-referenced statements were often found to be successful tactics, whereas disruptions, self-references, and attention-getting behaviors were tactics that had a relatively high probability of leading to failure. Waiting and hovering tactics led to neither success nor failure, but were usually ignored by peers. In addition, Dodge et al. found that children often string tactics together into sequences of behaviors during peer group entry. They called these sequences of tactics *strategies*. Several strategies were found to be highly successful, particularly one in which the child waited, hovered, moved closer to the peer group, and then made statements that maintained the focus on the peer group's activity without disrupting or calling attention away from that activity. This sequence may be called a socially competent peer group entry strategy. Not surprisingly, Dodge et al. also found that the children who most often employed these competent tactics and strategies were children who became popular in their peer group. Thus, there seems to be coherence in these various methods of identifying socially competent behaviors.

The Concept of Social Tasks

The study of competent behaviors has led us to emphasize the social task as a way of organizing and understanding the complex stream of behavior. This research has shown that it is useful to structure behaviors according to tasks, settings, situations, domains, contexts, or problems. We may find that we can describe competence *at a task* more easily than we can describe general competence. But, how do we define a social task? How do we know which social tasks are most important in development? Just as we found that the selection of critical social behaviors is often an arbitrary process, so too we may find that social tasks are selected arbitrarily. These questions bring us to the third facet of social interaction: the concept of the social task.

For Freud (1933), social tasks were very important, but they were defined in a broad manner and were concerned with stages of psychosexual development. For example, in the first year of life, the infant must master the task of oral gratification from his or her mother. Erikson (1950) extended this concept with a list of important life tasks, including becoming appropriately dependent in the first year of life, gaining autonomy and self-control in the second year, and so on. Tasks are defined by a set of stimuli (the parameters of which may include a time frame and a cast of other persons) and an end point, or a goal.

Social tasks could also be defined narrowly. For example, a child may face the following problem: What do you do if you are 6 years old and you are putting on your rain gear in your classroom and a peer laughs at you because you look funny; he throws your boot out the window just at the moment that your teachers tells you to hurry up because you have to catch the school bus? Would it make a difference if the peers were disliked by the teacher, or if the child had previously lost his or her umbrella? Obviously, tasks can be defined at a number of levels, varying in specificity of the situational parameters. At what level does it make most sense to conceptualize social tasks when one is examining a child's social competence? Also, which tasks are most important? A child could possibly respond quite competently in 99% of the tasks that he or she faces, but fail at a single critical task, and thus suffer deviant and tragic outcomes. So while the concept of tasks may

enlighten the assessment of socially competent behaviors, it also is fraught with
its own difficulties.

It seems to this writer that an appropriate level for the analysis of social tasks
is the level at which the task makes sense to the child. Both narrow tasks (such
as the one just defined) and broad tasks (making friends in school) thus may have
relevance for a child. Asking interested parties to describe tasks they face may
constitute a reasonable approach to determining the level at which tasks make
sense to a group. In the case of young children, verbal responses are more difficult to obtain, however, so other interested parties, such as parents and
teachers, may be appropriate sources of this information.

In addition to determining the level at which tasks are relevant for young
children, researchers must somehow determine the critical, common, and most
important tasks that this group faces. As stated by Freedman, Rosenthal,
Donahoe, Schlundt, and McFall (1978, p. 1449), "what is needed at this point is
research aimed at developing a taxonomy of the particular problem situations and
skill deficits most characteristic of clinical populations. . . . Clearly, basic tax-
onomic research is a prerequisite to further treatment-oriented research."

In order to develop a taxonomy of problematic social situations for elementary
school children, Dodge, McClaskey, and Feldman (in press) asked teachers and
child clinicians to identify frequently occurring social situations which they
thought were likely to eventuate in peer relationship problems among school
children. A total of 44 nonredundant situations were generated and transcribed
into a uniform format so that each was worded as a conditional premise such as
the following two examples: (a) when one child tries to join in with a group of
peers who are already playing a game, and they tell him or her to wait until they
are ready; and (b) when a peer starts playing with a toy or game that one child had
been using.

The resulting Taxonomy of Problematic Social Situations for Children (TOPS)
was then presented to a new group of teachers of aggressive and socially competent children who were asked to rate how much of a problem each situation
presented for each child. Factor analyses of responses yielded six meaningful and
distinct types of problematic situations: (a) attempting to initiate entry into the
peer play group; (b) responding to an ambiguous provocation by a peer; (c)
responding to one's own failure; (d) responding to one's own success; (e) responding to peer group norms and expectations; and (f) responding to a teacher's
expectations. Teachers rated each type of situation as more problematic for
aggressive children than for socially competent children.

In a subsequent study, these researchers presented these six types of social
situations to children to assess the competence of their behavioral responses.
Situations were presented hypothetically, and responses were role-played. The
responses were then scored as competent or deficient by trained observers using
a coding manual. The subjects included a group of children rated as aggressive
and socially incompetent by teachers and peers and a group of children rated as
nonaggressive and socially competent. The former group enacted responses that
were rated as less competent than those of the latter group in all six situation

types, and these children were particularly less competent in responding to provocations by a peer and in responding to peer group norms.

More importantly, the responding by aggressive children was quite heterogeneous across children and situations. It appeared that some aggressive children responded deficiently in one situation, whereas other aggressive children responded deficiently in a second situation, and so on. This point is supported by the fact that the responding by the socially competent group was more internally consistent (coefficient alpha = .82) than was the responding by the aggressive group (coefficient alpha = .54). One outcome of this heterogeneity was that the greatest discrimination between the aggressive and the competent groups occurred using a combined assessment of responding in each situation. That is, when the number of deficiencies in responding (across all situations) was tabulated for each child, it was found that two-thirds of the aggressive children gave at least two deficient responses, compared with only one-third of the nonaggressive, competent children.

These analyses suggest the following conclusions. First, social competence can be profitably assessed within specific tasks or domains. Second, it appears that a fair degree of divergence exists in children's responding across tasks, that is, a child may behave competently in one domain, such as peer group entry, while displaying incompetence in another domain, such as responding to failure. In order to gain a comprehensive evaluation of a child's social competence, assessments must be made in multiple social situations. Likewise, this divergence suggests that it may be possible to categorize subtypes of socially incompetent children according to the kinds of situations in which they behave incompetently. These subgroups (such as "group entry problem children" or "provocation problem children") may constitute relatively homogeneous units for research inquiry, diagnosis, and clinical intervention. Classification according to the domain in which behavior problems occur represents an alternative to the behavior-based, nonsituationally oriented classification systems now commonly used (Achenbach & Edelbrock, 1981; Quay, 1977).

The Role of Unconscious Influences

Thus far, this chapter has toured three of the five facets of social interaction proposed earlier. Two stops remain on the tour, both concerning the organismic components of social responding. These aspects may be divided into those features that the child brings to the situation and those processes that are activated within the situation. The latter consists of the processing of social information in response to a particular situation and has a direct effect on the behavioral response. The former has an indirect, probabilistic relation to behavioral outcomes, and thus may be referred to as "unconscious influences." Their action is to influence social processing, which then determines behavioral responding.

A good deal of research has emphasized those features a child brings to a social situation. For example, Harter (1982) has developed a concept of perceived self-

competence, which is based on Bandura's (1977) construct of self-efficacy. She
has developed a self-report scale consisting of items that tap a child's self-
appraisals and which apparently is related to individual differences in behavioral
outcomes. Wheeler and Ladd (1982) have refined this construct with a scale of
perceived self-efficacy specifically in situations in which the child wishes to persuade a peer to change his or her behavior. Their work is consistent with the
theme of this chapter—that heterogeneity exists across situations in the features
of social interaction. Masters, Barden, and Ford (1979) have studied the role of
mood in social information processing and behavior and have found it to have
dramatic effects. Asher and his colleagues (Parkhurst & Asher, in press; Renshaw
& Asher, 1982; Taylor & Asher, 1984) have studied the role of a child's goal in
his or her social behavior. They have shown that individual differences in goals
exist and that these differences relate to behavioral and sociometric status outcomes. For example, Taylor & Asher's (1984) assessment instrument includes
relationship, performance, and avoidant goals. They have found that popular
children endorse social goals more strongly than do socially incompetent (unpopular) children, whereas the latter group endorses avoidant goals more than the
former group.

These influences are important because they shape how a child is likely to
respond to a social task. They form the lens through which the child perceives the
task, or the format (in computer processing terms) with which the child reads the
"data" in the social environment. They help the child make sense of the environment and construct reality out of the overwhelming amount of information present in the social setting. Because of this overload of information, the child uses
prior experiences and "response sets" in a heuristic way to make sense of the cues
being presented. At the same time that these influences promote social understanding, they also limit what the child can perceive. For example, if we draw
from Asher's goal orientations, a child who displays a set to perceive every social
situation as a chance to achieve and to win (or lose) may fail to perceive opportunities for growth in social relationships. In this way, these unconscious influences have the characteristics of a "paradigm" for a child, bringing both insight
and encumbrances to the setting in the way that paradigms function in scientific
thought (Kuhn, 1962).

Many clinical theories of personality development focus on these unconscious
influences on behavior. Cognitive theories (Abramson, Seligman, & Teasdale,
1978; Beck, 1967) emphasize an individual's expectations for behavioral outcomes. Psychoanalytic theory emphasizes paradigmatic early experiences, such
as one's relationship with his or her mother, and the role that these experiences
play in structuring how the child construes the world subsequently, as in a trans-
ference relationship. Attachment theorists (Sroufe, 1983; Hartup, in press) suggest that one type of insecure early attachment to the mother may form the basis
for anxiety-based withdrawal in later social interactions (Rubin, Chapter 8 this
volume). The same problems that apply to these theories also apply to unconscious influences as described in the present context, that is, these theorists have
been unable to describe the mechanisms by which these influences have an effect

on behavior. Likewise, they have been relatively unsuccessful in making reliable predictions of behavior based on knowledge of these unconscious influences. An adequate model of the various kinds of unconscious influences has yet to be developed, so at this point we know neither the components involved nor their distinctive roles.

What are the empirical findings concerning the relation between these unconscious aspects and other aspects of social interaction, such as behaviors and status outcomes? Several of the most pertinent findings have already been reviewed here. Generally, like the other aspects, significant relations have been found, but the magnitude of these effects is not overwhelming. Does this mean that there may be great heterogeneity in unconscious influences, just as there is in other areas? This is quite possible. Asher (personal communication, October 1984), for example, reports that while rejected children as a group are more lonely than popular and average children, only about one-fourth of all rejected children are extremely lonely, compared with but a few percent of the other children.

Perhaps the most important problem with the concept of unconscious influences for the practicing clinician is that they are hard to change directly, just as their effect on behavior is indirect. How does one change a child's self-perception or goals? They are a vague consequence of prior experiences and so might be changed through direct experience. We might change a child's perceived self-competence, for example, by exposing the child to a set of success experiences. This increased self-competence, in turn, would presumably have a direct effect on how this child processes social informaion in the future and an indirect effect on future behavioral outcomes. Thus far, researchers have not adequately described how these unconscious influences are formed and changed, and so while they may be important, their use, like their formulation, is still in an early stage of development.

Social Information Processing

The action of unconscious influences is to alter the manner in which a child processes the information available in the social environment. It is this processing of social information that is hypothesized to determine directly the child's behavioral response in a situation and that forms the fifth and final aspect of social interaction to be reviewed here. This aspect is concerned with the mental processes occurring between the presentation of a social stimulus and the emission of a behavioral response. A number of researchers have assessed different processes in this domain, including social role taking (Chandler, 1973), impulsivity and verbal mediation (Camp, 1977), problem solving (Spivack & Shure, 1974), and intention-cue detection (Dodge et al., 1984). Recently, theorists have described how these processes might interact and have formulated general models of social information processing (Dodge, in press; Rubin & Krasnor, in press).

According to one model (Dodge, in press), the child must pass through several stages in the processing of information in order to respond competently. First, the child must encode the social cues in the environment, a step requiring attention, sensation, and perception of relevant cues. Second, the child must form a mental representation of these cues and make some interpretation of them. The child may do this by integrating the cues with past experiences and by applying some rule about which cues suggest which interpretation. Once the child has represented the social cues, the child then generates, accesses, or makes available one or more possible behavioral responses to the cues. The child then evaluates the potential consequences of each available response and selects an optimal response. Finally, the child enacts the chosen response in behavior and self-monitors its effects.

The model is based on several propositions that are worth articulating. It is proposed that processing occurs very rapidly, in real time, and often non-consciously. Because of the tremendous amount of information present in the social environment, the child could not possibly process all of it, so the child uses heuristics, rules, and characteristic patterns in responding. These patterns may be based on the unconscious influences described earlier (such as mood, self-esteem, and goals). The model describes processing in a single instance, but it can be applied to general patterns of processing as well. The model also describes processing in the ideal, that is, in a socially competent fashion. Incompetence may be assessed in relation to this ideal. Deviant processing is proposed to occur in the form of either deficits in processing skills or biases in processing patterns. Finally, while the five steps of processing are related sequentially, it is proposed that they are separable and can be assessed somewhat independently by holding preceding steps constant.

Assessments of these five steps have demonstrated that patterns in processing are related to patterns in social behavior, and that deficits and biases in processing are related to negative evaluations among peers. Socially incompetent children have been shown to display inadequate and biased encoding of social cues (Dodge, in press), inaccurate and biased interpretations of those cues (Dodge et al., 1984), and deficient response search, problem solving, and response evaluation patterns (Richard & Dodge, 1981; Dodge, in press; Rubin & Krasnor, in press). However, as with other aspects of social interaction, the magnitude of any single difference between competent and incompetent children has been found to be relatively small. The proportions of aggressive, socially incompetent children displaying deficits at any single step of processing are found in Figure 1.2, accord-ing to reanalyses of data by Dodge (in press). Basing an intervention program on any single aspect of social information processing seems to be unwarranted.

At the same time, Dodge (in press) and Feldman (1983) have shown that an aggregated assessment of all five steps of processing leads to strong predictions of actual social behavioral success and ratings of competence by peers. A multi-ple regression analysis reveals that several steps provide unique increments to the prediction of ratings of competence and that the combined assessments yield multiple correlations with ratings of competence on the order of .74 (in a domain involving processing of information about a provocation by peers) to .82 (in a domain involving peer group entry information). When deficits in social infor-

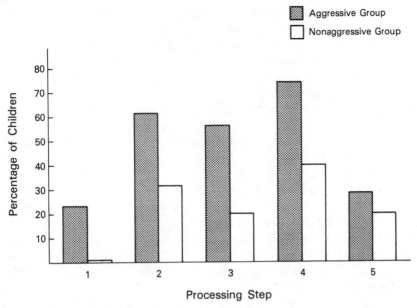

FIGURE 1.2. Percentages of children displaying processing deficits.

mation processing by a child in these two domains are counted, 63% of aggressive and socially incompetent children are found to display three or more deficits, whereas only 21% of nonaggressive children display this many deficits. It appears then, that one incompetent child may be deficient in one aspect of processing and a second child may be deficient in a second aspect of processing, but that an aggregated assessment of patterns across the five stages of processing can yield powerful predictions about social behavior and ratings of competence.

Conclusions

This discussion of the various aspects of social interaction has revealed that each aspect is relevant to a comprehensive understanding of social competence in children. Each aspect is apparently related to other aspects of social interaction, but any single measure is only related in a weak to moderate magnitude. Multiple measures seem to yield stronger relations.

The implications of this pattern of findings for researchers interested in assessing children's social competence are several. First, researchers must use statistical procedures other than analyses of variance to gain maximal understanding of social patterns. Multivariate procedures, such as multiple regression and discriminant function analyses, and other methods of aggregating measures, such as chi-square analyses, seem more likely to reveal these patterns. Also, correlational analyses of subject group tendencies often fail to tell us much about the social process itself. A few examples from other substantive areas may help to explain this point. An epidemiological researcher may find a positive correlation between unsanitary conditions and the spread of a disease. While interesting, this correlation reveals little about the process of disease itself. Microbiological analyses may be required for this understanding. Likewise, an educational researcher may find a positive correlation between the number of magazines in a child's home and the reading level acquired by that child. This interesting finding does not tell us how a child learns to read; process analyses may be required here as well. Baer (1984) articulated this point quite succinctly: "group designs yield only actuarial conclusions, and you cannot study *process* in behavior when your data represent actuarial combinations of unknown and possibly very different processes in an equally unknown mix" (p. 192). Baer also suggested an alternative: "If you want to study process, you have to study it one process at a time . . . . Single-subject designs can systematically let you see one process operating at a time; group designs cannot (except by unusually good luck)" (p. 192). Most research in the field of social competence has consisted primarily of actuarial predictions about social interaction. The scheme offered in this chapter may take us one step closer to understanding social process itself, if researchers will dare to attempt novel designs.

The findings reviewed in this chapter also have important implications for practitioners interested in the assessment and treatment of social incompetence. A first implication is that clinicians may benefit from the consideration of subtypes of incompetent children. Subtyping may occur across the facets of social interaction (such as a distinction between the processing-skill-deficient child and the child suffering from a biased and prejudiced evaluation by others) or within facets (such as the group entry problem child vs. the provocation problem child or the encoding-deficient child vs. the response-search-deficient child). A second implication is that the multiple ways in which a child can be socially incompetent suggest that even subtyping of incompetent children may yield heterogeneous groups. There are many possible reasons why a child is rated by others as incompetent. The most appropriate level of assessment, therefore, may be the individual child. A third implication is that clinicians may benefit from a profile approach to the assessment of social competence in which all five facets of social interaction are evaluated. This profile approach might start with an analysis of relevant social tasks or situations for a child. Assessments of social behaviors and ratings of competence by others within those situations may reveal a list of problematic situations for this particular incompetent child. Assessments of unconscious influences and social information processing patterns within those problematic situations may yield a profile of biases, deficits, and adverse influences. This profile might consist of a grid, in which the problematic situations are listed on one axis and the sources of difficulty within those situations (unconscious influences, social information processing patterns, biased ratings by others) are listed on the other axis.

Such a profile grid may provide a comprehensive assessment of all aspects of a child's social functioning. The proposed intervention for that child may follow directly from this profile, in that the areas of a child's social incompetence have been identified in a rather detailed fashion. Unfortunately, the intervention itself may be very difficult and more complex than the assessment. While most current interventions seem to be unsuccessful in improving a child's level of social competence, the more successful forms have been those that have attended to the specific cognitive or behavioral problems displayed by an individual child or subgroup. Ladd (1981), for example, targeted specific behavioral skill areas for his interventions (question asking, leadership behavior, support, aggression, and prosocial behaviors), and also targeted the same areas for his assessments. Coie and Krehbiel (1984) restricted their subject sample to those socially rejected children who also displayed academic achievement deficits, and then directed their intervention specifically toward ameliorating those deficits. Both interventions are reasonably individualized. The present analysis suggests that future interventions may be even more individualized, based on a comprehensive assessment of the socially incompetent child.

References

Abramson, L. Y., Seligman, M. E. P., & Teasdale, J. D. (1978). Learned helplessness in humans: Critique and reformulation. *Journal of Abnormal Psychology*, *87*, 49-74.

Achenbach, T. M., & Edelbrock, C. S. (1981). Behavioral problems and competencies reported by parents of normal and disturbed children aged four through sixteen. *Society for Research in Child Development Monographs*, *46*, No. 1.

Asher, S. R. (1983). Social competence and peer status: Recent advances and future directions. *Child Development*, *54*, 1427-1433.

Asher, S. R., & Hymel, S. (1981). Children's social competence in peer relations: Sociometric and behavioral assessment. In J. D. Wine & M. D. Smye (Eds.), *Social competence*. New York: Guilford Press.

Asher, S. R., Hymel, S., & Renshaw, P. D. (1984). Loneliness in children. *Child Development*, *55*, 1456-1464.

Asher, S. R., Markell, R. S., & Hymel, S. (1981). Identifying children at risk in peer relations: A critique of the rate-of-interaction approach to assessment. *Child Development*, *52*, 1239-1245.

Asher, S. R., Singleton, L. C., Tinsley, B. R., & Hymel, S. (1979). A reliable sociometric measure for preschool children. *Developmental Psychology*, *15*, 443-444.

Asher, S. R., & Wheeler, V. A. (1985). Children's loneliness: A comparison of rejected and neglected peer status. *Journal of Consulting and Clinical Psychology*, *53*, 500-505.

Baer, D. M. (1984). Review of *Single-case research designs*. *Behavioral Assessment*, *6*, 191-193.

Bandura, A. (1977). Self-efficacy: Toward a unifying theory of behavioral change. *Psychological Review*, *84*, 191-215.

Beck, A. T. (1967). *Depression: Clinical, experimental, and theoretical aspects*. London: Staples Press.

Beck, S., Forehand, R., Neeper, R., & Baskin, C. H. (1982). A comparison of two analogue strategies for assessing children's social skills. *Journal of Consulting and Clinical Psychology*, *50*, 596-598.

Bierman, K. L., & Furman, W. (1984). The effects of social skills training and peer involvement on the social adjustment of preadolescents. *Child Development*, *55*, 151-162.

Bornstein, M., Bellack, A. S., & Hersen, M. (1977). Social skills training for unassertive children: A multiple-baseline analysis. *Journal of Applied Behavior Analysis*, *10*, 183-195.

Bower, E. M. (1969). *Early identification of emotionally handicapped children in school*. Springfield, IL: Charles C Thomas.

Camp. B. (1977). Verbal mediation in young aggressive boys. *Journal of Abnormal Psychology*, *86*, 145-153.

Chandler, M. J. (1973). Egocentrism and antisocial behavior: The assessment and training of social perspective-taking skills. *Developmental Psychology*, *9*, 326-337.

Coie, J. D., Dodge, K. A., & Coppotelli, H. (1982). Dimensions and types of social status: A cross-age perspective. *Developmental Psychology*, *18*, 557-570.

Coie, J. D., & Krehbiel, G. (1984). Effects of academic tutoring on the social status of low-achieving, socially rejected children. *Child Development*, *55*, 1465-1478.

Coie, J. D., & Kupersmidt, J. (1983). A behavioral analysis of emerging social status in boys' groups. *Child Development*, *54*, 1400-1416.

Corsaro, W. A. (1981). Friendship in the nursery school: Social organization in a peer environment. In S. R. Asher & J. M. Gottman (Eds.), *The development of children's friendships*. New York: Cambridge University Press.

Cowen, E. L., Pederson, A., Babigian, H., Izzo, L. D., & Trost, M. D. (1972). Longterm follow-up of early detected vulnerable children. *Journal of Consulting and Clinical Psychology*, *41*, 438-446.

Dodge, K. A. (1980). Social cognition and children's aggressive behavior. *Child Development*, *51*, 162-170.

Dodge, K. A. (1983). Behavioral antecedents of peer social status. *Child Development*, *54*, 1386-1399.

Dodge, K. A. (in press). A social information processing model of social competence in children. In M. Perlmutter (Ed.), *Minnesota Symposium in Child Psychology*. Hillsdale, NJ: Erlbaum.

Dodge, K. A., Coie, J. D., & Brakke, N. P. (1982). Behavior patterns of socially rejected and neglected preadolescents: The roles of social approach and aggression. *Journal of Abnormal Child Psychology*, *10*, 389-409.

Dodge, K. A., & Frame, C. L. (1982). Social cognitive biases and deficits in aggressive boys. *Child Development*, *53*, 620-635.

Dodge, K. A., McClaskey, C. L., & Feldman, E. (in press). A situational approach to the assessment of social competence in children. *Journal of Consulting and Clinical Psychology*.

Dodge, K. A., Murphy, R. R., & Buchsbaum, K. (1984). The assessment of intention-cue detection skills in children: Implications for developmental psychopathology. *Child Development*, *55*.

Dodge, K. A., Schlundt, D. G., Schocken, I., & Delugach, J. D. (1983). Social competence and children's sociometric status: The role of peer group entry strategies. *Merrill-Palmer Quarterly*, *29*, 309-336.

Erikson, E. H. (1950). *Childhood and society*. New York: Norton.

Feldman, E. H. (1983). *The assessment of social information processing patterns in popular, average, neglected, and rejected girls and boys*. Unpublished doctoral dissertation, Indiana University, Bloomington, IN.

Flavell, J. H. (1974). The development of inferences about others. In T. Mischel (Ed.), *Understanding other persons*. Totowa, NJ: Rowman and Littlefield.

Freedman, B. J., Rosenthal, L., Donahoe, C. P., Jr., Schlundt, D. G., & McFall, R. M.

(1978). A social-behavioral analysis of skills deficits in delinquent and nondelinquent adolescent boys. *Journal of Consulting and Clinical Psychology, 46,* 1448-1462.

Freud, S. (1933). *New introductory lectures on psychoanalysis.* New York: Norton.

Furman, W., Rahe, D. F., & Hartup, W. W. (1979). Rehabilitation of socially withdrawn preschool children. *Child Development, 50,* 915-922.

Gesten, E. L. (1976). A health resources inventory: The development of a measure of the personal and social competence of primary-grade children. *Journal of Consulting and Clinical Psychology, 44,* 775-786.

Goldfried, M. R., & d'Zurilla, T. J. (1969). A behavioral-analytic model for assessing competence. In C. D. Spielberger (Ed.), *Current topics in clinical and community psychology* (Vol. 1). New York: Academic Press.

Gottman, J. M., Gonso, J., & Rasmussen, B. (1975). Social interaction, social competence, and friendship in children. *Child Development, 46,* 709-718.

Harter, S. (1982). The perceived competence scale for children. *Child Development, 53,* 87-97.

Hartup, W. W. (in press). On relationships and development. In W. W. Hartup & Z. Rubin (Eds.), *Relationships and development.* Hillsdale, NJ: Erlbaum.

Hartup, W. W., Glazer, J. A., & Charlesworth, R. (1967). Peer reinforcement and sociometric status. *Child Development, 38,* 1017-1024.

Kohn, M., & Rosman, B. L. (1972). A social competence scale and symptom checklist for the preschool child: Factor dimensions, their cross-instrument generality and longitudinal persistence. *Developmental Psychology, 6,* 430-444.

Kuhn, T. S. (1962). *The structure of scientific revolutions.* Chicago: The University of Chicago Press.

Kupersmidt, J. B. (1983, April). Predicting delinquency and academic problems from childhood peer status. In J. D. Coie (Chair), *Strategies for identifying children at social risk: Longitudinal correlates and consequences.* Symposium conducted at the biennial meeting of the Society for Research in Child Development, Detroit.

Ladd, G. W. (1981). Effectiveness of a social learning method for enhancing children's social interaction and peer acceptance. *Child Development, 52,* 171-178.

Lefkowitz, M. M., Eron, L. D., Walder, L. O., & Huesmann, L. R. (1977). *Growing up to be violent.* New York: Pergamon.

Masters, J. C., Barden, R. C., & Ford, M. E. (1979). Affective states, expressive behavior and learning in children. *Journal of Personality and Social Psychology, 37,* 380-390.

McFall, R. M. (1982). A review and reformulation of the concept of social skills. *Behavioral Assessment, 4,* 1-35.

O'Connor, R. D. (1969). Modification of social withdrawal through symbolic modeling. *Journal of Applied Behavior Analysis, 2,* 15-22.

Oden, S., & Asher, S. R. (1977). Coaching children in social skills for friendship making. *Child Development, 48,* 495-506.

Ogbu, J. H. (1981). Origins of human competence: A cultural ecological perspective. *Child Development, 52,* 413-429.

Parkhurst, J. T., & Asher, S. R. (in press). Goals and concerns: Implications for the study of children's social competence. In B. Lahey & A. E. Kazdin (Eds.), *Advances in clinical child psychology.* New York: Plenum.

Pekarik, E. G., Prinz, R. J., Liebert, D. E., Weinraub, S., & Neale, J. M. (1976). The pupil evaluation inventory: A sociometric technique for assessing children's social behavior. *Journal of Abnormal Child Psychology, 4,* 83-97.

Phillips, L. (1953). Case history data and prognosis in schizophrenia. *Journal of Nervous and Mental Disease*, *117*, 515-525.

Phillips, E. L., Shenker, S., & Ravitz, P. (1951). The assimilation of the new child into the group. *Psychiatry*, *14*, 319-325.

Putallaz, M. (1983). Predicting children's sociometric status from their behavior. *Child Development*, *54*, 1417-1426.

Putallaz, M., & Gottman, J. M. (1981). Social skills and group acceptance. In S. R. Asher & J. M. Gottman (Eds.), *The development of friendship: Description and intervention*. New York: Cambridge University Press.

Putallaz, M., & Gottman, J. M. (1983). Social relationships problems in children: An approach to intervention. In B. Lahey & A. E. Kazdin (Eds.), *Advances in clinical child psychology* (Vol. 6). New York: Plenum.

Quay, H. C. (1977). Measuring dimensions of deviant behavior: The Behavior Problem Checklist. *Journal of Abnormal Child Psychology*, *5*, 277-289.

Renshaw, P. D., & Asher, S. R. (1982). Social competence and peer status: The distinction between goals and strategies. In K. H. Rubin & H. S. Ross (Eds.), *Peer relationships and social skills in childhood*. New York: Springer-Verlag.

Richard, B. A., & Dodge, K. A. (1981). Social maladjustment and problem solving in school-aged children. *Journal of Consulting and Clinical Psychology*, *50*, 226-233.

Robins, L. N. (1966). *Deviant children grown up*. Baltimore: Williams & Wilkens.

Roff, M., Sells, S. B., & Golden, M. M. (1972). *Social adjustment and personality development in children*. Minneapolis: University of Minnesota Press.

Rubin, K. H., & Krasnor, L. R. (in press). Social-cognitive and social behavioral perspectives on problem-solving. In M. Perlmutter (Ed.), *Minnesota Symposium on Child Psychology* (Vol. 18). Hillsdale, NJ: Erlbaum.

Spivack, G., & Shure, M. B. (1974). *Social adjustment of young children: A cognitive approach to solving real life problems*. San Francisco: Jossey-Bass.

Sroufe, L. A. (1983). Infant-caregiver attachment and patterns of adaptation in preschool: The roots of maladaptation and competence. In M. Perlmutter (Ed.), *Minnesota Symposium on Child Psychology* (Vol. 16). Hillsdale, NJ: Erlbaum.

Taylor, A. R., & Asher, S. R. (1984, April). *Children's interpersonal goals in game situations*. Paper presented at the meeting of the American Educational Research Association in New Orleans, LA.

Walker, H. M., Hops, H., Greenwood, C. R., & Todd, N. (1979). Differential effects of reinforcing topographic components of free play social interaction: Analysis and direct replication. *Behavior Modification*, *3*, 291-321.

Wheeler, V., & Ladd, G. W. (1982). Assessment of children's self-efficacy for social interactions with peers. *Developmental Psychology*, *18*, 795-805.

Whittman, M. P. (1941). A scale for measuring prognosis in schizophrenic patients. *Elgin State Hospital Papers*, *4*, 20-33.

Zigler, E., & Trickett, P. K. (1979). The role of national social policy in promoting social competence in children. In M. W. Kent & J. E. Rolf (Eds.), *Primary prevention of psychopathology: Vol. 3. Social competence in children*. Hanover, NH: University Press of New England.

CHAPTER 2

Social Competence and Skill: A Reassessment

Hyman Hops and Melissa Finch

This chapter reports on a study of social and nonsocial variables hypothesized to contribute to social competence among preschool children. Three areas of basic skill in the child's repertoire were examined—language, motor, and social. We also examined a sample of parents' child-rearing skills in the home setting. As a measure of social competence, the judgments of children by social agents in their environment—parents, peers, and teachers—were used.

Children's relationships with the peer group has once again become a legitimate focus for research and treatment (Hartup, 1983; Lewis & Rosenblum, 1975). As a consequence, a substantial literature on children's competence in social relationships has developed over the past decade (e.g., Hops, 1983; Rubin & Ross, 1982; Wine & Smye, 1981). However, there remains considerable disagreement on the specific, objective, specifiable criteria for social competence. Where agreement exists, the criteria are vague and/or global (Anderson & Messick, 1974). We have taken the position, therefore, that social competence can best be measured on the basis of the judgments of social agents in the child's environment (Hops, 1983). If the manner in which children's social competence is exhibited has an impact on others, their judgments should provide a summary measure of the children's level of successful social functioning or adaptation.

Peers, teachers, and parents comprise the primary groups of social agents whose judgments have been measured or examined (Hops & Greenwood, 1981; Hops & Lewin, 1984). The judgment of peers has been shown to have both short- and long-term predictability for a variety of mental health and social difficulties (Cowen, Pederson, Babigian, Izzo, & Trost, 1973; Roff, Sells, & Golden, 1972). Parents' judgments have also been shown to discriminate between children referred to mental health centers and nonreferred children (Achenbach & Edelbrock, 1982). Additionally, teachers' ratings have a long history of identifying problematic children in school settings (e.g., Walker et al., 1983).

Not surprisingly, the correlations between measures of social competence based on these sources of data are not very high (Hops & Finch, 1982; Gresham, 1981; McConnell & Odom, in press). The data simply reflect the different criteria upon which each of the assessments are based. The settings in which behavior is observed, the opportunity to observe, and the standards used by social agents can all affect judgments of social competence (McConnell & Odom, in press). For example, in the preschool, the settings in which social behavior is observed by a child's teachers and peers are identical. Consequently, we find moderate and significant correlations based on the ratings of these two groups (Connolly & Doyle, 1981; Greenwood, Walker, Todd, & Hops, 1979). In the elementary school, the settings in which peers and teachers observe a child's social behavior decrease in similarity, reflected in lower relationships (McConnell, 1982). Where settings and raters differ completely, for example, parents observing at home versus teachers at school, the relationships are quite low (Becker, 1960).

Social agents may differ markedly in the standards they use for evaluating a child's social competence. Teachers' ratings may be biased by a child's academic behavior in the classroom; parents' ratings may be affected by the child's compliance to parental commands. Thus, both settings and standards may affect the judgments of these social agents. We have suggested that a comprehensive cross-setting measure of social competence should incorporate the combined judgments of all of these agents (Hops, 1983). Some will argue, however, that this procedure may confound the meaningfulness of the specific judgments made in specific settings. We will examine this issue more thoroughly in this study.

Comprehensive View of Skills Underlying
Social Competence

From the previous discussion, it follows that one important goal of research in social competence is to delineate those factors that contribute to (a) a general measure of social competence based on the multiple judgments of parents, peers, and teachers, and (b) the specific judgments of each of the groups. In taking this position, we assume there is a set of specific skills that accounts for a substantially large proportion of social agents' judgments of a child's social competence (Hops, Finch, & McConnell, in press). Specific behaviors that children emit or exhibit in social situations affect the perceptions and judgments of these social agents (Hops, 1983). Children judged less socially competent by others are more likely to show deficits in specific skill areas (e.g., Gottman, Gonso, & Rasmussen, 1975).

As attested to by the chapters in this volume, the most comprehensive literature accumulated in the past few years has focused on the contribution of children's *social* skills to judgments of social competence. Studies have examined the impact of both behavioral (for example, indices of low social interaction, Greenwood et al., 1979; entry skills, Dodge, 1983; Putallaz & Gottman, 1981) and cognitive deficits (for example, social information processing, Dodge, Chapter 1 this volume); problem-solving strategies (Krasnor, Chapter 4 this volume).

However, the increasing number of studies on the impact of specific behavioral and cognitive social skills has not explained much of the variance in social competence measures. A definite shortcoming has been the paucity of research on the various *nonsocial* skills, which must also be considered to be important prerequisites for successful social interaction. Two examples will suffice.

Several studies have shown that motor skill performance is directly and positively related to children's social competence as measured by peer sociometric status. In a study conducted in the early 1970s, Broekhoff (1977) demonstrated that ball throwing for distance was the best predictor of social status in elementary school boys; furthermore, these relationships between motor performance and sociometric scores remained stable from fourth through seventh grade. A decade later, it would not be surprising to find motor skill performance as a significant predictor of girls' social acceptance. Boys and girls with limited motoric ability may not find willing playmates on the playground or in settings in which motor performance plays an important role. Similarly, children with language and comprehension difficulty may be hampered in their ability to communicate and interact with the peer group. As the frequency of child-adult speech decreases and child-child directed speech increases between the ages of 2 and 5 (Schachter, Kirshner, Klips, Friedricks, & Sanders, 1974), language assumes increasing importance for social relationships.

The lack of attention to motor and language skills is one possible explanation for the limited impact of treatment programs designed to increase a child's social skills and subsequent acceptance by the peer group. Such programs may fail with children who lack the prerequisite motor and language skills that would optimize the treatment effects of the social skills training programs.

Any investigation of potentially significant factors must consider the effect of familial variables on children's extrafamilial behavior, especially where the young are concerned. The skills a very young child brings to a social situation are likely to have been learned at home. But, the impact of familial relations on peer relations has not been extensively examined (Hartup, 1983). The meager data base that exists is primarily dependent upon the attachment literature. For example, in a longitudinal study, Waters, Wippman, and Sroufe (1979) found a definite relationship between "secure" attachments at 15 months of age and peer interaction 2 years later. Thus, the variables that account for secure attachment in children may also provide the necessary base for successful entry into the peer group (Hartup, 1983).

Conceptually, the child's social relationship skills may be accounted for in part by the parents' child-management skills (Sherman & Farina, 1974; Patterson & Reid, 1970). Clarke-Stewart (1973) found that maternal stimulation *contingent* upon infants' social behavior was positively related to the children's scores on measures of language and social competence. Parents of socially low competent children may not have the child-rearing skills necessary to teach their children socially adaptive behaviors.

In addition, as Hartup (1983) has noted, the impact of familial stress can also have a significant effect on extrafamilial behavior. For example, Hetherington (1979) found that children of divorced parents showed significant deficits in social behavior when compared with a normal control group. These differences, however, disappeared over time with a return to stable family conditions, especially for boys. Taken together, these data suggest that familial conditions may have an impact on a child's behavior in other settings over the course of a child's lifetime.

A more comprehensive view of factors that may contribute to children's social competence should include: (a) specific social skills that enable a child to establish and maintain social contact, (b) language skills that form the essential prerequisites for effective social communication, (c) physical or motor skills that allow children to explore more effectively the world of objects with the peer group, and (d) specific parent child-rearing skills that provide the child with socially adaptive behavior necessary for entering and adapting to the social milieu outside the home setting.

We shall now report on a study that examined the impact of preschool children's social, language, and motor skills on their social competence (Hops & Finch, 1982). Social competence was assessed by the judgments of peers, parents, and teachers, in the children's environment. In addition, home observations of family interactions on a subset of the larger sample provided some data on the impact of parenting behavior on children's social competence (Finch, 1984; Hops & Finch, 1985).

The Study

Approximately 240 children were recruited from 17 classrooms in 10 preschools in the Eugene-Springfield, Oregon, area. They ranged in age from 2½ to 6 years and represented a broad range of SES from Headstart classrooms to private preschools.

Indices of Social Competence

Estimates of social competence were obtained from three relevant sources of information, each presumed to provide a unique source of variance. These consisted of data obtained from (a) peer sociometrics, (b) parent ratings, and (c) teacher ratings.[1] A description of each measure follows.

Because of the generally low test-retest reliability scores based on the restricted-nomination procedure (Greenwood et al., 1979; Hops & Greenwood, 1981), the paired-comparison procedure (Cohen & Van Tassel, 1978) was used. Each child was shown all possible pairs of classmates' pictures (excluding pairs with the subject's own picture) and asked to select the child with whom he or she preferred to play.

Two scores were computed for inclusion in the composite measure of sociability: (a) overall popularity, calculated as the proportion of all possible peer nominations the subject received; and (b) number of friends, calculated as the number of peers whom the subject had selected, and who had selected the subject in turn on at least 50% of all possible occasions. (To increase the probability that the

---

[1]It should be noted here that our measures of social competence were primarily designed to discriminate socially withdrawn children from their nonwithdrawn, normal peers. Consequently, low competence scores on the dependent variables are more likely to refer to withdrawn rather than aggressive acting-out children.

children were indeed friends, the combined percentage was required to sum to at least 110%, based on a procedure adopted from Cohen and Melson, 1979.) This measure of *reciprocated* sociometric choices took into account the mutuality inherent in friendship (Hartup, 1983; Hops & Lewin, 1984). Reciprocated choices were used here because they have been shown to have higher test-retest reliability (Busk, Ford, & Schulman, 1973) and they account for more of a child's social behavior than unreciprocated choices (Hops & Finch, 1985).

Parental input to the composite measure of social competence was obtained using a 64-item, 7-point, bipolar adjective rating scale devised by Becker (1960) for preschool children. Reliability estimates for both teachers and parents were moderate to high. In the present study, two of the five available factors, the withdrawn-sociable scale and the submissive-dominant scale (Becker & Krug, 1964), were used. Both of these factors were presumed to assess a child's level of overt sociability or withdrawal. In intact families, the mean of the parents' ratings on each scale was used.

Teacher judgments were assessed using two instruments previously developed to screen low social interactors in the preschool setting (Greenwood, Walker, & Hops, 1977; Greenwood et al., 1979): (a) the teacher verbal frequency ranking procedure (TVFR), and (b) the social behavior rating scale (SBRS) (Greenwood, Todd, Walker, & Hops, 1978). The TVFR requires the teacher simply to rank-order all the children in the classroom on the basis of an estimate of each child's verbal behavior output. Greenwood and his colleagues (Greenwood et al., 1977, 1978, 1979) found the procedure to be (a) stable across a 1-month period, (b) significantly correlated with directly observed rates of social interactions, and (c) accurate at identifying the child with the lowest rate of interaction in each classroom. The SBRS is a 9-item, 7-point rating scale. Both individual scores and the total scale score are significantly correlated with (a) observed rates of interaction, and (b) sociometric acceptance. Test-retest reliabilities over a 1-month period for both measures ranged from .72 to .85 in a series of studies involving several hundred preschoolers over a 3-year period (Greenwood et al., 1978).

Predictor Social and Nonsocial Skills

Social skill variables were derived from observations of the children during freeplay periods using a variation of the Peer Interaction Recording System (Garrett, Hops, & Stevens, 1977). This 6-s interval coding system distinguishes verbal and nonverbal, as well as positive and negative, interactive behavior. A "no response" code indicates a lack of response to peer initiation. Nonsocial coding categories included the *proximity* of the subject to peers, whether they were involved in the *same activity*, whether the subject merely *observed* a peer, and whether the subject was *alone* and away from other peers. Children in each classroom were observed until a minimum of 15 min of data was collected per subject over a 5-day period. Observers were required to achieve at least 80% agreement with the observer coordinator on at least three separate occasions before their data were used in the study. Over the entire study, 54 agreement checks were made between the observer coordinator and all observers. The average agreement was 82%.

A 14-item battery of tests based on the work of Vogt (1978) and Broekhoff (1977) was used to assess each child's motor ability. They included measures of speed, motor coordination, agility and strength, and complex as well as single movements.

The Basic Concept Inventory (Engelmann, Ross, & Bingham, 1982) assessed each child's listening vocabulary, knowledge of linguistic study, and logic. The test taps both expressive and receptive language and analogies. The concepts measured here have been shown to be important prerequisites for teaching problem-solving skills to preschoolers (Spivack & Shure, 1974).

Home Observations Recording Procedure

Families of children with scores from the low, middle, and high thirds on a composite score of social competence[2] were initially invited by letter to participate in the home observation portion of the larger research project. Each participating family was paid a total of $50. Five consecutive 1-h observation sessions were required, in which all family members were present, and with the following stipulations: (a) all members must confine themselves to specific rooms so that they may be visible to the observer; (b) no television viewing, outgoing telephone calls, or guests are allowed; and (c) incoming calls may be answered briefly.

Family interaction was recorded using the MOSAIC (measurement of social adjustment in children) observation coding system developed at the Oregon Social Learning Center (Toobert, Patterson, Moore, & Halper, 1982). The MOSAIC categorizes behavior on four simultaneous levels: (a) context, (b) activity, (c) content, and (d) valence. It also identifies the subject of the interaction and the recipient of the behavior. For this study, content codes were collapsed into three categories: *positive* (pleasing behavior with high impact, e.g., approve physical affection), *normative* (the majority of prosocial behaviors that are facilitative, instructional, and communicative, e.g., request, general statement), and *aversive* (displeasing behaviors with high impact, e.g., disapprove, physical negative, criticize). Positive and normative child behavior were also summed to reflect overall rates of child *prosocial* behavior.

Several levels of parenting behavior were examined in this study to determine the level of specificity of parent interaction required to predict social competence in children. These were: (a) overall rates of parent behavior to reflect the family's "social energy level," (b) overall rates of parent behavior directed specifically toward the target child to reflect the level of attention the child receives from the

---

[2]The composite score upon which this group of families was selected also included two global variables based upon direct observation. These were percent social behavior and initiation ratio. In previous analyses, both of these were shown to be related to the teacher factor. Thus, it is unlikely that the social competence variable differs much from the composite index used previously.

parents, and (c) the *contingent* relationship between parent and child behavior, that is, the reinforcement of prosocial behavior, and the punishment of aversive behavior.

Indices of Social Competence

All scores were standardized by classroom to control as much as possible for effects due to age, sex, SES, and other classroom variables. Each of the two scores obtained from the three sets of social competence measures was averaged, providing scores based on peer sociometrics, and parent and teacher ratings. In addition, the three scores were summed to provide a general measure of social competence.

Skill Variables

To control for possible differences due to sex of the child, the analyses were conducted separately for boys and girls. Each set of predictor variables (motor, social, and language) was factor analyzed with varimax rotation to reduce the total number of variables in the analysis. Only those variables loading on the factors at .40 or greater were considered. Factors were included based on eigenvalues greater than 1 and on the Scree test (Cattell, 1966).

Six factors representing social skill variables based on direct observation of the children's behaviors were extracted for each sex. The factor loadings are presented in Tables 2.1 and 2.2. Four of the six factors for each sex were quite similar. Two factors represented positive interaction with girls, and positive interaction with boys. Two hovering factors, one related to each sex, were also extracted, based on high loadings on being proximal to and observing others. The fifth factor for boys had high loadings on same activity as girls and positive nonverbals to boys. It appears to represent a rather passive, noninteractive behavior pattern that we called passive responder. The sixth boys' factor was loaded highly on positive and negative verbal behavior to girls and is referred to as verbal interaction/girls. For girls, a fifth factor represented nonverbal behavior to girls and the sixth positive nonverbal response to boys' initiations. Both are similar to the passive responder factor noted for the boys except that they represent that style of interaction separately for each sex.

A factor analysis of the motor skill variables produced three factors each for boys and girls (see Tables 2.3 and 2.4, respectively). The three boys' factors represented (a) general motor coordination, (b) arm strength, and (c) speed and ball throwing form (underhand is scored lower than overhand). Ball throwing form is usually correlated with age and can thus be referred to as one aspect of physical maturity. The girls' factors were quite similar, representing (a) general motor coordination, (b) leg strength and speed, and (c) arm strength. For both sexes, the general motor factor accounted for most of the variance in motor performance.

A single language factor was extracted with high loadings on the four scores obtained from the basic concept inventory.

TABLE 2.1. Factor loadings on social skill variables after varimax rotation for boys.

	Positive interaction with girls	Positive interaction with boys	Hover/ boys	Passive responder	Hover/ girls	Verbal interaction with girls
Positive verbal/ girls	0.868					
Positive verbal initiations/girls	0.756					
Positive nonverbal/ girls	0.733					
Alone	−0.827					
Positive nonverbal/ boys		0.674				
Positive verbal/ boys		0.622				
Positive verbal initiations/boys		0.479				
Proximal/boys			0.854			
Observe/boys			0.846			
$_p$(PosVerbal$_S$/ PosVerbal$_B$)				−0.871		
$_p$(PosNonVerbal$_S$/ PosVerbal$_B$)				0.793		
Same activity/girls				0.407		
Observe/girls					0.906	
Proximal/girls					0.878	
$_p$(PosNonverbal$_S$/ PosVerbal$_G$						−0.861
$_p$(PosVerbal$_S$/ PosVerbal$_G$)						0.615
Negative verbal/ girls						0.533
Percent variance explained	14.8	−11.8	9.4	8.1	7.0	5.9

Relationship of Child Skill to a Composite Measure of Social Competence

First, the factor loadings for the entire set of social, motor, and language factors were entered into a stepwise regression analysis to predict the level of social competence for each sex independently.[3] For boys, 20.7% of the variance in social competence was accounted for by general motor coordination ($p < .001$). No other skill variables entered the equation.

---

[3]Despite the standardization of scores within classrooms to control for settings or developmental variables, a preliminary correlational analysis indicated that age was modestly correlated with some of the skill variables, for example, motor skills. Thus, to remove

TABLE 2.2. Factor loadings on social skill variables after varimax rotation for girls.

	Positive inter-action with boys	Positive inter-action with girls	Passive responder girls	Hover/boys	Hover/girls	Passive responder boys
Positive verbal/ boys	0.872					
Positive nonverbal/ boys	0.755					
Positive verbal initiations/boys	0.738					
Positive verbal/ girls		0.805				
Alone		−0.762				
Positive verbal initiations/ girls		0.745				
p(PosNonverbal$_S$/ PosVerbal$_G$)			0.918			
p(PosVerbal$_S$/ PosVerbal$_G$)			−0.891			
Positive nonverbal/ girls	−0.400	0.409	0.598			
Interaction/ teacher		−0.401	−0.433			
Observe/boys				0.917		
Proximal/boys				0.904		
Observe—girls					0.909	
Proximal/girls					0.867	
p(PosNonverbal$_S$/ PosVerbal$_B$						0.913
p(PosVerbal$_S$/ PosVerbal$_B$)						−0.811
Percent variance explained	17.0	11.9	9.8	6.5	6.2	6.0

In contrast, 36% of the variance in girls' social competence was accounted for by two motor and two social variables. As with boys, general motor coordination entered the equation first, accounting for almost 15% of the variance. This was followed in turn by hovering/boys, speed and leg strength, and passive respond-ing/girls, accounting for 8%, 8%, and 6% of additional variance, respectively. The beta weights, however, for the hovering and passive responding factors were negative, indicating that both of them acted as suppressor variables. Girls who hovered around boys and who did not respond verbally to initiations by girls were likely to be judged less socially competent overall.

any variance due to age-related or developmental factors, age was forced into each equation first. At no time did it prove to be a significant predictor of any measure of social competence.

TABLE 2.3. Factor loadings on motor skill variables after varimax rotation for boys.

	General motor	Arm strength	Speed maturity
Standing long jump	0.804		
Run 8 m	−0.517		0.477
Run 6 m	−0.712		0.439
Walk and clap	0.516		
Agility	−0.684		
Open/close hands	0.556		
Forward roll	0.583		
Ball throw distance	0.722		
Ball throw form			0.770
Catch and toss	0.695		
Balance beam	0.451	0.400	
Under flex arm hang		0.839	
Straight arm hang		0.679	
Over flex arm hang		0.789	
Percent variance explained	34.7	10.7	9.7

Relationship of Child Skill to Individual Measures of Social Competence

The entire set of skill factors was entered into three independent regression equations for each sex to predict parent, teacher, and peer judgments. Here, we attempted to answer the question of which specific skills accounted for the social judgments of specific social agents. The beta weights and the amount of variance

TABLE 2.4. Factor loadings on motor skill variables after varimax rotation for girls.

	General motor	Speed & leg strength	Arm strength
Standing long jump	0.678	−0.409	
Run 8 m		0.855	
Run 6 m		0.886	
Walk and clap	0.710		
Agility	−0.516	−0.464	
Forward roll	0.453		
Ball throw distance	0.670		
Catch and toss	0.616		
Balance beam	0.565		
Under flex arm hang			0.838
Straight arm hang			0.638
Over flex arm hang			0.830
Percent variance explained	29.9	12.5	8.5

TABLE 2.5. Stepwise regression of skill factors on boys' social competence factors after age forced in.

Skill factor	Beta	Variance	p	Competence factor	Overall R²
General motor coordination	0.35	0.12	< .05	Peer	0.13
General motor coordination	0.39	0.14	< .01	Teacher	0.22
Passive responding/ boys	−0.24	0.05	< .10		

accounted for by each factor, and the overall R^2 for each measure of social competence is presented in Tables 2.5 and 2.6.

None of the social, motor, or language variables was found to be a significant predictor of parent ratings for boys. Two factors predicted the parent ratings of girls. Hovering/boys (negatively weighted) and speed/leg strength accounted for approximately 18% of the variance. As with overall social competence ratings, hovering/boys was a negative predictor.

General motor coordination was the only predictor of sociometric scores for boys, accounting for 12% of the variance. However, hovering/boys was also a significant negative predictor for girls' popularity and, combined with general motor coordination, accounted for 14% of the variance. The two factors were approximately equal in their contributions.

TABLE 2.6. Stepwise regression of skill factors on girls' social competence factors after age forced in.

Skill factor	Beta	Variance	p	Competence factor	Overall R²
General motor coordination	0.50	0.20	< .001	Teacher	0.36
Hover/boys	−0.29	0.08	= .01		
Speed/leg strength	0.29	0.07	< .01		
Passive responding/ girls	−0.24	0.06	< .05		
Hover/boys	−0.32	0.10	< .05	Parent	0.18
Speed/leg strength	0.30	0.09	< .05		
General motor coordination	0.28	0.09	< .05	Peer	0.14
Hover/boys	−0.26	0.08	< .05		

Twenty-two percent of the variance in teachers ratings and rankings of the boys' social competence was predicted by two factors. These were general motor coordination and passive responding/boys, accounting for 14% and 5% of the variance, respectively. Passive responding/boys was also a negative predictor; boys who are nonverbal in their response to verbal initiations are less likely to be seen as socially competent by their teachers.

Four factors accounted for 36% of the variance in teacher ratings and rankings of girls' social competence. General motor coordination, hovering/boys, leg speed and strength, and passive responding/girls entered the equation in that order. General motor coordination accounted for as much variance as the three other factors combined.

The Relationship of Parenting Behavior
to Child Social Competence

As we indicated earlier, a small subset of children representing the broad range of children's social competence were observed in the home during interactions with their families (Finch, 1984; Hops & Finch, 1985). Correlations between social competence levels of children and parenting behavior were examined for the entire sample of 42 families, and for a subset of the 28 intact families. The latter allowed us to compare the impact of fathers and mothers to their children's social competence.

Neither the overall rates of parental behavior (i.e., total, positive, normative, or aversive) nor the parental contingent behaviors (i.e., reinforcement of prosocial and punishment of aversive behaviors) were found to be significant predictors of social competence. However, the total amount of parental attention directed to the child was a significant predictor ($r = .351, p < .01$); more specifically, it was the parent rate of normative behavior that accounted for most of the variance in social competence ($r = .391, p < .001$).

Examining the parental behavior within intact families revealed some important differences between the contribution of mothers and fathers to child social competence. None of the fathers' behaviors at any level was found to be significantly related. In contrast, mothers' total behavior directed to the child ($r = .332, p < .01$) and specifically, her normative behavior ($r = .386, p < .01$) was found to be significantly correlated to children's social competence levels. Thus, it was mothers', rather than fathers', behavior that accounted for most of the predictive power noted in the larger sample.

A close examination of the structure of the families revealed that family size, more specifically, the number of siblings, was also significantly correlated with social competence levels $r = .397, p < .01$, and $r = .462, p < .01$, for the large and intact samples, respectively. However, the number of siblings was also significantly related to the total amount of parental behavior directed at the child ($r = -.772, p < .001$) and the total amount of maternal behavior directed at the child ($r = .598, p < .001$). Thus, it appears that children in larger families receive proportionally less parental attention than in smaller families.

Discussion

The results of this study appear to have important theoretical and practical implications for the study of children's social competence and for the design of treatment procedures to improve the relationships of those who are socially incompetent or withdrawn. The data presented here have shown that motor skill performance is a more powerful predictor of how the child is perceived by social agents in the environment than was performance in social skills. Moreover, this was true for the judgments of peers, teachers, and parents about both boys *and* girls. Even when age effects are controlled for, the impact of motoric proficiency is clear. Yet there are virtually no studies that have included a motor proficiency component as part of a treatment to improve children's social relationships. As we have suggested previously (Hops, 1983; Hops et al., in press), interventions that focus solely on social skills training may not be productive for those children who are also deficient in the necessary prerequisite motor skills. It can no longer be argued that these data simply reflect the powerful influences of physical and physiological development since, after general developmental level had been controlled for by entering age first into the regression analyses, motor skills remained significant predictor variables. Several studies have shown that well-designed training programs can increase the physical proficiency of preschoolers (Werner, 1974), even those who are developmentally delayed (DuBose & Folio, 1977). Whether training in motor skills has a *functional* relationship to social competence remains an empirical question, for the possibility remains that there is some other factor mediating the relationship between motor skills and social competence. At the very least, studies of social skills interventions must consider motor performance levels in their analysis when judging the impact of their training programs.

A second finding that has important implications for the design of future research and treatment programs is the data showing that the predictors of boys' and girls' social competence as judged by social agents in their environment are somewhat different. For example, judgments by teachers and peers of boys' social competence was based primarily on the children's general motor coordination. Only one social behavior variable increased the predictive power of motoric skills and only for teacher ratings. In contrast, judgments of social competence in girls was dependent upon both motor and social variables. Girls who were not socially active, who hovered around boys, and who were nonverbal and reactive in their interactions with girls were less likely to be seen by their teachers as socially competent.

It may also be somewhat surprising that peers' ratings of boys *and* girls were predicted by their level of motor coordination. Boys activities are usually more physical and boisterous than girls (see Halverson & Waldrop, 1973; Hartup, 1983). A decade ago, Broekhoff (1977) found social status could be predicted by boys' motor coordination but not girls'. However the present studies suggests that currently proficiency in motor skills is as important a predictor of girls' social competence as it is of boys'.

The influence of the home on children's social competence has received little attention in the past (Hartup, 1983; Hops, 1983). The results presented here, although correlational, indicate that parental influences do affect children's social relationships outside the home. Furthermore, the finding that it is mothers, rather than fathers, whose influence is significant, is not surprising. Recently, Patterson (1980) noted that fathers' most appropriate role label is that of "guest." They tend not to operate as crises managers. Fathers in normal families do not appear to behave differently than those in distressed families. Similar findings have been obtained recently in another study we have conducted on the familial interactions of depressed mothers (Hops et al., 1985). The implications for the treatment of socially withdrawn or incompetent children are clear. Parental involvement may increase the power of the intervention and providing a role for fathers may have a more significant impact than using mothers only.

One issue that requires some clarification is the finding that social factors more representative of deficits rather than skills in the children's repertoires were significant predictors of social competence. As indicated, it was not the factors representing positive social interactions that accounted for portions of the variance in social competence, but rather those variables that represented non-responsiveness or hovering. There is at least one possible reason for this effect. The correlations between the significant motor skill predictors and the positive social interaction factors tended to be significant, although the magnitude of these relationships were not large. However, since the relationships between the dependent variables and the motor skill variable were larger than that with the positive social interaction variable, the motor skill factor entered the equation first. Thus, even had we eliminated the factors indicating deficiencies in social skills from the analyses, motor performance would still have accounted for larger proportions of the variance.

The issue of the relationship between a composite measure of social competence and one based on the individual components remains somewhat unclear. The correlations between the different measures were relatively low and the factors that predict each, while similar, account for different amounts of variance. It appears that teachers' judgments are affected by a wider range of information than that of peers or parents. Teachers' judgments of children's social interaction among preschoolers is surprisingly good (Greenwood et al., 1979) and further research will be required to determine whether they are more valid assessors of children's social behavior than are peers. Certainly, parents' judgments, especially of boys' social competence, are minimally affected by those variables examined in this study.

One final caveat: To the extent that the measures of social functioning in this study were sensitive only to one specific type of social problem, namely withdrawal, caution should be used in generalizing these findings to other socially impaired groups or different measures of social competence. For example, it may be the case that for aggressive children other factors besides motor skills would prove to be most strongly related to ratings of social competence.

Acknowledgments. This manuscript was prepared with the assistance of NIMH Grant #MH33205 and BRSG Grant #RR05612. The authors wish to acknowledge the contributions of Tuck Stevens who coordinated both home and school observations, the home and school observers, and the parents, teachers, and children who graciously participated in this study. We also thank Virginia Osteen for her assistance in the preparation of this manuscript.

References

Achenbach, T. M., & Edelbrock, C. S. (1982). *Manual for the Child Behavior Checklist and Child Behavior Profile*. Burlington, VT: Child Psychiatry, University of Vermont.

Anderson, S., & Messick, S. (1974). Social competency in young children. *Developmental Psychology, 10*, 282-293.

Becker, W. C. (1960). The relationship of factors in parental ratings of self and each other to the behavior of kindergarten children as rated by mothers, fathers, and teachers. *Journal of Consulting Psychology, 24*, 507-527.

Becker, W. C., & Krug, R. S. (1964). A circumplex model for social behavior in children. *Child Development, 35*, 371-396.

Broekhoff, J. (1977). A search for relationships: Sociological and social-psychological considerations. *The Academy Papers, 11*, 45-55.

Busk, P. L., Ford, R. C., & Schulman, J. L. (1973). Stability of sociometric responses in classrooms. *Journal of Genetic Psychology, 123*, 69-84.

Cattell, R. B. (1966). The meaning and strategic use of factor analysis. In R. B. Cattell (Ed.), *Handbook of multivariate experimental psychology*. Chicago: Rand McNally.

Clarke-Stewart, K. A. (1973). Interactions between mothers and their young children: Characteristics and consequences. *Monographs of the Society for Research in Child Development, 38*(6-7,Serial No. 153).

Cohen, A. S., & Melson, G. F. (1979, May). *The influence of friendship on children's communication*. Paper presented at the annual meeting of the Midwestern Psychological Association, Chicago. IL.

Cohen, A. S., & Van Tassel, E. (1978). A comparison: Partial and complete paired-comparisons in sociometric measurement of preschool groups. *Applied Psychological Measurement, 2*, 31-40.

Connolly, J., & Doyle, A. (1981). Assessment of social competence in preschoolers: Teachers versus peers. *Developmental Psychology, 17*, 454-462.

Cowen, E. L., Pederson, A., Babigian, H., Izzo, L. D., & Trost, M. A. (1973). Long-term follow-up of early detected vulnerable children. *Journal of Consulting and Clinical Psychology, 41*, 438-446.

Dodge, K. A. (1983). Behavioral antecedents of peer social status. *Child Development, 54*, 1386-1399.

DuBose, R. F., & Folio, R. (1977, April). Investigation of short-term gains in motor skill achievement in delayed and non-delayed preschool children. *Peabody Journal of Education*, pp. 181-184.

Engelmann, S., Ross, D., & Bingham, V. (1982). *Basic language concepts test*. Tigard, OR: C. C. Publications.

Finch, M. (1984). *Childhood social competence and parental variables: A direct observation study*. Unpublished doctoral dissertation, University of Oregon, Eugene, OR.

Garrett, B., Hops, H., & Stevens, T. (1977). *Peer interaction recording system II (PIRS II)*. Eugene, OR: Center at Oregon for Research in the Behavioral Education of the Handicapped.

Gottman, J. M., Gonso, J., & Rasmussen, B. (1975). Social interaction, social competence, and friendship in children. *Child Development, 46*, 709-718.

Greenwood, C. R., Todd, N. M., Walker, H. M., & Hops, H. (1978). *Social assessment manual for preschool level (SAMPLE)*. Eugene, OR: Center at Oregon for Research in the Behavioral Education of the Handicapped, University of Oregon.

Greenwood, C. R., Walker, H. M., & Hops, H. (1977). Some issues in social interaction/withdrawal assessment. *Exceptional Children, 43*, 490-499.

Greenwood, C. R., Walker, H. M., Todd, N. M., & Hops, H. (1979). Selecting a cost-effective screening device for the assessment of preschool social withdrawal. *Journal of Applied Behavior Analysis, 12*, 639-652.

Gresham, F. M. (1981). Validity of social skills measures for assessing social competence in low-status children: A multivariate investigation. *Developmental Psychology, 17*, 390-398.

Halverson, C. F., & Waldrop, M. F. (1973). The relations of mechanically recorded activity level to varieties of preschool play behavior. *Child Development, 44*, 681-687.

Hartup, W. W. (1983). The peer system. In E. M. Hetherington (Ed.), *Handbook of child psychology: Vol. 4. Socialization, personality, and social development*. New York: Wiley.

Hetherington, E. M. (1979). Divorce: A child's perspective. *American Psychologist, 34*, 851-858.

Hops, H. (1983). Children's social competence and skill: Current research practices and future directions. *Behavior Therapy, 14*, 3-18.

Hops, H., Biglan, A., Sherman, L., Friedman, L. S., Arthur, J., & Osteen, V. (1985). *Home observations of family interactions of depressed women*. Manuscript submitted for publication.

Hops, H., & Finch, M. (1982, May). *A skill deficit view of social competence in preschoolers*. Paper presented at the annual meeting of the Association for Behavior Analysis, Milwaukee, WI.

Hops, H., & Finch, M. (1985). *The relationship between observed social behavior and reciprocated sociometric choices: A dyadic view of friendship*. Manuscript submitted for publication.

Hops, H., & Finch, M. (1985, April). *Parental contributions to childhood social competence*. Paper presented at the biennial meeting of the Society for Research in Child Development, Toronto.

Hops, H., Finch, M., & McConnell, S. R. (in press). Social skills deficits. In P. H. Bornstein & A. E. Kazdin (Eds.), *Handbook of clinical behavior therapy with children*. Homewood, IL: Dorsey Press.

Hops, H., & Greenwood, C. R. (1981). Social skills deficits. In E. J. Mash & L. G. Terdal (Eds.), *Behavioral assessment of childhood disorders*. New York: Guilford Press.

Hops, H., & Lewin, L. (1984). Peer sociometric forms. In T. H. Ollendick & M. Hersen (Eds.), *Child behavioral assessment: Principles and procedures*. New York: Pergamon.

Lewis, M., & Rosenblum, L. A. (1975). *Friendship and peer relations*. New York: Wiley.

McConnell, S. (1982). *Identifying social skills for handicapped boys: Evaluation of teacher rating, peer sociometric, and direct observation measures*. Unpublished doctoral dissertation, University of Oregon, Eugene, OR.

McConnell, S., & Odom, S. L. (in press). Sociometrics: Peer-referenced measures and the assessment of social competence. In P. S. Strain, M. J. Guralnick, & H. M. Walker (Eds.), *Children's social behavior: Development, assessment, and modification*. New York: Academic Press.

Patterson, G. R. (1980). Mothers: The unacknowledged victims. *Monographs of the Society for Research in Child Development, 45* (5, Serial No. 186).

Patterson, G. R., & Reid, J. B. (1970). Reciprocity and coercion: Two facets of social systems. In C. Neuringer & J. Michael (Eds.), *Behavior modification in clinical psychology*. New York: Appleton-Century-Crofts.

Putallaz, M., & Gottman, J. M. (1981). Social skills and group acceptance. In S. R. Asher & J. M. Gottman (Eds.), *The development of children's friendships*. New York: Cambridge University Press.

Roff, M., Sells, S. B., & Golden, M. M. (1972). *Social adjustment and personality development in children*. Minneapolis: University of Minnesota Press.

Rubin, K. H., & Ross, H. S. (1982). *Peer relations and social skills in childhood*. New York: Springer-Verlag.

Schachter, F. F., Kirschner, K., Klips, B., Friedricks, M., & Sanders, K. (1974). Everyday preschool interpersonal speech usage: Methodological, developmental, and sociolinguistic studies. *Monographs of the Society for Research in Child Development, 39*(3).

Sherman, H., & Farina, A. (1974). Social adequacy of parents and children. *Journal of Abnormal Psychology, 83*, 327-330.

Spivack, G., & Shure, M. B. (1974). *Social adjustment of young children*. San Francisco: Jossey-Bass.

Toobert, D. J., Patterson, G. R., Moore, D. R., & Halper, V. (1982). *MOSAIC (measurement of social adjustment in children)*. Eugene, OR: Castalia.

Vogt, U. (1978). *Die motorik 3-bis 6jahrigerKinder*. Schorndorf, W. Germany: Verlag Karl Hofman.

Walker, H. M., McConnell, S. R. Holmes, D., Todis, B., Walker, J. L., & Golden, N. (1983). *A curriculum for children's effective peer and teacher skills (ACCEPTS)*. Austin, TX: Pro-Ed.

Waters, E., Wippman, J., & Sroufe, L. A. (1979). Attachment, positive affect, and competence in the peer group: Two studies in construct validation. *Child Development, 50*, 821-829.

Werner, P. (1974). Education of selected movement patterns of preschool children. *Perceptual and Motor Skills, 39*, 795-798.

Wine, J. D., & Smye, M. D. (Eds.). (1981). *Social competence*. New York: Guilford Press.

CHAPTER 3

What's the Point? Issues in the Selection of Treatment Objectives

Wyndol Furman and Philip Robbins

A number of intervention programs have been developed to teach children the skills necessary for effective interactions with others (see Furman, 1984; Hops, 1982). Some investigators have developed programs to improve the sociometric status of children who are not liked or who are disliked by their peers. Others have designed interventions to increase the rates of peer interaction of children who are isolated from their peers. Although there is considerable controversy concerning which of these approaches is more appropriate, the objective of both is to enhance children's relationships with their *peers*.

Social skills training programs could, however, have other objectives. For example, rather than change peer relationships in general, one might want to foster close friendships with one or two peers. Alternatively, one might want to enhance children's relationships with any significant other in their social networks, rather than focus on relationships with peers per se. In the present chapter, we consider the relative merits of these alternative objectives and their implications for designing intervention programs. Our intention, however, is not to argue that one treatment objective is preferable to another. Efforts to enhance general peer relationships, close friends, or relationships with other individuals in the social network are all commendable. A careful examination of the objectives of social skills programs may, however, lead to more effective interventions.

Friendships and Peer Relationships

A child's relationships with his or her peers may vary considerably. Some may be close friends; others may be playmates; still others may be casual acquaintances; and a few may even be antagonists. Commonly, however, clinical investigators have not differentiated among these different relationships, and instead they have relied on global indices of the general quality of peer relationships. For example, the most common index of the quality of peer relationships is sociometric status, which is often measured by averaging peer ratings is likeability.[1] Similarly, most

---

[1] Sociometric status is also measured by having children name their three best friends or the three they like the most. Although this is technically a measure of the size of friendship cliques, it is commonly considered to be a measure of sociometric status or popularity. Most importantly, it is not an accurate measure of the *quality* (vs. number) of close friendships.

observational measures of reinforcing, punishing, or other types of peer interaction are also global measures of the general quality of peer relationships, because investigators typically code children's interactions without differentiating among the peers with whom they are interacting.

As has been shown by a number of recent investigators, children's interactions with their friends differ from their interactions with other peers (see Furman, 1982; Hartup, 1978). Moreover, the quality of children's close friendships may not correspond closely to the quality of their relationships with other peers. For example, some popular children do not even have best friends (Hymel & Asher, 1977), and many children with best friends are not particularly popular. In fact, "controversial" children are liked the most by some peers and liked the least by other peers (Coie, Dodge, & Coppotelli, 1982). Additionally, the quality of the one close friendship one child has may be superior to that of any of a number of close friendships another child has. Although it is not known empirically how different they are, the group of children without close friendships or with unsatisfactory close friendships is probably not exactly the same as those who generally have poor peer relationships.

Hence, one should distinguish between the quality of children's close friendships and the quality of their peer relationships in general. This distinction becomes particularly important in the preadolescent and adolescent years when the characteristics and functions of friendships and other peer relationships become more differentiated (Buhrmester & Furman, in press). The descriptions in subsequent sections refer particularly to these "mature" forms of friendships.

The Functions of Peer Relationships and Friendships

Should the primary objective of a social skills training program be to enhance children's peer relationships in general or should the objective be to promote and enhance close freiendships? One way to address this question is to consider the functions served by peer relationships in general and those served by close friendships. Weiss's (1974) theory of social provisions provides a useful framework for understanding the functions of different relationships. He hypothesized that individuals seek specific social provisions or types of social support in their relationships with others. He listed six specific provisions, but in our research on children's relationships (e.g., Furman & Buhrmester, in press), we have found it useful to include eight provisions. These are: (a) affection, (b) intimacy, (c) reliable alliance, (d) instrumental aid, (e) nurturance, (f) companionship, (g) enhancement of worth, and (h) a sense of inclusion. Weiss thought that different types of relationships supplied different provisions. For example, children may primarily turn to their parents for instrumental aid, whereas they may primarily turn to their friends and peers for companionship. In the following paragraphs, we compare the provisions obtained in friendships and those obtained in peer relationships in general.

Affection. Although the need for love and affection lasts across the life cycle, it is especially strong in childhood. Theorists have long thought that children's friendships are characterized by feelings of love or affection. In fact, the defining feature of a friendship is usually considered to be a mutual affective bond (Hartup, 1978). Sullivan (1953) particularly stressed the importance of preadolescent' "chumships" in providing them with their first experience of genuine affection.

The affective ties in most peer relationships are not as strong as those in preadolescent and adolescent friendships. In some respects, one could characterize the difference as that between liking and loving. Certainly, there may be benefits from being liked by a number of peers, yet the experience of love and affection in those friendships seems unique. At the very least, the experiences of being loved by one and being liked by many seem qualitatively different. Thus, one would expect them to have different effects on children's socioemotional development. For example, Weiss (1974) hypothesized that the absence of a strong affective bond may lead to the experience of emotional loneliness. Hence, children, or at least adolescents, without close friendships seem more prone to experience such feelings than those who do not have a large network of peers who like them.

Intimacy. As is true with adults, children and adolescents are likely to share their secrets and personal aspects of themselves with close friends. In fact, Sullivan (1953) viewed the experience of intimacy in preadolescent chumships as one of the hallmarks of the children's love and affection for each other. Of course, children may also share information about themselves in their other peer relationships, but the level of disclosure is likely to be less intimate than that in close friendships.

The experience of having a friend in whom one can confide may promote feelings of trust, acceptance, and a sense of being understood. Additionally, being a confidant for another can provide a child with the opportunity to give help and support to another individual. The long-term consequences of such intimate interchanges in childhood friendships have not been studied, but Sullivan (1953) suggested that these experiences were a precursor to the development of intimate heterosexual relationships in early adolescence. Finally, investigators studying adult relationships have suggested that intimate interactions are a key element in the salubrious effects of social support for adults experiencing stress (Reis, 1984). Perhaps the same will prove to be true for adolescents and perhaps even preadolescents.

Reliable Alliance. In Weiss' theory, the concept of reliable alliance referred to the individual's sense of the other's loyalty or continued availability for the provision of resources and assistance. Clearly, the expectations concerning loyalty and availability are much greater in friendships than in other peer relationships. Having a loyal and reliable resource is of considerable benefit itself, but it can also promote feelings of security and the absence of such can cause feelings of anxiety and vulnerability. Additionally, the experience of being a reliable ally for one's friends can teach the child the value of being loyal and the importance of being able to set aside one's own desires to be able to respond to a friend's needs.

Because children may rely upon their friends more than their peers, the loss of a friend may have a more profound effect on them than the loss of other peer relationships. The loss of a friendship can even be a growth-inducing experience sometimes. Undesirable as it is, the experience may help the child to learn how to cope with pain and loss.

Instrumental Aid. Are friends or peers more important sources of instrumental aid or tangible help? Children expect friends to be more helpful than acquaintaintces (Furman & Bierman, 1984) and in some, but not all, circumstances they are more helpful (Berndt, in press). On the other hand, children are likely to have more acquaintances than close friends. Hence, there are a greater number of potential sources of aid among acquaintances than among close friends. Moreover, some types of assistance require specialized skills; for example, not all children could help others with their arithmetic homework. Hence, children may find an appropriate helper in a large and diverse pool of acquaintances more often than in a small pool of close friends. In light of these considerations, it appears fruitless to try to juxtapose the help provided by friends against that provided by peers. Instead, the principal conclusion to draw is that both can be important sources of instrumental aid.

Nurturance. Nurturance refers to providing comfort, solace, or aid to others. Following a line of reasoning similar to that outlined in the previous paragraph, we expect that both friends and other peers could be potential recipients of nurturance. Providing assistance and comfort to other children may promote feelings of competence and self-esteem and give children a sense of being needed.

Companionship. The provision of companionship or social integration refers to having someone with whom to share activities. Such activities are often rewarding, and the absence of companionship may lead to feelings of social isolation and boredom (Weiss, 1974). Both friends and other peers can provide these rewarding experiences and help children avoid the negative feelings. Much as was the case for instrumental aid and nurturance, close friends are frequent and regular sources of companionship, whereas there are many different sources of companionship among the group of other peers.

The companionship experience may, however, be different in the two cases. Friendships are characterized more by positive affect and social responsiveness than other peer relationships are. For example, while performing a cooperative task together, friends talk more and express more affect than acquaintances do (Newcomb, Brady, & Hartup, 1979). Thus, even when children engage in similar activities with their friends and other peers, the friendship bond may make the experience of the activity qualitatively different.

Enhancement of Worth. Weiss used the term "enhancement of worth" to refer to the affirmation by another of one's competence or value. Enhancement of worth promotes feelings of pride, self-esteem, and self-acceptance. The quality of both close friendships and other peer relationships has been found to affect children's self-worth (see Hartup, 1983; Mannarino, 1978). It is unclear which type of relationship has a stronger influence, but more importantly, it is likely that the kind of enhancement of worth received from close friends and peers is qualitatively different. Friends have a greater knowledge of each other than acquaintances do. Accordingly, they can affirm more central aspects of each other's personality than acquaintances do (Duck, 1973).

Sense of Inclusion. Sense of inclusion refers to the feeling that one belongs to and is accepted by a group larger than oneself. Several of the preceding provisions are more likely to be obtained in close friendships than in other types of peer relationships, but the reverse is true here. Close friendships are dyadic phenomena, and cannot really be considered groups. On the other hand, being part of a club, team, or other peer group can foster a sense of inclusion. Belonging to such groups may have a positive effect on children's self-esteem as they learn that others approve of certain aspects of them enough to want to share a group identity with them. The need for inclusion becomes particularly salient in the adolescent years (Veroff & Veroff, 1980). As adolescents make the transition to adult roles and responsibilities, groups provide them with opportunities to try out different roles as well as to interact with others of varying status simultaneously. Finally, groups provide opportunities to develop new relationships; for example, heterosexual dating relationships may emerge out of interactions between adolescent groups of same-sex peers (Dunphy, 1963).

Summary. In examining the relative contributions of close friendships and other peer relationships, we find two general patterns. Some provisions are primarily obtained in one type of peer relationship. For example, affection, intimacy, and a sense of reliable alliance are primarily obtained in close friendships, particularly preadolescent and adolescent ones, whereas feelings of inclusion are likely to result from peer group relationships. At the same time, we find that many of the provisions can be obtained in both friendships and other peer relationships, although the specific nature of the provision is different in the two. In the preceding paragraphs, we have principally described the functions of these relationships in terms of the social provisions that are obtained in them. A similar picture would emerge, however, if we thought of functions in terms of the social skills or competencies that are acquired in these relationships (Burhmester & Furman, in press). Some skills, such as intimacy skills, are likely to be developed in close friendships, whereas other skills, such as leadership skills, are likely to be acquired in peer group interactions. Finally, many skills, such as prosocial or activity skills, are acquired in both. Thus, both types of peer relationships are important, but they are not interchangeable.

It should be noted, however, that this conclusion is principally based on intuition and common sense. Although the effects of popularity and unpopularity have been studied extensively, we know remarkably little about the effects of close friendships. Moreover, only a few investigators have tried to distinguish between the effects of the two (e.g., McGuire & Weisz, 1982). To what extent are children without close friends at risk? Are they at greater risk than those who are unpopular? Can the presence of a close friendship or two buffer children from the deleterious effects of peer isolation or rejection? Clearly, these issues need to be addressed in the near future.

Implications for Social Skills Programs

Our discussion of the functions of friendships and other peer relationships highlights the importance of promoting both types of relationships. One might think that teaching children social skills that apply to most peer relationships would promote close friendships, but this does not appear to be the case. In many, although not all, instances, social skills programs have been successful in changing unaccepted children's general likeability (see Furman, 1984; Hops, 1982). Yet even when changes in general likeability have occurred, changes in the number of best friends have not (Gresham & Nagle, 1980; Oden & Asher, 1977). If we are to be successful in fostering close friendships, as well as general peer relationships, changes in the assessment strategies, program content, and treatment mechanisms are required.

Assessment Strategies. In the preceding, we described a number of benefits that result from having a close friendship. These benefits, however, do not result from the simple existence of such a friendship as much as they result from certain experiences that tend to occur in close friendships. Hence, it seems important to assess the qualitative features of these relationships. Simply asking children whether they have close friends is not sufficient. Our experience has been that most children will name close friends, even if they do not have particularly close relationships with any peer. Some investigators have limited close friendships to those where both children have nominated it as a close friendship. Even here, however, we believe that the quality of the friendship varies from dyad to dyad.

One measure that assesses the quality of friendships is Mannarino's (1976) Chumship Checklist in which children indicate whether they have engaged in each of 17 activities with their peer. Recently, we have developed a Friendship Relationship Questionnaire (FRQ), which assesses 13 qualities of children's friendships. Preliminary analyses revealed that three factors underlie these qualities: (a) Warmth/Closeness, composed of affection, intimacy, prosocial behavior, acceptance, loyalty, similarity, and the admiration of and by friend scales; (b) Conflict, composed of quarreling, antagonism, and competition scales; and (c) Exclusivity of the Relationship, composed of two scales that assess how much the child and friend want the other to be friends only with him or her (Furman, Adler, & Buhrmester, 1984). Finally, information about friendships can be derived from the Network of Relationships Inventory (NRI), a measure that assesses the characteristics of different relationships in children's social networks (Furman & Buhrmester, in press). Later in this chapter, some of the initial research with the NRI is presented.

Not only is it important to include measures of friendship quality, but also the timing of the assessments may require reevaluation. Changes in friendships may occur more slowly than changes in peer acceptance. Hence, lengthy follow-ups may be required to determine if the interventions are effective.

Program Content. Typically, social skills interventions focus on training skills that are important for effective interactions in most peer relationships. In particular, programs often include training in conversational skills, prosocial behavior, and cooperative play. Although training in these skills may be necessary for fostering friendships, that may not be enough. The traditional coaching program may need to be supplemented with training in other skills that related specifically to the development or enhancement of friendships.

The preceding discussion of the provisions specifically obtained in friendships provides some clues concerning what these skills may be. Because intimate self-disclosure is important in preadolescent and adolescent friendships, it may be important to help children learn how and when to self-disclose and how to be a supportive listener. Learning appropriate means of sharing affectionate feelings with a peer may also prove valuable. It may be useful to include discussions of the expectations and obligations of friendships, so that children are aware of the importance of being a reliable ally or good listener. Finally, children could be taught the conflict-resolution skills needed to avoid losing friendships as well as the skills needed to promote and enhance them.

Treatment Mechanisms. In most social skills training programs, investigators have tried to change the behavior or attitudes of the target children *directly* by the use of reinforcement, modeling, and behavioral rehearsal techniques. It is also possible to bring about such changes *indirectly* by changing peers' behaviors or attitudes (see Furman, 1984). For example, Bierman and Furman (1984) demonstrated that having the peer group involved in the treatment can be an effective means of enhancing the impact of the program. Children who participated in a social skills training program showed changes in conversational skills, but not in sociometric status. Children who participated in cooperative peer group activities as well as the social skills training program displayed changes in both. The peers who had been involved in the programs were particularly likely to change their attitudes toward the target children with whom they had participated.

The inclusion of peers in the treatment program seems particularly promising when the objective is to develop or enhance friendships. After all, friendships are dyadic phenomena. Greater change may occur if both members of a dyad are involved than if only one is. One way this could be done is to have both children receive training in friendship-enhancement skills. One could also try to promote a particular friendship between two children by having them participate in a series of experiences together as a dyad. These experiences may involve having the dyad perform a cooperative task involving a superordinate goal (Bierman & Furman, 1984; Sherif, Harvey, White, Hood, & Sherif, 1961), or alternatively having the two engage in a particularly rewarding or special experience together (e.g., visiting an amusement park or going on a camping trip). Such activities may not only foster that particular friendship, but also may provide children with experience in the skills required to develop or enhance other friendships.

Summary. Our comments are largely speculative in nature because there has been little empirical research pertaining to these issues. Yet, it does appear that changes in assessment techniques, program content, and treatment mechanisms may be required if the objective is to promote friendships. Ideally, it should be possible to incorporate these changes into existing programs so that we can develop a training program that promotes and enhances both close friendships and other peer relationships.

Peer Relationships and Other Personal Relationships

In the previous section, we discussed whether our objective should be to enhance the quality of the relationships children have with their peers generally or to enhance the quality of their relationships with specific kinds of peers—namely, close friends. Why focus on peer relationships, however? Children have close relationships with many others, including siblings, parents, relatives, and other adults. Perhaps it would be worthwhile to try to enhance the quality of these relationships as well. In this section, we discuss whether our objective should be to enhance children's peer relationships or to enhance their close relationships in general.

The Functions of Personal Relationships

Piaget (1932), Sullivan (1953), and other developmental theorists have discussed the different contributions of parent-child and peer relationships, but few investigators have examined this issue empirically. Recently, we compared and contrasted the social provisions obtained in different relationships in children's social networks (Furman & Buhrmester, in press). Approximately 200 fifth- and sixth-grade children competed Network of Relationships Inventories that assessed the characteristics of their relationships with their friends, mothers, fathers, grandparents, siblings, friends, and teachers[2] Children were asked how much each of six social provisions were obtained in each type of relationship. Based on Weiss' (1974) theory, the six were: (a) intimacy, (b) companionship, (c) affection, (d) reliable alliance, (e) enhancement of worth, and (f) instrumental help. Four other

---

[2]Unfortunately data were not obtained on other peer relationships, although the descriptions of friendships should provide some information concerning the functions of peer relationships.

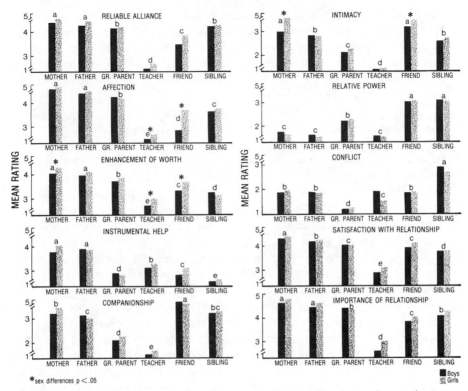

FIGURE 3.1. Mean quality scores of each relationship. Scores are mean item ratings on 5-point scales with higher scores indicating more of the characteristic. (Higher scores on relative dominance indicate greater dominance by the subjects. Scores of 3 indicated equal power by subject and other.) Scores with different superscripts are significantly different, $p < .05$. From "Children's Perceptions of the personal relationships in their networks by W. Furman and D. Burmeister, in press, *Developmental Psychology*. Copyright by the American Psychological Association. Reprinted by permission.

Qualities were assessed: relative power of the child and other, conflict, satisfaction, and importance of the relationship.[3]

Figure 3.1 presents the mean item ratings for each quality in each type of relationship. Friendships were particularly important sources of two provisions. Ratings of companionship with friends were higher than those for anyone else, and the ratings of intimacy with friends were equalled only by those with mothers. In subsequent research, we have found that the ratings of companionship and intimacy with friends increase further in adolescence and early

---

[3]In subsequent research, children have also been asked to rate four additional relationship qualities: (a) nurturance, (b) sense of inclusion, (c) similarity, and (d) punishment.

adulthood. Several other provisions, particularly affection, also displayed developmental increases. Additionally, opposite-sex friendships and romantic relationships emerged as important sources of provisions. At the same time, there is some decrease in the social provisions obtained in relationships with parents and other family members, although the increasing significance of friendships is more striking than these decreases.

The ratings of relative power in friendship are also noteworthy. Most children reported that the distribution of power was relatively equal in friendships (scores of 3 on a 5-point scale), whereas the distribution of power was skewed in relationships with adults and even most siblings.[4] Many developmental theorists have argued that the egalitarian nature of friendships and other peer relationships has a major effect on the characteristics of these relationships and their influence on development (Hartup, 1976; Piaget, 1932; Youniss, 1980). In particular, the egalitarian nature of these relationships is thought to contribute to moral development, the control of aggression, and the acquisition of norms and values.

It would be misleading, however to overemphasize the special properties of friendships or peer relationships. As Figure 3.1 depicts, children also turn to a number of other individuals for many of the social provisions that can be obtained in friendships. For example, affection and reliable alliance are important characteristics of friendships, yet children obtain these provisions from parents, siblings, and grandparents more often than they do from friends. The important point is that there are multiple sources of each provision. All can be obtained from more than one person. In fact, the mean ratings of some provisions, such as enhancement of worth, are high for almost all relationships. Functionally, it seems important for children to be able to obtain a provision from more than one person in case a specific person is unwilling or unable to supply it.

What implications does this have for the selection of treatment goals in social skills interventions? The answer parallels the one given in the previous section on friendships and peer relationships. There are some particular reasons for enhancing peer relationships and friendships specifically, yet strong arguments can be made for enhancing other relationships as well.

Implications for Social Skills Programs

Assessment. Not only should relationships with friends and peers be assessed, but also we should assess children's relationships with parents, siblings, relatives, and other network members. Do children who are rejected, isolated, or lacking close friendships show deficits in other close relationships? Previous investigators have found the characteristics of peer and parental relationships to be

---

[4]Mean rating of sibling relationships also approximates 3, but this is misleading. Relative power is actually a function of the relative age of the two children. As one would expect, when they are older, siblings are perceived as having more power than the subjects. When they are younger, siblings have less power than the children. The distribution of power is only relatively equal when the age difference is small or when the children are twins.

moderately positively correlated (see Hartup, 1983). Hence, children with poor relationships may be more likely to have interpersonal difficulties in other relationships, but not all do. In some cases, difficulties may arise in sibling and adult relationships as well as peer relationships, although the specific nature of the problem may vary from one relationship to another. For example, children who are aggressive toward their peers may be noncompliant with their parents' requests. In other cases, the difficulties the children are experiencing may occur primarily in their peer relationships. Perhaps many shy or neglected children have peer-specific problems, whereas many aggressive or rejected children may have general interpersonal difficulties.

Based on these considerations, it is likely that the children who have been targeted in skills training program are a heterogenous group. Detailed assessments of these children's social networks should help identify those children who are experiencing difficulties in many interpersonal relationships. Such children may be at greater risk for psychological problems than those whose difficulties are specific to peer relationships. If so, we may want to invest our resources in developing intervention programs for those who have interpersonal problems in many relationships. At the very least, it may be necessary to design different interventions for these peer-specific and general interpersonal difficulties.

Program Content. Will changes in peer relationships generalize to other relationships? Although this question has not been addressed empirically, one should not be too optimistic. As noted previously, changes in general peer relationships usually do not even lead to changes in close friendships. Thus, it is unlikely that changes occur in other relationships.

Programs need to be designed to foster generalization across relationships to insure that such effects occur. The expressions of some skills are relationship-specific. For example, the appropriateness of different expressions of affection varies from relationship to relationship. Other skills, such as most conversational skills, are expressed similarly in most relationships. Generalized effects may be more likely to occur if these latter skills are trained than if the former are. Regardless of which skills are taught, one might be able to foster generalization by providing the children with instruction and practice in applying the skills in different relationships.

As noted in a previous section, children can obtain most provisions from more than one person in their networks. For example, children may turn to either their peers or siblings for companionship. Children with inadequate peer relationships may be able to compensate for the provisions they lack in these relationships by turning to their other social relationships. Such compensation may not be complete, but it may reduce the difficulties they are experiencing. Thus, children should be taught this concept of multiple agency so that they learn to turn to others if they encounter problems in one relationship. This point may be particularly important for children who are very unattractive, obese, or otherwise have some difficulty that makes it hard to improve the quality of their peer relationships.

Program Mechanisms. Previously, we saw that peer involvement in the intervention program may be an effective means of enhancing peer relationships. Similarly, parents, teachers, and siblings could be important therapeutic agents (see Guerney, 1969). Their participation in the programs should be cost-effective, may foster changes in those specific relationships, and should promote generalization to the natural environment. The involvement of siblings warrants particular consideration. Although there is marked diversity among sibling relationships, some sibling relationships resemble friendships (Furman & Buhrmester, 1985). Enhancing these sibling relationships may prove to be an effective way of helping children compensate for peer relationship difficulties.

Conclusion

Should our treatment objective be to enhance children's general peer relationships? Their close friendships? Other personal relationships? It seems pointless to pit these goals against each other. All three seem very reasonable. Instead, our point is that we have tried to enhance peer relationships without really considering these other potential objectives. Today, a significant amount of research is being conducted on children's friendships and on children's social networks. We investigators who have been studying social skills and peer relationships need to be more aware of this research and its potential implications for intervention programs.

As clinicians, we routinely consider children's relationships with their close friends, other peers, their siblings, their parents, and other significant persons in their social network. It is simply good clinical practice. Now we need to do the same as clinical researchers.

Acknowledgment. Portions of the research described in this chapter were supported by a grant from the National Institute of Child Health and Human Development (1R01 HD 16142), and preparation of the manuscript was facilitated by a W. T. Grant Faculty Scholar Award to W. Furman.

References

Berndt, T. J. (in press). Sharing between friends: Contexts and consequences. In E. Mueller & C. Cooper (Eds.), *Peer relations: Process and outcome*.

Bierman, K. L., & Furman, W. (1984). The effects of social skills training and peer involvement on the social adjustment of preadolescents. *Child Development, 55,* 151-162.

Buhrmester, D., & Furman, W. (in press). The changing functions of friends in childhood: A neo-Sullivanian perspective. In V. Derlega & B. Winstead (Eds.), *Friendship and social interaction*. New York: Springer-Verlag.

Coie, J., Dodge, K., & Coppotelli, H. (1982). Dimensions and types of social status: A cross-age perspective. *Developmental Psychology, 18,* 557-571.

Duck, F. W. (1973). *Personal relationships and personal constructs: A study of friendship formation*. London: Wiley.

Dunphy, D. C. (1963). The social structure of urban adolescent peer groups. *Sociometry*, *26*, 230-246.

Furman, W. (1982). Children's friendships. In T. Field, G. Finley, A. Huston, H. Quay, & L. Troll (Eds.), *Review of human development* (pp. 327-342). New York: Wiley.

Furman, W. (1984). Enhancing children's peer relations and friendships. In S. Duck (Ed.), *Personal relationships: V. Repairing personal relationships* (pp. 103-126). London: Academic Press.

Furman, W., Adler, T., & Buhrmester, D. (1984, July). *Structural aspects of relationships: A search for a common framework*. Paper presented at the Second International Conference on Personal Relationships, Madison, WI.

Furman, W., & Buhrmester, D. (1985). Children's perceptions of the qualities of sibling relationships. *Child Development*, *56*, 448-461.

Furman, W., & Bierman, K. L. (1984). Children's conceptions of friendship: A multimethod study of developmental change. *Developmental Psychology*, *20*, 925-931.

Furman, W., & Buhrmester, D. (in press). Children's perceptions of the personal relationships in their networks. *Developmental Psychology*.

Gresham, F. M., & Nagle, R. J. (1980). Social skills training with children: Responsiveness to modeling and coaching as orientation. *Journal of Consulting and Clinical Psychology*, *48*, 718-729.

Guerney, B. G., Jr. (1969). *Psychotherapeutic agents: New roles for nonprofessionals, parents and teachers*. New York: Holt, Rinehart, & Winston.

Hartup, W. W. (1976). Peer interaction and the behavioral development of the individual child. In E. Schopler & R. J. Reichler (Eds.), *Psychopathology and child development* (pp. 203-218). New York: Plenum.

Hartup, W. W. (1978). Children and their friends. In H. McGurk (Ed.), *Childhood social development*. London: Methuen.

Hartup, W. W. (1983). The peer system. In E. M. Hetherington (Ed.), *Carmichael's manual of child psychology* (4th ed., Vol. 4, pp. 103-196). New York: Wiley.

Hops, H. (1982). Social skills training for socially withdrawn/isolated children. In P. Karoly & J. Steffan (Eds.), *Advances in child behavior analysis and therapy: Vol. 2. Intellectual and social deficiencies*. New York: Gardner Press.

Hymel, S., & Asher, S. P. (1977, March). *Assessment and training of isolated children's skills*. Paper presented at the meeting of the Society for Research in Child Development, New Orleans, LA.

Mannarino, A. P. (1976). Friendship patterns and altruistic behavior in preadolescent males. *Developmental Psychology*, *12*, 555-556.

Mannarino, A. P. (1978). Friendship patterns and self-concept development in preadolescent males. *Journal of Genetic Psychology*, *133*, 105-110.

McGuire, K. D., & Weisz, J. R. (1982). Social cognition and behavioral correlates of preadolescent chumship. *Child Development*, *53*, 1478-1484.

Newcomb, A. F., Brady, J. E., & Hartup, W. W. (1979). Friendship and incentive condition as determinants of children's task-oriented social behavior. *Child Development*, *50*, 878-881.

Oden, S., & Asher, S. R. (1977). Coaching children in social skills for friendship making. *Child Development*, *48*, 495-506.

Piaget, J. (1932). *The moral judgment of the child*. Glencoe, IL: The Free Press.

Reis, H. T. (1984). Social interaction and well being. In S. Duck (Ed.), *Personal relationships: V. Repairing personal relationships* (pp. 21-46). London: Academic Press.

Sherif, M., Harvey, O. J., White, B. J., Hood, W. R., & Sherif, C. W. (1961). *Intergroup conflict and cooperation: The Robbers Cave experiment*. Norman, OK: University of Oklahoma Press.

Sullivan, H. S. (1953). *The interpersonal theory of psychiatry*. New York: W. W. Norton.

Veroff, J., & Veroff, J. B. (1980). *Social incentives: A life-span developmental approach*. New York: Academic Press.

Weiss, R. S. (1974). The provisions of social relationships. In Z. Rubin (Ed.), *Doing unto others*. Englewood Cliffs, NJ: Prentice-Hall.

Youniss, J. (1980). *Parents and peers in social development: A Sullivan-Piaget perspective*. Chicago: University of Chicago Press.

PART II

Assessing Social Behavior

CHAPTER 4

Observational Assessment of Social Problem Solving

Linda Rose-Krasnor

Social competence is an elusive construct, and there has been relatively little agreement on its operational definition. Recently, however, there as been some convergence on social effectiveness and acceptability as critical components of the competency construct (Foster & Ritchey, 1980; O'Malley, 1977; Weinstein, 1969). Ford (1982), for example, defined social competence as "the attainment of relevant social goals in specified social contexts, using appropriate means and resulting in positive developmental outcomes" (p. 324). This definition may also be used to describe the phenomenon known generally as social problem solving.

A child who is an effective social problem solver is one who is able to gain desired resources. These may be social resources such as attention or information, or physical resources such as food or toys. In contrast, an unsuccessful child is relatively deprived of these resources, and thus may be at considerable developmental risk. Repeated social failure may interfere with the development of self-effectance and mastery (Goetz & Dweck, 1980; Harter, 1980), and may also promote a maladaptive generalized social response such as aggression or withdrawal. In addition, a child who uses socially unacceptable means to achieve goals may become isolated or rejected, and thus be unlikely to form supportive social relationships.

The predominant approach to identifying and remediating social problem-solving deficits has focused on the cognitive aspects of problem solving that are assumed to *underlie* competent social behavior (e.g., Elardo & Caldwell, 1979; Spivack & Shure, 1974). In this approach, children are asked to generate alternative strategies or consequences for common hypothetical dilemmas (e.g., making friends). More recently, researchers have developed procedures to measure social problem-solving skill through observation (Rickel, Eshelman & Loigman, 1983; Sharp, 1981; Weissberg et al., 1981).

Observational assessments offer several advantages over hypothetical-reflective methods (Krasnor & Rubin, 1981). Researchers using the latter techniques have found that children's responses to hypothetical dilemmas do not directly correspond to their social behavior (Rubin & Krasnor, in press). In addition, it is difficult to evaluate the likelihood of a strategy's success in an interview context. The child's actual social effectiveness is captured in an observational approach, however, and the validity problems characteristic of hypothetical-reflective methods are not a major issue, given adequate representative sampling.

The observer can identify the goals and strategies actually used by the child. One problem with presenting hypothetical dilemmas to children is that the goals and strategies suggested in response to hypothetical dilemmas are only *potentially* representative of competence. Given the pressures of actual interactions, these verbally derived goals and strategies may never be employed (Damon, 1977).

Naturalistic approaches also allow assessment of the environmental influences that might maintain maladaptive social problem solving. In particular, the general responsivity of social partners can be observed. An individual's high failure rate, for example, may be explained by her frequent interaction with a child who only rarely complies with *anyone*. Finally, the unstructured nature of the observational method allows individual priorities in goals and targets to emerge as reflected by high frequency, emotional intensity, and persistence. This potentially important information is not available when the goals are predetermined or the situation is tightly structured by the tester. The major focus of this chapter is to present an observational methodology for the study of naturalistic social problem-solving skills.

General Framework

Much of the recent research into the thinking and behavioral aspects of social problem solving has been guided by an information-processing model (e.g., Dodge, in press; Spivack & Shure, 1974). A model of social problem solving recently developed by Rubin and Krasnor (Krasnor & Rubin, 1981; Rubin & Krasnor, in press) is representative of this approach (see Figure 4.1). Social problem solving begins with the selection of a goal and target, and ends with either success or abandonment of the goal. Within this model, several important areas of observational assessment can be identified: (a) the frequency, type, and diversity of social goals and targets; (b) the breadth, type, and distribution of strategies; (c) the linkage between strategy and situation, as revealed by effectiveness, social acceptability, and the systematic differentiation of strategies across situations; and (d) persistence, flexibility, and responsiveness to feedback following failure.

In order to illustrate these components, two social problem-solving sequences are presented in Tables 4.1 and 4.2. A transcript of two first-grade girls participating in a study of social problem-solving and friendship (Krasnor, 1984) is presented in Table 4.1. In this example, Anne attempts to get Tammy to watch her puppet. Table 4.2 is a narrative observation of preschool free play. Marty's attempts to get some blocks from Jenny dominate this exchange. Anne and Marty were randomly selected as focal problem solvers: Tammy and Jenny were the social targets.

Observational Methods for Assessing Social Problem Solving

The first step in an observational analysis is to identify social problem-solving attempts as they occur in the stream of behavior. Three criteria have been proposed (Krasner, 1982; Krasnor & Rubin, 1983). The behavior must be:

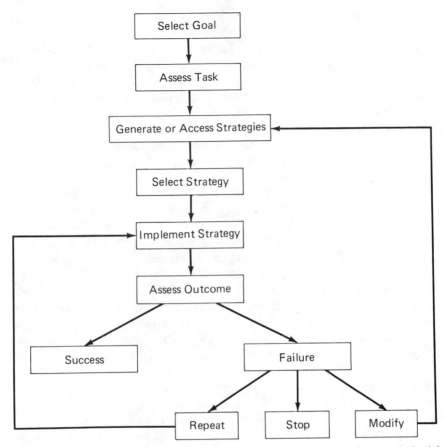

FIGURE 4.1. Social problem-solving model. From "Social Cognitive and Social Behavioral Perspectives in Problem Solving" in *The Minnesota Symposium on Child Psychology Vol. 18*, in press, Hillside, NJ: Erlbaum. Copyright by Lawrence Erlbaum Associates, Inc.

(a) socially oriented, indicated by a look, orienting act, or calling; (b) directive in nature, consisting of a physical or verbal directive (Ervin-Tripp, 1976), or initiation of interaction; and (c) initiated by the focal child. For example, a statement such as "I want to play house" would be coded as a social problem-solving attempt, unless it were uttered in responses to another child's question "What do you want to do now?" Once social problem-solving attempts have been identified from these criteria, goal, strategy and outcome variables are coded.

Social Goals

Goal analysis is an important component in social interaction analysis (Ford, 1982; Meichenbaum, Butler, & Gruson, 1981; Renshaw & Asher, 1982). If an individual's goals are known, his or her behavior can be put into context, and the appropriateness and effectiveness of social actions can be judged. Differences between the goals of participants within a specific social situation are an important source of potential conflict (Graham, Argyle, & Furnham, 1980).

Most of the research work on goal assessment has been hypothetical-reflective. For example, developmental increases in self-reported performance goals during games was positively correlated with social status in elementary school (Asher & Taylor, 1984). In addition, Ford (1982) found that adolescents judged by their peers as socially effective tended to rate social goals as more important than nonsocial ones.

Hypothetical-reflective analysis of goals requires inferences by the problem solver about his or her own intent; the observational assessment of goals requires inference by the observer. The problem solver's and observer's inferences may or may not coincide, however. The distinction between external judgments and internal reports of goals parallels those made between actor and spectator perspectives (Beck, 1975), etic versus emic approaches (Pike, 1967), and objective and subjective aspects of social competence (see Ford, 1982). The question of who is the "real" judge of social intent may never be determined (see Rubin & Krasnor, in press), and both approaches are likely to be important. The adequacy of "observer" interpretations of behavior should be judged on the basis of their reliability and success in generating scientifically useful theories, rather than upon an inherent superiority of one method over the other (Harris, 1979).

Goal judgments have been an important component of many observational taxonomies. Researchers have assessed information goals (Forbes, Katz, Paul, & Lubin, 1982; Gottman, 1983; Lefebvre-Pinard, Bufford-Bouchard, & Feidler, 1982); affiliative, intruding, activity-oriented, and relational goals (Forbes et al., 1982); permission and specific action goals (Lefebvre-Pinard et al., 1982); caretaking, object possession, and joint object use goals (Holmberg, 1980); as well as gaining access to activities and protecting space (Corsaro, 1981). Some observational systems sample a wide range of social goals (Charlesworth, 1983; White, Kaban, Shapiro, & Attanucci, 1977); others sample only one or two goals. The most common of these are group entry attempts (Corsaro, 1981; Forbes et al., 1982; Phinney, 1979; Putallaz & Gottman, 1980), and getting others to share objects or cooperate (Berndt, 1983; Richard & Dodge, 1982; Newcomb & Brady, 1982).

The following goal taxonomy is relatively broad, and has been useful in observing interactions of preschool to fifth-grade children, with consistently acceptable reliability (Krasnor & Rubin, 1983; Krasnor, 1984). Goal categories include: (1) *stop action* (attempts to stop or prevent another's action, such as "Don't touch that" or pushing a child away); (2) *self-action* (attempts to elicit permission, such as "Can I help you?" or "Let me play now"); (3) *other action* (attempts to evoke a specific action from another which cannot otherwise be coded, such as "Close the door"); (4) *object acquisition* (attempts to obtain sole use of an object, such as "Give me that truck!" or grabbing); (5) *attention* (attempts at eliciting attention toward a specific object or event, such as showing or "Look at what I can do"); (6) *information seeking* (attempts at obtaining information, such as "How do you play this?"); and (7) *comfort/affection* (attempts to give or elicit prosocial

TABLE 4.1. Grade 1 social problem-solving transcript.

Tape Position	Attempt	Goal	Strategy	Affect	Outcome	Anne	Attempt	Goal	Strategy	Affect	Outcome	Tammy
2882	52	5	2	2	0	Tammy, Look it (smile)				1		(No apparent response, plays with game)
	53	5	2 9	1	0	Watch this (shows puppet; lightly touches Tammy)				1		(No apparent response)
2883	54	5	2	1	0	Tammy, watch this				1		(No apparent response)
	55	5	13 14	0	0	Tammy (growls, frowns)				1		(Moves eyes slightly)
2884	56	5	9	1	0	(taps Tammy)				1		(No apparent response)
	57	5	14	1	0	Tammy				1		(No apparent response)
2885	58	5	13 14	0	0	Tammy (growls loudly)				1		(No apparent response)
	59	5	2 9	1	0	Look it (holds puppet up)				1		(No apparent response)
2886	60	5	13 9	1	1	Tammy (shows puppet)				1		(looks very briefly)

TABLE 4.2. Preschool social problem-solving transcript.

Tape #	At-tempt	Goal	Strat-egy	Af-fect	Out-come	Marty	At-tempt	Goal	Strat-egy	Af-fect	Out-come	Jenny
129	1	4	3		0	Can I have a block so I can make a choo choo train?						No this is for a house (builds house for three bears)
	2	4	3 9		0	Can I use a block that's in there? (points with toy dog)						No, you might shake it and bother the thing over
130	3	4	4		0	Well, I'll take it and leave you the rest of them						No, because the bear's going to go "Ahh"
131	4	4	1		0	Well I need one to make a choo choo train for myself						(No apparent response; builds)
133	5	4	1 5		0	So I need me to make a train cause my Robbie [dog] will get mad at you and will take one from you						Oh yeah (looks in box of blocks)

135	6	4	1	0	I need a train. I just can't run on my blocks. I got six and I can't just use the blocks so I need another block	(Looks away)
136	7	4	4	0	Now what you'll get if you don't give me a block	Oh yeah
137	8	4	1 3	1	I need a block when you're all finished with making it cleared out. I can have a block when you're all done playing?	Okay (but doesn't give blocks)

contact, such as hugging or "Don't worry, it'll be okay"). The goal coding in Tables 4.1 and 4.2 corresponds to these categories.

It is important to note the separation of goal from strategy in the above taxonomy. There are many strategic paths to the same goal; similarly, there are many goals that might be achieved using the same strategy. In order to distinguish intent and method, strategy codes were based primarily on form rather than content.

Social Strategies

Strategies are means to achieve a goal. Two strategy dimensions typically have been evaluated: (1) the size of the strategy repertoire, defined by number of strategies; and (2) the diversity of the repertoire, measured by the number of different types of strategies. It generally has been assumed that the more strategies an individual has available, the better his or her social problem solving. For example, a child with only one social strategy (e.g., crying) cannot adapt if the strategy fails or is socially unacceptable. At the other extreme, a child with an infinitely large repertoire can continue to generate new strategies until an effective one is found. Some of the individual variation in strategy diversity is illustrated by the difference between the relatively narrow repertoire shown in Table 4.1 and the richer range of strategies apparent in Table 4.2. In the episode transcribed in Table 4.1, Anne uses only very simple orienting strategies (showing, tapping), play noises, callings, and commands. Marty, however, shows an elaborate set of strategies including permission requests, commands, statements of personal need, threats, compromises, and orienting acts.

Strategy taxonomies can be drawn from a number of reserach domains, including ethology (e.g., Strayer, 1981), sociolinguistics (e.g., Ervin-Tripp, 1976), and persuasion (e.g., Clark & Delia, 1976). Strategy taxonomies have been based on dimensions such as risk-taking (Dodge, Schlundt, Shocken, & Delugach, 1983; Forbes et al., 1982), perspective-taking (e.g., Abrahami, Selman, & Stone, 1981), and information level (e.g., Lefebvre-Pinard et al., 1982). In the strategy taxonomy outlined in the following, however, categorization is based primarily on strategy form, although the separation between form and function is not complete. The taxonomy includes both verbal nonverbal components.

Fourteen strategy categories are distinguished: (1) *need statements* (personal need, desire, or normative statements such as "I want to play checkers," and "You shouldn't do that"); (2) *commands* (direct imperatives, such as "Gimme that"); (3) *requests* (imbedded and direct requests, such as "Would you pass the crayons"); (4) *suggestions* (activity propositions, such as "Let's play house" or "Wanna paint now?"); (5) *conditionals* (threats and bribes, such as "If you be my friend, I'll let you wear my watch"); (6) *statements* (descriptive utterances, such as "That's the garage for the truck"); (7) *questions* (interrogative forms, such as "Are you my friend?"); (8) *claims* (statements asserting ownership or right of access, such as "It's my turn"); (9) *orienting acts* (pointing, showing, and other visually directive gestures); (10) *object aggression* (physically forceful acts directed at objects, such as grabbing or pulling); (11) *person aggression* (physically forceful acts directed at others, such as hitting or pulling); (12) *affiliative* (prosocial physical acts, such as giving or holding hands); (13) *play noise* (play vocalizations within fantasy role, such as "Grrrr"); and (14) *callings* (isolated names, titles, pronouns, or exclamations, such as "Andrea" or "Teacher!"). Examples of this coding are provided in Tables 4.1 and 4.2.

In theory, an individual who has a large and diverse strategy repertoire has the basis for adaptive social problem solving. Actual social success, however, depends on choosing the "right" strategy and goal for a specific situation. The next area of assessment, therefore, focuses on the matching of strategy and goal to situation, as reflected in social acceptability, effectiveness, and systematic variation.

Linking Strategy and Goal to Situation

The social acceptability of a behavior depends on situational factors such as physical setting or group demography. Aggressive behavior, for example, may be tolerated in the playground, but not in the school. Seeking attention from teachers might be appropriate in some classes, but not in others.

Adult or peer ratings of the social acceptability of specific strategies or goals could be used as an assessment measure, although this approach has rarely been employed. The ratings are themselves subject to social acceptability biases. It is difficult to judge the acceptability of a behavior outside its physical and temporal context, however. Ratings may need, therefore, to be made for each specific occurrence of a behavior, creating an unwieldy system.

An observational measure of social acceptability focuses on the target's overt affective reactions. Three affective categorizations were made on the basis of facial expressions: (0) *negative* (frown, cry, etc.); (1) *neutral* (no overt affect); and (2) *positive* (smile, laugh, etc.). Social unacceptability would be indicated by negative affect and/or disapproving verbal statements (e.g., "That's not polite," "You're awful"). Using this criterion, Anne's persistent attempts to get attention provoked surprisingly little overt negative reaction from Tammy (Table 7.1). Even if negative affect is observed, however, it may be difficult to distinguish between the social unacceptability of the strategy or goal and other causes of negative reactions (e.g., dislike of the person or reluctance to comply).

A strategy or goal that is well matched to the situation is effective, as well as acceptable. Outcome taxonomies have generally included success and failure categories as well as codes for partially compliant or neutral outcomes (e.g., Levin & Rubin, 1983; Putallaz & Gottman, 1981; Richard & Dodge, 1982).

The outcome taxonomy that we (Krasnor & Rubin, 1983; Krasnor, 1983; 1984) used in naturalistic observations includes the following codes: (0) *failure* (self-solutions, delayed compliance, inability, no apparent response, and active noncompliance); (1) *partial success* (partial compliance or clarification requests); and (2) *success* (compliance within 10 s). The 10-s interval was an operational limit for contingent social behavior (Mueller & Brenner, 1977). Outcome codes are illustrated in Tables 4.1 and 4.2.

A third aspect of the linkage between goals and strategy and situation is the degree of predictable differentiation across situations. The situational requirements of competence will vary across tasks, and competent children will vary their behavior accordingly (Makamura & Finck, 1980). Socially competent children should therefore show greater differentiation across social tasks than their less competent peers. This differentiation can be measured by the reduction in uncertainty in predicting strategy or goal given situational information, over the predictions made using baseline probabilities alone. Reduction of uncertainty coefficients can be calculated for each individual as an index of his or her systematic situational variation. Using this index, differentiation of strategies, and goals across targets have been found to be positively related to preschool social success, once the effects of receptive vocabulary were removed (Krasnor, 1982).

Strategy Sequencing After Failure

It is common for children to fail in social problem-solving interactions. Across samples, observations indicate that approximately 40% of attempts do not succeed (Krasnor, 1984; Krasnor & Rubin, 1983; Rubin & Borwick, 1984) and the failure probabilities are considerably higher for some goals (e.g., object acquisition) and strategies (e.g., suggestions). The child's reaction to social failure, therefore, can be critical to his or her social adjustment.

Children's responses to social failure have been studied in the context of causal attributions (e.g., Goetz & Dweck, 1980) and communication skills (e.g., Garvey, 1975; Levin & Rubin, 1983). These results suggest that flexibility, persistence, and responsiveness to feedback are important dimensions of a child's reaction to failure.

In order to study sequencing after failure, the level of analysis should shift from that of single strategies to episodes. A social problem-solving episode is defined as a series of strategies directed at the same goal (Krasnor & Rubin, 1981, 1983). Tables 4.1 and 4.2 show two partial episodes (attention and object acquisition, respectively).

Episode coding uses a looser categorization of behavior than the coding of single attempts, due to greater reliance on sequences for understanding over all intent. Thus attempts that are coded with different individual goals may be judged as part of the same episode. Consider the following sequence, for example:

Sarah: "Stop that, Jesse!"
Jesse (walking on table):   "Go away Sarah."
Sarah: "Teacher, look at that!" (Points to Jesse.)

At the single strategy level, Sarah's two attempts would have been coded with different goals (stop action and attention, respectively). At the episodic level, they would be judged as having the same overall goal of stopping Jesse's action.

Episode coding begins with the first failed strategy in a transcript. The nature of the target's response is coded in order to determine sequential dependencies. It may be adaptive, for example, to persist only after perceiving that the target responses indicated potential capitulation. Wilcox and Webster (1980), for example, found that young preschoolers were more likely to repeat a request if the listener ignored them, than if the listener responded without complying.

Three categories of target responses are coded: (1) inadequate (partial compliance, clarifications, delays, acknowledgments); (2) no apparent response; and (3) explicit refusal (other noncompliance circumstances). The conditional probability that a child will persist after these specific forms can be calculated. For example, the probabilities of a reattempt given active refusals and inadequate responses were found to decrease with age over middle childhood, although the probability of persisting after no apparent response showed little developmental change (Krasnor, 1984).

If a second strategy (located at any point in the transcript) is judged to be directed at the same goal as the first failed attempt, it is considered the second attempt in the first episode. When a pair of related attempts are identified, flexibility in strategy sequencing can be asessed. If the second attempt is the same as the first, it is coded as a "repeat." If there is a substantive change within the same strategy category, a "within-category" shift is coded. An example of the latter sequence can be found between the first two attempts in Table 4.2, in which one unsuccessful request ("Can I have a block so I can make a choo choo train?") is followed by another ("Can I use a block that's in there?"). "Between-category" shifts are coded when the child changes strategy types. An example of a between-category sequence is between the third and fourth attempts in Table 4.2, in which there is a change from a suggestion to a personal need statement.

If the second attempt was successful, it ends the episode. If not, other attempts at the same goal may be present and are coded for target responses. Flexibility between each pair of sequential strategies in an episode is also coded. Overall flexibility can be assessed across episodes. The probability of within-category changes is indexed by dividing the number of within-category shifts by the number of reattempts. The probabilities of between-category changes and strategy repetitions are similarly assessed.

A child's overall persistence after failure can be measured by the number of reattempts divided by the number of failures. A child who gave up after each failure would have no reattempts, and would have a persistence index of .00. A child who tried again after every failure would have a persistence index of 1.00. Anne, for example (see Table 4.1), showed approximately three times more persistence after failure than was the average for her peer group.

Assessment Criteria

In the previous section, an observational taxonomy of social problem solving was outlined. Assessments of individual skills using this approach can only be interpreted meaningfully within a well-specified frame of reference.

The correlational analyses characteristic of much of the recent research reflects an underlying assumption that socially competent children will have "more" of each of the social problem-solving components than less-competent children (e.g., more flexibility, more strategies, more goal diversity). In fact, a much more complex and curvilinear relationship may exist between these components and competence. More social success, for example, is not necessarily better.

Success in every interaction would be neither possible nor desirable. Similarly, a large number of strategies may not be adaptive, if they are all ineffective, age-inappropriate, or not adequately matched to the situation. A few general-purpose, effective strategies may be more desirable than struggling to decide among an excess of ineffective strategies.

Too little persistence after failure would not be adaptive, since the child would fail to achieve many social goals. Too much persistence would also be maladaptive. Successive reattempts at the same goal may be wasteful of time and energy since the probability of success after a prior failure is remarkably low (Krasnor & Rubin, 1983). In addition, high persistence ("nagging") may alienate others. Adaptive persistence is likely to be moderate and selective, continued on the basis of either high investment in the success of the goal or encouraging responses by the target. High flexibility may also not be particularly important for social effectiveness. Individual levels of flexibility, for example, were not found to correlate with overall success in preschoolers (Krasnor & Rubin, 1983). On the basis of this analysis, it is clear that "the more, the better" is not an adequate model for interpreting observed social problem solving. In the following, four evaluation models will be considered: absolute, self-report, empirical, and normative.

Absolute Criteria

It would be possible to determine an absolute level of adequate social problem-solving skill (e.g., 40% success, at least five different strategies per 10-min observation). A child who falls below specified levels would be targeted for training. Similar procedures have been used in targeting isolates for social skills programs (Keller & Carlsen, 1974; O'Connor, 1972). This approach is arbitrary and relatively weak, however, and should generally not be used if alternatives are available.

Self-Report Criteria

A second approach to assessment criteria would be based on self-reports. Children would be targeted on the basis of their reported dissatisfaction with their social problem-solving outcomes. Although some assessment tools are available (e.g., Ford, 1982), the method has not been widely used. These measures are subject to the biases characteristic of self-reports. In addition, the method would be inappropriate for use with young children.

Empirical Criteria

A third approach to individual assessment can be based on empirical relationships. Variables that show significant concurrent or predictive relationships with other indices of competence would form the evaluation criteria. White and his colleagues (White et al., 1977), for example, found that the percentage of time spent in attempting to procure a service and gaining attention at 1 year of age was positively correlated to competence at 3 years. Rubin and Krasnor (in press) found that social success in kindergarten predicted first-grade popularity, and Putallaz (1983) found that the relevance of social strategies to ongoing activities predicted first-grade social status 4 months later. Concurrent correlations between social problem-solving elements and social status have also been found (e.g., Putallaz & Gottman, 1981; Richard & Dodge, 1982; Rubin & Borwick, 1984). Precise cutoff levels for targeting are not clearly established by this method, however, and the correlations tend to be much too low for accurate individual predictions.

Normative Criteria

At present, the most appropriate method for targeting children with social problem-solving deficits is one that takes normative data into account. In this approach, children who fall significantly below peer group averages would be identified, and individual strengths and weaknesses could be evaluated. A relatively high percentage of a specific goal, for example, might indicate that the goal has special importance for the child, and a high failure rate would indicate that needs were unmet.

An example of a normative assessment was presented by Krasnor (1983). A preschool child, "Jason", was selected on the basis of low social success (> 2 *SD* below same-sex mean). The relative frequency of Jason's goals, targets, and strategies were compared to those of his peers, and found to be within 1 *SD* of the norm. The profiles of Jason's success with specific goals, targets, and strategies, however, showed greater divergence. This interindividual comparison indicated particularly poor success with object acquisition, stop action, and other action goals. An intraindividual analysis showed Jason was relatively successful when he used orienting strategies. His behavior showed relatively low systematic variation over targets, indicating a lack of appropriate differentiation in strategies and goals. Similar profile analyses were recently presented by Rubin and Krasnor (in press) for two children targeted on the basis of rejected peer status and low observed sociability, rather than for high observed failure. As with Jason, specific areas of strengths and weaknesses were pinpointed by inter- and intraindividual analyses, and remediation strategies were suggested.

Normative criteria should be used cautiously, however, because norms are sensitive to age and setting variables. For example, developmental differences in goals (e.g., Forbes et al., 1982; Holmberg, 1980; Whiting & Whiting, 1975), strategies (Krasnor, 1984), outcomes (Levin & Rubin, 1983; Krasnor, 1984), and persistence (Forbes et al., 1982; Krasnor, 1984) have already been documented. Children clearly vary their strategic behavior in response to partner characteristics such as age (Garvey, 1975; Holmberg, 1980; Levin & Rubin, 1983), sex (Maccoby & Jacklin, 1980; Krasnor & Rubin, 1983), friendship (Berndt, 1983; Gottman, 1983; Krasnor, 1984), and social status (Putallaz, 1983; Putallaz & Gottman, 1980). The presence of such situational influences makes the choice of an appropriate setting, relevant reference group, and representative sampling important in interpreting an observational assessment. In the next section, some issues related to these decisions will be discussed.

Some Additional Issues

Social problem-solving skills have been observed in a number of different settings, which have varied in degree of experimental control. At the naturalistic end are observations of social problem solving in unconstrained interactions (e.g., Charlesworth, 1983; Corsaro, 1981; Holmberg, 1980; Lefebvre-Pinard et al., 1982; Krasnor & Rubin, 1983). Goals, strategies, outcomes, sequencing, and targets are free to vary. At the controlled end are constrained, scripted social interactions (e.g., Putallaz, 1983), in which the targets, outcomes, and goals are externally restricted. Only strategies are under subject control.

Toward the middle of this continuum, two less-extreme assessment settings can be identified. On the "controlled" side of the middle are settings in which the social goal (and usually target) are externally determined, but strategies, outcomes, and sequencing are free to vary. Examples of this approach include studies of group entry goals (e.g., Putallaz & Gottman, 1980) and object acquisition goals (e.g., Richard & Dodge, 1982). On the "uncontrolled" side of the midpoint are "concentrated encounters" (Cazden, 1977), in which the situation is manipulated so that social problem-solving behaviors are more likely to occur. Goals, strategies, outcomes, and sequencing are uncontrolled once the situation is set "in motion." Targets may be preselected or left to vary. Common manipulations include providing only limited resources for use (e.g., Sharp, 1981) or introducing a cooperative task (e.g., Krasnor, 1984; Sharp, 1981; Rickle et al., 1983).

The experimental control of social problem-solving components has been useful in showing the effects of social status and friendship (Gottman, 1983; Krasnor, 1984; Richard & Dodge, 1982; Sharabany & Hertz-Lazarowitz, 1981), but the use of unconstrained settings provides an important balance and replication of these findings.

In addition to the careful choice of setting, observational assessment of social problem-solving requires complex sampling and recording decisions. Event sampling techniques assume that the observer can record all occurrences of a behavior. For this reason, this approach does not tend to be used for behaviors that are very frequent. Social problem-solving attempts occur at high rates (see Krasnor & Rubin, 1983) and therefore group-based event sampling procedures are inappropriate. In a pilot study comparing group-based event sampling with a focal-child method, the focal method produced longer average episodes than did the event sampling. Brief episodes were apparently missed during the scanning of the group, and thus the event-sampling data were biased toward longer interactive sequences.

Since outcomes and sequencing after failure are important components of the social problem-solving process, time sampling is not appropriate unless the intervals are at least 5 min in length. Even at this length, much sequential and contextual information will be sacrificed.

Focal individual sampling methods appear to be most appropriate for studying social problem solving. Individuals can be observed for extended periods and interactions are likely to be followed until their conclusion. Prior research (Krasnor, 1984; Krasnor & Rubin, 1983) indicates that 15- to 20-min observations during concentrated or unconstrained interactions will yield sufficient data and adequate sequencing information for an assessment session. The number of sessions needed for a stable individual assessment will depend on both situational and person-specific variability.

Both narrative audio recording (Krasnor & Rubin, 1983) and videotape recording (Krasnor, 1984; Rubin & Krasnor, in press) methods have been used successfully to study social problem-solving interactions. The former method, however, is difficult and requires extensive observer training before adequate reliability is achieved. In addition, fine distinctions between strategies (e.g., "Wanna do it?" vs. "Do it") are very difficult for the observer to make "on the spot." Videotaping is preferable for this finer-grained analysis and for the simultaneous coding of affect and other nonverbal behaviors. It is also time-consuming, expensive, and can be intrusive. A balance between these approaches would be the use of an elaborated coding system for goals, strategies, target response, and outcome, which could be recorded as the interaction unfolds without losing contextual and sequencing information.

Conclusion

Early assessments of social problem solving tended to focus on the cognitive skills presumed to underlie effective and acceptable social behavior. In recent years, there has been a marked shift toward observational assessments, and there are few current social problem-solving programs that do not include a direct observational component. Valid criteria for the interpretation of these assessments are lacking, however.

Social competence was defined as effective and acceptable social problem solving. In this chapter, several specific points for observational evaluation were outlined, including goals, targets, strategies, linkages between goals and strategies and situation, and responses to failure. Observations of carefully chosen, controlled variations in social situations as well as unconstrained, naturalistic interactions, have yielded important normative information, and are beginning to provide a basis for individual assessment and remediation.

References

Abrahami, A., Selman, R., & Stone, C. (1981). A developmental assessment of children's verbal strategies for social action resolution. *Journal of Applied Developmental Psychology, 2*, 145-163.

Asher, S., & Taylor, A. (1984, June). *Children's goals and social competence*. Paper presented at the conference on Research Strategies in Children's Social Skills Training, Ottawa.

Beck, L. (1975). *The actor and the spectator*. New Haven: Yale University Press.

Berndt, T. (1983). Social cognition, social behavior, and children's friendships. In E. Higgins, D. Ruble, & W. Hartup (Eds.), *Social cognition and social development* (pp. 158-189). Cambridge: Cambridge University Press.

Cazden, C. (1977). Concentrated versus contrived encounters: Suggestions for language assessment in early childhood education. In A. Davies (Ed.), *Language and learning in early childhood* (pp. 40-54). London: Heinemann.

Charlesworth, W. (1983). An ethological approach to cognitive development. In C. Brainerd (Ed.), *Recent advances in cognitive-development research* (pp. 237-258). New York: Springer-Verlag.

Clarke, R., & Delia, J. (1976). The development of functional persuasive skills in childhood and early adolescence. *Child Development, 47*, 1008-1014.

Corsaro, W. (1981). Friendship in the nursery school: Social organization in a peer environment. In S. Asher & J. Gottman (Eds.), *The development of children's friendships* (pp. 207-241). Cambridge: Cambridge University Press.

Damon, W. (1977). *The social world of the child*. San Francisco: Jossey-Bass.

Dodge, K. (in press). A social information processing model of social competence in children. In M. Perlmutter (Ed.), *The Minnesota Symposia on Child Psychology* (Vol. 18). Hillsdale, NJ: Erlbaum.

Dodge, K., Schlundt, D., Schocken, I., & Delugach, J. (1983). Social competence and children's sociometric status: The role of peer group entry strategies. *Merrill-Palmer Quarterly, 29*, 309-336.

Elardo, P., & Caldwell, B. (1979). The effects of an experimental social development program on children in the middle childhood period. *Psychology in the Schools, 16*, 93-100.

Ervin-Tripp, S. (1976). Is Sybil there? The structure of some American English directives. *Language in Society, 5*, 25-66.

Forbes, D., Katz, M., Paul, B., & Lubin, D. (1982). Children's plans for joining play: An analysis of structures and function. In D. Forbes & M. Greenberg (Eds.), *New directions for child development. Children's planning strategies* (pp. 61-79). San Francisco: Jossey-Bass.

Ford, M. (1982). Social cognition and social competence in adolescence. *Developmental Psychology, 18*, 323-340.

Foster, S., & Ritchey, W. (1980). Issues in the assessment of social competence in children. *Journal of Applied Behavioral Analysis, 12*, 625-638.

Garvey, C. (1975). Requests and responses in children's speech. *Journal of Child Language, 2*, 915-922.

Goetz, T., & Dweck, C. (1980). Learned helplessness in social situations. *Journal of Personality and Social Psychology, 39*, 246-255.

Gottman, J. (1983). How children become friends. *Monograph of the Society for Research in Child Development, 48* (3, Serial No. 201).

Graham, J., Argyle, M., & Furnham, A. (1980). The goal structure of situations. *European Journal of Social Psychology, 10*, 345-366.

Harris, M. (1979). *Cultural materialism: The struggle for a science of culture*. New York: Vantage.

Harter, S. (1980). A model of intrinsic mastery motivation in children: Individual differences and development change. In W. Collins (Ed.), *Minnesota Symposium on Child Psychology* (Vol. 14). Hillsdale, NJ: Erlbaum.

Holmberg, M. (1980). The development of social interchange patterns from 12 to 42 months. *Child Development, 51,* 557-569.

Keller, M., & Carlsen, P. (1974). The use of symbolic modelling to promote social skills in preschool children with low levels of social responsiveness. *Child Development, 45,* 912-919.

Krasnor, L. (1982). An observational study of social problem solving in children. In K. Rubin & H. Ross (Eds.), *Peer relationships and social skills in childhood* (pp. 113-132). New York: Springer-Verlag.

Krasnor, L. (1983). An observational case study of failure in social problem solving. *Journal of Applied Developmental Psychology, 4,* 81-98.

Krasnor, L. (1984). *Social problem solving between friends in middle childhood.* Manuscript submitted for publication, Brock University, St. Catharines, Ontario.

Krasnor, L., & Rubin, K. (1981). Assessment of social problem-solving in young children. In T. Merluzzi, C. Glass, & M. Genest (Eds.), *Cognitive assessment* (pp. 452-478). New York: Guilford Press.

Krasnor, L., & Rubin, K. (1983). Preschool social problem solving: Attempts and outcomes in naturalistic interaction. *Child Development, 54,* 1545-1558.

Lefebvre-Pinard, M., Bufford-Bouchard, T., & Feidler, H. (1982). Social cognition and verbal requests among preschool children. *Journal of Psychology, 10,* 133-143.

Levin, E., & Rubin, K. (1983). Getting others to do what you want them to do: The development of children's requestive strategies. In K. Nelson (Ed.), *Children's language* (Vol. 4). Hillsdale, NJ: Erlbaum.

Maccoby, E., & Jacklin, C. (1980). Sex differences in aggression. A rejoinder and reprise. *Child Development, 51,* 964-980.

Meichenbaum, D., Butler, L., & Gruson, L. (1981). Toward a conceptual model of social competence. In J. Wine & H. Smye (Eds.), *Social competence* (pp. 36-60). New York: Guilford Press.

Mueller, E., & Brenner, J. (1977). The origins of social skills and interaction among play group toddlers. *Child Development, 48,* 854-861.

Nakamura, C., & Finck, D. (1980). Relative effectiveness of socially oriented and task oriented children and predictability of their behavior. *Monographs of the Society for Research in Child Development, 45* (Serial No. 185).

Newcomb, A., & Brady, J. (1982). Mutuality in boys' friendship relations. *Child Development, 53,* 382-395.

O'Connor, R. (1972). Relative efficacy of modeling, shaping, and the combined procedures for modification of social withdrawal. *Journal of Abnormal Child Psychology, 79,* 327-334.

O'Malley, J. (1977). Research perspective on social competence. *Merrill-Palmer Quarterly, 23,* 29-44.

Phinney, J. (1979). Social interaction in young children. Initiation of peer contact. *Psychological Reports, 45,* 489-490.

Pike, K. (1967). *Language in relation to a unified theory of the structure of human behavior* (2nd ed.). Paris: Mouton.

Putallaz, M. (1983). Predicting children's sociometric status from their behavior. *Child Development, 54,* 1417-1426.

Putallaz, M., & Gottman, J. (1981). Social skills and group acceptance. In S. Asher & J. Gottman (Eds.), *The development of children's friendships* (pp. 116-149). Cambridge: Cambridge University Press.

Renshaw, P., & Asher, S. (1982). Social competence and peer status: The distinction between goals and strategies. In K. Rubin & H. Ross (Eds.), *Peer relationships and social skills in childhood* (pp. 375-396). New York: Springer-Verlag.

Richard, B., & Dodge, K. (1982). Social maladjustment and problem solving in school-aged children. *Journal of Consulting and Clinical Psychology, 50*, 226-233.

Rickel, A., Eshelman, A., & Loigman, A. (1983). Social problem-solving training: A follow-up study of cognitive and behavioral effects. *Journal of Abnormal Child Psychology, 11*, 15-28.

Rubin, K., & Borwick, D. (1984). The communication skills of children who vary with regard to sociability. In H. Sypher & J. Applegate (Eds.), *Social cognition and communication*. Hillsdale, NJ: Erlbaum.

Rubin, K., & Krasnor, L. (in press). Social cognitive and social behavioral perspectives in problem solving. In M. Perlmutter (Ed.), *The Minnesota Symposium on Child Psychology* (Vol. 18). Hillsdale, NJ: Erlbaum.

Sharabany, R., & Hertz-Lazarowitz, R. (1981). Do friends share and communicate more than non-friends? *International Journal of Behavioral Development, 4*, 45-59.

Sharp, K. (1981). Impact of interpersonal problem-solving training in preschoolers' social competency. *Journal of Applied Developmental Psychology, 2*, 129-143.

Spivack, G., & Shure, M. (1974). *Social adjustment of young children*. San Francisco: Jossey-Bass.

Strayer, F. (1981). The organization and coordination of asymmetrical relations among young children: A biological view of social power. In M. Watts (Ed.), *Ethological and physiological approaches. New directions for methodology of social and behavioral science* (No. 7, pp. 33-50). San Francisco: Jossey-Bass.

Weinstein, E. (1969). The development of interpersonal competence. In D. Goslin (Ed.), *Handbook of socialization theory and research* (pp. 753-775). Chicago: Rand McNally.

Weissberg, R., Gesten, E., Carnrike, C., Toro, P., Rapkin, B., Davidson, E., & Cowen, E. (1981). Social problem-solving skills training: A competence-building intervention with second- to fourth-grade children. *American Journal of Community Psychology, 9*, 411-423.

White, B., Kaban, B., Shapiro, B., & Attanucci, J. (1977). Competence and experience. In C. Uvgiris & F. Weizmann (Eds.), *The structuring of experience* (pp. 115-152). New York: Plenum Press.

White, B., & Whiting, J. (1975). *Children of six cultures: A psychocultural analysis*. Cambridge, MA: Harvard University Press.

Wilcox, M., & Webster, E. (1980). Early discourse behavior: An analysis of children's response to listener feedback. *Child Development, 51*, 1120-1125.

CHAPTER 5

Children's Peer Relations: Assessing Self-Perceptions

Shelley Hymel and Sylvia Franke

Graham was a fourth-grader who appeared to be socially rejected by his peers. Several pieces of information supported this conclusion. For example, on a rating-scale sociometric measure, Graham received an average rating of 1.5 from his classmates, with 1 being the lowest possible rating one could receive on a 5-point scale. In addition, the classroom teacher had intercepted a note being passed around class which read, "Everybody who hates Graham, sign here." The page was filled with signatures. Graham's social rejection, then, seemed quite clear. However, Graham characterized himself as the most popular child in the class, based on several pieces of seemingly convincing behavioral evidence. For instance, he was always chosen first for teams on the playground and was often voted leader for group projects. According to the teacher, Graham was quite competent in sports and highly intelligent, and peers often "used" him to their own advantage, leading Graham to believe he was well-accepted by his peers. Graham's apparent misperception of his own social status clearly influenced his social behavior as well as his interpretations of peer behavior directed toward him. His self-perceptions also appeared to be quite different from those of other socially rejected children who seemed both aware of their poor peer acceptance and unhappy about it.

Anecdotal evidence such as this suggests that children may differ considerably in the way they themselves view their social situations. The focus of the present chapter is on the assessment of children's social self-perceptions, with particular emphasis on individual differences in the self-perceptions of socially isolated and rejected children. These children have come to be viewed as "socially at risk," owing primarily to both recent and rediscovered research indicating that children who are not well accepted by their peers are more likely to face adjustment problems in later adolescent and adult life (e.g., Cowen, Pederson, Babigian, Izzo, & Trost, 1973; Kupersmidt, 1983; Roff, Sells, & Golden, 1972; Ullmann, 1957). In light of this evidence, we have devoted considerable research efforts toward understanding the nature and causes of children's early peer difficulties and to developing effective intervention techniques aimed at ameliorating children's social problems. Within this literature, however, surprisingly little attention has been given to how the children themselves feel about their own relationships with peers. For example, children are typically targeted for social skills intervention programs on the basis of outside or external sources of information, including teachers, peers, or adult observers (see Hymel & Rubin, 1985, for a review). Notably absent within the assessment literature is consideration of the child's own perspective on his or her social situation. Our ultimate aim is to help these children function more effectively or positively within their social worlds, yet we know very little about how they themselves perceive that social world, and how self-perceptions influence subsequent interpersonal behavior and the effectiveness of intervention programs.

This failure to consider the child's perspective is reminiscent of an earlier criticism of the child-rearing literature made by Dubin and Dubin (1965) 20 *years ago*. At that time, Dubin and Dubin argued that, within the parent-child literature, there existed potentially erroneous assumptions that the adult view of parental behavior was identical to that of the child and that all children tended to perceive and respond to similar parental behavior in a similar manner. Dubin and Dubin referred to such assumptions as the "classic observer-actor dilemma which particularly haunts child-development research" (1965, p. 810).

Similar criticisms can be made within the social skills literature to date. First, it is not necessarily the case that children's perceptions of their relations with classmates are the same as those of the children's peers or teachers or outside observers (see Ledingham and Younger, Chapter 4 this volume). However, individual differences in the correspondence between these various perspectives may be an important consideration in future research. Second, and perhaps more important, it is not necessarily the case that all socially isolated or rejected children perceive their own social relations in a similar way. Even children who exhibit similar patterns of social behavior may perceive and interpret their social situations differently.

In a recent review of research on socially isolated and rejected children, Hymel and Rubin (1985) argued that children who are not well accepted by their peers and who are believed to be at risk for future adjustment difficulties constitute a rather heterogeneous sample, and that there appear to be multiple pathways for the development of social difficulties. Our own research on children's self-perceptions (to be described in the following sections) is based, in part, on the hypothesis that individual differences in self-perceptions may be an important mediator in this developmental process. Indeed, at present there is clearly no one-to-one correspondence between early peer difficulties and later social maladjustment. The predictive longitudinal research on which this link is based is suggestive at best. The magnitude of the predictive correlations is sufficiently low as to suggest that not all poorly accepted children are destined to face adjustment difficulties in later life. Our hunch is that how children themselves perceive and interpret their social difficulties may influence subsequent behavior and, in turn, the likelihood of negative interpersonal outcomes. Unfortunately, at present, we have no data that speak directly to this issue.

Nevertheless, consideration of children's feelings and perceptions about their own peer relations may be important within this literature for several reasons. First, in terms of issues of identification and assessment, it seems surprising that children are seldom, if ever, given a voice in targeting procedures. Despite the fact that self-perceptions, self-reports, and self-referrals are frequently utilized as indices of social difficulties in *adult* populations (e.g., see Peplau & Perlman, 1982, on adult loneliness), we tend to question more critically the validity of children's self-reports. Are adult self-reports more valid than those of children?

Developmental changes in children's ability to evaluate or estimate their own competence have been documented in previous research. For instance, research by Harter (1982) and by Nicholls (1978, 1979) demonstrated that children's estimations of their own *academic* competence become increasingly accurate with age, as compared with teacher judgments or achievement test scores. Within the social domain, Ausubel and his colleagues (e.g., Ausubel, Schiff, & Gasser, 1952) examined developmental changes in children's awareness of their own acceptance among peers, an ability they referred to as "sociempathy." In this research, sociempathy was measured by the correspondence between socio-metric ratings received from peers and ratings children expected to receive from peers on such a measure. They found that accuracy of awareness of peer acceptance did increase with age. Thus, developmental changes cannot be ignored in considering the validity of children's self-reports.

Individual differences, however, may be more important than developmental differences. Particularly relevant to this discussion is research by Kagan, Hans, Markowitz, Lopez, & Sigal (1982) that directly addressed the question of the validity of children's self-reports. They conducted a series of studies examining third-grade children's self-reports in a number of domains, including popularity among classmates. On the basis of their results, Kagan and his colleagues concluded that children's self-reports did provide a relatively valid data source, as compared with teacher and peer assessments, *when self-reports acknowledged negative or undesirable attributes*. Positive self-evaluations were suspect in about one-third of the cases in which children overestimated their own abilities relative to the perceptions of teachers and peers. The point here is that when children do admit to undesirable characteristics in themselves, their self-reports appear to provide a valid source of information. Failure to utilize such information, then, is to ignore a theoretically important data source that could contribute substantially to our understanding of children's social difficulties.

The accuracy of children's self-perceptions, however, may not be the most important issue. Instead, it may be more useful to consider how children's self-perceptions, *regardless of validity*, affect subsequent interpersonal behavior and the effectiveness of intervention efforts. For example, Meichenbaum, Bream, and Cohen (1984) argued for the application of a cognitive-behavioral perspective to the treatment of social isolation in children, emphasizing the need to consider the interaction of children's own thoughts and feelings with observable social behavior. Indeed, consideration of children's social self-perceptions may permit greater understanding of the child's own role in his or her social difficulties.

To illustrate this point, consider recent evidence on children's social problem-solving skills. With younger children, quantitative, and especially qualitative, differences in children's solutions to hypothetical social dilemmas have been found to distinguish children varying in terms of social adjustment and/or peer acceptance, with unpopular and/or less socially adjusted children offering more aggressive and/or nonnormative behavioral solutions (e.g., Shure & Spivack, 1980; Spivack & Shure, 1974; Rubin & Krasnor, in press). With older samples, results have been more equivocal, with discrepant findings reported across studies (e.g., Butler, 1979; Deluty, 1981; Krasnor, 1983; Richard & Dodge, 1982; Vosk, Forehand, Parker, & Rickard, 1982). More recent evidence, however, has indicated that children's own perceptions of the intentions behind a given peer behavior were the best predictors of the type of behavioral solutions offered (Dodge, Murphy, & Buchsbaum, 1984) and that unpopular children tend to express more negatively biased perceptions of peer intentionality (Bream, Franke, & Hymel, 1984). These data suggest that considering the child's perspective may be particularly critical in unravelling the processes involved in the development of inadequate peer relations, especially as children get older.

Variations in children's own perceptions of their social worlds may also be an important consideration in the design of effective intervention strategies. Consistent with these arguments are results of intervention research conducted during the mid-70s by Evers-Pasquale (Evers-Pasquale, 1978; Evers-Pasquale & Sherman, 1975). She found that intervention effectiveness varied as a function of the value that target children themselves placed on peer interaction. In these studies, peer value was assessed in terms of children's expressed preferences for performing varous activities with peers, adults, or alone. Socially withdrawn children who valued peer interaction more and who, therefore, may have been more motivated to increase their own peer interactions, were significantly more likely to benefit from a modeling intervention procedure aimed at reducing socially isolated behavior.

Assessing Children's Self-Perceptions

The arguments presented thus far serve to underscore the importance of considering the child's perspective within the peer relations literature. While children's self-perceptions have been relatively neglected within this literature, they have not been totally unrecognized. Indeed, within the past 5 years, there has been a growing body of research emphasizing the development of valid and reliable means of assessing children's self-perceptions. In addition to the research reviewed thus far, several self-report measures have been developed that attempt to assess children's perceptions of their own relationships with peers. Within the published literature, at least two different domain-specific self-concept scales have recently been developed, both of which include an assessment of children's perceptions of their own social competence and peer relations. One such scale is the Perceived Competence Scale for Children (Harter, 1982); the other is the Self-Description Questionnaire developed by Marsh and his colleagues (Marsh, Smith, & Barnes, 1983; Marsh, Barnes, Cairns, & Tidman, in press). In addition, Ladd and Wheeler (1982) have developed a self-report measure of perceived social difficulty, derived from Bandura's (1977) theory of self-efficacy, assessing the degree to which children view various social situations as easy or difficult. Asher and his colleagues (e.g., Taylor & Asher, 1984; in press) have attempted to assess children's goals in social interactions and how such goals influence subsequent social behavior. Finally, Sobol and Earn (Chapter 6 this volume) have considered the assessment of children's social attributions in peer interactions. Given the recency of the development of these measures, it is not surprising that such self-perceptions have seldom been included as either assessment or outcome measures in intervention research, with the exception of intervention research by Bierman and Furman (1984).

In the paragraphs that follow, our own research on the assessment of children's self-perceptions of their peer relations is considered. This research has focused on two different aspects of children's feelings and perceptions of their social difficulties: feelings of loneliness and social anxiety.

Loneliness in Children

Initial research in this area focused on children's feelings of loneliness and social dissatisfaction (Asher, Hymel, & Renshaw, 1984). Our interest here was stimulated in part by social psychological research on loneliness in adults. Like research on children's peer relations, research on adult loneliness has increased dramatically within the last decade. In much of this literature, loneliness is assessed through self-report measures such as the UCLA loneliness scale (Russell, 1982). Similarly, we developed a 16-item self-report measure of loneliness and social dissatisfaction for children (see Asher et al., 1984). The primary purpose of this initial research was to examine the question of whether unpopular children, particularly those targeted for intervention, were indeed dissatisfied with their own peer relations. The measure itself evidenced good internal reliability and consistency (Asher et al., 1984) and a fair degree of stability over time (Hymel et al., 1983). For example, among third- through sixth-grade children, Hymel et al., (1983) reported a test-retest reliability coefficient of .55 over a 1-year period (N=111).

Research including this measure has indicated that a substantial number of children express dissatisfaction with their own peer relations and extreme feelings of loneliness. As hypothesized, unpopular children, defined on the basis of peer sociometric ratings, expressed significantly greater loneliness and social dissatisfaction than did popular children (Asher et al., 1984; Hymel, 1983). Subsequent research by Asher and Wheeler (1983) indicated that self-reported loneliness was greater among sociometrically *rejected* as opposed to *neglected* elementary-school-age children.

Particularly interesting, however, were findings that self-reported loneliness was associated with a generally negative pattern of self-perceptions (Hymel, 1983; Hymel et al., 1983). Lonelier children exhibited lower *social* perceived competence (Harter, 1982), perceived social situations as more difficult, and had less positive expectations for social outcomes and peer sociometric evaluations.

It seemed quite clear that a child who actually experienced such negative expectations and self-perceptions might be particularly debilitated in his or her social behavior; perhaps explainable by notions of negative self-fulfilling prophecies.

Borrowing again from research on loneliness in adults, we then considered an attributional analysis of loneliness in children (Hymel et al., 1983). Previous research (Anderson, Horowitz, & French, 1983; Peplau, Russell, & Heim, 1979) demonstrated that lonely adults tended to attribute social *success* to external and unstable causes and tended to attribute social *failure* to internal and stable causes. These findings have been interpreted as supportive of a cognitive model of loneliness in adults (Peplau et al., 1979) in which the individual's own cognitions and self-evaluations are viewed as mediating factors in the relationship between loneliness and social behavior. According to this model, the negative attributional pattern exhibited by lonely adults affects subsequent expectations, motivation for social interaction, and ultimately, actual social performance.

In a 2-year study of loneliness among third- through sixth-grade children, Hymel et al. (1983) examined whether a similar model would apply to lonely children. Particularly evident in the second year of results (following methodological improvements in assessing children's social attributions), we found that lonelier children were significantly more likely to view social failure as internally caused and as stable or likely to occur again. These findings are consistent with results of other researchers in the area of children's social attributions (e.g., Ames, Ames, & Garrison, 1977; Goetz & Dweck, 1980; Sobol & Earn, Chapter 6 this volume), with a similar pattern of results obtained across studies that differ considerably in terms of methodology. Children experiencing social difficulties, variously defined as unpopular, lacking in friends, or highly lonely, tend to perceive social success as unstable and externally caused and view social failure as stable and internally caused.

As Peplau and her colleagues (1979) suggest, this negative attributional pattern may have direct implications for subsequent social behavior. Lonely adults, who view their loneliness as stable and as internally or personally caused, are less likely to attempt to change their social situations. With children, a similar relationship is suggested by results of research by Goetz and Dweck (1980). They found that children who attributed their failure to be accepted into a pen-pal club to personal causes were indeed debilitated in subsequent attempts to gain entry into the club.

These data demonstrate that the negative attributional pattern associated with loneliness in children clearly parallels that exhibited by lonely adults. It may be the case that feelings of loneliness and the negative pattern of self-perceptions associated with them may be quite stable over time. The emergence of such feelings and self-perceptions in childhood may begin a negative cycle of perceptions and behavior that contributes to the continued experience of loneliness throughout the life span (Hymel, Franke, & Freigang, in press). In other words, lonely children may become lonely adults. Evidence such as this demonstrates the importance of a life-span perspective in studying the development of social difficulties and underscores the need for longitudinal studies of loneliness and social maladjustment.

Within this research, however, it is also important to keep in mind the notion of individual differences. Although many unpopular and/or lonely children evidenced this negative attributional pattern, not all of them did. Moreover, in our own research we have identified a few cases in which average status or even popular children evidenced a similarly negative pattern of self-perceptions and causal attributions. However, for those children who *did* interpret their social failures as stable and internally caused, an important consideration in ameliorating their social difficulties may be modification of their own perceptions or attributional interpretations. It seems unlikely that such children will readily modify their social behaviors or will generalize newly acquired social behaviors unless they first believe that such changes will indeed lead to greater social success. Such concerns may be less crucial for children who do not evidence this negative pattern of attributional bias.

Social Anxiety

Loneliness, however, is only one affective concomitant of poor interpersonal relations. Subsequent research on children's self-perceptions has focused on the assessment of children's attitudes toward peers and their feelings of social anxiety and social avoidance. Of particular interest here was the assessment of social anxiety. At a general level, the effects of anxiety have been a major concern of clinical researchers and practitioners for many years. In fact, Quay and Werry (1979) have argued that anxiety disorders form one of the two most common types of psychological problems in childhood. Anxiety in social situations may be manifested in various ways, but it is generally conceded that anxiety has a detrimental effect on interpersonal interactions.

Within the area of children's peer relations, a number of authors have suggested that feelings of social anxiety may mediate poor peer relationships (e.g., Asarnow, 1983; Hartup, 1970, 1983; Rubin, Chapter 9 this volume). However, there has been little empirical evidence to support this association. The few studies that have addressed this issue do lend some support to this hypothesized link, but these studies are somewhat limited. For example, McCandless, Castenada, and Palermo (1956) reported that general (trait) anxiety was negatively related to peer status among middle elementary school children. Similarly, Ollendick (1981) found that trait anxiety was negatively related to sociometric acceptance in elementary school boys, but not girls. Cowen, Zax, Klein, Izzo, and Trost (1965) also found anxiety to be related to peer rejection which, in turn, predicted later mental health problems.

These data do support the hypothesis that feelings of anxiety are related to poor interpersonal relations. However, previous research on anxiety and social behavior in children has tended to focus almost exclusively on general or trait anxiety (e.g., McCandless et al., 1956; Ollendick, 1981), but not *social* anxiety, per se.

There is evidence to suggest that more domain- or situational-specific measures of anxiety appear to be better predictors of anxiety states and subsequent behavior in relevant situations (e.g., Finch & Kendall, 1978; Finch, Kendall, & Montgomery, 1974). Although several self-report measures of *social* anxiety have been developed for use with adults (e.g., Curran, Corriveau, Monti, & Hagerman, 1980; Watson & Friend, 1969), similar, domain-specific measures have not been developed for use with younger populations.

One exception here is the Children's Concerns Inventory (CCI) developed by Buhrmester (1981, 1982). The CCI was designed as a short, domain-specific, self-report measure of anxiety in children, tapping feelings of anxiety in a number of areas, including peer acceptance. While the peer acceptance subscale of the CCI does evidence good internal consistency and a moderate degree of stability, the reported factor structure of this particular subscale is somewhat weak, with three out of seven items evidencing factor loadings of .40 or less. Moreover, the peer acceptance subscale of the CCI was found to be only moderately related to self-reports (Harter, 1982) of social perceived competence, $r(89) = -.28$, and to peer acceptance as indexed by sociometric nominations, $r(89) = -.40$ (Buhrmester, 1982). Currently, Buhrmester (personal communication, September, 1984) is attempting to revise the CCI to provide a more valid and reliable index of children's anxieties or concerns. Until such revisions are complete, however, the need for a measure of social anxiety in children remains.

Our first task, then, was the development of a more fine-grained assessment of children's feelings of social anxiety. In constructing this scale, we were guided, in part, by adult self-report measures of social anxiety (e.g., Watson & Friend, 1969), which tap a number of different dimensions including social anxiety, social avoidance, and fear of negative evaluation. In addition, we also considered children's general attitudes toward peer interaction, given previous research findings by Evers-Pasquale (described earlier). The resulting self-report measure included three distinct subscales: Social Anxiety, Social Avoidance, and Negative Peer Attitudes, with six items in each (see Franke & Hymel, 1984; 1985). Factor analytic results provided strong support for the distinctiveness of these three dimensions, with no significant cross-loadings for any of the items included in the scale.

In examining the psychometric properties of these three subscales (see Franke & Hymel, 1985), we found that all three scales evidenced good internal reliability and consistency and a reasonable degree of stability (test-retest reliability) over a 4-week interval. Over a *1-year* period, however, it became apparent that feelings of social anxiety were considerably more stable, $r(36) = .61$, $p < .001$, than were self-reports of social avoidance, $r(36) = .38$, $p < .05$, or negative attitudes toward peers $r(36) = .12$, NS, the latter subscale evidencing the least stability over a 1-year period. Moreover, although scores on the Social Anxiety and Social Avoidance subscales were nonsignificantly correlated, scores on the Social Avoidance and Negative Peer Attitudes subscales were significantly and positively correlated, suggesting considerable overlap in the two (Franke & Hymel, 1985). On the basis of these data, it appeared that two of the three subscales evidenced sufficient psychometric strength to warrant their use. The Negative Peer Attitudes sucscale, however, was subsequently deleted from the scale (see Franke & Hymel, 1985). It should also be noted that in a separate sample, the social anxiety subscale was found to be significantly related to more general feelings of anxiety, as measured by the children's Manifest Anxiety Scale (CMAS, McCandless et al., 1956), lending support to the validity of this measure (Franke & Hymel, 1985).

In subsequent research (Franke & Hymel, 1985) we examined the relationship among the Social Anxiety and Social Avoidance subscales and a variety of self-report and peer assessment indices of social competence among elementary school children. A brief review of the findings will be presented here. In examining these results it becomes clear that gender-related differences are a critical consideration, with different patterns of interrelations being obtained for boys and girls. In many cases, however, the pattern of relations obtained was similar for male and female subjects. For instance, self-reported loneliness (Asher et al., 1984) was found to be significantly related to greater social avoidance in both boys and girls. Similarly, low social perceived competence (Harter, 1982) was associated with greater social anxiety and greater social avoidance in both sexes.

Gender-related differences in the patterns of relationships obtained were readily apparent, particularly for self-reported social anxiety. Relative to males, female subjects in the present sample tended to report significantly greater social anxiety. This finding is not surprising, given previous research which also indicates that females are more susceptible to anxiety than males (Block, 1983). Perhaps of greater interest were sex-related differences in the correlates of social anxiety. Socially anxious females in the present sample were less popular among their same-sex peers and were perceived by same-sex peers as exhibiting more isolated social behavior. Moreover, social anxiety in females was associated with a negative pattern of self-perceptions, including greater feelings of loneliness and social dissatisfaction. For male subjects, however, these relationships were all nonsignificant. Interestingly, only the relations between social anxiety and social perceived competence were similar for both males and females, with greater social anxiety associated with lower social perceived competence, although even here, the correlation was greater in the case of girls than boys.

These data clearly suggest that feelings of social anxiety may differentially influence the social perceptions and interactions of male and female children. Indeed, such findings may be interpreted as indicating that social anxiety is a more important consideration for females than males. However, such a conclusion may be premature, since other studies have indicated a significant relationship between anxiety and social difficulties in males. For example, Trent (1957) found that among institutionalized delinquent boys, anxiety was related to greater peer rejection. Furthermore, Ollendick (1981) found that self-reported trait anxiety was associated with lower peer acceptance and less positive social interaction among boys, but not girls. Thus, it is not necessarily the case that anxiety is only a problem experienced by females. The discrepancies in results obtained across studies are difficult to reconcile, given considerable variations in samples, methodologies, and assessments employed across studies. However, variations in self-perceptions and their associations with other indices of social competence as a function of gender appear to be important considerations in future research.

Individual Differences

The research reviewed thus far constitutes an initial examination of the nature of children's self-perceptions of their own interpersonal relations. These data clearly indicate that subject variables, especially gender, must be considered in attempting to unravel the relationship between self-perceptions and social functioning. With regard to social skills intervention, however, perhaps the most important issue in terms of assessing children's social self-perceptions is a healthy concern for individual differences in how children perceive, interpret, and feel about their own relations with peers. In our own research within this area, we have repeatedly noted clear differences in social self-perceptions, especially among children who appear to be experiencing social difficulties.

The magnitude of these individual differences and the utility of inclusion of self-report measures in the assessment of socially isolated and/or rejected children is perhaps best demonstrated by examining several case examples. Relevant data are presented in Table 5.1, in which we have summarized assessment results obtained for six children included in our recent sample (Franke & Hymel, 1984). All scores reported in the table were standardized within each sex group ($Z = X - \overline{X}/SD$) to simplify comparisons across measures. Included here are both peer assessment and self-report measures of children's social functioning. Peer assessment measures included (a) the average rating received from same-sex peers on a rating-scale sociometric measure, and (b) peer perceptions of typical aggressive, isolated, and sociable behavior, derived from same-sex peer nominations on the Revised Class Play (Masten & Morison, 1981).

On the basis of peer assessment data, all six children would be considered unpopular and highly rejected by their same-sex classmates, receiving peer ratings that were at least one standard deviation below class means. In addition, all six children were perceived by peers as exhibiting extremely isolated behavior, again at least one standard deviation above class means. In intervention studies, relying exclusively on peer assessment measures for targeting, all six children might be classified similarly, as both socially rejected and isolated in their behavior. Considering peer perceptions of aggressive-disruptive behavior, the first three cases would also be classified as nonaggressive, while the latter three cases were clearly perceived by peers as aggressive-disruptive in their social behavior (as well as isolated). Recent research by Serbin and her colleagues (Serbin, Lyons, Marchessault, & Morin, 1983) has suggested that these isolated-aggressive children may be particularly victimized within their social groups.

Despite the general similarities obtained in peer assessments of these six children, however, they differed considerably in terms of peer perceptions of

TABLE 5.1. Individual differences in social difficulties and self-perceptions.

Case	Sex	Grade	Peer Acceptance (Sociometric ratings)	Peer assessment measure (Revised Class Play, Masten & Morison, 1982) Peer perceptions of behavior		
				Aggressive-disruptive	Sensitive-isolated	Sociable-leadership
S_1	F	5	-1.53	0.18	1.31	-0.91
S_2	F	6	-1.37	-1.36	2.12	-1.24
S_3	M	4	-1.22	-0.54	1.99	0.00
S_4	M	6	-1.08	1.14	1.06	-0.41
S_5	F	6	-1.87	2.34	1.92	-1.35
S_6	M	5	-1.83	1.83	1.40	-1.07

	Sex	Grade	Social perceived competence (Harter, 1982)	Loneliness (Asher et al., 1984)	Self-report assessments Social anxiety (Franke & Hymel, 1984)	Social avoidance (Franke & Hymel, 1984)	Negative peer attitudes (Franke & Hymel, 1984)	Children's action tendency scale (Deluty, 1979)		
								Aggressive	Assertive	Submissive
S_1	F	5	-1.34	2.33	1.94	1.38	2.09	0.30	-1.89	1.98
S_2	F	6	-0.62	-0.59	-1.18	-0.84	-1.19	1.63	0.11	-2.32
S_3	M	4	-0.93	-0.52	2.26	-0.66	-0.94	-1.83	0.69	2.01
S_4	M	6	-0.57	0.51	-0.23	-0.37	1.34	0.81	-0.46	-0.75
S_5	F	6	-1.34	2.40	0.58	0.50	1.84	0.06	-0.29	0.32
S_6	M	5	-0.72	-0.21	-0.23	0.77	1.34	-0.15	-0.08	0.28

Note. All scores presented were standardized ($Z = X - \overline{X}/SD$) to simplify comparisons across measures. Peer assessment measures were standardized with class and sex groups, while self-report measures were standardized within sex groups.

their sociable behavior, with some children perceived as below average in sociability and others perceived as average. More striking, perhaps, are individual differences in these children's own perceptions and feelings about their social situations. Most of these children expressed low social perceived competence, evidencing at least some awareness of their own poor status among peers. Two of the six children, however, scored particularly low on this measure, accompanied by fairly extreme feelings of loneliness and social dissatisfaction (S_1 and S_5). Only two of the six children, however, reported extreme feelings of social anxiety about peer interactions (S_1 and S_3). Interestingly, the most extreme feelings of social anxiety were reported by S_3, a fourth-grade *male*.

Variations in children's social self-perceptions are clearly evident if one compares assessment results obtained for S_1 and S_2, both of whom would be classified as unpopular females, perceived by peers as extremely isolated but neither highly aggressive nor highly sociable in their behavior. By peer assessments, then, these two children appear to be somewhat similar in terms of their social difficulties. However, their self-perceptions of their own social situations differ markedly. The first subject, S_1, appeared to be both aware of her poor peer acceptance (low social perceived competence) and unhappy about it (high loneliness and social dissatisfaction), and expressed an understandably negative pattern of self-perceptions including high social anxiety and social avoidance and fairly negative attitudes toward peer interactions. This child also saw herself as being submissive in her response to social conflict. Such self-perceptions are consistent with peer perceptions of her as isolated but nonaggressive. In contrast, S_2, also an unpopular and isolated female, did not exhibit extremely low social perceived competence, nor did she express extreme feelings of loneliness or social anxiety. She expressed fairly positive attitudes toward peers and did not prefer to avoid social interaction. Her preferred response to social conflict situations tended to be aggressive rather than submissive, which is quite discrepant with peer perceptions of her being relatively nonaggressive. In contrast to S_1, S_2 appeared to be either unaware of her poor peer acceptance, or denied it, or tended toward the provision of socially desirable responses to self-report measures. While these possibilities cannot be assessed on the basis of the present data, this child (S_2) may certainly respond quite differently to a particular social skills training program than would the first case considered (S_1).

Similarly, one might contrast S_4 and S_6, both of whom are unpopular males, perceived by peers as both aggressive *and* isolated in their social behavior. In both cases, results of self-perception assessments suggested only minimal awareness of their poor peer acceptance (or denial of it), both reporting only slightly below average perceived social competence and nearly average feelings of loneliness. Neither of these boys saw themselves as socially anxious, which is not surprising in light of results reported earlier with regard to social anxiety in males in this sample. Both boys, however, reported fairly negative attitudes toward peers. The interesting contrast between these two boys comes from an examination of their responses to the CATS measure (Deluty, 1979). The first, S_4, tended to emphasize relatively aggressive responses to social conflict while the second, S_6, did not, and, if anything, advocated relatively submissive responses to social conflict. Given that both these boys were perceived by peers as aggressive as well as isolated, it is interesting that each tended to emphasize different aspects of their social tendencies. How such individual differences in self-perceptions influence subsequent social relationships or the effectiveness of social skills intervention programs is as yet unknown. The potential effects of these varying self-perceptions clearly warrants consideration in future research on social skills training.

Comparisons of these six children clearly illustrates the need to consider individual differences in self-perceptions when assessing children's social difficulties. Even children who might be classified as experiencing similar social problems on the basis of external assessments, exhibit considerable variations in their own feelings and perceptions of their own social difficulties. Our hope is that the present chapter will encourage greater consideration of the uniqueness of each child's self-perceptions in future assessment and intervention research. It should be stressed, however, that it is *not* our intention to suggest that self-perception assessments be used in lieu of more traditional assessment procedures within this literature. The issue of validity of children's self-reports is still an important, yet unresolved, consideration. Nevertheless, the need to consider the unique perspective of each target child both in terms of assessment and the design and evaluation of intervention procedures appears unquestionable.

In this respect, the research reported herein may have implications for social skills training in a broader sense. Relevant here is a quote that Michael Rutter (1982) included in a recent paper on the myths of primary prevention programs. In this paper, he quotes the writing of Lewis Thomas who presents a rather skeptical view of intervention attempts. Lewis writes:

You cannot meddle with one part of a complex system from the outside without the most certain risk of setting off disastrous events that you hadn't counted on in other, remote parts. If you want to fix something, you are first obliged to understand, in detail, the whole system. (cited in Rutter, 1982, p. 884.)

At present we are only now beginning to understand the complexities of children's peer relations and their impact on development and adjustment throughout the life span. As we have attempted to illustrate, one aspect of this system, which is not well understood, is the impact of peer relations, especially poor peer relations, on the children themselves. For example, we do not as yet understand whether feelings of social anxiety mediate or cause social difficulties, or result from them, or both. Nor do we as yet understand the development or emergence of such negative feelings and self-perceptions across age. Nevertheless, these seem to be important issues for intervention research. Consider, for instance, reinforcement procedures utilized to increase sociable behavior and decrease isolated behavior by manipulating external consequences. While such procedures may effectively increase rates of social interaction, we have not seriously considered their potential effects on other aspects of the individual. In the case of an isolated, socially anxious child, would such treatments inadvertently lead to greater social anxiety? Questions of this sort have yet to be answered, and have only recently begun to be addressed.

References

Ames, R., Ames, C., & Garrison, W. (1977). Children's causal ascriptions for positive and negative interpersonal outcomes. *Psychological Reports, 41*, 595-602.

Anderson, C. A., Horowitz, L. M., & French, R. (1983). Attributional style of lonely and depressed people. *Journal of Personality and Social Psychology, 45*, 127-136.

Asarnow, J. (1983). Children with peer adjustment problems: Sequential and nonsequential analyses of school behaviors. *Journal of Consulting and Clinical Psychology, 51*, 709-717.

Asher, S. R., Hymel, S., & Renshaw, P. D. (1984). Loneliness in children. *Child Development, 55*, 1456-1464.

Asher, S., & Wheeler, V. (August 1983). *Children's loneliness: A comparison of rejected and neglected peer status*. Paper presented at the annual meeting of the American Psychological Association, Anaheim, CA.

Ausubel, D., Schiff, H., & Gasser, E. (1952). A preliminary study of developmental trends in sociempathy: Accuracy of perception of own and others' sociometric status. *Child Development, 23*, 111-128.

Bandura, A. (1977). Self-efficacy: Toward a unifying theory of behavior change. *Psychological Review, 84*, 191-215.

Bierman, K. L., & Furman, W. (1984). The effects of social skills training and peer involvement on the social adjustment of preadolescents. *Child Development, 55*, 151-162.

Block, J. H. (1983). Differential premises arising from differential socialization of the sexes: Some conjectures. *Child Development, 54*, 1335-1354.

Bream, L., Franke, S., & Hymel, S. (May 1984). *Social problem solving in children: The mediation of intentionality inferences*. Paper presented at the biennial University of Waterloo Conference on Child Development, Waterloo, Ontario.

Buhrmester, D. (April 1981). *A new measure of elementary-aged children's anxieties: The development and validation of the Children's Concerns Inventory*. Paper presented at the biennial meeting of the Society for Research in Child Development, Boston, MA.

Buhrmester, D. (1982). *Children's Concerns Inventory Manual*. Unpublished manuscript, University of Denver, Denver, CO.

Butler, L. (April 1979). *Social and behavioral correlates of peer reputation*. Paper presented at the biennial meeting of the Society for Research in Child Development, San Francisco, CA.

Cowen, E., Pederson, A., Babigian, H., Izzo, L., & Trost, M. (1973). Longterm follow-up of early detected vulnerable children. *Journal of Consulting and Clinical Psychology, 41*, 438-446.

Cowen, E., Zax, M., Klein, R., Izzo, L., & Trost, M. (1965). The relation of anxiety in school children to school records, achievement and behavioral measures. *Child Development, 36*, 685-695.

Curran, J. P., Corriveau, D. P., Monti, P. M., & Hagerman, S. B. (1980). Social skill and social anxiety: Self-report measurement in a psychiatric population. *Behavior Modification, 4*, 493-512.

Deluty, R. H. (1979). The Children's Action Tendency Scale: A self-report measure of aggressiveness, assertiveness and submissiveness in children. *Journal of Consulting and Clinical Psychology*, *47*, 1061-1071.

Deluty, R. (1981). Alternative-thinking ability of aggressive, assertive, and submissive children. *Cognitive Therapy and Research*, *5*, 309-312.

Dodge, K., Murphy, R., & Buchsbaum, D. (1984). The assessment of intention-cue detection skills in children: Implications for developmental psychopathology. *Child Development*, *55*, 163-173.

Dubin, R., & Dubin, E. (1965). Children's social perceptions: A review of research. *Child Development*, *36*, 809-838.

Evers-Pasquale, W. (1978). The Peer Preference Test as a measure of reward value: Item analysis, cross-validation, concurrent validation, and replication. *Journal of Abnormal Child Psychology*, *6*, 175-188.

Evers-Pasquale, W., & Sherman, M. (1975). The reward value of peers: A variable influencing the efficacy of filmed modeling in modifying social isolation in preschoolers. *Journal of Abnormal Child Psychology*, *3*, 179-189.

Finch, A. J., & Kendall, P. C. (1978). Anxiety in children: Theoretical views and research findings. In L. E. Beutler & R. Greene (Eds.), *Special problems in child and adolescent behavior* (pp. 75-98). CT: Technomic.

Finch, A. J., Jr., Kendall, P. C., & Montgomery, L. E. (1974). Multidimensionality of anxiety in children: Factor structure of the Children's Manifest Anxiety Scale. *Journal of Abnormal Child Psychology*, *2*, 331-336.

Franke, S., & Hymel, S. (May 1984). *Social anxiety in children: Development of self-report measures*. Paper presented at the Third Biennial Meeting of the University of Waterloo Conference on Child Development, Waterloo, Ontario.

Franke, S., & Hymel, S. (1985). *Social anxiety and social avoidance in children: The development of a self-report measure*. Manuscript submitted for publication.

Goetz, T., & Dweck, C. (1980). Learned helplessness in social situations. *Journal of Personality and Social Psychology*, *39*, 246-255.

Harter, S. (1982). The perceived competence scale for children. *Child Development*, *53*, 87-97.

Hartup, W. W. (1970). Peer interaction and social organization. In P. H. Mussen (Ed.), *Carmichael's Manual of Child Psychology* (3rd ed., Vol. 2). New York: Wiley.

Hartup, W. W. (1983). The peer system. In E. M. Hetherington (Ed.), *Handbook of child psychology: Vol. 4. Socialization, personality, and social development*. New York: Wiley.

Hymel, S., Franke, S., & Freigang, R. (in press). Peer relationships and their dysfunction: Considering the child's perspective. *Journal of Social and Clinical Psychology*.

Hymel, S., Freigang, R., Franke, S., Both, L., Bream, L., & Borys, S. (1983). *Children's attributions for social situations: Variations as a function of social status and self-perception variables*. Paper presented at the annual meeting of the Canadian Psychological Association, Winnipeg, Manitoba.

Hymel, S., & Rubin, K. H. (1985). Children with peer relationship and social skills problems: Conceptual, methodological and developmental issues. In G. J. Whitehurst (Ed.), *Annals of child development* (Vol. 2). Greenwich, CT: JAI Press.

Hymel, S. (April 1983). *Social isolation and rejection in children: The child's perspective*. Paper presented in the biennial meeting of the Society of Research in Child Development, Detroit, MI.

Kagan, J., Hans, S., Markowitz, A., Lopez, D., & Sigal, H. (1982). Validity of children's self-reports of psychological qualities. In *Progress in experimental personality research* (Vol. II). New York: Academic Press.

Krasnor, L. (April 1983). *Peer status differences in social problem solving*. Paper presented at the biennial meeting of the Society for Research in Child Development, Detroit, MI.

Kupersmidt, J. (April 1983). *Predicting delinquency and academic problems from childhood peer status*. Paper presented at the biennial meeting of the Society for Research in Child Development, Detroit, MI.

Ladd, G., & Wheeler, V. (1982). Assessment of children's self-efficacy for social interaction with peers. *Developmental Psychology, 18*, 795-805.

Marsh, H. W., Barnes, J., Cairns, L., & Tidman, M. (in press). The Self-Description Questionnaire (SDQ): Age and sex effects in the structure and level of self-concept for preadolescent children. *Journal of Educational Psychology*.

Marsh, H. W., Smith, I. D., & Barnes, J. (1983). Multitrait-multimethod analysis of the Self-Description Questionnaire: Student-teacher agreement on multidimensional ratings of student self-concept. *American Educational Research Journal, 20*, 333-357.

Masten, A. S., & Morison, P. (1981, April). *The Minnesota revision of the class play: Psychometric properties of a peer assessment instrument*. Paper presented at the biennal meeting of the Society for Research in Child Development, Boston, MA.

McCandless, B. R., Castaneda, A., & Palermo, D. S. (1956). Anxiety in children and social status. *Child Development, 27*, 385-391.

Meichenbaum, D., Bream, L. A., & Cohen, J. S. (1984). A cognitive-behavioral perspective of child psychopathology: Implications for assessment and training. In R. J. McMahon & R. D. Peters (Eds.), *Childhood disorders: Behavioral-developmental approaches*. New York: Brunner/Mazel.

Nicholls, J. G. (1978). The development of the concepts of effort and ability, perception of academic attainment, and the understanding that difficult tasks require more ability. *Child Development, 49*, 800-814.

Nicholls, J. G. (1979). Development of perception of own attainment and causal attributions for success and failure in reading. *Journal of Educational Psychology, 71*, 94-99.

Ollendick, T. H. (1981). Assessment of social interaction skills in school children. *Behavioral Counseling Quarterly, 1*, 227-243.

Peplau, L. A., & Perlman, D. (1982). *Loneliness: A sourcebook of current trends, research and therapy*. New York: Wiley.

Peplau, L. A., Russell, D., & Heim, M. (1979). An attributional analysis of loneliness. In I. Frieze, D. Bar-Tal, & J. S. Carroll (Eds.), *New approaches to social problems*. San Francisco: Jossey-Bass.

Quay, H. C., & Werry, J. S. (1979). *Psychopathological disorders of childhood* (2nd ed.). New York: Wiley.

Richard, B., & Dodge, K. (1982). Social maladjustment and problem solving among school aged children. *Journal of Consulting and Clinical Psychology, 50*, 226-233.

Roff, M., Sells, S., & Golden, M. (1972). *Social adjustment and personality development in children*. Minneapolis: University of Minnesota Press.

Rubin, K., & Krasnor, L. (in press). Social cognitive and social behavioral perspectives on problem solving. In M. Perlmutter (Ed.), *Minnesota Symposium on Child Psychology* (Vol. 18). Hillsdale, NJ: Erlbaum.

Russell, D. (1982). The measurement of loneliness. In L. A. Peplau & D. Perlman (Eds.), *Loneliness: A sourcebook of current theory, research, and therapy*. New York: Wiley.

Rutter, M. (1982). Prevention of children's psychosocial disorders: Myth and substance. *Pediatrics, 70*, 883-894.

Serbin, L., Lyons, J., Marchessault, K., & Morin, D. (April 1983). *Naturalistic observations of peer-identified aggressive, withdrawn, aggressive-withdrawn and comparison children*. Paper presented at the biennial meeting of the Society for Research in Child Development, Detroit, MI.

Shure, M. B., & Spivack, G. (1980). Interpersonal problem solving as a mediator of behavioral adjustment in preschool and kindergarten children. *Journal of Applied Developmental Psychology, 1*, 29-44.

Spivack, G., & Shure, M. B. (1974). *Social adjustment of young children*. San Francisco: Jossey-Bass.

Taylor, A., & Asher, S. (April 1984). *Children's interpersonal goals in game situations*. Paper presented at the annual meeting of the American Educational Research Association, New Orleans, LA.

Taylor, A., & Asher, S. (in press). Children's goals and social competence: Individual differences in a game-playing context. In T. M. Field (Ed.), *Friendships among normal and handicapped children*. Norwood, NJ: Ablex.

Trent, R. D. (1957). The relationship of anxiety to popularity and rejection among institutionalized delinquent boys. *Child Development, 28*, 379-384.

Ullmann, C. (1957). Teachers, peers, and test predictors of adjustment. *Journal of Educational Psychology, 48*, 257-267.

Vosk, B., Forehand, R., Parker, J., & Rickard, K. (1982). A multimethod comparison of popular and unpopular children. *Developmental Psychology, 18*, 571-575.

Watson, D., & Friend, R. (1969). Measurement of social-evalutive anxiety. *Journal of Consulting and Clinical Psychology, 33*, 448-457.

CHAPTER 6

Assessment of Children's Attributions for Social Experiences: Implications for Social Skills Training

Michael P. Sobol and Brian M. Earn

A considerable amount of research has been generated linking attributions for achievement success and failure to expectations about and production of future behavior (cf. Dweck, 1975; Weiner, 1979). Very little effort, however, has been directed toward studying the relations between attributions and success and failure in the realm of social relationships. It seems likely, as Weiner (1979) has suggested, that the same or similar cognitive mediators as those that have been identified as being important in the achievment sphere would also be important in determining reactions and behavior in any situation where one can succeed or fail. As has been previously noted in this volume, one set of situations that has crucial implications for children is social relationships. By examining children's attributions for social success and failure the causal and maintenance conditions of sociometric status should become more apparent.

The developmental literature pertaining to attributional analyses of social behavior is relatively scant. Indeed, until recently we could find only two published studies that examined aspects of children's social attributions. In the earlier of the two studies, Ames, Ames, and Garrison (1977) asked children to endorse one of three causes, either an external, internal, or neutral one that typified the child's reasons for achieving social successes and failures. Overall, they found that social failure was more frequently attributed to external factors than was social success. While this result is consistent with findings from the achievement sphere, the conclusions that can be drawn from the study are restricted in that the causes that Ames et al. used were confounded on the dimensions of locus and stability. According to Weiner (1979), the separation of these two dimensions appears to be crucial when attempting to assess the relationships between attributions, behavior, and affect. In the only other published study that examined children's social attributions Goetz and Dweck (1980), as part of a larger investigation, obtained children's spontaneous explanations for social failure. The reasons that children offered appear to be compatible with the dimensions of locus and stability suggested by Weiner. For example, children discriminated between internal, stable causes such as ability and external, and unstable causes such as mood of the rejector. In addition, Goetz and Dweck also provided some support for linkage between endorsement of stable causes and future expectations and behavior. They found that children who attributed social rejection to internal and stable causes manifested greater disruption of goal-directed behavior than did children who attributed rejection to other types of causes. It should be noted that although the Goetz and Dweck study was clearly methodologically sound, in terms of an attributional analysis of social experience it was limited in that no information was gathered regarding children's attributions for social success. As we will note later, one factor that may relate to the production of future successful social behavior on the part of children may be their assigning previous success to internal factors.

Children's Spontaneous Attributions for
Social Success and Failure

As a first step toward applying an attributional analysis to the social relationships of children, Earn and Sobol (1984) measured the spontaneous attributions of fourth- and fifth-grade children by placing them in an open-ended interview format in which children offered reasons for a variety of successful and unsuccessful social outcomes. These attributions were then rated according to Elig and Frieze's (1975) categorical coding scheme for attributions and Weiner's (1979) dimensional analysis of locus, stability, and controllability. Besides attempting to identify those categories that children typically use to explain social outcomes, a major goal of the study was to determine whether or not patterns of attributions would covary with social experience. In the achievement area, Raviv, Bar-Tal, Raviv, & Bar-Tal (1980) found that previous experience as represented by such factors as race and ability level appears to be related to the types of attributions that individuals use in order to explain success and failure. In the area of social relationships, Anderson, Horowitz, and French (1983) showed that the extremely lonely manifest a particular attributional style. Specifically, they tend to attribute interpersonal failure to their own characterological defects. Given the quite different behavior and experience patterns that children in groups differing on peer acceptance and rejection nominations appear to have (Dodge, 1983), we expected that these groups would tend to use different types of causes when explaining various social outcomes.

In our study, 56 participants were selected from 262 fourth- and fifth-grade children who filled out a sociometric modeled after Gronlund (1959). Each child was asked to nominate three children from their classes whom they would choose to sit near, play with, not sit near, not play with. The sums of the acceptance and rejection scores were then converted separately to z scores determined by class in order that relative positions within class would be equivalent. Based on their sociometric status, children were placed into one of four groups. These groups (each consisting of 14 children) were classified as controversial (high acceptance, high rejection), popular (high acceptance, low rejection), rejected (low acceptance, high rejection), and neglected (low acceptance, low rejection).

In the open-ended interview each child was presented with a series of 12 social situations that varied as to outcome (successful or unsuccessful) and initiator of the activity (self or other). For example, a successful self-initated outcome would read, "You ask a child to go to the movies with you and he does. Why do you think this would happen?" The Elig and Frieze (1975) Coding Scheme of Perceived Causality was used to code the children's audiotaped responses to the interview questions. This involved a two-step process. First, the causal responses were coded along the dimensions of locus (internal, mutual, or external), stability (stable or unstable), and controllability (controllable, mediate, or uncontrollable). This was followed by assigning the causal responses to one of the categories that fell within the dimensional domain of the response. For example, if the child gave the answer "because I always try to be friendly" this was scored internal, stable, and controllable and was categorized as Stable Effort.

Categories of Causes Used to Explain Social Outcomes

A clear picture of general category usage emerges when the data are collapsed across sociometric groups and situations. Six categories, luck (36.9%), other's assessment of self (17.1%), other's motives (14.3%), personality interaction (10.4%), third-party intervention (10.4%), and other's personality (4.9%), accounted for over 90% of the causes offered to explain the outcomes in the various situations. As in the achievement area, children tended to use external causes considerably more often when explaining failure situations than when explaining success. Luck, for instance, was used 49.4% of the time when explaining failure but only 24.4% of the time when explaining success. The opposite was true for success situations where internal causes were used more often to explain outcomes. Personality interaction (defined as mutual compatability) was used considerably more often when explaining success (17.3%) than when explaining failure (3.6%).

Differences in Category Usage Among the Sociometric Groups

Although these results will be discussed later in this chapter, one important trend should be noted. In general, popular children used causes that suggested that they undertook a more sophisticated analysis of social situations than did the other three sociometric groups. Luck, for example, was used as an explanation for outcomes considerably less often by popular children (28%) than by controversial (42.9%), neglected (36.9%), or rejected children (39.9%). Popular children used the category other's motives, on the other hand, more often (19%) than did neglected (14.3%), rejected (12.5%), or controversial (11.3%) children. Similar types of differences were also reflected in the explanations provided for social success versus failure.

Linkages Between Self-Esteem, Expectation of Future Success, and Attributions

In order to assess the possible linkages between attributions, self-esteem, and expectations of future success that Weiner (1979) has suggested exist in the achievement domain, measures of social self-esteem (adapted from Kokenes,

1974) and expectations of future success were also obtained from the children in our sample. Although the attributions in the study were for hypothetical rather than real outcomes and thus the likelihood of obtaining any linkages ought to be reduced, some significant relationships were found. The more that children saw their failure as being determined by stable causes, the more likely it was that they did not expect success in future social relationships. In addition, the more that children endorsed controllable causes, the higher their self-esteem.

Children's Assessments of the Meanings of Social Causes

The study just described attained the goal of assessing children's spontaneous attributions for social experience and determining if social status was related to the use of certain causal categories. However, we soon realized that we had set out to examine children's pespectives of their social world but had done so only from an adult's point of view. The main problem with the study was that although we had discovered the causes that children themselves use to explain social outcomes, we had assigned adult's meaning to the causes by having adult raters categorize and place the causes on the dimensions of locus, stability, and controllability. This approach is consistent with what Russell (1982) has called the "fundamental attribution researcher error," that is, researchers have inappropriately assumed that the meanings of the causes that subjects provide for outcomes are identical for both researchers and subjects alike. The evidence gathered by Russell (1982) suggests that this is clearly not always the case. To insure that we were not making the same error, we decided to obtain children's own placement of these causes on the three attributional dimensions. Since we had found social experience to be related to the types of causes that children use to explain social experience, we wanted to determine whether the four sociometric groups might also differ in the meaning that they assign to the same causes. If social experience does play a role in dimensional placement, then causal categories can no longer be viewed as having absolute meaning. Thus, we (Sobol & Earn, 1985) designed measures to determine whether children differing in social experience would see a category such as luck, for example, as being internal, stable, and uncontrollable, that is, reflective of a personality trait, or external, stable, and uncontrollable, and therefore reflective of an uncertain and unpredictable social environment.

The subjects in this study were 164 children from grades 4, 5, and 6. All children were tested in a group setting within their classrooms. On the basis of their acceptance and rejection z scores, 22 children were assigned to the popular, 17 to the neglected, 10 to the controversial, and 18 to the rejected sociometric groups. All of the children rated dimensional characteristics of eight social attributions. Six of these causes (luck, third-party intervention, personality interaction, other's motives, personality, and behavioral sociability) had been shown in the previously discussed study to be ones that were offered at least 5% of the time by children of the same age and grade. Two additional causes, effort and mood, were included in the questionnaire since Weiner (1979) thought them to be of some importance in achievment situations.

Children were asked to evaluate the eight causes along the dimensions of locus, stability, and controllability. For example, in evaluating third-party intervention, the children first read the following sentence: "Sometimes the way you get along with other kids depends on what other kids say about you." They then rated the cause on three 10-point scales. The end points for *locus* were "What other kids say about me has to do with things about me" and "What other kids say about me has nothing to do with things about me." For *stability* the end points were "What other kids say about me changes all the time" and "What other kids say about me never changes." Finally, *controllability* was measured on a scale defined by the endpoints "I can do something about what other kids say about me" and "I can do nothing about what other kids say about me."

Differences in Assessment of Causal Meaning
Among the Sociometric Groups

For each of the eight causes, separate analyses of variance were carried out for ratings of locus, stability, and controllability, respectively. All analyses of variance were of a 2×2 (Acceptance $\times$ Rejection) between-groups design. Scores on the dimensions could range from 1 to 10 with low scores being indicative of internal, unstable, and controllable evaluations. A summary of the significant effects is to be found in Table 6.1.

Table 6.1 graphically illustrates that social experience, as measured by a peer sociometric, is related to dimensional placement of a cause. Social causes appear to have different meanings depending upon one's sociometric group. On seven of the eight causes sociometric status has a significant effect on at least one of the dimensions. Perhaps most interesting is the fact that five of the effects are expressed as Acceptance $\times$ Rejection interactions. Thus, it is necessary to have both acceptance and rejection nominations in order to predict dimensional placement of causes.

Some Conclusions Concerning Children's
Social Attributions

Two distinct groups of conclusions emerge. The first set relates to the measurement of children's social attributions while the second group addresses the relationship between social experience and social attributions. We will consider both of these areas in turn.

Measurement of Children's Social Attributions

The Need for Ecologically Valid Causes, Categories, and Situations. One thing that is quite evident from our data is that it is essential to insure that the attribu-

TABLE 6.1. Summary of effects of sociometric status on dimensional evaluation of causes.

Cause	Dimension	Effect p level	Group means
Other's motives	Controllability	Acc < .05	HiA = 3.15, LoA = 4.59
Personality	Locus	A × R < .02	P = 5.05, R = 5.44, N = 3.59, C = 3.30
	Controllability	Rej < .05	HiR = 3.93, LoR = 5.48
Behavioral sociability	Controllability	Acc < .02	HiA = 5.27, LoA = 3.56
Mood	Locus	A × R < .02	P = 5.55, R = 5.72, N = 3.65, C = 4.20
	Controllability	A × R < .02	P = 4.82, R = 3.50, N = 5.82, C = 6.70
Third party intervention	Locus	Acc < .02	HiA = 6.64, LoA = 4.79
	Stability	A × R < .02	P = 6.41, R = 5.00, N = 3.90, C = 4.00
Personality interaction	Stability	Acc < .07	HiA = 5.60, LoA = 4.26
Effort	Locus	A × R < .05	P = 5.68, R = 4.83, N = 3.59, C = 4.10

Note. Low scores indicate Internal, Unstable, and Controllable ratings. A = Acceptance; P = Popular (High Acceptance, Low Rejection); R = Rejected (Low Acceptance, High Rejection); N = Neglected (Low Acceptance, Low Rejection); C = Controversial (High Acceptance, High Rejection).

tional causes either elicited from or provided for subjects be ecologically valid. In our own work, we addressed this issue by having children spontaneously generate causes in response to a variety of situations and outcomes. In the achievement area, in spite of Weiner's (1983) cautions, much of the work has required that children differentially endorse one of four predetermined attributions representing ability, effort, luck, and task difficulty. Clearly had we restricted ourselves to only these four, our research would not have been representative of the causes that children typically use to explain social outcomes since only one of the four (luck) appears on our list of spontaneously generated causes. In addition, because social situations have many more varied possibilities than does, for example, test taking, it is imperative that the researcher insure that the situations provided make up a broad range of social behaviors. Finally, in extending an attributional analysis to the social domain, researchers must be aware of the limits of available coding schemes developed primarily for achievement situations.

The Need for an Idiosyncratic Approach to the Dimension of Causes. Rather than researchers placing their own meanings on the causes that children generate, children must be asked for their own phenomenological or idiosyncratic interpretations of these causes in terms of their placement on the attributional dimensions. In addition to finding that the dimensional placement of causes varied with social experience the other results from the second study, discussed earlier, suggested that children do not use the stability dimension in the same way as adult researchers. Thus, it cannot be assumed, a priori, then that when children say an outcome is due to, for example, "personality" that they mean it is caused by an internal, stable, and uncontrollable factor as suggested by the Elig and Frieze (1975) coding scheme. One final cautionary note on the use of dimensions must be raised. While the causal dimensions used in our studies appear to be useful analytical tools, it cannot be assumed, a priori, that children themselves spontaneously use these or any other dimensions when thinking about causes.

Definition and Use of the Controllability Dimension. Another point that should be made about our approach to the measurement of attributions concerns our use of the controllability dimension. Weiner (1979) has defined controllability as not emanating merely from the perspective of the actor. From this perspective, a cause is controllable if anyone could do something about it. One consequence of this approach is that those causes that subjects see as personally controllable cannot be distinguished from those that are controllable by others. Given research that links attributions of personal controllability to coping (Silver & Wortman, 1980), this seems a crucial distinction to be able to make. For this reason we have defined controllability in terms of personal control; children are asked whether *they* can do something about the cause of an outcome. Other support for this approach comes from Forsyth and McMillan (1981) who found that the controllability dimension (as defined by personal control) was more strongly linked with self-esteem than was locus. Combining the personal control definition of controllability with the idiosyncratic approach to the meaning of causes also removes the problem of confounding the attributional dimensions since it leaves open the possibility of finding external, personally controllable causes. For example, in our research children defined other's motives as being both external and personally controllable.

The Importance of Using Age-appropriate Techniques. Clearly, as in all research with children, attribution researchers must insure that the measurement techniques they are using are appropriate for the age of the sample they are studying. In another of our studies we decided that rather than spending excessive time interviewing each child individually, we would provide a questionnaire that varied situations and outcomes and let the children place the causes on the dimensions. Thus, children were presented with a situation and outcome, such as not being invited to a birthday party, and were asked to place the cause or causes of this outcome on the three attributional dimensions. The locus dimension, for example, asked if this outcome occurred "because of things about me" or "because of things that have nothing to do with me." The results of our study strongly suggested that the children did not understand what was demanded of them. Apparently to place causes on the dimensions it was necessary for them to concentrate on a single cause.

    In summary, as a result of our research we have come to believe that, at least for children up to the age of 12, an interview is necessary for assessing social attributions. The interview should utilize a two-stage approach in which the child is first read a description of a social situation with a successful or unsuccessful outcome and then is asked to provide a single cause to explain the event. Immediately following this, the child is asked to place the cause on the three attributional dimensions. Finally, it should be restated that in assessing children's social attributions, it is important to present a full range of social situations and outcomes in order to increase the content validity of the task.

Sociometric Status and Attributions

The Relationship Between Sociometric Status and Explanations of Social Outcomes. Our results clearly indicate that groups that differ in sociometric status use different causes when explaining social success and failure. Popular children appear to employ a more sophisticated social analysis and thus use more sophisticated social explanations. One example of this tendency is that they used luck less and personality interaction more than did the other groups when explaining social success and therefore, compared to the other groups, appear to take more credit for success. The popular group's approach to failure is also interesting in that, as do the other sociometric groups, the group members tend to externalize failure but not in the same simple way. That is, rather than only using luck to explain their failures (as do the members of other groups) they are more likely to use external, but more sophisticated reasons such as other's motives. Finally it is interesting, but perhaps not surprising, to note that popular children tend to see their social world as being more controllable than do the members of other sociometric groups.

The Relationship Between Sociometric Status and the Meaning of Causes. Too much should not be made of the difference between sociometric groups in the use of causes since our data also suggest that even when children offer the same cause as an explanation for an outcome it may mean very different things to them depending upon their previous social experience. The argument that social experience is related to the dimensional placement of social causes is perhaps best supported by the form of the Acceptance × Rejection interactions obtained in the second study reported earlier. For all five of the interactions (summarized in Table 6.1) there is a recurring similarity between the popular and rejected groups on the one hand and the neglected and controversial children on the other. These results suggest that consistency of social feedback may have an impact on the dimensional placement of causes. For both the popular and rejected children, social feedback should be relatively consistent, positive in the case of the popular children and negative in the case of the rejected children. Thus, there should be less uncertainty about the meaning of particular causes. The social world of the neglected and controversial children is, however, not nearly as consistent with feedback, being either mixed, as in the case of the controversial group, or virtually nonexistent, as in the case of neglected children. The potential effects of feedback consistency are best demonstrated by the significant Acceptance × Rejection interaction on the stability dimension for interpretations of third-party intervention. It should not be surprising that given their consistent social experience both rejected and, especially in this case, popular children see what other people say about them as being more stable than do either the neglected or controversial children. Taken together then, the pattern of results seems to suggest a strong connection between social experience and the meaning or dimensional placement of causes.

The Use of Acceptance and Rejection Scores in Sociometric Measurement. The fact that many of the differences obtained on the dimensional placement of causes by the sociometric groups were expressed as Acceptance × Rejection interactions calls into question (if there was still any question about it) the practice in the literature of considering the effects of sociometric positions in terms of acceptance alone (Asher, 1978). Had we placed the neglected and rejected children into one sociometric group and the popular and controversial children into another, our results would have been obscured.

Attributions and Social Skills Training

In his model, developed earlier in this volume (Chapter 1), Dodge suggested that one area that both practitioners and researchers in the social skills area might focus on is "what children bring to the task." The research that we have just presented supports the notion that children who differ in sociometric status bring different attributions and meanings for these attributions when they appear at a social skills training session. What implications does this have for the practice of social skills training? This question, particularly as it applies to the enhancement of skill concepts and performance and the issues of skill maintenance and generalization, will now be addressed.

Enhancing Skill Concepts

Using Ladd & Mize's (1983) cognitive social learning model as a guide for social skills training, it follows that prior to behavioral skill acquisition, the child must first be cognizant of social concepts that underlie successful interaction. One means of fostering these skill concepts involves increasing the child's awareness of the "strategic value or usefulness of that which is to be learned" (p. 133). Using this as a goal, the therapist will try to persuade the child that a specific set of behaviors will lead to a valued outcome. However, the ease by which a child comes to accept the therapist's view of a social means-ends relationship is in all likelihood moderated by the degree to which the therapist and the child share a common attributional perspective. One can imagine, for example, a situation in which the therapist is explaining to a child the merits of sharing and cooperation in overcoming social rejection. The therapist says to the child "when you act nicely to other people, they will act nicely to you." However, if the child's interpretation of his lack of social success runs something like "People don't like me because I'm fat and ugly," then there is little chance that simple didactic instruction will lead the child to accept the therapist's view of means-ends relationships in social interaction. We must always begin not only with an assessment of what the child knows about goals, plans, and concepts; we must also determine what it is that the child believes are the causes of social success and failure.

A primary role for attribution is suggested, for if the child holds stable and uncontrollable explanations for social failure, then his or her goals, being self-protective, may be different from the socially successful child, his or her plans for achieving his or her goals may incorporate strategies outside of the training regimen, and his or her concepts may not include those deemed necessary for successful social functioning.

Another point for consideration at the enhancement of social concepts stage centers on the meaning of the attributions that the child holds for social outcomes. In our work, we have attempted to ascertain the meaning of social attributions by having children place causes on the dimensions of locus, stability, and controllability as suggested by Weiner (1979). These dimensions allow us to understand whether children view the cause as being due to factors inside or outside of themselves, as being stable or changeable in time, and finally as being under or not under their control. By assessing attributions and their dimensional meaning we believe that social skill concepts themselves will become more apparent. Weiner (1979) has suggested that "attributional inferences are often quite retrospective, summarize a number of experiences, [and] take place below a level of awareness" (p. 4). By directly assessing attributions and their dimensional meanings, we assume that the salience of an attributional perspective is enhanced. From this perspective, the act of assessment helps the child to conceive of a social means-ends relationship. Opportunities exist to allow for the consideration of the dimensions and their related linkages that underlie an attributional structure. The child may be challenged to trace the causes of causes, to consider the standing dimensional meaning, and finally, to assess the possibility of movement in meaning along the dimensions in light of social information provided by the therapist.

Finally, the assessment and discussion of attributions at the concept enhancement stage may prepare the child for a greater acceptance of therapeutic manipulations at the skill enhancement stage. This notion is based upon several factors. The consideration of multiple causes for outcome may increase the probability that the child will not view behavior-outcome sequences as being rigidly determined. Instead, several sources of input may be more easily considered. Furthermore, awareness of the dimensional meaning of causes opens up the possibility for the children to evaluate performance-related outcomes as being reflective of factors about themselves, not fixed but variable, and possibly being brought under their own control. By moving the child in the direction of internal, unstable, and controllable attributions, the child is perhaps more able to accept the idea that there is something that can be done to change negative outcomes. Thus, through direct assessment, from an attributional perspective, children may be more prepared to learn appropriate social skills.

Enhancing Skill Performance

Ladd and Mize's (1983) second stage of training concentrates on the acquisition of specific social-behavioral skills. A role for an attributional approach is apparent at this stage. Either the training program can be matched to the attributional style of the child or the child's attributional style may be modified in line with more effective social functioning. These two approaches will be dealt with in turn.

Bugental, Whalen, and Henker (1977) have argued that the effectiveness of a therapeutic intervention is in part determined by a match between the child's attributional style and the implicit attributional emphasis of the intervention. They hypothesized that if the child held an internal attribution for academic success, such as effort, then this child would benefit most from a remediational program that stressed self-control and self-instructional procedures. On the other hand, external control children, holding teacher bias and luck attributions, would show better improvement in a program that systematized feedback from the external environment. The results of their study supported this hypothesis, that is, internal children responded more positively to self-control procedures, while external children displayed more improvement when given directed, external feedback.

On the basis of this study one is easily led to the suggestion that the strategy used to modify social behavior ought to reflect the attributional style of the child. In one of our studies (Sobol & Earn, 1985), we found that neglected children tend to view causes as being more internal than do rejected children. As such, we are able to hypothesize that perhaps neglected children would respond more effectivly to a self-instructional and self-control program. On the other hand, a social skills program designed for rejected children ought to begin with an emphasis on a more conventional operant approach utilizing external reinforcement procedures.

This hypothesis concerning a match between the child's attributional style and the implicit attributional emphasis of the training program does not, however, lead to the conclusion that self-control training is inappropriate for children who hold an external attributional perspective. Following Bandura (1977), for successful maintenance and generalization of behavior the child must ultimately accept an attributional style in which outcome is viewed as being internal controllable. Thus, strategies that stress an external orientation must eventually be modified in order that the child is able to take on a more self-efficacious perspective (Wheeler & Ladd, 1982).

The notion that the child's attributional style ought to be modified in line with more effective social skills performance finds support in the work of Dweck and Repucci (1973), Dweck (1975), Goetz and Dweck (1980), and Ladd (1981). Exactly what the most effective approach for the modification of attributional style is remains a question yet to be addressed. However, it is possible to give a catalog of strategies that may prove to be efficacious.

In many ways, current social skills training using modeling, coaching, and instruction incorporates, implicitly, a social, attributional perspective. We say implicitly since the stated goals of such training do not include the direct eliciting of attributional statements about outcome from the child. Asher and Renshaw (1981), for example, see coaching as meeting four objectives: (a) the transmission of general interactional principles, (b) knowledge of behavioral sequences, (c) the setting of social goals, and (d) an awareness of one's social impact on others. In meeting these goals, it would seem that they are also conveying to the child that the cause of a social success is based upon the child's appropriate assessment and behavioral response to a given situation. However, it is left to the child to draw this cause-effect relationship.

We believe that children in training programs should not be left to draw attributional conclusions on their own. Instead, they should be guided toward accepting responsibility for success by attributing outcome to the appropriateness of their behavior within the social context. Furthermore, social failure should perhaps be attributed to their behavior, which did not meet the demands of the social situation. Elsewhere (Earn & Sobol, 1984), we referred to such an attribution as behavioral sociability. This is usually coded as internal, unstable, and controllable and bares a resemblance to another important attributional category, that of effort. In fact, Dweck (1981) suggested that this is the primary attribution needed to meet failure with adaptation, self-confidence, and perseverance.

How does one shift the child in the direction of effort-based, behaviorally related attributions? One way is to provide such attributional information within a modeling sequence. If the child observes a model complete a behavioral sequence and state that success was caused by trying hard to act in a way that met the demands of the situation, then perhaps the child will be more likely to use a similar attribution. Another approach using coaching would be to sensitize the child directly to the possibility that social success is the result of appropriate action. When reviewing the success of an interaction the coach should first question the child about the reasons for the success. Then feedback can be given that success was the direct result of the child's effort-based behaviors. This would also be a good place to expand on the dimensional meaning of the attribution, that is, that effortful, appropriate behavior reflects something about the child that can change over time and also remain within the control of the child. Finally, if the trainer utilizes a more operantly oriented contingency program, then the child should be given more than the simple feedback that the behavior was successful. The child should also be told that success was caused by the displaying of an appropriate sequence of behaviors.

This emphasis on an attributional component for operantly based programs is especially important when one considers the finding of some studies (Kirby & Toler, 1970; O'Connor, 1972) that with the withdrawal of feedback, the targeted behaviors returned to baseline. It is easy to imagine the child saying to him- or herself: "I succeeded because the teacher helped me—now that he's not helping me, I can't do it." In such a circumstance, the child must be encouraged to shift the attribution from third-party intervention to something about him- or herself, over which he or she feels a sense of control.

So far, possibilities have been presented for attributional retraining under the conditions of success. However, the work of Dweck and her colleagues would suggest that neglected and rejected children are most at risk when dealing with failure experiences. For these children, two attributional patterns emerge: Either they view failure as being caused by personal characteristics and lack of ability or they believe that negative outcomes are the result of a luckless and hostile environment. In both cases, these attributions are distinguished by the fact that the child believes that the cause of failure cannot be controlled. As a result, these children, when faced with failure, do not meet the situation with adaptability and perseverance. Instead, their behavior is marked by either withdrawal or rigidity and intensification.

Dweck (1975, 1981) has dealt with this issue of reactions to failure by including in an attributional retraining program experiences with both success and failure. One group of children received materials structured so that only success resulted. The second group, however, sometimes failed the task, with the experimenter noting that "this means that you should have tried harder." Following 25 training sessions, all children were tested for performance in a failure situation. Dweck found that only the group that received mixed success and failure training both improved performance after failure and displayed a change in attributions for task outcome.

The study by Goetz and Dweck (1980) also points out the need to consider an attributional analysis of failure. Children were first asked to endorse one of a list of reasons for social rejection in hypothetical situations. They then individually tried out for membership in a pen-pal club by writing a sample "getting-to-know-you" letter they were told would be evaluated by a peer who was a member of the pen-pal committee. Shortly after completing the letter, the child was informed that the initial attempt had been rejected but that a second opportunity would be allowed. This second attempt was enthusiastically accepted in all cases and the child was given the name of an actual pen-pal in another school.

Two important results emerged from this study. First, Goetz and Dweck found that children who either gave up or failed to modify their letter on the second round were the ones who held attributions for failure that stressed personal inadequacy. On the other hand, children who held effort-based attributions for failure met the rejection with attempts to overcome this negative outcome. One is, thus, led to the conclusion that if children are to meet failure with adaptability, then they must be taught to construe the outcome as something they can potentially control through appropriate action. The second finding of this study was that across popularity groups, the same link between attributions and coping style was found. This must alert us then to the possibility that there are some popular children, who not having had experiences with failure, may be quite vulnerable to the inevitable social rejections that everyone is likely to encounter at some point. It is not enough simply to have good social skills; one must also have matching internal and controllable attributions to deal with the ups and downs of social interaction.

Finally, there may be certain social situations in which effort-based attributions for rejection will *not* serve the child well. One can think, for example, of circumstances in which children are rejected by peers, not on the basis of what they do, but because of some enduring personal characteristic such as physical appearance, motor disability, or racial features. If the social environment will not bend to accept such children, in spite of any changes in their behavior, then the holding of effort-based attributions for rejection will lead to frustration, a sense of lowered self-efficacy, and decreased self-esteem. In such a circumstance, it would be better for such children to hold failure attributions that make an accommodation with certain inevitable factors. These would not be reflective of self but of an unaccepting environment. Examples of such a self-serving bias would include attributions such as "They rejected me because they don't know any better or they don't know the good things about me." This shift to external attributions may help to avoid the debilitating, affective consequences of holding internal, stable, and uncontrollable attribution for inevitable failure.

Skill Maintenance and Generalization

The major task of the child at this stage of social skills training is to be able to utilize previously learned concepts and behaviors in new and varied settings. At this point, the use of cognitive mediators ought to be well-entrenched. The child should be actively considering the demands of the social situation, the requisite skills needed for successful outcome, and the standards for determining the achievement of success. As an indirect consequence of this cognitive endeavor and as a direct result of training, the child should also possess an attributional style that stresses internal and controllable factors. Such an attributional style serves to remind the child that he or she is able to undertake response initiation. Also, it shifts the responsibility for responding from external sources, such as the trainer, to the child him- or herself. If such a causal perspective is combined with experience with success, then the result should be a heightened sense of self-efficacy (Bandura, 1977; Wheeler & Ladd, 1982). This, in turn, should mediate continued successful functioning.

Weiner (1979) argued along similar lines, but placed his emphasis upon the stability dimension of attributions. For Weiner, the child's expectation of future outcome in periods of nonreinforcement is a direct function of the stability of the causal ascription. If the child believes that failure is caused by stable factors such as ability or the bias of others, then there is little to be gained by persisting in the face of nonreinforcement. On the other hand, if failure is thought to be due to unstable factors such as lack of effort, then there will be minimizing of expectancy decrements, inasmuch as effort can be increased volitionally. Such unstable attributions are hypothesized to result in the sustaining of hope and increased persistence toward a goal. These are assumed, by Weiner, to be conditions that cement response maintenance in situations of minimal reinforcement, and are probably quite reflective of the experience of children who are learning to use a new response repertoire.

Another strategy for increasing generalization, that of widening the range of situations in which social skills are used, also has attributional implications. Borrowing from Kelley's (1967) covariation model, we would expect that as children encounter experiences of success across several different social situations, they will come to realize, at least implicitly, that there is a sense of consistency in their behavior and related outcomes. The child will become aware that success is less a result of random external factors and more the result of internal and controllable qualities that may be brought to bare across situations. As such, an interesting circular pattern emerges: Internal and controllable attributions influence appropriate responding and such behavior in turn further strengthens an attribution style based on effort and behavioral sociability. We believe that the mutual interaction of these two systems will further enhance maintenance and generalization.

An alternative approach to generalization places emphasis upon the training of appropriate social entrance skills for use in naturalistic settings. Before a child is able to establish an ongoing interactional relationship with a group, the child must possess a set of skills that allows for acceptance into the group (Putallaz & Gottman, 1982). These include acting in a way consistent with the frame of reference of the group and displaying an agreeable interactional style. Once entrance has been achieved, it is assumed that the child will be caught up in what Baer and Wolf (1970) referred to as a "behavioral trap." That is, the child's behavior will be brought under the natural contingencies of the peer group. If targeted children are to be caught up in such a behavioral social trap, one must change not only the behavior of the targeted child, but also the perceptions of the peer group. One aspect of such a perceptual change must incorporate modifications in peers' attributions about the targeted child's behavior, for as Dodge, Murphy, and Buchsbaum (1984) found, behavior in a provocative situation is determined more by the attribution of intent perceived by the observer than by the veridical intention of the actor. One means of accomplishing a shift in peer perceptions and evaluations may be, as Bierman and Furman (1984) suggested, to provide opportunities for positive peer interaction under superordinate goals. Another tack would be to prime the peer for a change in attribution and behavior through the use of cognitive restructuring materials.

Finally, if the effect of social skills training is to be spread, then the entire social network of the child ought to provide information to the child that is in line with the goals and structure of the training program. In order to accomplish this, parents, teachers, sibs, and peers must all not only reinforce appropriate social behavior, but must also give feedback that is compatible with and complimentary of the newly established attributional style of the targeted child.

So far, we have dealt with stimulus generalization, that is, the increasing of the probability of appropriate social behavior across several situations. However, the second form of generalization, that of response generalization, also should be considered. It is expected that if training has been successful, then there ought to be a change, not only in the range of situations in which the target behavior is displayed but also in other response domains related to the target behaviors.

One such example of response generalization is the child's sense of self-esteem. Weiner (1979) has argued that affect is related to outcome in three ways. First, there are emotions experienced as a direct result of an outcome. One feels "good" when success has been achieved and "badly" given a failure. The second level of affective reaction is made up of attribution-linked emotions. For example surprise is experienced when outcome is attributed to luck. The last level, for Weiner, involves the interaction of the dimensional placement of the cause on the locus dimension and outcome. Thus, competence and pride are thought to be the result of internal attributions for success, such as ability and effort, while a sense of shame is linked to an internal attribution for failure.

If these dimensionally linked affective reactions are placed within the context of social skills training, then it can be seen that an important component of the child's experience has been consistently ignored. We have argued in this chapter that attribution plays an important role in the development and modification of social skills. Furthermore, following Weiner (1979), it has been postulated that attribution mediates affective reactions. Yet of the social skills training studies only one, that by Bierman and Furman (1984), has considered children's self-evaluations as a consequence of training. Obviously there is a need for further investigation of this issue. A partial list of appropriate response generalization measures includes social self-efficacy, social anxiety, loneliness, and attributions for nonsocial experience such as academic performance. Until researchers and therapists alike are prepared to address this issue of response generalization, specifically directed toward a sense of self, important information concerning the effectiveness of skill training programs will not be forthcoming.

In conclusion, it is suggested that as social skills research has made the turn from a narrow behavioristic to a wider social cognitive perspective, a consideration of the influence of attribution will open up new vistas. By taking account of the child's phenomenological understanding of social cause and effect, we will be able to provide better interventions for children who occupy deviant roles within their social networks.

Acknowledgment. The research reported in this chapter was supported by the Social Sciences and Humanities Research Council of Canada Grant 410-81-0389. While working on this chapter Brian Earn was supported by a Leave Fellowship from the same agency. Order of authorship was determined randomly.

References

Ames, R., Ames, C., & Garrison, W. (1977). Children's causal ascriptions for positive and negative interpersonal outcomes. *Psychological Reports*, *41*, 595-602.

Anderson, C. A., Horowitz, L. M., & French, R. D. (1983). Attributional style of lonely and depressed people. *Journal of Personality and Social Psychology*, *45*, 127-136.

Asher, S. (1978). Children's peer relations. In M. Lamb (Ed.), *Social and personality development*. New York: Holt, Rinehart, & Winston.

Asher, S., & Renshaw, P. (1981). Children without friends: Social knowledge and social skill training. In S. R. Asher & J. M. Gottman (Eds.), *The development of children's friendships*. New York: Cambridge University Press.

Baer, D. M., & Wolf, M. M. (1970). The entry into natural communities of reinforcement. In R. Ulrich, T. Stachnik, & J. Mabry (Eds.), *Control of human behavior* (Vol. 2, pp. 319-324). Glenview, IL: Scott, Foresman.

Bandura, A. (1977). Self efficacy: Towards a unifying theory of behavior change. *Psychological Review, 84,* 191-215.

Bierman, K., & Furman, W. (1984). The effects of social skills training and peer involvement on the social adjustment of preadolescents. *Child Development, 155,* 151-162.

Bugental, D., Whalen, C., & Henker, B. (1977). Causal attributions of hyperactive children and motivational assumptions of two behavior-change approaches: Evidence for an interactionist position. *Child Development, 48,* 874-884.

Dodge, K. A. (1983). Behavioral antecedents of peer social status. *Child Development, 53,* 1386-1399.

Dodge, K. A., Murphy, R. R., & Buchsbaum, K. (1984). The assessment of intention-cue detection skills in children: Implications for developmental psychopathology. *Child Development, 55,* 163-173.

Dweck, C. (1975). The role of expectations and attributions in the alleviation of learned helplessness. *Journal of Personality and Social Psychology, 31,* 674-685.

Dweck, D. (1981). Social cognitive processes in children's friendships. In S. R. Asher & J. M. Gottman (Eds.), *The development of children's friendships* (pp. 322-333). New York: Cambridge University Press.

Dweck, C., & Repucci, D. (1973). Learned helplessness and reinforcement responsibility in children. *Journal of Personality and Social Psychology, 25,* 109-116.

Earn, B. M., & Sobol, M. P. (1984). *A categorical analysis of children's attributions for social experience.* Manuscript submitted for publication.

Elig, T., & Frieze, I. (1975). A multi-dimensional scheme for coding and interpreting perceived causality for success and failure events. The coding scheme of perceived causality (CSPC). *JSAS: Catalog of Selected Documents in Psychology, 5,* 313.

Forsyth, D. R., & McMillan, J. H. (1981). Attributions, affects and expectations: A test of Weiner's three-dimensional model. *Journal of Educational Psychology, 73,* 393-403.

Goetz, T. E., & Dweck, C. (1980). Learned helplessness in social situations. *Journal of Personality and Social Psychology, 39,* 246-255.

Gronlund, N. E. (1959). *Sociometry in the classroom.* New York: Harper.

Kelley, H. (1967). Attribution theory in social psychology. In D. Levine (Ed.), *Nebraska Symposium on Motivation* (Vol. 15, pp. 192 240). Lincoln: University of Nebraska Press.

Kirby, F., & Toler, H. (1970). Modification of preschool isolation behavior: A case study. *Journal of Applied Behavior Analysis, 3,* 309-314.

Kokenes, B. (1974). Grade level differences in factors of self esteem. *Developmental Psychology, 10,* 954-958.

Ladd, G. W. (1981). Effectiveness of a social learning method for enhancing children's social interaction and peer acceptance. *Child Development, 52,* 171-178.

Ladd, G., & Mize, J. (1983). A cognitive-social learning model of social skill training. *Psychological Review, 90,* 127-157.

O'Connor, R. D. (1972). Relative efficacy of modeling, shaping and the combined procedures for modification of social withdrawal. *Journal of Abnormal Psychology, 79,* 327-334.

Puttalaz, M., & Gottman, J. M. (1982). Social relationship problems in children: An approach to intervention. In B. Lahey & A. Kazdin (Eds.), *Advances in Clinical Child Psychology* (Vol. 6, pp. 3-43). New York: Plenum Press.

Raviv, A., Bar-Tal, D., Raviv, A., & Bar-Tal, Y. (1980). Causal perceptions of success and failure by advantaged, integrated and disadvantaged pupils. *British Journal of Educational Psychology, 50,* 137-146.

Russell, D. (1982). The causal dimension scale: A measure of how individuals perceive causes. *Journal of Personality and Social Psychology, 42,* 1137-1145.

Silver, R. L., & Wortman, C. B. (1980). Coping with undesirable life events. In J. Garber & M. E. P. Seligman (Eds.), *Human helplessness: Theory and applications* (pp. 279-340). New York: Academic Press.

Sobol, M. P., & Earn, B. M. (1985). What causes mean: An analysis of children's interpretations of the causes of social experience. *Journal of Social and Personal Relationships, 2,* 137-149.

Weiner, B. (1979). A theory of motivation for some classroom experiences. *Journal of Education Psychology, 71,* 3-25.

Weiner, B. (1983). Some methodological pitfalls in attribution research. *Journal of Educational Psychology, 75,* 530-543.

Wheeler, V. A., & Ladd, G. (1982). Assessment of children's self-efficacy for social interactions with peer. *Developmental Psychology, 18,* 795-805.

CHAPTER 7

The Influence of the Evaluator on Assessments of Children's Social Skills

Jane E. Ledingham and Alastair J. Younger

In the field of assessment of social skills, a great deal of attention has been paid to the issue of what behaviors or skills to assess, while relatively little attention has been paid to the question of *who* should do the assessing. In the absence of consensual agreement as to what constitutes social competence (Anderson & Messick, 1974; Foster & Ritchey, 1979; O'Malley, 1977), which might foster the development of a more objective index, most individuals in the field have relied upon the judgments of significant others in the natural environment, often in combination. It is our contention that the type of evaluator that we choose can have important implications for the picture of social skills that emerges. It is also our contention that we have too little information at present on the impact of the type of evaluator to allow for unambiguous interpretations of our data.

Our interest in this area of research developed out of a project designed to identify children at risk by virtue of their high rates of aggression and withdrawal (Ledingham, 1981). The first important decision we faced was a highly pragmatic one involving the selection of a method for identifying target subjects. Should teachers', parents', or clinicians' ratings be used to select targets, or would ratings by peers, or self-ratings, yield more sensitive or more stable estimates of deviance? We also wondered whether ratings made by boys were similar to those made by girls, whether fathers reported behavior in a fashion similar to mothers, and whether the age of the person making the evaluations was a significant factor.

The existing literature provided few clear and unambiguous answers to these questions. It is common for studies that contrast evaluations made by different types of raters to lack an additional criterion measure against which the relative predictive power of each type of evaluation may be assessed. Furthermore, comparisons between ratings by different types of evaluators are frequently confounded with differences in the content of the assessment instrument, since different kinds of assessors are often asked to complete different measures. This is particularly true when the context in which the rater makes observations changes, such as from home to school.

The most frequently used raters in research reports are teachers and peers, perhaps reflecting both researchers' predominant interest in extrafamilial social relationships, and the greater ease of obtaining samples through centralized, universal-access institutions. In general, measurements taken within the same setting show moderate agreement: correlations between ratings by teachers and peers, and ratings by mothers and fathers are of the magnitude of .60 (Burrows & Kelley, 1983; Jacob, Grounds, & Haley, 1982; Kazdin, French, & Unis, 1983; Ledingham, Younger, Schwartzman, & Bergeron, 1982; Semler, 1960). Inter-rater agreement generally drops when ratings from the home are compared with ratings from the school (Touliatos & Lindholm, 1981).

Probably because of their susceptibility to social desirability response sets, self-ratings are rarely used alone to index social behavior. Although at least one study has indicated that agreement between parent ratings and self-ratings by children can be very high (up to 80%) under some conditions (Herjanic, Herjanic, Brown, & Wheatt, 1975), there is, apart from this, general agreement that self-ratings of children's social behavior are correlated only to a very limited extent with other measures (Ledingham et al., 1982; Semler, 1960). Yet, despite the lack of any demonstrated concurrent validity for self-ratings, several writers have underlined the importance of self-evaluations for designing treatment programs and have stressed the fact that the person himself has access to more behavior than does any other observer (Monson & Snyder, 1977; O'Leary & Johnson, 1979). Moreover, some information, including knowledge about goals and plans, is only accessible through self-ratings.

Parents provide the means of assessment that is of special significance in the preschool years and that taps a very important intimate relationship. While data from mothers may be more readily available, and while mothers' and fathers' experiences with their children are quite different (Lamb, Frodi, Hwang, Frodi, & Steinberg, 1982), there has been a high degree of agreement demonstrated between mothers and fathers (Burrows & Kelley, 1983). In comparison to teachers, parents report more problems and show less-marked developmental trends (Touliatos & Lindholm, 1981), perhaps suggesting that parents' greater emotional involvement with their children and less extensive experience with other children make their reports less valid. Lobitz and Johnston (1975) have suggested that parental attitudes and tolerance for deviance are more strongly related to reporting behavior problems for the child than is the degree of behavior problems exhibited by the child. Agreement between parents and teachers in describing children's behavior is low to moderate (Touliatos & Lindholm, 1981).

The role of clinicians in the assessment of social competence has been minimal. However, in at least one study there is some evidence that clinicians' judgments are not more powerful than those of untrained observers in the natural environment. Mednick and Schulsinger (1970) reported that peer relations provided a better predictor of adult maladjustment than did ratings by a psychiatrist. This is perhaps not surprising given that professionals' experience with children is much more circumscribed than that of significant others.

The question of whether teacher ratings or peer ratings provide the more accurate measure of children's social behavior is unclear. At least three studies have demonstrated that teacher ratings correlate more highly with observational measures than do peer ratings (Connolly & Doyle, 1981; Greenwood, Walker, &

Hops, 1977; Liem, Yellott, Cowen, Trost, & Izzo, 1969). However, two other impressive studies indicate that peer ratings are more sensitive than teacher ratings in the discrimination of poorly adjusted children (Cowen, Pederson, Babigian, Izzo, & Trost, 1973; Rolf, 1972).

Overall, the arguments, both logical and empirical, in support of the utility of any of these assessment methods are equivocal, and interrater agreement is at best moderate. There is clearly a substantial degree of nonoverlap between judgments by different types of observers. There is some shared variance across raters, but not a lot. Moreover, confounded with different methods of evaluation are frequently a variety of other factors, such as the context in which judgments are made, the number of evaluators, and the age and history of the evaluator, all of which make extrapolation from these findings even more difficult.

Apart from the practical knowledge inherent in knowing exactly how different types of evaluators compare, it is of theoretical interest to understand the dimensions on which perspectives by different raters differ. If peers prove to be superior to other types of raters simply by virtue of the fact that ratings by multiple observers cancel out individual rater bias, then combining ratings across observers should prove to be a more effective strategy. However, to the extent that the validity of evaluations is a function of more complex factors than number of raters, then characteristics of the rater (such as age, sex, intelligence, and socioeconomic class), characteristics of the person being rated (including his specific behavioral profile), and characteristics of the interactional interface of rater and target (specifically the typical nature of their interchanges) will have to be considered in order to interpret these evaluations meaningfully.

To resolve our original dilemma about whom to choose to identify target subjects, in the end we elected to identify our target subjects by means of peer ratings, primarily because of the fact that this method is almost unique in involving multiple evaluators. We assumed that this at least would "wash out" individual rater biases, and that individual bias was one significant determinant of measurement error. However, we took out an insurance policy by collecting teacher, parent, and self-ratings, too. The analyses we present here focus primarily upon the teacher-peer contrasts we have carried out.

Teachers Versus Peers

A second impetus to our investigation of rater differences emerged out of preliminary data analyses indicating that, when we did select our target subjects, there were many more aggressive targets and withdrawn targets identified by peers in seventh grade than in first grade (Ledingham, 1981). In contrast, members of a third target group of subjects high on *both* aggression *and* withdrawal were much more frequent in first grade than in seventh grade. In sum, aggression and withdrawal were co-occurring with far greater frequency among young children than among older children. Two plausible explanations existed for this finding. Either children's behavior was becoming more consistent over time, or the apparent increase in consistency was attributable to a change in the perspective of the peer evaluators. Our resulting efforts to disentangle actual behavioral change from changes only present in the perspective of the evaluator have led us to explore the basis of teacher and peer ratings in several ways. These analyses were performed on data collected from children and teachers from first, fourth, and seventh grade who completed the Pupil Evaluation Inventory (PEI; Pekarik, Prinz, Liebert, Weintraub, & Neale, 1976), an instrument that consists of 34 items loading on factors of aggression, withdrawal, and likeability.

The first data we examined were the correlations between teacher and peer ratings at different grade levels (Ledingham et al., 1982). We reasoned that, if changes in identification rates were solely the result of change in the evaluator's perspective, then this might be due to the greater cognitive capabilities of older peers. In this case, older children's ratings should agree with teachers' ratings to a greater extent than ratings of younger children. However, this interpretation was made less likely by the fact that teacher-peer correlations did not change in magnitude as grade level increased. Evidently, differences between the ratings of teachers and peers cannot be attributed solely to the child's lower cognitive abilities.

It was also clear that the extent of agreement between raters was higher for aggression than for withdrawal or likeability. This is in line with Kenrick and Stringfield's (1980) thesis that agreement between raters is higher for behaviors that have greater perceptual impact or are more publicly observable.

Age Trends in Peer Evaluations

Does the fact that we failed to find differences in teacher-peer agreement as grade level increased indicate that children rate their peers in a similar fashion at all ages? To answer this question, we used multidimensional scaling techniques (cf. Kruskal & Wish, 1978) to provide a spatial representation of the perceived similarity of items from the PEI. Using this procedure with peer ratings from first, fourth, and seventh grade makes it quite clear that the clustering and interrelationship of items from the aggression, withdrawal, and likeability factors of the PEI do change dramatically with age (Younger, Schwartzman, & Ledingham, 1985). In first grade, the items fanned out along a single dimension, apparently reflecting judgments of deviant versus nondeviant behavior. As grade level increased, withdrawal was increasingly differentiated from aggression, and a second dimension emerged that seemed to differentiate active from passive behavior. In addition, the withdrawal factor became increasingly cohesive at older ages.

These data seemed to indicate that there are important developmental changes involving increasing differentiation that take place in children's capacity to rate their peers. However, because these changes in peers' ratings are not accompanied by changes in teacher-peer agreement (Ledingham et al., 1982), it does not seem likely that these developmental changes alone are sufficient to explain the differences in ratings by peers and teachers.

The original intent of these studies had been to determine whether younger children were more likely to rate a peer simultaneously on aggression and withdrawal items merely because they were less capable of differentiating these categories. The results of multidimensional scaling analyses of peer ratings support this interpretation. However, in the study, the age of the peer rater was confounded with the age of the person being rated. Thus, it may have been the case that first-graders have the ability to differentiate aggression and withdrawal, but that these behaviors actually occurred together more often among their first-grade peers than among older children.

To separate rater-specific effects from those reflecting the influence of the person being rated, two additional studies were conducted (Younger, 1984). The first examined the organization underlying teacher ratings of first-, fourth-, and seventh-grade children. Had the effect found in the peer ratings actually reflected grade-related differences in how behaviors co-occur in children, then a similar trend should have been identified in the teacher ratings. Such was the not the case. Multidimensional scaling analyses of teachers' ratings at all three grades closely resembled the distribution of items for ratings by peers of seventh-grade children.

We then examined the ability of children to differentiate among aggression, withdrawal, and likeability categories of behavior in children who were not age-mates. In this study, first-graders rated the behavior of familiar seventh-graders and seventh-graders rated the behavior of familiar first-graders. First-graders' view of deviance in rating seventh-graders paralleled their undifferentiated view of deviance in their age-mates, while seventh-graders viewed deviance in first-graders from a more differentiated perspective similar to that emerging from their ratings of age-mates. However, especially for older raters, ratings of children who were not age-mates differed somewhat in organization from ratings of same-age peers, suggesting the importance of actual age-related changes in the behavior of the person being rated to account for the developmental shifts observed in children's peer ratings. Nevertheless, the increasing cohesiveness of withdrawal with age, the increasing differentiation of aggression and withdrawal in ratings by older children, and the lack of a similar pattern in the teacher ratings provided strong support for the notion that the age of the peer evaluator is also an important consideration in the assessment of social functioning in children.

Peer and Teacher Identification of Extreme Groups

The next question we asked concerned just what the extent of overlap was between teachers and peers in the identification of extreme groups. We created four classification groups of aggressive and withdrawn children based on peer ratings using the PEI, and an identical four groups based on teacher ratings using the PEI. Aggressive targets scored in the top 5% of scores on aggression and below the 75th percentile on withdrawal. Similarly, withdrawn targets scored above the 95th percentile on withdrawal, and below the 75th percentile on aggression. Aggressive-withdrawn children scored above the 75th percentile on

TABLE 7.1. Overlap between teacher and peer identification of deviant groups and controls.

| Peer classification | Teacher classification | | | | |
	Aggressive	Withdrawn	Aggressive-withdrawn	Control	Total
Aggressive	8	0	4	1	13
Withdrawn	0	23	3	1	27
Aggressive-withdrawn	3	1	19	3	26
Control	1	3	3	39	46
Total	12	27	29	44	112

both dimensions, and controls scored below the 75th percentile on both dimensions. Despite these stringently selected cutoff points, there was substantial agreement between teacher and peer classification systems as Table 7.1 indicates: Approximately 65% of subjects designated as aggressive targets, 85% of withdrawn targets, 70% of aggressive-withdrawn targets, and 87% of controls were assigned to that classification by both teacher and peer ratings. These results suggest that there is substantial agreement between teachers and peers for the identification of extreme groups. Surprisingly, despite the rather more diffuse nature of withdrawal among young children, and the developmental changes occurring on this dimension in children's ratings, this category was highly reliable across raters. Moreover, peers and teachers never disagreed on the differentiation of aggressive targets and withdrawn targets. These results indicate that interrater agreement for extreme group identification is in fact very good.

A different sort of question asks whether teacher or peer ratings are a more powerful predictor of later adjustment. At this point we have longitudinal information on one intermediate marker of some significance, that is, later school success. For 112 subjects, we have determined the academic placement 3 years

TABLE 7.2. Academic status after 3 years for teacher- and peer-identified deviant groups.

| Academic status | Classification of child | | | |
	Peer-identified deviant only, $n = 5$	Teacher identified deviant only, $n = 7$	Consensus target, $n = 61$	Consensus control, $n = 39$
Regular class, expected grade level	80%	100%	64%	95%
Special class placement and/ or behind at least one grade	20%	0	36%	5%

following subject classification. We looked to see whether teacher or peer ratings more successfully predicted outcome after 3 years. While the numbers are small for subjects selected as targets by only *one* type of rater, the direction of results, presented in Table 7.2, is surprising. We had expected teacher ratings to be more powerful predictors of school placement because of teachers' more direct involvement in this decision-making process. However, children identified as target subjects by teacher ratings alone seem somewhat less likely to have suffered some sort of academic setback than children identified as target subjects by peers only. It is also clear that combining these two types of ratings improves the prediction of academic success markedly over using either system alone, suggesting that these different kinds of ratings provide nonredundant, additive kinds of information about children.

Evaluator Differences in the Context of Interaction

To this point, several of the results have suggested that both peers and teachers make significant and at least partially unique contributions to the description of children's social behavior. Rather than dismissing this nonshared variance merely as method variance, hence a nuisance factor, we attempted to explore the possibility that these differences were a result of different behavioral repertoires on the part of the subject being rated. In other words, we believed it likely that the target children were engaging in different sorts of interactions with teachers and peers, and that the frequency of occurrence of behaviors was affecting the way they were rated. To investigate this possibility, we collected observational data on 34 elementary-school-aged children in free play at recess. These children were attending school at a treatment center for behavior-disordered children. For each child, 30 min. of playground observations were collected.

Two types of observational categories were coded in each interval. The first indicated with whom the child was interacting—either with a peer or with a teacher—and the second noted the type of activity in which he was involved. Interrater reliability exceeded 80%.

The rates of different activities were computed for intervals when the child was playing with a peer, and separately for those occasions when he was in the company of a teacher. To compensate for the much greater frequency of interactions with peers (eight times the rate of interactions with teachers), the total score for each activity is also presented in Table 7.3 as a percentage of the total observations within that association category.

It is evident that there are marked differences, both quantitative and qualitative, in the activities of the child, which depend upon who his companion was. With peers, children were more likely to be involved in gross motor activity, rough-and-tumble play, or engaged in cooperative activity with the other. Virtually all aggression occurred in the company of peers. In contrast, in the company of a teacher, children appear more controlled, less physically active, more verbal, and more likely to be in physical contact with their partner. These find

TABLE 7.3. Frequency of observed activities in the company of peers and teachers during recess.[a]

Activity category	Peers	Teachers
Unoccupied	578 (7%)	84 (8%)
Gross motor	1084 (14%)	53 (5%)
Watching	2541 (32%)	354 (34%)
Vocal	1114 (14%)	216 (21%)
Touching	503 (6%)	220 (21%)
Aggression	107 (1%)	4 (0%)
Rough and tumble play	921 (12%)	57 (5%)
Cooperation	1120 (14%)	54 (5%)
Total	7968 (100%)	1042 (100%)

[a] $X^2(7) = 426.16$.
$p < .0001$.

ings are virtually identical to results of crosscultural studies of children's interactions with peers and adults (Whiting & Whiting, 1975). Obviously such differences in the direct experiences of these two types of raters with a given child should result in quite different types of evaluations. It thus seems plausible that a substantial proportion of the nonshared variance in teacher and peer ratings is a function of the quite different behavioral picture presented to them. To explore this possibility further, playground observation category scores were entered into multiple regression analyses of activity, and then association, categories separately for peer and teacher ratings of aggression, withdrawal, and likeability using the PEI. These ratings were obtained from a children's treatment center in which classes were small (9-12 children) and each class had two teachers and a child-care worker. Thus, ratings by adult observers, like ratings by peers, reflected the averaged judgments of multiple observers.

The results of these analyses are presented in Table 7.4. It is evident that peer and teacher ratings are predicted by quite different sorts of behaviors. Activities that are more likely to be carried out in the company of peers, such as aggressive and motor acts, are better predictors of peer ratings than of teacher ratings, whereas activities that occurred more often with teachers, such as touching and talking, have a stronger connection with teacher ratings.

Conclusions

In summary, we have found some evidence that children's evaluations of others change and become more differentiated and complex with time. However, these developmental changes do not appear sufficient to explain the discrepancies between ratings by teachers and peers. Instead, the actual behavior of the person being rated appears to be of critical importance in determining the degree of agreement between raters. Behavior that is highly salient, and behavior that is so extreme as to be consistent across many situations and raters, will be

TABLE 7.4. Increase in multiple R values for observational categories that significantly predicted teacher or peer ratings of aggression, withdrawal, and likeability.

	Behavior factor					
Ratings	Aggression		Withdrawal		Likeability	
Peer ratings						
Activity categories			Motor	.51	Retaliatory aggression[a]	.42
			Initiates aggression	.09		
Association categories	Teacher	.42	Alone	.57	Teacher[a]	.35
Teacher ratings						
Activity categories	Touching	.54	Unoccupied	.41	Vocal[a]	.41
	Motor	.08				
	Rough and tumble[a]	.06				
Association categories			Peer[a]	.45		

[a] This observational category is negatively correlated with the behavior factor.

rated more reliably. However, to the extent that different types of raters elicit different behavioral repertoires, their evaluations of the same individual will be quite different.

These findings suggest several recommendations for choosing an appropriate evaluation. First, choose an evaluator who elicits a higher rate of the behavior you wish to assess. Ask peers to evaluate aggression and cooperation; choose teachers or parents to assess the capacity for appropriate demonstrations of physical affection. More direct experience with the behavior should lead to more accurate portrayals of it.

Second, match the format and content of the instrument to the rater you choose. Very simple, unidimensional judgments about whether behavior is good or bad, deviant or nondeviant, liked or disliked appear to be all that the early elementary-school-aged child can handle meaningfully. At the beginning of adolescence, withdrawal appears to become a much more meaningful, cohesive category for children and may lead to more useful judgments. Similar developmental trends may help to explain the seemingly paradoxical findings that measures that show little concurrent validity at one age turn out to have excellent predictive power later on. For example, Cowen and his colleagues (Liem et al., 1969) reported that peer ratings, in contrast to teacher and parent ratings, bore the "weakest and most variable" (p. 624) relationship to a composite measure of adjustment derived from psychological screenings, social work family interviews, and in-class observation. Remarkably, it was these same peer evaluations which, following an 11-year period, were found to predict psychiatric outcome "far more sensitively than teacher judgements, test data, etc." (Cowen et al., 1973, p. 445). It seems likely that evaluations made by children, despite the fact that they fail to conform very closely to adults' conceptualizations of what is critical to judgments of adjustment, are sensitive to additional parameters relevant to adjustment.

In a similar fashion, self-ratings, of goals and plans for example, may add significantly to our ability to predict future behavior, providing that they are obtained when the child has become more capable of guiding his own behavior, rather than merely reacting to the external world. Measures that at one point in time lack evidence for concurrent validity should not be rejected out of hand for all age groups. In general, additional longitudinal research is necessary in this area. We still know very little about how the specific characteristics of different types of evaluators affect assessments.

Further research on the nature of ratings by other types of evaluators such as siblings may yield a more complete picture of the child's social repertoire. Research on children for whom there is marked disagreement between raters in comparison to children for whom raters agree should also serve to advance our understanding of the significance of the evaluator for the assessment of social competence.

Acknowledgments. This research was supported in part by funds awarded to the Concordia High Risk Project from the Quebec Ministry of Social Affairs, the Quebec Ministry of Education, and the National Health Research and Development Program, Health and Welfare Canada. The authors would also like to thank the Commission des écoles catholiques de Montréal, and the Child Study Centre, University of Ottawa, for their extensive cooperation. Thanks also to Barry Schneider, who provided the observational data for the multiple regression analyses, and to Barbara Byrne, who carried out these analyses.

References

Anderson, S., & Messick, S. (1974). Social competency in young children. *Developmental Psychology, 10,* 282-293.

Burrows, K. R., & Kelley, C. K. (1983). Parental interrater reliability as a function of situational specificity and familiarity of target child. *Journal of Abnormal Child Psychology, 11,* 41-48.

Connolly, J., & Doyle, A. B. (1981). Assessment of social competence in preschoolers: Teachers versus peers. *Developmental Psychology, 17,* 454-462.

Cowen, E. L., Pederson, A., Babigian, H., Izzo, L. D., & Trost, M. A. (1973). Long-term follow-up of early detected vulnerable children. *Journal of Consulting and Clinical Psychology, 41,* 438-446.

Foster, S. L., & Ritchey, W. L. (1979). Issues in the assessment of social competence in children. *Journal of Applied Behavior Analysis, 12,* 625-638.

Greenwood, C. R., Walker, H. M., & Hops, H. (1977). Issues in social interaction/withdrawal assessment. *Exceptional Children, 43,* 490-499.

Herjanic, B., Herjanic, M., Brown, F., & Wheatt, T. (1975). Are children reliable reporters? *Journal of Abnormal Child Psychology, 3,* 41-48.

Jacob, T., Grounds, L., & Haley, R. (1982). Correspondence between parents' reports on the Behavior Problem Checklist. *Journal of Abnormal Child Psychology, 10,* 593-608.

Kazdin, A. E., French, N. H., & Unis, A. S. (1983). Child, mother, and father evaluations of depression in psychiatric inpatient children. *Journal of Abnormal Child Psychology, 11*, 167-180.

Kenrick, D. T., & Stringfeld, D. O. (1980). Personality traits and the eye of the beholder: Crossing some traditional philosophical boundaries in the search for consistency in all of the people. *Psychological Review, 87*, 88-104.

Kruskal, J. B., & Wish, M. (1978). *Multidimensional scaling*. Beverly Hills, CA: Sage.

Lamb, M. E., Frodi, A. M., Hwang, C.-P., Frodi, M., & Steinberg, J. (1982). Mother- and father-infant interaction involving play and holding in traditional and nontraditional Swedish families. *Developmental Psychology, 18*, 215-221.

Ledingham, J. E. (1981). Developmental patterns of aggressive and withdrawn behavior in childhood: A possible method for identifying preschizophrenics. *Journal of Abnormal Child Psychology, 9*, 1-22.

Ledingham, J. E., Younger, A., Schwartzman, A., & Bergeron, G. (1982). Agreement between teacher, peer and self ratings of children's aggression, withdrawal and likeability. *Journal of Abnormal Child Psychology, 10*, 363-372.

Liem, G. R., Yellott, A. W., Cowen, E. L., Trost, M. A., & Izzo, L. D. (1969). Some correlates of early-detected emotional dysfunction in the schools. *American Journal of Orthopsychiatry, 39*, 619-629.

Lobitz, G. K., & Johnston, S. M. (1975). Normal versus deviant children: A multimethod comparison. *Journal of Abnormal Child Psychology, 3*, 353-374.

Mednick, S., & Schulsinger, F. (1970). Factors related to breakdown in children at high risk for schizophrenia. In M. Roff & D. Ricks (Eds.), *Life history research in psychopathology, 1*. Minneapolis: University of Minnesota Press.

Monson, T. C., & Snyder, M. (1977). Actors, observers and the attributional process. Toward a reconceptualization of personality. *Journal of Experimental Social Psychology, 13*, 89-111.

O'Leary, K. D., & Johnson, S. B. (1979). Psychological assessment. In H. C. Quay & J. S. Werry (Eds.), *Psychopathological disorders of childhood* (2nd ed., pp. 210-246). New York: Wiley.

O'Malley, J. M. (1977). Research perspective on social competence. *Merrill-Palmer Quarterly, 23*, 29-44.

Pekarik, E. G., Prinz, R. J., Liebert, D. E., Weintraub, S., & Neale, J. M. (1976). The Pupil Evaluation Inventory: A sociometric technique for assessing children's social behavior. *Journal of Abnormal Child Psychology, 4*, 83-97.

Rolf, J. E. (1972). The social and academic competence of children vulnerable to schizophrenia and other behavior pathologies. *Journal of Abnormal Psychology, 80*, 225-243.

Semler, I. J. (1960). Relationships among several measures of pupil adjustment. *Journal of Educational Psychology, 57*, 61-64.

Touliatos, J., & Lindholm, B. W. (1981). Congruence of parents' and teachers' ratings of children's behavior problems. *Journal of Abnormal Child Psychology, 9*, 347-354.

Whiting, B. B., & Whiting, J. W. M. (1975). *Children of six cultures: A psychocultural analysis*. Cambridge, MA: Harvard University Press.

Younger, A. J. (1984). *Age-related changes in children's perceptions of social deviance*. Unpublished doctoral dissertation, Concordia University, Montreal.

Younger, A. J., Schwartzman, A. E., & Ledingham, J. E. (1985). Age-related changes in children's perceptions of aggression and withdrawal in their peers. *Developmental Psychology, 21*, 70-75.

PART III

Selecting Populations for Interventions

CHAPTER 8

Socially Withdrawn Children: An "At Risk" Population?

Kenneth H. Rubin

Recent years have seen the emergence of an interest in children who do not interact often with their peers. This interest has been sparked not only by theoretical considerations of the significance of early interaction for later development (Piaget, 1926; Sullivan, 1953), but also by data-derived suggestions that a deficiency in early peer interactive experiences may have implications for adolescent and adulthood disorders (see Wanlass & Prinz, 1982, for a relevant review).

The theoretical impetus for studying peer relationships and interactions stems from several distinct camps. Cognitive-developmentalists have long held that within the boundaries of peer interaction children (a) learn about, observe, and practice alternative social roles and rules, and (b) gain knowledge concerning social relationships and the skills necessary for the development and maintenance of these relationships (Shantz, 1983; Smollar & Youniss, 1982).

Learning and social learning theorists and researchers also have extolled the benefits of childhood peer interaction. Peers serve as control agents for each other, punishing or ignoring nonnormative behaviors and reinforcing prosocial or culturally appropriate activities (e.g., Lamb & Roopnarine, 1979). Prosocial, aggressive, and sex-typed behaviors, among others, can be modified by exposure to peer models (see Hartup, 1983, for a review). Furthermore, peers can serve directly as tutors; peer tutoring has been shown to accompany benefits in the areas of altruism (Staub, 1975), self-esteem, and academic prowess (East, 1976).

Although proponents of major developmental theories have waxed eloquent concerning the benefits of peer relational experiences, very little has been written vis-à-vis the possible effects of a *lack* of peer interaction on child development. The primary source of empirical information regarding the potential deficits associated with social withdrawal has, heretofore, been the classic work of Harlow and his colleagues (e.g., Harlow, 1969; Harlow, Dodsworth, & Harlow, 1965; Suomi & Harlow, 1972). These researchers found that rhesus monkeys raised by their mothers without access to peers displayed avoidant and aggressive behaviors when placed in peer group play situations. Moreover, the monkeys' abnormalities of wariness and aggression were long-standing.

To what may be the surprise of many readers, the correlates and consequences of social withdrawal in childhood are virtually unknown. Drawing from the oft-cited work of Cowen, Pederson, Babigian, Izzo, and Trost (1973) and Roff,

Sells, and Golden (1972), clinical child and applied developmental psychologists have suggested that withdrawn or isolated children are "at risk" for adolescent or adult psychopathology (e.g., Strain & Kerr, 1981; Wanlass & Prinz, 1982). Yet, in these studies the researchers actually targeted, as the "at risk" group, children rejected or negatively evaluated by peers; children *observed* to be extremely withdrawn have not yet been found to exhibit psychopathological disorders in adolescence and adulthood (e.g., Michael, Morris, & Soroker, 1957; Robins, 1966).

Despite this lack of an empirical basis for arguing that withdrawn children represent an "at risk" population, psychologists have developed, with ever-increasing regularity, a multitude of procedures designed to ameliorate or prevent the negative concomitants or consequences of early social withdrawal. One would assume that these negative associations of withdrawal are inferred from theoretical and empirical statements concerning the *benefits* of peer interaction, that is, the stream of thought may flow as follows—if peer encounters help develop social cognitions, social skills, and impersonal cognitions and skills, then a lack of peer interaction can only prove costly.

At any rate, regardless of the impetus for the sudden acceleration of intervention efforts on the behalf of withdrawn children, it is significant to note that the numbers of published treatment studies is of such a magnitude that the editors of *Psychological Bulletin*, a highly esteemed journal, have seen fit to publish, in the past 4 years, *two* reviews concerning the treatment of isolate children (Conger & Keane, 1981; Wanlass & Prinz, 1982). Furthermore, despite a general lack of knowledge concerning the *development* of behavioral sociability in childhood, social withdrawal has been implicated in three DSM III categories of psychological disturbance: shyness disorder, adjustment disorder with withdrawal, and introverted disorder. Social withdrawal also appears often as a factor on other indices of childhood clinical disorder (e.g., Achenbach & Edelbrock, 1981).

Given the obvious lack of data concerning negative outcomes of childhood social withdrawal, why has the area garnered so much attention in the intervention literature? More to the point, why have there been so few studies of isolate behavior, its development, and its correlates in childhood? The purpose of this chapter is to review the extant literature on the characteristics of socially withdrawn children. Since the data available are scant, the review will be brief. A second purpose of this chapter is to describe two recent studies concerning the characteristics of children who have been observed to be withdrawn during their early years. These studies should provide a reasonable start (or finish, as the case may be) for those who believe that early childhood isolation is of psychological and clinical significance.

Characteristics of Withdrawn Children

Perhaps the most obvious place to begin a discussion of withdrawn children is with the provision of a definition for the population of interest. For purposes of this chapter, the population of withdrawn children will be comprised of those who are *observed* to interact with their peers significantly *less* often than their age-mates. This particular definition precludes the possibility of targeting socio-metrically rejected and neglected children as the population of interest. The reason for the exclusion of these groups is quite simple: there are too few data to suggest that rejected and neglected children, if *observed* in natural settings, *would* be targeted as extremely withdrawn (see Hymel & Rubin, 1985, for a relevant review).

Given this expressed observational bias for targeting extremely withdrawn children, how can we describe this population? First, with regard to *preschool* social isolates, Greenwood, Todd, Hops, and Walker (1982) indicated that this group initiated and received fewer social initiations with peers, responded less frequently to peer initiations, and were observed to spend more time with adults than with their more sociable counterparts. Interestingly, withdrawn preschoolers were observed to be involved in fewer agonistic encounters than either middle or high rate interactors.

In perhaps the most extensive examination of the characteristics of withdrawn children, Rubin (1982) reported that preschool and kindergarten isolates engage in less mature forms of play and receive fewer social overtures from peers than their more sociable age-mates. During dyadic interaction with nonisolate children in a small playroom furnished with materials designed to "pull for" interactive behavior, withdrawn children are more likely to produce egocentered utterances, particularly those directed to inanimate objects (Rubin, 1982). Further analyses of dyadic interaction revealed that withdrawn preschoolers and kindergarteners produce fewer commands and their social requests are more likely to result in noncompliance than those of their more sociable counterparts (Rubin & Borwick, 1984). Discourse analyses indicate further that young isolates' social requests are generally less "costly" than those of their more sociable peers. For example, withdrawn children emit more requests for attention (low cost) and fewer bids for objects in the possession of their play partners (high cost) than do nonwithdrawn children. Taken together, the previously described data suggest the possibility that young, withdrawn youngsters are immature and nonassertive and may be perceived by peers as "easy marks." Further support for this characterization is taken from the finding that withdrawn children are *more* likely to comply with their partners' requests than are more sociable children (Rubin & Borwick, 1984).

During the early years of childhood, preschool and kindergarten isolates also evidence difficulties in the domain of social problem solving. They produce fewer relevant solutions to social dilemmas and are less able to suggest additional alternative solutions when confronted with failure (Rubin, 1982; Rubin, Daniels-Beirness, & Bream, 1984). They are also more likely to suggest that *adults* intervene on the behalf of hypothetical protagonists who are faced with social dilemmas (Rubin, 1982; Rubin et al., 1984). These data appear to be in keeping with the observation that withdrawn preschoolers and kindergarteners are less assertive than their more sociable peers.

The profiles painted previously of withdrawn children represent summaries based on the extant data base. Other researchers have provided rather circular descriptions of young, isolate children (e.g., they engage in less social play than nonisolates); the aforementioned descriptive characteristics thus represent much of what we know about social withdrawal in childhood.

The extant data pose two immediate concerns for developmental and clinical psychologists. First, we know little, if anything, about the correlates of social withdrawal in children older than five years of age. This is a major deficit in knowledge because it may well be that withdrawal in the middle and later years of childhood may bring with it more severe problems than it does in early childhood. We do know, for example, that children become increasingly social with age (Greenwood et al., 1982; Parten, 1932). We also know that solitary activity in early childhood is more the norm than the exception (Parten, 1932; Rubin, 1982). Thus, it might be reasonable to speculate that withdrawn seven-, nine-, or eleven-year olds are at greater risk than withdrawn four- or five-year olds.

Second and related to the first concern, is that we know little about the stability of early withdrawal in childhood. If solitary activity is viewed as a developmental phenomenon, it may well prove to be unstable from the early to the middle years. This might mean that children who remain withdrawn relative to their age group norms consistently throughout the early and middle years are at greater risk for associated problems than are children who were identified as withdrawn only in the early years.

In the first study described below I examine the psychological characteristics of children who have been targeted as withdrawn consistently over a 3-year-period, kindergarten to second grade.

Study I: Sociometric Status, Social-Cognitive Competence, and Self-Perceptions of Withdrawn Children

In the introduction to this chapter, I indicated that peer interaction has been viewed as an arena for the development of social-cognitive skills. That is, peer negotiation and conflict has been viewed as a means by which children learn about multiple social perspectives and varieties of ways to deal with their social milieus (Hartup, 1983). If this is the case, then one might predict that children who do not experience a "normal" amount of peer interaction consistently over a number of years may evidence deficits in social cognitive development.

It is also the case that children become increasingly interactive with age; consequently, those who stay on the periphery of the social group structure should become increasingly salient to their peers. In the early years, solitary activity is quite normal; consequently, there is little reason for solitary players to be singled out as displaying behaviors deviant from age-group play norms. However, in the middle years of childhood, individuals who continue to choose to remain alone in situations that strongly "pull for" social interaction may become increasingly noteworthy; consequently, their deviance from social play norms may result in the establishment of negative peer reputations and peer rejection.

Finally, it may well be that children who are extremely withdrawn relative to their peers choose to remain alone because of feelings of insecurity and incompetence vis-à-vis the social milieu (Cicchetti & Schneider-Rosen, in press). Such negative self-perceptions and feelings of insecurity may initially mediate isolate behavior; with time, however, the choice to remain alone precludes the possibility of achieving competence in domains relevant to children (e.g., in the academic, social, and physical/athletic realms). Thus, both isolation and negative self-perceptions, through their interplay, may become increasingly exacerbated.

The purpose of this study was to examine the social-cognitive, sociometric, and self-perception characteristics of children who have been targeted as "isolates" consistently over a 3-year period.

Targeting the Longitudinal Sample

The Waterloo Longitudinal Project began with the observation of 111 kindergarteners attending six different classes. These children were observed during classroom free-play for six 10-s intervals daily over a 25-day period (Rubin, 1982; Rubin & Borwick, 1984). Relevant behaviors coded for purposes of this chapter include isolate (ISO) and sociable (SOC) play. ISO consists of the sum of unoccupied and onlooker and solitary activity. SOC consists of the sum of group interactive behavior and peer conversations.

The procedures described earlier were replicated for 72 of the original children in first grade. In second grade, the children were reobserved using the same procedures (Rubin & Krasnor, in press). However, in second grade, because free-play activities could not be arranged in the classroom, each child was invited to play with three same-sex age-mates for four 12-min free-play sessions in a laboratory playroom. The child's playmates differed in each of the four sessions.

The children in each grade were targeted into one of three categories (Rubin, 1982; Rubin & Borwick, 1984; Rubin & Krasnor, in press). *Isolates* were those children whose nonsocial behavior exceeded their age group means by 1 *SD* and likewise exceeded their particular classroom means by 10%. Moreover, isolates produced SOC that was 1 *SD* below the age group mean and 10% below the class mean.

Sociable children were those whose SOC was 1 *SD* above the age group mean and 10% above the class mean; in addition, sociable children produced ISO that was 1 *SD* below the age group mean and 10% below the class mean. All other children were considered *average*.

By second grade, there were 8 children who were targeted as isolates in 2 of their 3 years in the study, one of those years being second grade (ISO2). A second group was comprised of all children identified as isolates in kindergarten and/or first grade, but *not* in second grade (ISO1). There were 11 children in this group.

The third group (AVG) consisted of those children whose sociability scores were "average" for *all* 3 years ($n=14$). Finally, second-grade sociable children (SOC) who were targeted as either average or sociable in the previous years ($n=10$) were targeted.

Measures

Sociometric status was assessed by administering a rating scale developed by Asher, Singleton, Tinsley, and Hymel (1979) individually to each child. Children were presented with color Polaroid photographs of each classmate. They were asked to assign each picture to one of three boxes on which there were drawn a happy face ("Children you like a lot"), a neutral face ("Children you kinda like"), or a sad face ("Children you don't like"). Thus, each child assigned a positive, neutral, or negative rating to each classmate. The ratings were accorded scores of 3, 2, or 1 (for positive, neutral, and negative ratings, respectively). Same-sex sociometric scores were then summed for each child and divided by the number of same-sex children in the class.

Social cognition was measured by administering to each child a test of social problem-solving skills. Children were individually presented with a series of hypothetical situations concerning two types of social dilemmas. One set of dilemmas centered around a cartoon protagonist's desire to obtain an object from a given target (see Rubin, 1982; Rubin et al., 1984; Rubin & Krasnor, in press, for detailed descriptions of methodology). Children's responses were scored for (a) the number of relevant solutions offered, and (b) the proportion of different types of strategies suggested by children to solve the problems. Strategy types included prosocial, agonistic, authority intervention, trade/bribe, and affect manipulation responses.

A second set of dilemmas concerned cartoon protagonists' attempts to initiate friendship with given targets (Rubin & Krasnor, in press). Once again, children's responses were scored for the number of relevant solutions and for quality of strategy. Specific categories included (a) invitation to join in play; (b) prosocial and complementary acts; (c) adult intervention; (d) conversational openers; (e) nonassertive, nondirective overtures; and (f) assertive, directive acts.

Children's perceptions of self-competence were assessed by individually administering Harter's (1982) Perceived Competence Scale. The scale taps three domains of competence: cognitive (e.g., "good at school work"), social (e.g., "have a lot of friends"), and physical (e.g., "do well at sports"). A fourth category, general self-worth (e.g., "happy the way I am"), is also measured. Finally, a total score of self-perceptions was computed by summing scores across all four categories.

Results

Group means for the sociometric and perceived self-competence data are presented in Table 8.1 (social problem-solving data are published in Rubin & Krasnor, in press). A one-way ANOVA comparing same-sex sociometric scores of the four groups, ISO_2, ISO_1, AVG, and SOC, was found to be nonsignificant. Similarly, Target Group (4) × Types of Categories (5 for object-acquisition dilemmas; 6 for friendship-initiation problems) ANOVAs revealed neither significant main effects nor interactions.

A 4 (Target Group) × 4 (Perceived Self-Competence Category) ANOVA produced significant main effects for target group, $F(3,39)=5.42, p<.003$ and self-competence category, $F(3,117)=8.13, p<.0001$, as well as a significant Group × Category interaction, $F(9,117)=1.96, p<.05$ (Greenhouse-Geiser, $p<.07$). Follow-up pairwise comparisons revealed that the ISO_2 children had significantly

TABLE 8.1. Sociometric and perceived self-competence means for each target group.

	Group			
	ISO$_2$ ($n = 8$)	ISO$_1$ ($n = 11$)	AVG ($n = 14$)	SOC ($n = 10$)
Sociometric	2.64	2.76	2.50	2.62
Perceived self-competence				
Cognitive	2.80	3.60	3.01	3.58
Social	2.83	3.46	3.14	3.46
Physical	2.46	2.69	3.03	3.28
General	3.07	3.58	3.32	3.70
Total	2.79	3.33	3.12	3.51

($p < .05$) lower *total* perceived self-competency scores than all other groups. Furthermore, the SOC children had higher M scores than the AVG group. No other comparisons for the total scores were significant.

Additional pairwise comparisons indicated that the ISO$_2$ children had significantly ($p < .05$) lower cognitive, social, physical, and general self-competency scores than the SOC children, and lower cognitive, social, and general scores than the ISO$_1$ children. Only in the physical self-competency area did the ISO$_2$ children differ significantly from the AVG group.

The AVG group scored lower than the ISO$_1$ and SOC children in the cognitive area. Finally, the SOC children had higher physical self-perceptions than the ISO$_1$ children.

Discussion

The purpose of this study was to examine whether children who were identified as extremely withdrawn consistently, over a 3-year period, evidenced difficulties in the domains of sociometric status, interpersonal cognitive problem-solving skills, and perceived self-competence. The data indicated quite clearly that negative peer status is not associated with social withdrawal, at least insofar as second-grade children are concerned. These results are consistent with the findings of earlier reports concerning *younger*, withdrawn children (Rubin, 1982). The data also support previous investigations in which rates of observed interaction have failed to relate significantly with peer rejection (see Asher, Markell, & Hymel 1981, for a relevant review). Given that peer rejection and other indices of negative peer status in childhood predict later psychopathology, delinquency, and academic dropout, and given the nonsignificant findings reported herein, it may be appropriate to dismiss social withdrawal as an "at risk" indicator in the early and mid-years of childhood. Furthermore, given these results, one may choose to follow the advice of Asher (1983), Gottman (1977), and others, by focusing intervention efforts, not on low rate interactors, but rather on rejected and aggressive children.

This conclusion gains added substance upon examination of the social problem-solving data. Despite the sound theoretical bases upon which the assumption is made that peer interaction plays a major causal role in cognitive and social-cognitive growth and development (Damon, 1983; Piaget, 1926; Sullivan, 1953), the present results indicated nonsignificant differences between consistently targeted withdrawn children and their more sociable counterparts. Indeed, pushing the comparison to the extreme, highly isolated second-grade children did not differ from highly sociable children in their abilities to *think about* solving social dilemmas. Drawing from Rubin and Krasnor (in press), these results have a number of significant implications. For years, psychologists have been concerned with the possibility that social withdrawal during the *early* years places children "at risk" for a variety of problems (e.g., Strain, Kerr, & Ragland, 1982). This may, in the long run, prove to be true; however, the sociometric and social-cognitive data reported in this chapter certainly do not support this proposition. Given these data, I should beg to differ from Spivack and Shure (1974) and others who have argued that the time, effort, and finance required to provide social problem-solving *cognitive* training to young withdrawn children is well-worthwhile. Instead, following from Rubin and Krasnor (in press), I would suggest the following.

It is quite probable that psychologists who study social withdrawal and who base their work on Piaget's or Sullivan's theories have actually misinterpreted the original theoretical speculations. Although it is true that Piaget and Sullivan implicated peer interaction as a causal agent vis-à-vis social, cognitive, and social-cognitive development, it is nevertheless the case that they did not expect such interactions to prove productive until, at least, the middle and later childhood years. Perhaps social withdrawal *does* have an impact on children's peer status and interpersonal cognitions, but not until later in childhood.

Yet, on the other hand, it is important to point out that in kindergarten, isolate children do tend to suggest, more often than their more sociable age-mates, that adults should intervene to aid children solve object conflict problems with peers (Rubin et al., 1984). Moreover, first-grade isolates are more likely than more sociable children to suggest the use of nonassertive strategies to initiate friendships (Rubin & Krasnor, in press). By second grade these findings appear to wash out; thus, despite initial leanings toward adult dependent, nonassertive strategies to meet social goals, isolate children do come eventually to suggest the use of strategies identical to those suggested by average and highly sociable children. In short, the cumulative impact of consistent isolate status is practically nil. It may be that a relatively low level of peer interaction is sufficient for stimulating the development of social problem-solving skills, or that children gain knowledge of social strategies by observing others or through conversing with adults. At any rate, by second grade, isolate children do not deviate from age-group "norms" concerning their social problem-solving skills or their sociometric status. Whether deficits in these areas emerge later on in childhood remains an open question.

Given these findings, it may be appropriate to suggest that withdrawn children will never be "at risk" for the kinds of problems generally associated with negative peer ratings and peer rejection. From a close reading of the extant literature, the critical "outcomes" of childhood rejection and negative peer status appear to fall into the domain of "externalizing" problems, that is, aggression, delinquency. These problems may well emanate from social-cognitive deficits (Dodge, in press; Rubin & Krasnor, in press) not found in the withdrawn population studied herein.

The present data, when taken together with other reports from the Waterloo Longitudinal Study, suggest that if withdrawn children were to be characterized as "at risk," the risk factors would be internalizing problems. Thus, withdrawn children may not interact regularly with their peers because of anxieties or fears concerning their social and academic milieus. Such negative affects may develop as a result of early socialization and family relationship factors. For example, the insecurely attached infant and toddler may be reticent to explore his or her social and impersonal worlds (Sroufe, 1983). This reticence, based on the lack of trust and felt security in the child's personal and impersonal environments may lead ultimately to anxiety-based withdrawal from interpersonal encounters (Hartup, in press). Furthermore, when these early activities and withdrawals remain unchecked, they may, in turn, lead to the development of negative self-perceptions regarding one's personal competencies in those environments that involve social interaction with others.

The data described in Study I are clearly supportive of this contention. Although the continuously withdrawn children were not actually disliked by their peers, and although they were able to *think* through the solution of social dilemmas with as much skill as their more sociable age-mates, they nevertheless *felt* that they were unpopular and socially incompetent. Indeed, they felt poorly about their cognitive and physical-motor skills as well. The bottom line is that if these children continue to feel poorly about their interpersonal and impersonal competencies, they may well be "at risk" for internalizing problems such as depression (Cicchetti & Schneider-Rosen, in press).

A final note worth mentioning with regard to Study I concerns those children who were targeted as extremely withdrawn in kindergarten and/or first grade but not in second grade (ISO$_1$). These children were as popular and as social-cognitively astute as all other groups. Furthermore, they did not evidence negative perceptions of self-competence relative to average children; indeed their perceived cognitive skills were greater than those of average children! These sociometric, social problem-solving, and self-perception data certainly do pose difficulties for those who believe that social isolation in *early* childhood should be taken as a "warning sign" for the onset of later disorders. It would appear as it only those children who are targeted consistently, *over several years*, as extremely withdrawn represent a potential "at risk" population. The present results may indicate also that extreme isolation in middle rather than early childhood should be taken as a "warning sign" of potential problems.

One question that merits attention at this time concerns the sorts of interpersonal experiences that may reinforce or, perhaps cause, the withdrawn second-grade child's negative self-perceptions. In the following study, I describe the roles that withdrawn children play and those they attempt to play when they interact

with more sociable age-mates during dyadic free play. The basic guiding expectations are that withdrawn children will play submissive roles during social encounters and, when they do attempt to play dominant roles, their efforts will be
rebuffed. Should these expectations be confirmed, the negative self-evaluations
reported previously will begin to take on added meaning.

Study II: The Role Relationships of Withdrawn Children

In earlier sections of this chapter it has been suggested that young, preschool and
kindergarten-age isolate children are adult-dependent, immature in their play
behavior, and that they exhibit nonconfrontational, unassertive styles of interaction. Second-grade data reveal, further, that withdrawn children have negative
self-perceptions. Given these data, it may be that withdrawn children are viewed
as "easy marks" by their peers. Thus, during peer interaction more sociable
children may attempt to "manage" or control the behaviors of their withdrawn
counterparts. Sociable children might also play the dominant role of "teacher"
more often than the role of "learner" when socializing with withdrawn children.
These speculations are drawn from research by Brody, Stoneman, and MacKinnon (1982; Stoneman, Brody, & MacKinnon, 1984) who investigated the
manager-managee and teacher-learner role relationships of siblings. Brody et al.
found that older siblings tended to take on the more dominant roles; consequently, it might be expected that the "teacher" and "manager" roles are indicative of dominance and superiority.

Method

Eighty-five second-grade children were observed in quartets during free play as
in Study I. Following the targeting procedures described earlier, 18 "isolates"
were identified. Each isolate was brought with a nonisolate, same-sex, same-age
peer to a laboratory trailer for two separate 15-min dyadic free-play sessions.
    The dyadic sessions were videotaped from behind a one-way mirror. The tapes
were later transcribed and coded according to a scheme outlined by Stoneman et
al. (1984). Teacher/learner and manager/managee behaviors were recorded as
present or absent in each taped 10-s interval. The success or failure of each
attempt to "teach" the partner or to "manage" the play partner's behavior was
noted as well. Any attempt to assume a dominant role was considered successful
if the partner complied with the "manager's" directions or attended to and/or
attempted to follow the "teacher's" instructions. Domination attempts were considered unsuccessful if the target child ignored the attempt or refused to comply.
    Reliability data (percent agreement) based on the coding of six 15-min
transcripts ranged from 77%-90% for the role categories and for success.

Results

The M number of times children were observed to play or attempt to play the
dominant roles of "teacher" and "manager" in each of the two sessions is
presented in Table 8.2.

TABLE 8.2. Role behaviors of isolate and nonisolate children.

Roles	Isolates			Nonisolates		
	1[a]	2	Total	1	2	Total
Teacher M	3.39	1.28	4.67	2.56	1.67	4.23
Teacher % success	72.13	73.91	72.62	67.39	83.33	73.68
Manager M	9.28	8.33	17.61	12.67	12.56	25.23
Manager % success	54.49	58.00	56.15	70.61	69.02	69.82
Dominant M[b]	12.67	9.61	22.28	15.23	14.23	29.46
Dominant % success	59.21	60.12	59.60	70.01	70.71	70.38

[a] Session.
[b] Dominant = teacher + manager.

A 2 (Isolate vs. Nonisolate) × 2 (Session) repeated measures ANOVA computed for teacher behaviors produced a significant main effect for the session data only. Teacher behaviors were more frequent in Session 1 ($M=2.97$) than in Session 2 ($M=1.47$), $F(1,34)=13.53, p<.001$. There were no other main effects or interactions. A similar ANOVA for percent of success rates produced nonsignificant results.

A 2 (Groups) × 2 (Sessions) repeated measures ANOVA calculated for managerial behaviors revealed a significant main effect for target group, $F(1,34)=4.16, p<.05$. Nonisolate children were more likely to enact managerial roles than the isolates. A similar ANOVA indicated also that the nonisolates were significantly more successful ($M=69.82\%$) than isolates ($M=56.15$) in having their managerial behaviors complied with, $F(1,34)=9.21, p<.01$.

Finally, the frequency of observed attempts to take on the dominant role in dyadic interaction was computed (i.e., manager and teacher). A Group × Session ANOVA revealed a significant main effect for group, $F(1,34)=4.16, p<.05$. Isolate children were significantly less dominant than their nonisolate counterparts. Another Group × Session ANOVA indicated that isolate children were less successful in attempting to play dominant roles than were their more sociable counterparts, $F(1,34)=7.40, p<.01$.

Discussion

In Study I, isolate second-grade children were found to have poorer perceived self-competencies than their more sociable age-mates. These poor self-perceptions, especially those in the domain of *social* competence, appear to exist despite contradictory evidence, that is, isolate children were *not* disliked by their peers and they were as able to think about solutions to social dilemmas as their more sociable peers. Given these latter data concerning sociometric status and social problem solving, it is not surprising that many researchers have questioned whether withdrawn children represent an "at risk" population (Asher, Markel, & Hymel, 1981; Gottman, 1977). However, the self-perception data provide an alternative perspective.

Study II was designed to examine possible reasons for the apparent discrepancy between the social competence and the perceived self-competence data. The results of Study II did provide some potential insights into the discrepancy. Isolate children were observed to enact dominant, social roles *less* frequently than their more sociable play partners. Furthermore, when they did attempt to enact dominant (particularly managerial) roles, their peers allowed them to do so approximately 60% of the time; the more sociable children were able to take on dominant roles successfully 70% of the time.

In short, isolate second-grade children, when interacting with nonwithdrawn peers, appear to be the less-dominant partners in their role relationships; they also receive less positive reinforcement when they attempt to take on dominant roles. This combination of social deference and social failure could well provide the beginnings of an answer to the dilemma posed earlier.

The present data support the recent findings of Rubin and Borwick (1984) who indicated that withdrawn preschool- and kindergarten-age children were less assertive, less successful at gaining compliance with their requests (a form of managerial behavior), and more compliant in responding to their partners' requests than were their more sociable age-mates.

Taken together, the data described herein and in other reports concerning the first 3 years of the Waterloo Longitudinal Study provide new insights and new directions for the investigation of social isolation in childhood. First, it seems clear that the "costs" of withdrawal may involve negative developments with regard to the *self*-system. It may well be that these negative self-perceptions eventually generalize to the social (peer) system. With continued experiences of peer domination and lack of social success, withdrawn children may develop increasingly negative images of themselves. The relative inability to gain compliance with their requests (Rubin & Borwick, 1984) and the lack of success in enacting dominant roles may lead the already withdrawn child to set him- or herself even further apart from the world of his or her peers. Moreover, this negative feedback may well exacerbate the already negatiave self-image of the withdrawn child.

The bottom line is that continued isolation into the later years of childhood is likely to become associated with adult and peer perceptions of abnormality (see DSM III characterizations of withdrawal given earlier). In turn, peer-perceived deviance from normality is likely to become eventually associated with rejection. The combination of peer rejection, social withdrawal, and poor self-perceptions may pave a clear path to the development of childhood depression. These speculations will be monitored in subsequent years of the Waterloo Longitudinal Study, that is, the affective variables associated with continued withdrawal as well as with rejection will come under close scrutiny in the project.

Finally, in another aspect of the Waterloo Longitudinal Study, procedures are being developed to provide data-based intervention experiences for extremely withdrawn children. Direction for these interaction efforts is being drawn liberally from the aforementioned work of Furman et al. (1979). If, as we are finding, withdrawn children are deferent and somewhat unsuccesful in their social relationships, and if they are feeling negatively about their social competencies, then it might be appropriate to provide them with confidence-building peer-group experiences. One procedure that might provide an avenue of support is to involve withdrawn children in unstructured dyadic encounters with play partners who are younger than them. This procedure has proven successful in one highly cited, but relatively small-scale project with preschoolers (Furman et al., 1979). The efficacy of such pairing procedures will be explored in research with preschool and second-grade isolates in future years of the Waterloo Longitudinal Study.

Acknowledgments. Preparation of this chapter and the collection of the data described herein were supported, in part, by grants from Health and Welfare Canada and the Ontario Mental Health Foundation. I wish to thank Anne Emptage and Ellen Peters for their help in the collection, coding, and analyses of data.

References

Achenbach, T. M., & Edelbrock, C. S. (1981). Behavioral problems and competencies reported by parents of normal and disturbed children aged four through sixteen. *Monographs of the Society for Research in Child Development, 46*(1).

Asher, S. R. (1983). Social competence and peer status: Recent advances and future directions. *Child Development, 54*, 1427-1434.

Asher, S. R., Markell, R. A., & Hymel, S. (1981). Identifying children at risk in peer relations: A critique of the rate-of-interaction approach to assessment. *Child Development, 52*, 1239-1245.

Asher, S. R., Singleton, L. C., Tinsley, B. R., & Hymel, S. (1979). A reliable sociometric measure for preschool children. *Developmental Psychology, 15*, 443-444.

Brody, G. H., Stoneman, Z., & MacKinnon, C. E. (1982). Role asymmetries in interactions among school-aged children, their younger siblings, and their friends. *Child Development, 53*, 1364-1370.

Cicchetti, D., & Schneider-Rosen, K. (in press). An organizational approach to childhood depression. In M. Rutter, C. Izard, & P. Read (Eds.), *Depression in children—Developmental perspectives*. New York: Guilford.

Conger, J. C., & Keane, S. P. (1981). Social skills intervention in the treatment of isolated or withdrawn children. *Psychological Bulletin, 90*, 478-495.

Cowen, E. L., Pederson, A., Babigian, H., Izzo, L. D., & Trost, M. A. (1973). Long-term follow-up of early detected vulnerable children. *Journal of Consulting and Clinical Psychology, 41*, 438-446.

Damon, W. (1983). *Social and personality development*. New York: Norton.

Dodge, K. (in press). A social information processing model of social competence in children. In M. Perlmutter (Ed.), *Minnesota Symposium on Child Psychology*. Hillsdale, NJ: Erlbaum.

East, B. A. (1976). Cross-age tutoring in the elementary school. *Graduate Research in Education and Related Disciplines, 8*, 88-111.

Furman, W., Rahe, D., & Hartup, W. (1979). Rehabilitation of socially withdrawn preschool children through mixed-age and same-age socialization. *Child Development, 50*, 915-922.

Gottman, J. M. (1977). Toward a definition of social isolation in children. *Child Development, 48*, 513-517.

Greenwood, C. R., Todd, N. M., Hops, H., & Walker, H. M. (1982). Behavior change targets in the assessment and treatment of socially withdrawn preschool children. *Behavioral Assessment, 4*, 273-297.

Harlow, H. F. (1969). Age-mate or peer affectional system. In D. S. Lehrman, R. A. Hinde, & G. Shaw (Eds.), *Advances in the study of behavior* (Vol. 2). New York: Academic Press.

Harlow, H. F., Dodsworth, R. O., Harlow, M. K. (1965). Total social isolation in monkeys. *Proceedings of the National Academy of Sciences, 54*, 90-96.

Harter, S. (1982). The perceived competence scale for children. *Child Development, 53*, 87-97.

Hartup, W. W. (1983). Peer relations. In E. M. Hetherington (Ed.), *Handbook of child psychology: Vol. 4. Socialization, personality and social development*. New York: Wiley.

Hartup, W. W. (in press). On relationships and development. In W. W. Hartup & Z. Rubin (Eds.), *Relationships and development*. Hillsdale, NJ: Erlbaum.

Hymel, S., & Rubin, K. H. (1985). Children with peer relationships and social skills problems: Conceptual, methodological, and developmental issues. In G. J. Whitehurst (Ed.), *Annals of child development* (Vol. 2). Greenwich, CT: JAI Press.

Lamb, M. E., & Roopnarine, J. (1979). Peer influences on sex-role development in preschoolers. *Child Development, 50*, 1219-1222.

Michael, C. M., Morris, C. P., & Soroker, E. (1957). Follow-up studies of shy, withdrawn children: 2. Relative incidence of schizophrenia. *American Journal of Orthopsychiatry, 27*, 331-337.

Parten, M. B. (1932). Social participation among preschool children. *Journal of Abnormal Psychology, 27*, 243-269.

Piaget, J. (1926). *The language and thought of the child*. London: Routlege & Kegan Paul.

Robins, L. N. (1966). *Deviant children grow up*. Baltimore: Williams & Wilkins.

Roff, M., Sells, S. B., & Golden, M. M. (1972). *Social adjustment and personality development in children*. Minneapolis: University of Minnesota Press.

Rubin, K. H. (1982). Social and social-cognitive developmental characteristics of young isolate, normal, and sociable children. In K. H. Rubin & H. S. Ross (Eds.), *Peer relationships and social skills in childhood*. New York: Springer-Verlag.

Rubin, K. H., & Borwick, D. (1984). The communicative skills of children who vary with regard to sociability. In H. E. Sypher & J. L. Applegate (Eds.), *Communication by children and adults*. Beverly Hills, CA: Sage.

Rubin, K. H., Daniels-Beirness, T., & Bream, L. (1984). Social isolation and social problem solving: A longitudinal study. *Journal of Consulting and Clinical Psychology, 52*, 17-25.

Rubin, K. H., & Krasnor, L. R. (in press). Social-cognitive and social behavioral perspectives on problem-solving. In M. Perlmutter (Ed.), *Minnesota Symposium on Child Psychology* (Vol. 18). Hillsdale, NJ: Erlbaum.

Shantz, C. U. (1983). Social cognition. In J. H. Flavell & E. Markman (Eds.), *Handbook of child psychology: Vol. 3. Cognitive development*. New York: Wiley.

Smollar, J., & Youniss, J. (1982). Social development through friendship. In K. H. Rubin & H. S. Ross (Eds.), *Peer relationships and social skills in childhood*. New York: Springer-Verlag.

Spivack, G., & Shure, M. B. (1974). *Social adjustment of young children*. San Francisco: Jossey-Bass.

Sroufe, L. A. (1983). Infant-caregiver attachment and patterns of adaptation in preschool: Roots of maladaptation and competence. In M. Perlmutter (Ed.), *Minnesota Symposium on Child Psychology* (Vol. 16). Hillsdale, NJ: Erlbaum.

Staub, E. (1975). To rear a prosocial child: Reasoning, learning by doing, and learning by teaching others. In D. DePalma & J. Foley (Eds.), *Moral development: Current theory and research*. Hillsdale, NJ: Erlbaum.

Stoneman, Z., Brody, G. H., & MacKinnon, C. E. (1984). Naturalistic observations of children's activities and roles when playing with their siblings and friends. *Child Development*, *55*, 617-627.

Strain, P. S., & Kerr, M. M. (1981). Modifying children's social withdrawal: Issues in assessment and clinical intervention. *Progress in Behavior Modification*, *11*, 203-248.

Strain, P. S., Kerr, M. M., & Raglund, E. U. (1982). The use of peer social initiations in the treatment of social withdrawal. In P. S. Strain (Ed.), *The utilization of classroom peer as behavior change agents*. New York: Plenum Press.

Sullivan, H. S. (1953). *The interpersonal theory of psychiatry*. New York: Norton.

Suomi, S., & Harlow, H. (1972). Social rehabilitation of isolate-reared monkeys. *Developmental Psychology*, *6*, 487-496.

Wanless, R. L., & Prinz, R. J. (1982). Methodological issues in conceptualizing and treating childhood social isolation. *Psychological Bulletin*, *92*, 39-55.

CHAPTER 9

Fitting Social Skills Intervention to the Target Group

John D. Coie

Much of the current research interest in the application of social skills training to samples of children is tied to the assumption that this is a potentially powerful approach to preventive intervention with children who are at future risk for various forms of disorder. Many of the contributors to this volume, including the present one, share this hope. Obviously those who share such a vision believe that social maladjustment, particularly with child peers, is a significant predictor of future disorder. They further presume that failure to resolve these social adjustment problems adequately is causally related to subsequent manifestations of disorder. Although evidence related to the first of these two assumptions will be considered in the next few pages, there is little existing evidence related to the second assumption.

Who Should Be Singled Out for Social Skills Intervention?

Most children who have been identified for programmatic social skills training have been selected either on the basis of sociometric or behavioral criteria. In some cases both criteria have been used. The two behavioral syndromes most often employed to identify children at social risk are aggression and social withdrawal or isolation. Evidence for assuming these two behavioral criteria as good predictors or disorder will be reviewed briefly before turning to a review of sociometric criteria.

There have been a number of longitudinal studies in which solid evidence for the continuity of aggressive behavior has been documented (Coie & Dodge, 1983; Lefkowitz, Eron, Walder, & Huesmann, 1977; Olweus, 1979). Since blatant physical aggression itself is a form of delinquency, these continuity data are themselves evidence of risk for future antisocial disorder. However, among elementary school children, most of the aggressive behavior observed among children labeled aggressive by their peers or teachers is verbal aggression (Dodge, Coie, & Brakke, 1982), so that some further evidence for the risk status of aggressive children is called for. Most of the outcome data on aggression are actually data on children whose aggressive antisocial behavior has been indexed by their delinquent status (Farrington, 1978; Robins, 1966; Wadsworth, 1979;

West & Farrington, 1973). Although the association between aggressive forms of delinquency and antisocial disorders in early adulthood is quite strong, there is evidence that it is not so much the aggressive aspect of early delinquency that predicts to later delinquency and antisocial behavior as much as it is stealing that is predictive (Moore, Chamberlain, & Menkes, 1979). A recent investigation of the relationship between aggression, not connected with stealing and delinquency, and delinquency in adolescence was carried out in a follow-up study of children named by their fifth-grade peers as frequently starting fights. Kupersmidt (1983) examined police and juvenile court files for names from the Coie and Dodge (1983) longitudinal sample and found that peer ratings of aggression predicted subsequent delinquency among members of this same sample. Thus, although some of the evidence for considering aggression to be a significant predictor of disorder is confounded by the blurring of the distinction between aggression and delinquency, there is a reasonable basis in fact for viewing antisocial aggression in childhood as an important predictor of disorder in later life.

The evidence for social withdrawal as a significant predictor of future disorder is not nearly so clear-cut. Child clinicians traditionally have placed more emphasis on the pathological implications of social isolation than other child caretakers, such as teachers (Wickman, 1928). Some of this bias can be traced to earlier retrospective studies of schizophrenic populations in which preschizophrenic adolescents were reported to have been isolated and reclusive (Kasanin & Veo, 1932; Pollack, Woerner, Goodman, & Greenberg, 1966; Stabenau & Pollin, 1969). Two other investigations provided support for the connection between social withdrawal and schizophrenia. The data on social behavior in childhood in these two studies was less contaminated by the informants' knowledge of disordered outcomes than was true in the preceding three studies. Bower, Shellhammer, and Renshaw (1960) interviewed teachers, who were unaware of the outcome status of schizophrenic and matched control samples, about the adjustment of these subjects when they were in high school. The preschizophrenic sample was described in adolescence as having been shy and not well liked by their peers. In the second study, Flemming and Ricks (1969) used clinic records to assess the childhood emotional patterns of samples of schizophrenic and socially adequate control subjects. The preschizophrenic group was described in the records as isolated and alienated from their peers. The records also reported that these adolescents experienced peers as ignoring or rejecting them. They, in turn, reported themselves as withdrawing from peers. An important point to keep in mind regarding the results of these two studies is that in each there is evidence that the preschizophrenic subjects were not merely social isolates, but were also disliked by their peers and tended to withdraw from peer contact because of this rejection.

While the preceding studies do provide a basis for hypothesizing a developmental linkage between earlier social isolation and withdrawal and subsequent schizophrenic disorder, the follow-back nature of the research designs precludes any clear assessment of the extent to which withdrawn children as a total group are at risk for schizophrenic relative to nonwithdrawn children. The follow-forward studies of shy, withdrawn children seen briefly at the Dallas Child Guidance Clinic prior to World War II provide some indication that shy, withdrawn children are not at risk for schizophrenia or other psychological disorders. Morris, Soroker, and Burris (1954) rated the adult psychological adjustment of a subset of this sample based on clinical interviews with them and found two-thirds of them making satisfactory adjustment and all but one subject having at least a marginal adjustment. In a second study of the larger sample (Michael, Morris, & Soroker, 1957), subjects were categorized on the basis of their childhood clinical intake records as introverts, extroverts, or ambiverts. These categories referred to patterns of social withdrawal, aggression, or a mix of withdrawal and aggression, respectively. The incidence of schizophrenia among the withdrawn group was less than among the other two groups, particularly the ambivert group, and was no greater than among the general population. While there are some methodological problems with these studies, including the distinct possibility that the introverted children may have come from higher SES families than the extroverted or ambiverted children, it must be concluded that the case for withdrawal and isolation as a predictor of later pathology has yet to be made.

The preceding point is underscored by Kupersmidt's findings regarding sociometrically neglected children, children who receive little or no mention by their peers. Many of these neglected children can be described as shy or isolated (Coie, Dodge, & Coppotelli, 1982; Coie & Kupersmidt, 1983; Dodge, 1983). While Kupersmidt found neglected children to be truant as much or more so than other status groups, on all other outcome measures they had fewer problems than other children, including dropping out of school.

Rubin argues in Chapter 8 in this volume that it is a mistake to equate extreme withdrawal solely with either the neglected or rejected sociometric status categories. His point is a valid one. To explore this point further, we used the peer assessment data obtained in the fifth grade for the longitudinal sample evaluated by Kupersmidt to identify a group of behaviorally shy and withdrawn children. A group of 18 children were identified as behavioral isolates using a standard score cut-off point of $Z = 1.0$. The sociometric status breakdown of these 18 was as follows: six neglected, five average, four rejected, two popular, and surprisingly, one controversial. Conversely, 29% of the neglected group qualified as withdrawn by this criterion and the next largest subset of any status group belong to the rejected group (19%). Thus Rubin's point is substantiated. When the outcome data on this withdrawn group is compared to Kupersmidt's findings for the sociometrically derived status groups, we find that they have outcome totals strikingly similar to the neglected group, however. That is, 50% of them were truant in two or more academic years, compared to 50% for the neglected, 55% for the rejected group, and 26% for the average group. None of them had police or juvenile court records, as opposed to 5% for neglecteds, 24% for rejecteds, and 11% for average children. The total problem index for the withdrawn group was only slightly higher than that of the average or neglected group and less than that of the rejected group. It is therefore not unreasonable to consider the withdrawn group as being similar to the neglected group in terms of risk for these kinds of problems.

As Rubin also notes in chapter 8 of this volume, it may be illogical to expect behaviorally withdrawn children to be at risk for externalizing problems. Instead they should be expected to be at risk for internalizing problems or those problems that are more continuous with the form of their social behavior in childhood. The truancy problem certainly fits this description since it entails a radical withdrawal of self from the school per context. Whether or not the withdrawn child is at risk for future depressive disorders, as Rubin also speculates, is not known, since except for the studies cited previously, there is no follow-forward data on socially withdrawn children. One point made in an earlier paper by Rubin (1982) should be kept in mind by those who would investigate the long-term consequences of isolated behavior. Rubin distinguished between those children whose solitary behavior was of a constructive nature and those whose solitary behavior could be characterized as immature and inappropriate. The former appear to be a socially well-adjusted group, but the latter are less so; and if there were to be a behaviorally isolated risk group, these latter children would be the more logical choice.

Thus, while there is evidence that some aggressive children are at risk for future problems, particularly sociopathy, there is little evidence that withdrawn children are an at-risk group for serious forms of disorders such as psychosis or sociopathy. On the basis of the work of Morris and colleagues cited earlier, Ledingham and Schwartzman began to follow longitudinally a group of children characterized by both aggressive and withdrawn behavior (Ledingham, 1981). Although no outcome data on these children are available at present, connections between this group and a risk group identified by sociometric criteria will be described in a following section.

A number of studies have pointed to poor childhood peer relations as a predictor of disorder without tying the problems of peer social adjustment to a particular behavioral syndrome. Roff used guidance clinic records to follow boys who had poor peer relations into young adulthood. These were boys whose records indicated that they were actively disliked by peers and were unable to make or sustain friendships. From the military service records of these clinic-referred boys, he found that those with earlier peer problems had more bad conduct discharges, and more psychoneurotic and psychotic disorders (Roff, 1957, 1959, 1961, 1963). Mednick and Shulsinger (1969) obtained teacher ratings of social acceptance among peers for boys at risk for schizophrenia because of diagnosis of parental schizophrenia. These ratings proved to be a significant predictor of the actual incidence of schizophrenia among this risk group. Though the Mednick and Schulsinger data were obtained in a follow-forward design, both the Roff sample and the Mednick and Schulsinger sample were not descriptive of risk in a general child population since one consisted of clinic-referred boys and the other was composed of children of schizophrenic parents. Yet each of these studies pointed up the importance of peer relations as a predictor of disorder.

Cowen and his colleagues (Cowen, Pederson, Babigian, Izzo, & Trost, 1973) demonstrated that peer-based assessments of childhood social relations could be a significant predictor of mental health problems in later life. They found that children who had received psychiatric services during a 10-year period following third grade were more likely to have been named to negative peer assessment items on the Bower class play than comparison children who had not received psychiatric treatment during this same period. The magnitude of the Cowen et al. sample and the surprising contrast between the effectiveness of sociometric indices and the more traditional psychological measures also included in the prediction battery served to alert many investigators to the importance of negative sociometric indices. However, it should be kept in mind that the items in the Bower class play were behavioral descriptions and not the evaluative items typically associated with sociometric questionnaires. The negative items in the Bower scale characterized a range of behaviors including aggression, disruption, hypersensitivity, social withdrawal, immaturity, and fearfulness.

In another large-scale study employing peer-based sociometric indices, Roff, Sells, and Golden (1972) found that a combination of negative and positive sociometric nominations ("liked most" and "liked least") was a significant predictor of delinquency among a young adolescent population.

These latter two studies prompted those of us at Duke to employ the same combination of negative and positive sociometric items as used by Roff, Sells, and Golden in a longitudinal study of children's peer social adjustment. Positive and negative peer nominations were combined into two indices of peer social adjustment: Social Preference or relative peer likeability (liked most nominations minus liked least nominations) and Social Impact or relative social visibility (liked most nominations plus liked least nominations). Because peer groups of different size were being compared in much of the research, all nomination totals were transformed into standard scores by procedures described by Coie et al. (1982). These procedures enabled us to identify groups of children of different types of social adjustment who could be followed longitudinally in outcome studies. A schematic of these types of adjustment and their relationships to the sociometric nominations is displayed in Figure 9.1.

The four extreme types of social status groups pictured in Figure 9.1 are described by their peers in behavioral terms that differentiate them from each other and average status children (Coie et al., 1982; Coie, Finn, & Krehbiel, 1984). The group most closely resembling in sociometric terms the risk groups of the Roff et al. (1972) and the Cowen et al. (1973) studies is the rejected group. The rejected group is composed of those receiving many negative nominations and few positive nominations. This group is described by their peers as being excessively disruptive and aggressive, lacking in socially facilitative behavior, more unhappy, and easily aroused to anger than most other children. Unbiased observers also report these rejected children to be frequently off-task and disruptive in the classroom, aversively aggressive with peers, inclined to initiate social approach inappropriately in academic contexts, and to be more inappropriately

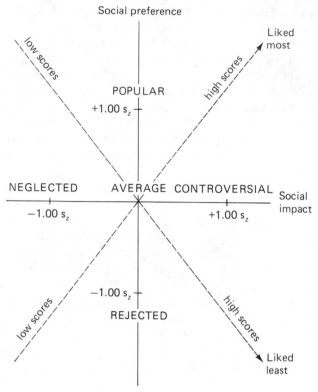

FIGURE 9.1. The relationships among positive and negative social choice measures, the dimensions of social preference and social impact, and five types of social status.

isolated in peer play contexts (Dodge et al., 1982). With new peers the play behavior of rejected boys is essentially the same as is their behavior among familiar school peers, although the inappropriate, isolated activity of rejected boys appears to emerge only after the boys clearly have become rejected by the new peer group (Coie & Kupersmidt, 1983; Dodge, 1983). Thus, in most regards, both peers and unbiased adult observers report the same social characteristics of socially rejected children and we find that these behavior patterns tend to transcend social contexts.

Neglected children are reported by their peers to be more shy and isolated than other children (Coie et al., 1982) and thus come closest to being the withdrawn and isolated group according to behavioral criteria. Unbiased observers tend to corroborate this picture in familiar peer contexts (Coie & Kupersmidt, 1983; Dodge, 1983; Dodge et al., 1982), but find a different pattern of social behavior in new and unfamiliar small group contexts. Although they almost never behave aggressively either verbally or physically, as is also the case for them with familiar peers, they are much more outgoing in the unfamiliar peer groups and are sometimes even viewed as leaders in these groups. This transient and context-bound aspect of the negelected group is mirrored in the data on status continuity. Neglected children often become average status children or even popular children as they grow older (Coie & Dodge, 1983).

Observational data suggests, therefore, that both rejected and neglected groups often isolate themselves from their peers. Neglected children do so in socially appropriate ways while the isolated activity of rejected children is more often inappropriate and seems to follow as a consequence of peer group rejection rather than simply reflecting a desire to play alone. There is a compelling parallel between the solitary activity of these two groups and Rubin's (1982) distinction between constructive and immature solitary play. This contrast between the solitary behavior of rejected and neglected status groups is reviewed more thoroughly elsewhere (Coie, Dodge, & Kupersmidt, in press).

Continuity of social status has been examined in two different ways. Longitudinal data on the continuity of social status across the period of elementary school to high school were acquired on the original elementary school samples of the Coie et al. (1982) study. Across a 5-year period, rejected group status was more stable than that of other groups. Of those children who were rejected in the fifth grade, about half were rejected at the last point of testing for them. Neglected children, on the other hand, tended to shift in their social status across time as noted previously, although never in a more negative or rejected direction. In the Coie and Kupersmidt study, boys who were rejected among their own school peers met weekly with four boys of different status, each from four different schools. By the end of the third weekly play group meeting almost all the rejected boys were the most rejected of the boys in their groups. Thus, even among totally unfamiliar boys, social rejection seems to be reestablished very quickly and seems to be determined by the behavioral characteristics of the boys rather than by contextual factors.

Finally, with respect to outcome, rejected children appear to be the social status group most at risk for negative outcomes. When the fifth-grade cohort from the Coie et al. sample entered the twelfth grade, Kupersmidt (1983) examined school and juvenile court records for data on this cohort. She compared groups on a weighted, combined problem index comprised of data on delinquency offenses, dropping out of school, retention in grade, and truancy. Children who were rejected by their peers in the fifth grade had significantly more problems over the next 7 years than did other status groups. Except for truancy, neglected children had no more problems than the most trouble-free group, the popular children.

At this time, then, the available evidence strongly indicates that children who are actively rejected by their peers are the group most at risk for future problems. They tend to continue to be rejected across time and upon entering new social peer groups. The same provocative and disruptive behavior patterns characterize their interactions in both well-established and new social situations. This pattern of acting-out behavior might suggest that these children are troublesome to others but do not necessarily feel badly about themselves. Two sources of data suggest this latter is not the case. Asher, Hymel, and Renshaw (1984) surveyed third-through sixth-grade children with a questionnaire designed to assess feelings of loneliness and social dissatisfaction. They found a moderate correlation between self-described loneliness and low sociometric ratings by peers.

In the second related study, Finn (1984) administered Harter's Perceived Competence Scale for Children to fourth-grade children and found that rejected children had lower self-concept scores than all other social status groups. In particular, they had lower feelings of general self-worth as well as in the areas of cognitive and social competence. There is evidence, therefore, that rejected children are more at risk for acting-out problems and are beleagured by feelings of lower self-worth and loneliness. The best available data would indicate that this is the group of children for whom preventive intervention programs are most appropriate.

Intervention with Children at Risk for Social Rejection

Remedial programs for children with social problems have taken many different forms; however some of this variety is a consequence of different bases for selecting children for intervention. Modeling, reinforcement for social approach, social perspective taking, and social skills training have been used with varying degrees of success. In none of the studies reported thus far have children been selected on the basis of negative sociometric nominations, however most investigators employing social skills training have identified intervention subjects using a peer rating measure that requries children to indicate how much they like to dislike playing or working with each of their classmates. In contrast to selection procedures based solely on positive sociometric choices, the peer rating measure does make it possible to identify most of the children referred to earlier as rejected children. Thus intervention studies in which the peer ratings scale have been employed will have the most information about the effects of intervention with rejected children. Nonetheless, it is important to keep in mind that about a third of the children who are categorized as unpopular on the basis of peer rating scales are likely to be neglected or controversial rather than rejected (Hymel & Asher, 1977). Since the behavior patterns of these two groups are not only different from each other but also from those of rejected children, one might expect that the same intervention procedures would not be equally effective for all low-rated children.

In four separate studies (Gresham & Nagle, 1980; Ladd, 1981; LaGreca & Santogrossi, 1980; Oden & Asher, 1977), children with low peer ratings received training in positive social interaction skills. Each of these studies presented evidence of some positive effects of the training procedure, however only one study (Ladd, 1981) documented significant improvements in both peer ratings and in the behaviors that were the focus of the coaching procedures. One factor that distinguished Ladd's design from the other three was his procedure for selecting subjects. Although he, too, used the peer rating scale to select unpopular children, he narrowed the intervention sample still further by taking only those low-rated children who were also observed to display low frequencies of the target behaviors for the coaching procedures. In so doing he identified children who were not well liked by their peers *and* who were also deficient in the positive interaction skills that his program was designed to teach to children. This close fit between the content of the intervention program and the social deficiencies of the intervention sample may be a major reason for the unusual degree of success Ladd was able to document in his study.

The idea that social skills interventions will be most successful if their content is geared to the primary behavior problems of the intervention sample is certainly not a novel one nor one that is counterintuitive. In fact, most investigators no doubt have proceeded on the assumption that that is just what they were doing. It is only in the hindsight of the Ladd study that we can begin to see why that may not have been the case in these other studies. Ladd's findings suggest the possibility that the group of children whose peer rating scores are in the lower third of the distribution is not a homogeneous group. We already know from the Hymel and Asher (1977) analyses cited earlier that this group contains both neglected and rejected children and that these two groups are not at all similar in their social behavior. By selecting subjects with low frequencies of prosocial behavior, Ladd inadvertently may have selected many of the neglected children in his sample since neglected children show low frequencies of any social behavior in familiar peer settings (Coie & Kupesmidt, 1983; Dodge et al., 1982).

In the other three studies that utilized social skills training with children selected only on the basis of low peer ratings, it is very likely that many of the children receiving social skills training were rejected rather than neglected. Rather than being children whose peer problems stem from a failure to interact sufficiently in prosocial ways, these children may have had problems with peers because of relatively high frequencies of aversive behavior. As a consequence, improvements in behavior based on the program criterion (frequency of prosocial activity) might not always lead to improvements on the selection criterion (low peer ratings). Conversely, children who improved on the selection criterion might not show improvements in the program criterion because they were already performing at adequately high levels. In the latter case, improvement in social standing may have resulted from other consequences of the social skills training program such as changes in social goals for interaction with peers (Renshaw & Asher, 1983). However, it is not likely that all of Ladd's sample were neglected children, given the numbers of children involved and the proportion of neglected subjects likely to fall below Ladd's selection score, given Hymel and Asher's data. Thus the possibility arises that the group of rejected children is not a homogeneous group either. This possibility is one that will be examined further in this chapter.

One of the consistent findings of observational studies of children in school settings is that unpopular or rejected children are more frequently not engaged in their academic work in the classroom in comparison to other children and that they are more often being disruptive (Dodge et al., 1982; Lahey, Green, & Forehand, 1980). Not surprisingly, then, these same children also are reported to have academic difficulties (Glick, 1972; Green, Forehand, Beck, & Vosk, 1980; McMichael, 1980; Yellott, Liem, & Cowen, 1969). The correlations between academic performance and social standing with peers, however, range from .2 to .4, suggesting that not all low status children have academic difficulty.

The connection between low academic achievement, off-task and disruptive classroom behavior, and low peer status prompted an investigation into the effects of academic tutoring on the social adjustment of children who are both rejected by their peers and having serious academic problems (Coie & Krehbiel, 1984). Thus, as with Ladd's study, only a subset of low status children was selected for intervention. Rejected children, as defined above by the combination of negative and positive sociometric nominations, with low California Achievement Test scores for reading or mathematics, were assigned to one of four intervention conditions. In one, they were just given academic tutoring focused on basic skills deficits and designed to enhance a sense of academic competence. In a second condition, they received a variant of Oden and Asher's social skills training program that added a series of group training sessions. In the third condition, both academic tutoring and social skills training were adminsitered, and the fourth was a non-treatment control condition.

The results of this intervention study were somewhat surprising since those children in the academic tutoring conditions not only improved in their academic achievement scores, but made dramatic gains in their social adjustment scores as well. These gains were fully sustained at a follow-up evaluation conducted 1 year after the completion of the intervention. Social skills training had some partial effects on social status but these disappeared by the 1-year follow-up. There was an effect of social skills training on reading comprehension that continued to be marginally significant at follow-up. Thus there were some crossover effects of training in the two skill areas, however the predominant effect was that academic skills intervention had substantial impact on both areas of competence.

One might conclude from these results that improvements in academic skill enabled the rejected, low-achieving children to stay on task more effectively in the classroom; as a result they were less disruptive to peers and became less disliked and more well liked by them. The observational data collected both before and after intervention provide partial support for this conclusion. The children in the academic skills training conditions did increase the proportion of time that they spent on task in the classroom. However, there was only a non-significant trend ($p < .11$) to their decreases in disruptive behavior. The failure to find improvement in disruptive behavior may be due to the fact that very little overtly negative behavior was observed at either preintervention or postintervention, on the part of either students or their teachers (teacher rebukes or corrections were almost never observed), suggesting that those who were observed were acutely aware of the presence of the observers and their hand-held microprocessor data collectors. Positive teacher attention did increase significantly for the academic skills training groups. This increase in teacher approval may have come about in recognition of the rejeced subjects' academic progress, but it may also have been an indirect reflection of improvements in appropriate classroom behavior. Teacher approval, in turn, may have had two positive consequences. It may have led class members to feel more positive about these children because the teachers felt this way (Coie & Pennington, 1976). On the other hand, the combination of increased academic skills and teacher approval may have enhanced the target children's self-confidence and self-esteem. These changes may have led them to interact more effectively with their peers and, in turn, led to improvements in their social standing in the peer group.

No matter which of these explanations for the positive consequences of academic tutoring on peer social adjustment is correct, the results of this study underscore the point made in Ladd's study. The programs that are most effective in bringing about improved social adjustment in low status children are those that are closely tailored to the needs and deficiencies of the children to be helped. In both studies only subsets of the total population of low status children were the subjects of intervention. The basis for selecting these subsets was derived from characteristics that distinguished the total group of rejected or unpopular children from their peers, however, instead of assuming that all rejected or unpopular children fit these criteria, only those rejected children who displayed those characteristics were selected. This selection process served to guarantee that the intervention procedures were highly relevant to the intervention group.

One implication that might be drawn from the preceding analysis is that for intervention purposes it is important to distinguish among subtypes of rejected children. It is not safe to assume that all children are rejected for the same reasons. This means that some observational data on rejected children may be slightly misleading if one takes group differences between rejected and average or popular children as the basis for intervention with the total group of rejected children. While as a group they are more aggressive, disruptive, and have more academic problems than other social status groups, not all rejected children have all these problems. Therefore the design of intervention programs, particularly social skills training programs, ought to be informed by an analysis of major subgroup patterns of behavior.

With this latter goal in mind, a follow-up of the Coie and Krehbiel study was undertaken to identify patterns of classroom and playground behavior among rejected children who differed in their academic performance levels. Krehbiel (1983) observed four groups of boys: (a) low-achieving, rejected boys, (b) high-achieving, rejected boys, (c) low-achieving, average status boys, and (d) high-achieving, average status boys. In part this study was designed to follow up questions regarding the relationship between classroom disruptiveness and low achievement that were unanswered in the earlier Coie and Krehbiel study because of the low frequency of disruptive behavior recorded in that study. In this study permission was obtained to have observers spend much more time in the classroom in order to allow students and teachers to become accustomed to the presence of the observers. This time, significant results for both disruptiveness and aversive or aggressive behavior were obtained in addition to the same pattern of findings for on-task and off-task behavior found in the earlier Coie and Krehbiel study. Low achievers were more disruptive in the classroom than high achievers, and rejected boys were more disruptive than average boys. As these two main effects would suggest, low-achieving, rejected status boys were far more disruptive in class than any of the other three groups. They were four times as disruptive as either the high-achieving, rejected group or the low-achieving, average status group and they were ten times more disruptive than the high-achieving, average status group. Insofar as aversive behavior was concerned, however, there were no differences between low- and high-achieving, rejected groups. Both rejected groups exhibited more aversive behavior than both of the average status groups. This was true both in the classroom and on the playground.

Further information on these four groups of boys comes from two other sources of information: behavior ratings from the subjects' peers and self-report information from the children themselves. The peer-assessed behavior descriptions reveal one interesting difference between the high- and low-achieving, rejected boys. The high achievers are reported by their peers to be more unhappy than either the low achievers or the two average social status groups (Krehbiel, 1983). The irony in this finding is that the low achievers would appear to have more to be unhappy about, since they are not only rejected by peers but also are having serious problems with their school tasks.

The self-report data (Finn, 1984) provide further corroboration of the fact that high-achieving, rejected boys experience more unhappiness and internal distress than their low-achieving counterparts. On the Harter (1982) scale, high-achieving, rejected children had the lowest scores on the general self-worth subscale. Surprisingly, the high-achieving, rejected boys also had scores on the cognitive competence scale, items reflecting on their self-perceived academic ability, that were equally as low as those of the low-achieving, rejected boys. Only the high-achieving, average boys had high scores on the cognitive competence scale. For some reason the high-achieving, rejected boys do not even give themselves credit for their academic achievments and have a uniformly self-derogatory view of themselves in all of the areas of competence tapped by the Harter self-report inventory. It is not surprising, therefore, that their peers see them as more unhappy than most other children.

For about half of the high-achieving, rejected boys this unhappiness and dissatisfaction with self may come to be translated into aggressive behavior with peers since 47% of this group was named by their peers as starting fights at a level greater than 1 SD beyond the mean. In the low-achieving, rejected group, only 13% were named as starting fights at that level. For boys of mixed academic achievement, the aggressive ratio is about the same as that of the high achievers. Thus aggression as well as internal distress may be more strongly connected with high academic achievement among rejected boys than with problems in academic achievement.

The point being made here is that status group comparisons on behavioral measures can be misleading with respect to the picture one gets of the total group of rejected children. As we have just noted, less than half of all the rejected boys in the preceding study were described by their peers as being extremely aggressive and yet one aspect of rejected children's behavior that most readily distinguishes them from other groups on some peer assessment inventories is aggressiveness and disruptiveness. Hymel and Rubin (in press) presented correlations between peer sociometric ratings and peer ratings for the three factors of the Revised Class Play (Masten & Morrison, in press) for children in grades 2 through 6. In grades 2 and 3 the aggressive-disruptive factor and the sensitive-isolated factor are equally correlated at a moderately negative level with status ($r = .30$ to $.40$). At Grade 4 the correlation of status with the aggressive-disruptive factor goes down to $-.49$, but the correlation with the sensitive-isolated factor is $-.71$. After this point only the sensitive-isolated factor is significantly correlated with low status. These findings certainly support the contention that aggression is not the basis for rejection among all children and they suggest a developmental shift in the correlates of rejected status. This shift is one that can be interpreted, in light of the observational data cited previously (Coie & Kupersmidt, 1983; Dodge, 1983), as reflecting the increasing withdrawal of children whose behavior has made them unwelcome among their peers.

Interestingly enough, Masten and Morrison found that scores on their sensitive-isolated scale were correlated with low academic performance records and teacher ratings of problems of comprehension and attention. Thus the low-achieving, rejected children may be the ones who are also characterized as sensitive and isolated. If this is true, we have further reason for thinking that their social isolation is less a cause of their poor peer status than it is a correlate of social and academic inadequacy. One thing we know about this group is that they are frequently engaged in solitary, off-task, inappropriate activity in the classroom and their bids for peer attention and interaction are more frequently ignored than are those of other children (Krehbiel, 1983). It is not unreasonable to speculate that this low-achieving rejected group would be rated highly on the sensitive-isolated scale of the Revised Class Play.

All of this information supports the strategy of devising different intervention programs for high- and low-achieving, rejected boys. The latter group appears to be more disruptive than aggressive and their disruptiveness may be a function of their inability to cope with the tasks of the classroom. Rejected children who do not have academic problems are a group about which we know somewhat less. Half of them appear to have problems with aggression. Some of the nonaggressive, high-achieving, rejected children seem to be unhappy and down on themselves for reasons that are not apparent from the available data. More needs to be known about this latter group. Some of them may have social skill deficits that are not related to aggression, such as peer group entry skills or some of the prosocial skills in the Oden and Asher or the Ladd programs. If we are to be more successful in applying intervention techniques to the problems of rejected children, we must know the children in this group better than we now do. However, we do know enough about the large majority of them to tailor intervention programs to their needs. This does not mean that our programs must be devised one by one for each individual, but it does mean that the target group for intervention must be assessed on some of the major dimensions of competency that are related to social rejection before setting out an intervention plan for them.

References

Asher, S. R., Hymel, S., & Renshaw, P. D. (1984). Loneliness in children. *Child Development, 55,* 1456-1464.

Bower, E. M., Shellhammer, T. A., & Daily, J. M. (1960). School characteristics of male adolescents who later became schizophrenic. *American Journal of Orthopsychiatry, 30,* 712-729.

Coie, J. D., & Dodge, K. A. (1983). Continuities and changes in children's social status: A five-year longitudinal study. *Merrill-Palmer Quarterly, 29,* 261-282.

Coie, J. D., Dodge, K. A., & Coppotelli, H. (1982). Dimensions and types of social status: A cross-age perspective. *Developmental Psychology, 18,* 557-570.

Coie, J. D., Dodge, K. A., & Kupersmidt, J. B. (in press). Peer group behavior and social status. In S. R. Asher & J. D. Coie (Eds.), *Peer rejection in childhood.* New York: Cambridge University Press.

Coie, J. D., Finn, M., & Krehbiel, G. (August, 1984). *Controversial children: Peer assessment evidence for status category distinctiveness.* Paper presented at annual meeting of the American Psychological Association, Toronto.

Coie, J. D., & Krehbiel, G. (1984). Effects of academic tutoring on the social status of low-achieving, socially rejected children. *Child Development, 55,* 1465-1478.

Coie, J. D., & Kupersmidt, J. (1983). A behavioral analysis of emerging social status in boys' groups. *Child Development, 54,* 1400-1416.

Coie, J. D., & Pennington, B. F. (1976). Children's perceptions of deviance and disorder. *Child Development, 47,* 651-657.

Cowen, E. L., Pederson, A., Babigian, H., Izzo, L. D., & Trost, M. A. (1973). Long term follow-up of early detected vulnerable children. *Journal of Consulting and Clinical Psychology, 41,* 438-446.

Dodge, K. A. (1983). Behavioral antecedents of peer social status. *Child Development, 54,* 1386-1399.

Dodge, K. A., Coie, J. D., & Brakke, N. P. (1982). Behavior patterns of socially neglected and rejected preadolescents: The roles of social approach and aggression. *Journal of Abnormal Child Psychology, 10,* 389-409.

Farrington, D. P. (1978). The family backgrounds of aggressive youths. In L. Herson, M. Berger, & D. Schaffer (Eds.), *Aggression and antisocial disorder in children.* Oxford: Pergamon.

Flemming, P., & Ricks, D. F. (1969). Emotions of children before schizophrenia and before character disorder. In M. Roff & D. F. Ricks (Eds.), *Life history research in psychopathology.* Minneapolis: University of Minnesota Press.

Finn, M. G. (1984). *Being disliked: Self-report and social status.* Unpublished doctoral dissertation, Duke University, Durham, NC.

Glick, O. (1972). Some social-emotional consequences of early inadequate acquisition of reading skills. *Journal of Educational Psychology, 63,* 253-257.

Green, K. D., Forehand, R., Beck, J., and Vosk, B. (1980). An assessment of the relationship among measures of children's social competence and children's academic achievement. *Child Development, 51,* 1149-1156.

Gresham, F., & Nagle, R. (1980). Social skills training with children's responsiveness to modeling and coaching as a function of peer orientation. *Journal of Consulting and Clinical Psychology, 48,* 718-729.

Harter, S. (1982). The perceived competence scale for children. *Child Development, 53,* 87-97.

Hymel, S., & Asher, S. R. (April, 1977). *Assessment and training of isolated children's social skills.* Paper presented at the biennial meeting of the Society for Research in Child Development, New Orleans, LA. (ERIC Document Service Reproduction Service No. ED 136930).

Hymel, S., & Rubin, K. H. (in press). Children with peer relationships and social skills problems: Conceptual, methodological, and developmental issues. In G. J. Whitehurst (Ed.), *Annals of child development* (Vol. 2). Greenwich, CT: JAI Press.

Kasanin, J., & Veo, L. (1932). A study of the school adjustment of children who later became psychotic. *American Journal of Orthopsychiatry, 2,* 212-230.

Krehbiel, G. (1983). *Sociometric status- and academic achievement-based differences in behavior and peer-assessed reputation.* Unpublished doctoral dissertation, Duke University, Durham, NC.

Kupersmidt, J. (April, 1983). *Predicting delinquency and academic problems from childhood peer status.* Paper presented at the meeting of the Society for Research in Child Development, Detroit, MI.

Ladd, G. (1981). Effectiveness of a social learning method for enhancing children's social interaction and peer acceptance. *Child Development, 52,* 171-178.

LaGreca, A., & Santogrossi, D. (1980). Social skills training with elementary school students: A behavioral group approach. *Journal of Consulting and Clinical Psychology, 48,* 220-227.

Lahey, B. B., Green, K. D., & Forehand, R. (1980). On the independence of ratings of hyperactivity, conduct problems, and attention deficits in children: A multiple regression analysis. *Journal of Consulting and Clinical Psychology, 48,* 566-574.

Ledingham, J. E. (1981). Developmental patterns of aggressive and withdrawn behavior in childhood: A possible method for identifying preschizophrenics. *Journal of Abnormal Child Psychology, 9,* 1-22.

Lefkowitz, M., Eron, L., Walder, L. O., & Huesmann, L. R. (1977). *Growing up to be violent.* New York: Pergamon.

Masten, A., Morison, P., & Pelligrini (1985). A revised class play method of peer assessment. *Developmental Psychology, 3,* 523-533.

McMichael, P. (1980). Reading difficulties, behavior, and social status. *Journal of Educational Psychology, 72,* 76-86.

Michael, C. M., Morris, D. P., & Soroker, E. (1957). Follow-up studies of shy, withdrawn children. II. Relative incidence of schizophrenia. *American Journal of Orthopsychiatry, 27,* 331-337.

Mednick, S. A., & Schulsinger, F. (1969). Factors related to breakdown in children at high risk for schizophrenia. In M. Roff & D. F. Ricks (Eds.), *Life history research in psychopathology.* Minneapolis: University of Minnesota Press.

Moore, D. R., Chamberlain, P., & Menkes, L. H. (1979). Children at risk for delinquency: A follow-up comparison of aggressive children and children who steal. *Journal of Abnormal Child Psychology, 7,* 345-355.

Morris, D. P., Soroker, E., & Burris, G. (1954). Follow-up studies of shy, withdrawn children. I. Evaluation of later adjustment. *American Journal of Orthopsychiatry, 24,* 743-754.

Oden, S., & Asher, S. R. (1977). Coaching children in social skills for friendship making. *Child Development, 48,* 495-506.

Olweus, D. (1979). Stability of aggression reaction patterns in males: A review. *Psychological Bulletin, 86,* 852-875.

Pollack, M., Woerner, M. G., Goodman, W., & Greenberg, J. W. (1966). Childhood development patterns of hospitalized adult schizophrenic and nonschizophrenic patients and their siblings. *American Journal of Orthopsychiatry, 36*, 492-509.

Renshaw, P. D., & Asher, S. R. (1983). Children's goals and strategies for social interaction. *Merrill-Palmer Quarterly, 29*, 353-374.

Robins, L. N. (1966). *Deviant children grown up: A sociological and psychiatric study.* Baltimore: Williams & Wilkins.

Roff, M. (1957). *Preservice personality problems and subsequent adjustment to military service: The prediction of psychoneurotic reactions* (Report No. 57-151). School of Aviation Medicine, USAF.

Roff, M. (1959). *Preservice personality problems and subsequent adjustment to military service: A replication of "The prediction of psychoneurotic reactions* (Report No. 57-151). School of Aviation Medicine, USAF.

Roff, M. (1961). Childhood social interaction and young adult bad conduct. *Journal of Abnormal and Social Psychology, 63*, 333-337.

Roff, M. (1963). Childhood social interactions and young adult psychosis. *Journal of Clinical Psychology, 19*, 152-157.

Roff, M., Sells, S. B., & Golden, M. M. (1972). *Social adjustment and personality development in children.* Minneapolis: University of Minnesota Press.

Rubin, K. H. (1982). Non-social play in preschoolers. Necessary evil? *Child Development, 53*, 651-657.

Stabenau, J., & Pollin, R. (1969). Experiential differences for schizophrenics as compared to their non-schizophrenic siblings: Twin and family studies. In M. Roff & D. F. Ricks (Eds.), *Life history research in psychopathology.* Minneapolis: University of Minnesota Press.

Wadsworth, M. (1979). *Roots of delinquency: Infancy, adolescence and crime.* Oxford: Martin Robinson.

West, D. J., & Farrington, D. P. (1973). *Who becomes delinquent?* London: Heinemann Educational.

Wickman, E. K. (1928). *Children's behavior and teacher's attitudes.* New York: Commonwealth Fund.

Yellott, A., Liem, G., & Cowen, E. L. (1969). Relationships among measures of adjustment, sociometric status, and achievement in third graders. *Psychology in the Schools, 6*, 315-321.

CHAPTER 10

An Evolving Paradigm in Social Skill Training Research With Children

Steven R. Asher

Social skill training research with children has accelerated rapidly with more than 30 studies published in the last 7 years (Ladd & Asher, 1985). This research has been extensively reviewed of late (e.g., Asher & Renshaw, 1981; Conger & Keane, 1981; Ladd & Mize, 1983; Wanlass & Prinz, 1982), and it is clear that considerable diversity exists under the general rubric of social skill training research with children.

In conceptualizing this diversity, it is useful to think of the literature as composed of several different paradigms. These paradigms vary in the particular intervention procedures employed, the types of program content taught, and the types of selection criteria and outcome measures used. For example, in one paradigm, children are selected based on low rates of interaction with peers and a variety of operant procedures are used to promote increased peer interaction (see Wanlass & Prinz, 1982, for a review). This paradigm has typically focused on children's interaction rate without regard to more qualitative aspects of children's social interaction.

In a second paradigm, the emphasis has been on one qualitative aspect of interaction, namely the extent to which children are assertive in their approaches and responses to others. Here children are selected based on self-report and role-play measures of assertiveness, and various instructional procedures are used to increase assertive ways of handling a variety of problematic situations (see Bornstein, Bellack, & Hersen, 1977; Michelson, Sugai, Wood, & Kazdin, 1983; Michelson & Wood, 1980).

This chapter focuses on a third paradigm, one that involves the selection of children based on sociometric criteria, teaches skills that previous research has found to correlate with sociometric status, and employs cognitively based, direct instruction procedures in which children are verbally instructed concerning the importance of various social interaction concepts. This sociometrically oriented social skill training paradigm is quite recent, with the first studies published less than a decade ago (Gottman, Gonso, & Schuler, 1976; Oden & Asher, 1977). Yet despite its relative youth, this paradigm has considerable promise. One of its strong features is the rationale for subject selection. Although the children selected are functioning in regular class situations, they are poorly accepted by peers and appear to be "at risk" in terms of later life adjustment (see Putallaz &

Gottman, 1982). Furthermore, as will be discussed, studies within this emerging paradigm have been quite successful in promoting immediate and lasting changes in children's status in the peer group. This chapter highlights the success of studies within the sociometrically oriented social skill training paradigm. However, its purpose is to do more than provide an overview of successful outcomes to date. Rather, it is intended to raise a fundamental question about the kinds of children who benefit from social skill training. In particular, the focus here is on whether sociometrically rejected as well as neglected children benefit from social skill training. The distinction between these two types of low-status children is a critical one, yet it has rarely been made in the social skill training literature. The problem is that making the distinction has traditionally required administering a type of sociometric measure that many researchers and practitioners view as objectionable. This chapter will describe these objections and then indicate alternative measurement strategies that are now available.

The plan for this chapter is as follows. First, each of the features that characterize the sociometrically oriented social skill training paradigm will be described. Following this, there is a brief review of research on the effectiveness of skill training with unpopular children. Next, the differences between rejected and neglected children will be summarized. It will be proposed that it is critical to learn whether rejected as well as neglected children benefit from intervention. Finally, new approaches to classifying children as rejected versus neglected will be presented.

Social Skill Training With Unpopular Children

There are now at least nine published papers and conference papers (Bierman & Furman, 1984; Coie & Krehbiel, 1984; Gottman et al., 1976; Gresham & Nagle, 1980; Hymel & Asher, 1977; Ladd, 1981; La Greca & Santogrossi, 1980; Oden & Asher, 1977; Siperstein & Gale, 1983) that present research on the effectiveness of social skill training within the sociometrically oriented paradigm. These nine studies share an emphasis on sociometric assessment, teach program content based on behavioral-correlates-of-status research, and employ cognitively based, direct instruction training procedures. Each of these elements will be briefly discussed.

Sociometric Assessment

Two types of sociometric measures are typically employed to assess status within this paradigm. One is a rating-scale procedure, in which children rate each of their classmates on a 1-5 scale in terms of how much they would like to play (or work) with each child (see Figure 10.1). This type of measure, developed originally for descriptive research on peer relations in school settings (e.g., Roistacher, 1974; Singleton & Asher, 1977; Thompson & Powell, 1951), has been used in virtually all social skill training research with unpopular children. The second type of sociometric measure is the traditional limited-choice nomination mea-

Name _____

EXAMPLES: How much do you like to play with this
                              person at school?

	I don't like to				I like to a lot
Louise Blue	1	2	3	4	5
Russell Grey	1	2	3	4	5
John Armon	1	2	3	4	5
Andrea Brandt	1	2	3	4	5
Sue Curtis	1	2	3	4	5
Sandra Drexel	1	2	3	4	5
Jeff Ellis	1	2	3	4	5
Bill Fox	1	2	3	4	5
Diane Higgins	1	2	3	4	5
Harry Jones	1	2	3	4	5
Jill Lamb	1	2	3	4	5
Steve Murray	1	2	3	4	5
Jo Anne Norman	1	2	3	4	5
Pam Riley	1	2	3	4	5
Jim Stevens	1	2	3	4	5

HOW MUCH DO YOU LIKE TO PLAY WITH

THIS PERSON AT SCHOOL?   1   2   3   4   5
                          I don't   I like
                          like to   to a lot

FIGURE 10.1. Sample rating-scale sociometric measure.

sure in which children indicate their best friends or most preferred playmates in class. This measure, too, has a long history of use in descriptive research (e.g., Gottman, Gonso, & Rasmussen, 1975; Hartup, Glazer, & Charlesworth, 1967; Moreno, 1934) and has often been used in intervention research as well (e.g., Coie & Krehbiel, 1984; Gresham & Nagle, 1980; Oden & Asher, 1977).

Several investigators have combined sociometric measures with other criteria in selecting their focal sample. For example, Ladd (1981) administered a sociometric measure and observed children in class to select unpopular peers who were also low on particular types of peer interactive behavior (offering suggestions, asking questions, and offering support). Coie and Krehbiel (1984) used a combination of sociometric and achievement test data to select unpopular, low-achieving children. Still, the common feature of the studies within this paradigm is their use of sociometric criteria to select children. This emphasis on sociometric status is based primarily on a widely cited set of studies that suggest a relationship between peer status in childhood and later dysfunction in adolescence and adulthood (e.g., Cowen, Pederson, Babigian, Izzo, & Trost, 1973; Roff, Sells, & Golden, 1972; Ullmann, 1957; also see Parker & Asher, 1985, and Kupersmidt, 1983, for reviews and recent data). That unpopular children seem to be "at risk" for later adjustment problems has provided the foundation for intervention efforts within this paradigm.

Program Content

The studies within the sociometrically oriented social skill training paradigm share an emphasis on teaching skills found in previous research to correlate with sociometric status. This has been termed a competence-correlates approach to selecting program content (Asher & Markell, 1979) and differs from other paradigms which derive content from theoretical perspectives or from commonsense intuition. In an early social skill training study using this competence-correlates approach, Gottman et al. (1976) focused on the concepts of giving and receiving positive interaction, how to start up a friendship, and taking the listener's perspective. Each of these skills was found in an earlier study (Gottman et al., 1975) to correlate with sociometric status. In a later training study, Oden and Asher (1977) taught four broad social interaction concepts: participation, communication, cooperation, and validation-support. The focus on these particular concepts emerged from comprehensive reviews of literature on the behavioral correlates of status (Asher, Oden, & Gottman, 1977; Hartup, 1970). Still later, Ladd (1981) focused on three particular behavioral categories found in previous research to relate to peer status: offering suggestions, asking questions, and offering support. Although the particular skills being taught vary in these studies, there is the shared assumption that program content should be based on prior evidence concerning the behavioral correlates of status.

Training Procedures

The studies in this paradigm use cognitively based, direct instruction procedures to teach program content. Typically this takes the form of verbal interaction between a "coach" and the child in which the coach provides ideas or concepts about social interaction, has the child generate specific behavioral examples of each concept, and encourages the child to use the concepts to monitor his or her own behavior. The assumption underlying this approach is that children can use general principles of social interaction to guide their own behavior in specific situations. For example, in the Oden and Asher (1977) study, children played six games with six different classmates, over a 2-3 week period. Before each of the last five sessions, the coach discussed with the child certain ideas that "might make games more fun to play." The child was encouraged to try out the ideas during each play session. After each play session the coach met with the child, reviewed the ideas, asked the child whether the ideas helped make the game more fun, and asked for specific examples concerning how each idea was or was not used. In later sessions an attempt was made to relate the concepts to everyday school situations.

Although all of the nine studies listed earlier use a direct instruction approach, they vary in ways that are probably significant. For example, studies differ in the number of sessions held, the spacing of sessions (e.g., once a week versus every few days), the size of the training group (i.e., one-to-one instruction versus teaching a dyad or small group), the inclusion of other training components (e.g., reinforcement, modeling), the degree of professional training of the person providing instruction, and whether the training includes opportunities to interact or practice with classmates or other peers. Concerning the last factor, there is now evidence that providing peer interaction opportunities with classmates may be critical to the success of the intervention. A recent study by Bierman and Furman (1984) as well as an earlier unpublished paper by Covill-Servo (1978) suggest this conclusion. Clearly, research is needed on particular aspects of instructional procedure. Ladd and Mize (1983) took the important step of suggesting a framework in which such research could be carried out.

Evidence Concerning Effectiveness

The evidence concerning the effectiveness of intervention within the sociometrically oriented skill training pardigm was reviewed recently by Ladd and Asher (1985). Here, some general points will be made. First, of the nine studies, seven have found that the sociometric status gains of children in experimental conditions exceed children's gains in control conditions (Bierman & Furman, 1984; Coie & Krehbiel, 1984; Gottman et al., 1975; Gresham & Nagle, 1980; Ladd, 1981; Oden & Asher, 1977; Siperstein & Gale, 1983). Furthermore, positive results seem to depend on instruction, since peer interaction opportunities alone (e.g., Oden & Asher, 1977) or simple attention from an adult (e.g., Ladd, 1981) usually do not produce lasting changes in sociometric status.

A second point is that the most consistent evidence of change has been on the rating-scale measure but not the limited-choice nomination measure (Coie & Krehbiel, 1984; Gresham & Nagle, 1980; Oden & Asher, 1977; Siperstein & Gale, 1983). Asher and Hymel (1981) suggested that rating-scale measures in the form of "How much do you like to play with this child?" can be seen as measures of acceptance, whereas limited-nomination measures seem to assess best friendship. Apparently, existing interventions are helping unpopular children to become better accepted or more liked but not to gain best friends. Teaching particular content that is focused on the domain of forming friendships seems needed to achieve this objective.

A third important finding is that when follow-up evaluations have been obtained on rating-scale measures, there is evidence of maintenance of change in sociometric status. The longest follow-up assessment to date found maintenance 1 year after intervention (Oden & Asher, 1977). The children in this study, initially among the three least-liked children in their class, were nearly average in their status at 1-year follow-up. Other studies have conducted 1-month follow-up assessments and found maintenance of change (e.g., Gresham & Nagle, 1980; Ladd, 1981). Even these 1-month follow-up findings are meaningful in light of evidence that short-term maintenance of changes in status is difficult to achieve with other types of interventions (Lilly, 1971; Rucker & Vincenzo, 1970).

Fourth, it is clear that not all studies have obtained unequivocably positive sociometric results from social skill training. La Greca and Santogrossi (1980) found that trained children made positive gains on behavioral observation measures and measures of social knowledge but no sociometric effects were obtained. Hymel and Asher (1977) found sociometric status change in two different coaching conditions but these gains were no greater than those made by children in a peer-pairing condition in which children were paired together for play but received no instruction. Due to the lack of a non-treatment control gorup it is unclear whether the gains in each condition were due to regression toward the mean or to comparable treatment effects. Bierman and Furman (1984) found that the children who served as play partners during the skill training gave higher sociometric ratings to the target children. However, other classmates (i.e., nonpartners) did not change in their acceptance of the target children.

Close inspection of even the successful studies suggests that as many as 40%-50% of the children may be unaffected by skill training (Asher & Renshaw, 1981). Furthermore it is possible that a disproportionate number of nonreplications of training effects exists in unpublished studies.

There are several factors that could explain success or failure in particular studies. One possibility discussed in the literature (e.g., Bierman & Furman, 1984; Hymel & Asher, 1977) is that intervention with older children (fifth- and sixth-graders) is less effective than with younger children (third- and fourthgraders). Another possibility, noted earlier, is that opportunities to practice with classmates may be critical (Bierman & Furman, 1984). Still other factors include the extent to which training sessions are concentrated versus spread out, the degree of training of coaches, and individual differences in the way coaches relate to children.

Factors such as these could be used to explain why some intervention studies work and others do not. They would not explain, however, the fact that even within studies with a narrow age focus and one coach some children benefit and others do not. The answer here must be found in the way characteristics of children interact with the mode of treatment. Thus far we know remarkably little about the children selected for training. However, investigators within the sociometrically oriented paradigm are beginning to include information about achievement (Coie & Krehbiel, 1984) and behavioral style (e.g., Bierman & Furman, 1984; Ladd, 1981) in their selection and/or description of target samples. Certainly the call for process-oriented inquiry into social skill training effects is becoming stronger (Asher & Taylor, 1983; Ladd, Chapter 5, this volume). Surprisingly, however, one issue that has been widely overlooked in sociometrically oriented training research actually is within the domain of sociometric assessment itself. Adequate information is not yet available concerning whether the children selected for training and influenced by training include sociometrically rejected as well as sociometrically neglected chidlren. The importance of this issue is discussed next.

Which Low-Status Children are Changing?

Sociometrically neglected children are those who have no best friends in their class but are not especially disliked. Sociometrically rejected children both lack friends and are actively disliked. The distinction between rejected and neglected status, although long recognized (e.g., Gronlund, 1959), has only recently come to be fully appreciated. Thanks primarily to the work of Coie, Dodge, and their colleagues (e.g., Coie, Dodge, & Coppotelli, 1982; Coie & Dodge, 1983; Dodge, 1983; Dodge, Coie, & Brakke, 1982), there is now a growing body of evidence concerning the distinguishing features of these two groups of children.

First, it is clear that rejected children are much more stable in their status over time. This is evident from research in which new groups of children are brought together for the first time (Coie & Kupersmidt, 1983) and from longitudinal studies that follow children from one grade level to the next (Coie & Dodge, 1983; Newcomb & Bukowski, 1984). Rejected children tend to remain rejected whereas neglected children become more popular over time.

It is also clear that rejected and neglected children differ behaviorally from one another. In particular, rejected children exhibit more antisocial behavior and other forms of behavior that are disruptive to group life. This generalization is supported by direct observations (e.g., Coie & Kupersmidt, 1983; Dodge, 1983), as well as by information from parents (French & Waas, 1985) and peers (Coie, Dodge, & Coppotelli, 1982). Rejected children are more aversive in their interactional style and it is therefore not surprising that their status is more stable over time.

Self-report data also indicate the importance of distinguishing between neglected and rejected status. Asher and Wheeler (in press) recently administered a questionnaire to learn whether children from various status groups differ in their feelings of loneliness and social dissatisfaction. The questionnaire (see Figure 10.2) consisted of 16 primary items focusing on children's feelings of loneliness (e.g., "I'm lonely at school"), feelings of social adequacy versus inadequacy (e.g., "I'm good at working with other children at school"), or subjective estimations of peer status (e.g., "I have lots of friends in my class"). The questionnaire also contained 8 "filler" items focusing on children's hobbies or preferred activities. These items were included to help children feel more open and

1. It's easy for me to make new friends at school.
2. I like to read.
3. I have nobody to talk to in my class.*
4. I'm good at working with other children in my class.*
5. I watch TV a lot.
6. It's hard for me to make friends at school.
7. I like school.
8. I have lots of friends in my class.
9. I feel alone at my school.*
10. I can find a friend in my class when I need one.
11. I play sports a lot
12. It's hard to get kids in school to like me.*
13. I like science.
14. I don't have any to play with at school.*
15. I like music
16. I get along with my classmates.
17. I feel left out of things at school.*
18. There's no other kids I can go to when I need help in school.*
19. I like to paint and draw.
20. I don't get along with other children in school.*
21. I'm lonely at school.*
22. I am well-liked by the kids in my class.
23. I like playing board games a lot.
24. I don't have any friends in class.*

FIGURE 10.2. Questionnaire Items from Asher and Wheeler. Items with an asterisk were those for which response order was reversed in scoring. Items 2, 5, 7, 11, 13, 15, 19, and 23 were classified as hobby or interest items. From S. R. Asher & V. A. Wheeler (in press). Children's loneliness: A comparison of rejected and neglected peer status. *Journal of Consulting and Clinical Psychology*. Copyright © by the American Psychological Association. Adapted by permission of the publisher.

relaxed about indicating their feelings about various topics. Children responded to each of the 24 items on a 5-point scale in terms of how true each item was about them. The questionnaire is similar to an earlier version developed by Asher, Hymel, and Renshaw (1984) except that in the Asher and Wheeler study each of the 16 primary items contains a clear school focus. As in the previous study, a factor analysis revealed that all 16 primary items loaded on 1 factor and that the scale had satisfactory internal reliability (Cronbach's Alpha = .90). With respect to the major question of interest, results indicated that rejected children were considerably more lonely than the other status groups, and that neglected children did not differ from their more accepted peers. Here too, then, is evidence that rejected children are quite distinct from other status groups.

Finally, it appears that rejected and neglected children differ in the extent to which they are at risk for serious later-life adjustment problems. Parker and Asher (1985) recently reviewed literature on the various long-term correlates of early peer relationship problems. Their review consisted of a detailed examination of the relationship between early peer relations and later outcomes such as dropping out of school, juvenile delinquency, and serious mental health problems. Although individual studies have particular weaknesses and more comprehensive follow-up research with broadly representative populations is needed, an overall pattern can nonetheless be discerned. Rejected children rather than neglected children seem to be most "at risk" for serious adjustment problems in later life.

To summarize, then, compared to other status groups, rejected children are more aversive in their interactions with peers, report greater feelings of loneliness and social dissatisfaction, are more stable in their status over time, and are more likely to experience a variety of serious later-life problems. Given this profile, this group might be difficult to change. It is especially important, therefore, to determine whether rejected as well as neglected children benefit from social skill training. If rejected children benefit, the line of studies within the sociometrically oriented skill training paradigm would come to assume particular importance. Should investigators find, however, that it is mainly neglected children whose status changes, then the accomplishments to date are clearly more modest and claims made in the research literature and the practitioner-oriented literature should be moderated accordingly.

The traditional way of distinguishing between neglected and rejected children is to administer a negative nomination sociometric measure in addition to the traditional positive nomination measure. The negative nomination measure involves asking children to indicate the names of children they would not want as friends. Although this measure has been used in perhaps 10%-15% of descriptive studies of peer status (e.g., Coie et al., 1982; Gottman et al., 1975; Gronlund & Anderson, 1957; Hartup et al., 1967; Newcomb & Bukowski, 1984; Peery, 1979), the measure has rarely been used in intervention research.

An exception is a recent study by Coie and Krehbiel (1984). They included a negative nomination measure as part of the subject selection process and assigned low-achieving, sociometrically rejected children to one of four conditions: academic tutoring, social skill training, a combination of treatments, or a no-treatment control. Results indicated that academic tutoring had very impressive effects on both academic and sociometric outcomes. Indeed, Coie and Krehbiel's findings indicate that one way to improve low-achieving, unpopular children's social relationships is through an effective *academic* intervention. The Coie and Krehbiel results were more complex with regard to social skill training. Here, training produced nonsignificant effects on a social preference score (i.e., "like most" standard scores minus "like least" standard scores), and on positive nomination and negative nomination scores analyzed separately. However, the most critical question, in light of previous social skill training findings, concerns the impact of training on acceptance as indexed by a rating-scale measure. As discussed earlier, this measure has been most sensitive to treatment effects in previous research. Here Coie and Krehbiel's results were more encouraging. The social skill training condition differed significantly from the control condition 3 weeks after intervention. No long-term follow-up data were collected using this measure. Although the academic tutoring results were most impressive in this study, the social skill training effects on the rating-scale measure, as Coie and Krehbiel note, were comparable to those obtained by several other investigations in which significant sociometric outcomes were obtained. Accordingly, the Coie and Krehbiel study provides some evidence that skill training can be effective with rejected children.

Two earlier sources of data provide indirect evidence on the issue of what kinds of children benefit from training. One source is the lack of change among control group children in successful studies. If there were a large proportion of neglected children in target samples, considerable drift toward the mean would be expected among control group children, given the demonstrated tendency of neglected children to become more popular over time (Coie & Dodge, 1983). Even within the school year, neglected status is unstable; certainly control group children should improve over a 1-year period if their ranks were heavily composed of sociometrically neglected youngsters. The fact that significant improvement among control group children has not been observed suggests that target samples contain a high percentage of rejected children. The other source of evidence comes from a study by Hymel and Asher (1977). They studied children who received a low average play rating on the rating-scale sociometric, and either no nominations or just one nomination on the positive nomination measure. These are the kind of children typically selected for intervention. When Hymel and Asher (1977) brought negative nomination data into the picture, they found that over half of those in the sample were classified as rejected.

There is, then, reason to believe that social skill training has been effective with rejected and not just neglected children. Inferences from previous research suggest that focal samples are composed of a significant number of rejected children. Furthermore, the one study that explicitly selected rejected children (Coie & Krehbiel, 1984) found evidence of skill training effectiveness with children who were not only rejected but had serious school achievement problems as well. Further research on the issue is needed, but there is cause for optimism.

Alternatives to the Negative Nomination Measure

Why are negative nomination measures not included more often in sociometrically oriented skill training research? The primary reason is that these measures elicit concerns from some researchers and practitioners that administering the measures can have some negative effects. The concerns are that unpopular children will feel badly knowing that this sort of information is being gathered, that such measures will implicitly sanction saying negative things about others, and that the children who are asked to name a specified number of disliked peers will come to view certain children more negatively than they already do.

Actually, little research has been done concerning the effects of administering negative nomination measures to children. In a first study addressed to this issue, Hayvren and Hymel (1984) observed preschool children both before and after sociometric testing. Children's conversations were recorded and their interactions with liked and disliked peers were categorized. Results indicated that, following sociometric testing, children talked about who they liked best but did not talk at all about their negative nominations. Furthermore, children did not change in the way they interacted with liked and disliked peers as a result of the sociometric testing experience. These results are encouraging. Nonetheless, additional research is needed with older children who are more reflective about their relationships and may be more likely to gossip or perhaps tease a child who is viewed unfavorably by peers.

Hesitancy about administering negative nomination measures suggests the need for alternative ways of distinguishing neglected from rejected children. One approach used recently by Ladd (1983) involves having teachers make the distinction between different types of unpopular children. Ladd (1983) first identified children as unpopular using a rating-scale sociometric measure and then had teachers indicate which of these children were rejected. This is a promising approach since it seems plausible that most teachers could reliably identify rejected children. However, information is needed concerning the degree to which teachers' classifications agree with those based on positive and negative peer nomination data. There may be large individual differences in the accuracy with which teachers can make this classification. Furthermore, Ladd (1983) noted that teachers were less confident in their ability to identify neglected as opposed to rejected children.

Another approach to identifying rejected children was recently proposed by Asher and Dodge (in press). They administered the rating-scale sociometric measure but instead of using the typical score, the average rating received from classmates, they summed the number of "1" ratings each child received on the 1-5 scale. One advantage of the rating-scale technique is that children are not required to nominate anyone as disliked; in fact they can give high ratings to everyone if that is the way they feel. As such, the measure is less ethically and politically sensitive than the traditional negative nomination measure. Asher and Dodge examined whether the number of "1" ratings could serve as a replacement for the number of negative nominations. Specifically, they examined whether children would be accurately identified as rejected using a combination of the "1" rating score and a positive nomination score. Results indicated that 91% of rejected children, traditionally classified by positive and negative nomination measures, were accurately identified using the substitute procedure. Furthermore, the stability of rejected status, identified using the new method, was similar to that obtained in previous research. Also of importance was that only a small percentage of children were "overidentified" using this procedure. Thus the method seems to be a satisfactory alternative for identifying rejected children. Interestingly, the method was not very successful in identifying neglected children. This is because neglected children do not receive a distinctive pattern of ratings on the rating-scale measure (French & Wass, 1985).

In concluding this discussion, it is important to emphasize that acknowledging concerns about negative nomination measures and suggesting alternatives, do not imply a conclusion that the measure is by itself harmful. As Asher and Dodge (in press) commented:

There is no evidence available to support that claim. Furthermore, it seems doubtful that the administration of this type of measure adds much beyond the trauma of everyday classroom life for rejected children. Indeed, using appropriate sociometric measures and implementing an appropriate intervention would seem to be a better course of action than failing to measure for fear of causing further embarrassment to an already stigmatized child. Further research is needed to learn whether negative nomination measures actually have adverse effects on children. At present, we only intend to conclude that a politically less sensitive procedure is now available.

Conclusion

In this chapter, the focus has been on one paradigm that has emerged within the social skill training literature. This paradigm involves the use of sociometric criteria to select children, focuses on skills known to correlate with sociometric status, and employs cognitively based, direct instruction training procedures as the mode of intervention. The frequent success of these studies with unpopular children suggests that this intervention approach needs to be taken quite seriously and that we need to learn the limits of the intervention's effectiveness and the reasons for its effectiveness. The time seems right for a second generation of studies within the sociometrically oriented social skill training paradigm. This second generation of research would examine the effects of training on subgroups of children. The distinction between neglected and rejected status is especially vital and future training studies need to define the focal population more adequately. It is hoped that new ways of identifying rejected children will contribute to this next generation of social skill training research.

Acknowledgment. The author acknowledges the support of NICHHD Grant numbers 07205 and 05951 in the research and writing of this chapter. The chapter was written while the author was on sabbatical in the Department of Human Development, University of Maryland, College Park.

References

Asher, S. R., & Dodge, K. A. (in press). Identifying children who are rejected by their peers. *Developmental Psychology*.

Asher, S. R., & Hymel S. (1981). Children's social competence in peer relations:

Sociometric and behavioral assessment. In J. D. Wine & M. D. Smye (Eds.), *Social competence* (pp. 125-157). New York: Guilford.

Asher, S. R., Hymel, S., & Renshaw, P. D. (1984). Loneliness in children. *Child Development, 55,* 1456-1464.

Asher, S. R., & Markell, R. A. (1979). *Peer relations and social interaction: Assessment and intervention.* Unpublished manuscript, University of Illinois, Champaign.

Asher, S. R., Oden, S. L., & Gottman, J. M. (1977). Children's friendships in school settings. In L. G. Katz (Ed.), *Current topics in early childhood education* (Vol. 1, pp. 33-61). Norwood, NJ: Ablex.

Asher, S. R., & Renshaw, P. D. (1981). Children without friends: Social knowledge and social skill training. In S. R. Asher & J. M. Gottman (Eds.), *The development of children's friendships* (pp. 273-296). New York: Cambridge University Press.

Asher, S. R., & Taylor, A. R. (1983). Social skill training with children: Evaluating processes and outcomes. *Studies in Educational Evaluation, 8,* 237-245.

Asher, S. R., & Wheeler, V. A. (in press). Children's loneliness: A comparison of rejected and neglected peer status. *Journal of Consulting and Clinical Psychology.*

Bierman, K. L., & Furman, W. (1984). The effects of social skills training and peer involvement on the social adjustment of preadolescents. *Child Development, 55,* 151-162.

Bornstein, M. R., Bellack, A. S., & Hersen, M. (1977). Social-skills training for unassertive children: A multiple-baseline analysis. *Journal of Applied Behavior Analysis, 10,* 183-195.

Coie, J. D., & Dodge, K. A. (1983). Continuities and changes in children's social status: A five-year longitudinal study. *Merrill-Palmer Quarterly, 29,* 261-281.

Coie, J. D., Dodge, K. A., & Coppotelli, H. (1982). Dimensions and types of status: A cross-age perspective. *Developmental Psychology, 18,* 557-570.

Coie, J. D., & Krehbiel, G. (1984). Effects of academic tutoring on the social status of low-achieving socially rejected children. *Child Development, 55,* 1465-1478.

Coie, J. D., & Kupersmidt, J. (1983). A behavioral analysis of emerging social status in boy's groups. *Child Development, 54,* 1400-1416.

Conger, J. C., & Keane, A. P. (1981). Social skills intervention in the treatment of isolated or withdrawn children. *Psychological Bulletin, 90,* 478-495.

Covill-Servo, J. L. (1978). *The modification of low peer status from a socio-psychological perspective.* Unpublished manuscript, University of Rochester.

Cowen, E. L., Pederson, A., Babigian, H., Izzo, L. D., & Trost, M. A. (1973). Long-term follow-up of early detected vulnerable children. *Journal of Consulting and Clinical Psychology, 41,* 438-446.

Dodge, K. A. (1983). Behavioral antecedents of peer social status. *Child Development, 54,* 1386-1399.

Dodge, K. A., Coie, J. D., & Brakke, N. P. (1982). Behavioral patterns of socially rejected and neglected preadolescents: The roles of social approach and aggression. *Journal of Abnormal Child Psychology, 10,* 389-410.

French, D. C., & Waas, G. A. (1985). Behavior problems of peer neglected and rejected elementary-age children: Parent and teacher perspectives. *Child Development, 56,* 246-252.

Gottman, J. M., Gonso, J., & Rasmussen, B. (1975). Social interaction, social competence, and friendship in children. *Child Development, 46,* 709-718.

Gottman, J. M., Gonso, J., & Schuler, P. (1976). Teaching social skills to isolated children. *Journal of Abnormal Child Psychology, 4,* 179-197.

Gresham, F. M., & Nagle, R. J. (1980). Social skills training with children: Responsiveness to modeling and coaching as a function of peer orientation. *Journal of Consulting and Clinical Psychology, 18*, 718-729.

Gronlund, N. E. (1959). *Sociometry in the classroom*. New York: Harper.

Gronlund, N. E., & Anderson, L. (1957). Personality characteristics of socially accepted, socially neglected, and socially rejected junior high school pupils. *Educational Administration and Supervision, 43*, 329-338.

Hartup, W. W. (1970). Peer interaction and social organization. In P. H. Mussen (Ed.), *Carmichael's manual of child psychology* (Vol. 2, pp. 361-456). New York: Wiley.

Hartup, W. W., Glazer, J. A., & Charlesworth, R. (1967). Peer reinforcement and sociometric status. *Child Development, 38*, 1017-1024.

Hayvren, M., & Hymel, S. (1984). Ethical issues in sociometric testing. The impact of sociometric measures on interactive behavior. *Developmental Psychology, 20*, 844-849.

Hymel, S., & Asher, S. R. (1977). *Assessment and training of isolated children's social skills*. Paper presented at the biennial meeting of the Society for Research in Child Development, New Orleans, LA. (ERIC Document Reproduction Service No. ED 136 930)

Kupersmidt, J. B. (1983). Predicting delinquency and academic problems from childhood peer status. In J. D. Coie (Chair), *Strategies for identifying children at social risk: Longitudinal correlates and consequences*. Symposium conducted at the biennial meeting of the Society for Research in Child Development, Detroit, MI.

Ladd, G. W. (1981). Effectiveness of a social learning method for enhancing children's social interaction and peer acceptance. *Child Development, 52*, 171-178.

Ladd, G. W. (1983). Social networks of popular, average, and rejected children in school settings. *Merrill-Palmer Quarterly, 29*, 283-307.

Ladd, G. W., & Asher, S. R. (1985). Social skill training and children's peer relations. In L. L'Abaté & M. A. Milan (Eds.), *Handbook of social skills training and research* (pp. 219-244). New York: Wiley.

Ladd, G. W., & Mize, J. (1983). A cognitive-social learning model of social skill training. *Psychological Review, 90*, 127-157.

La Greca, A. M., & Santogrossi, D. A. (1980). Social skills training with elementary school students: A behavioral group approach. *Journal of Consulting and Clinical Psychology, 48*, 220-227.

Lilly, M. S. (1971). Improving social acceptance of low sociometric status, low-achieving students. *Exceptional Children, 37*, 341-347.

Michelson, L., Sugai, D. P., Wood, R. P., & Kazdin, A. E. (1983). *Social skills assessment and training with children*. New York: Plenum.

Michelson, L., & Wood, R. (1980). A group assertive training program for elementary school children. *Child Behavior Therapy, 2*, 1-9.

Moreno, J. L. (1934). *Who shall survive? A new approach to the problem of human interrelations*. Washington, DC: Nervous and Mental Disease Publishing.

Newcomb, A. F., & Bukowski, W. M. (1984). A longitudinal study of the utility of social preference and social impact sociometric classification schemes. *Child Development, 55*, 1424-1447.

Oden, S., & Asher, S. R. (1977). Coaching children in social skills for friendship making. *Child Development, 48*, 495-506.

Parker, J., & Asher, S. R. (1985). *Peer acceptance and later personal adjustment: Are low-accepted children "at risk"?* Unpublished manuscript, University of Illinois, Urbana-Champaign.

Peery, J. C. (1979). Popular, amiable, isolated, rejected: A reconceptualization of sociometric status in preschool children. *Child Development, 50,* 1231-1234.

Putallaz, M., & Gottman, J. M. (1982). Conceptualizing social competence in children. In P. Karoly & J. J. Steffen (Eds.), *Improving children's competence: Advances in child behavioral analysis and therapy* (pp. 1-37). Lexington, MA: D. C. Heath.

Roff, M., Sells, S. B., & Golden, M. W. (1972). *Social adjustment and personality development in children.* Minneapolis: University of Minnesota Press.

Rostacher, R. C. (1974). A microeconomic model of sociometric choice. *Sociometry, 37,* 219-238.

Rucker, C. N., & Vincenzo, F. M. (1970). Maintaining social acceptance gains made by mentally retarded children. *Exceptional Children, 36,* 679-680.

Singleton, L. C., & Asher, S. R. (1977). Peer preferences and social interaction among third-grade children in an integrated school district. *Journal of Educational Psychology, 69,* 330-336.

Siperstein, G. N., & Gale, M. E. (1983). *Improving peer relationships of rejected children.* Paper presented at the biennial meeting of the Society for Research in Child Development, Detroit, MI.

Thompson, G. G., & Powell, M. (1951). An investigation of the rating-scale approach to the measurement of social status. *Educational and Psychological Measurement, 11,* 440-455.

Ullmann, C. A. (1957). Teachers, peers, and tests as predictors of adjustment. *Journal of Educational Psychology, 48,* 257-267.

Wanlass, R. L., & Prinz, R. J. (1982). Methodological issues in conceptualizing and treating social isolation. *Psychological Bulletin, 92,* 35-55.

PART IV
Developing Intervention Procedures

CHAPTER 11

Children's Social Skills Training: A Meta-Analysis

Barry H. Schneider and Barbara M. Byrne

Social skills training (SST) programs for children have been inspired by convincing evidence that childhood social competence is related to psychological adjustment in later years. It has not been clearly established, however, that interventions aimed at increasing childhood competence can improve the outcome for the children involved. Nevertheless, the number and variety of social skills training programs emerging in both the professional literature and commercial market attest to the appeal of this form of therapy. As is the case for most other forms of therapy, little data are available with regard to the relative effectiveness of the various training approaches or the child characteristics that may be associated with successful intervention. Several review articles on social skills training have focused on a given intervention modality (e.g., Combs & Slaby, 1977; Urbain & Kendall, 1980) or target population (e.g., Conger & Keane, 1981; Gresham, 1981). All have concluded that despite conflicting results and methodological problems, there is empirical evidence that provides some support for the positive impact of social skills training.

These review articles have used a qualitative approach. While this approach is useful, it is highly subjective. No common metric is required as a standard for comparison of studies. Therefore, conclusions regarding trends in the literature must be made without established methodological rigor. Glass, McGaw, and Smith (1981) summarized the conclusions of several investigators who have systematically scrutinized traditional review articles in psychology and education. It has frequently been found that different reviews of the same data yield diametrical results. This may occur for several reasons. Reviewers have been found to rely too heavily on a small, subjectively selected subset of studies in their discussions and analyses. Indeed, most traditional review articles contain so little information about the methods of reviewing that it is difficult to evaluate the validity of the conclusions. They generally fail to examine the possibility that the results of individual studies are mediated by methodological features of the studies including the inherent differences among the statistical techniques utilized. Reviewers have also paid too much attention to conclusions expounded at the end of research article rather than the weight of the data.

The purpose of this chapter is to provide a more quantitative summary of social skills training for children. Meta-analysis is a quantitative alternative to the qualitative approach characteristic of narrative review papers (Glass, 1976). Reviewers employing the meta-analysis technique use (a) objective procedures to locate studies; (b) quantitative features to describe study features and outcomes; and (c) statistical methods to summarize overall findings and explore relations between study features and outcomes. As might be expected, meta-analysis refers to the analysis of analyses. More specifically, it is the statistical analysis of a large collection of results from individual studies conducted with the purpose of integrating the findings. Meta-analysis research is multivariate in nature, with individual studies forming the units upon which measurements are taken, study findings comprising the dependent variables and study features comprising the independent variables (Glass et al., 1981). Through meta-analysis, the researcher is able to reduce the findings of disparate studies to a common value that can subsequently be related to various independent variables in a particular research area.

Study Selection

The meta-analysis approach used in this review was modeled after that described by Glass et al. (1981). An initial pool of approximately 200 studies was generated by conducting standard literature searches of *Psychological Abstracts, PSYSCAN-Developmental Psychology*, and *PSYSCAN-Clinical Psychology*. Computer searches of the ERIC documents and *Social Science Citation Index* were undertaken to locate additional studies. The following criteria were used to determine final inclusion in the data base:

1. The researchers had to investigate the effect of a planned intervention procedure specifically designed to enhance children's social behavior.

2. The study had to include a control group (either no-treatment or quasi-treatment). This criterion reduced the pool by approximately one-half, since the many studies that utilize small-n, within-subjects designs cannot be included in current forms of meta-analysis even though descriptive statistics have been developed for such data. This eliminated most unpublished studies as well.

3. The study had to include a quantitative measure of social behavior, such as rate of interaction with peers, social cognition, or aggression. This resulted in the elimination of several studies in which social skills training was conducted, but the only outcome measures were academic achievement or attending behavior while performing perceptual matching tasks.

4. The results had to be reported in a format appropriate for meta-analysis. In 22 studies, it was apparent that the data required were available to the investigators although they were not reported in the tables of the published text. For example, in several studies, mean values were provided, but not standard deviations. In these cases, complete data descriptions were requested by correspondence.

The final data pool included 51 studies that met the above criteria. The studies are listed in Appendix A.

Study Features

Preliminary inspection of the studies indicated that there were seven major attributes on which quantitative representation was both feasible and potentially useful to researchers and practitioners. These were:

1. treatment technique (e.g., modeling, coaching, operant or social-cognitive; these are defined below);
2. duration of treatment;
3. age and sex of subjects;
4. subject population (e.g., normal, sociometric isolates, learning disabled, behavior disordered, or developmentally handicapped);
5. therapist characteristics (e.g., teacher or research staff);
6. outcome variable (social interaction, aggression, social-cognition); and
7. reliability of outcome measure.

Each of 86 variables was coded by two trained, independent raters. Interrater agreement exceeded 90% on all variables. We originally hoped to examine each of the previously mentioned study features in terms of its impact on short-term (pre vs. post) and long-term behavior change. However, the paucity of follow-up data precluded meaningful analysis of the long-term effects of social skills training.

Statistical Analysis

The basic statistic used in meta-analysis is the effect size (ES), which is defined by Glass (1976) as the mean difference between experimental and control groups of a study divided by the control group standard deviation. In all meta-analyses, a number of arbitrary decisions must be made in applying this formula because of the variety of research designs and different ways in which data are reported. The following rules were used in calculating the ESs in our analyses:

1. In many of the published articles, statistics were reported only for those variables on which there were significant findings. The results for the nonsignificant variables were requested by letter. Where no response was received, an F value of 1.00, which is below the value that would be needed to achieve significance in any of the studies reviewed, was entered for the nonsignificant variables. This arbitrary decision avoided the elimination of a large number of well-designed studies, as well as the excessive elimination of unsuccessful results from the data pool.

2. In most of the studies, multiple outcome measures were used. If an ES was calculated for each of the outcome measures, studies that utilized a large number of dependent measures would receive disproportionate representation in the final analysis. As well, the assumption of independence would be violated. Therefore, where multiple outcome measures were reported, the ESs of each were combined

to yield a mean *ES* for the study. The exception was the analysis of the effects of social skills training on each type of outcome measure. For that analysis only, a separate *ES* was entered for each dependent measure.

3. Where only *p* values were reported and additional information could not be obtained from the authors, estimated appropriate test statistic values were used (see Glass et al., 1981).

4. Where covariance-adjusted mean score or gain scores were reported as well as raw score differences, the covariance-adjusted scores were used.

5. Where means and standard deviations were reported as well as a test statistic, the *ES* was calculated on the basis of the means and standard deviations.

6. Where there was more than one treatment group or where there was more than one control group (e.g., nontreatment and placebo), the data were combined to yield one *ES* for experimental subjects and one *ES* for control subjects per study.

Analyses of variance were performed for each major attribute. Post hoc comparison of mean *ES*s was effected using Tukey's HSD procedure.

Training Technique

The intervention techniques used were coded according to four major categories: coaching, modeling, operant conditioning, and social-cognitive. The analysis of variance compared the differences in mean *ES* among these four categories. Each of the categories was subdivided into more specific techniques as indicated in Table 11.1; these smaller categories were not compared statistically. The

TABLE 11.1. Means and standard errors of effect sizes by intervention technique.

Technique	M	SE	n of *ES*s
Modeling			
Live models	.63	.17	5
Film or videotape	.79	.12	29
Audiotape	.56	.10	3
Total	.75	.09	37
Operant procedures			
Social reinforcers	.89	.24	6
Material reinforcers	.85	.25	5
Social + material reinforcers	.65	.07	4
Total	.85	.22	15
Coaching	.65	.09	21
Social-cognitive			
Problem solving	.54	.10	30
Role-taking	.61	.06	28
Self-statements	.45	.12	6
Total	.55	.04	64

classification of the techniques was complicated by the fact that more than one training technique was used in about half the studies. The *ES*s for these studies were included under each technique that was used. Therefore, the *n* of *ES*s exceeds the *n* of studies in this analysis.

Operational definitions for each category were developed to facilitate coding. "Coaching" was coded when direct verbal instruction, accompanied by discussion, was the major medium of intervention (see Asher, chapter 10 this volume). "Modeling" was coded when the training focused on filmed, taperecorded, videotaped, or live demonstrations of the skills to be acquired. "Operant" was coded when the intervention consisted primarily of providing social or material reinforcement of targeted prosocial behavior in naturalistic or analog settings. "Social-cognitive" was coded when the intervention focused on any of the cognitive processes that have been associated with social competence. As indicated by the subcategories displayed under "social-cognitive" in Table 11.1, this included a number of diverse procedures including training in role taking (the ability to assume the perspective of another person in an interpersonal situation), problem solving (the ability to generate a number of different solutions to troublesome interpersonal problems, to predict the consequences of these solutions, and plan their implementation), and use of self-statements (essentially brief overt or covert mental contemplation of troublesome situations prior to action). While there are important conceptual distinctions among these social-cognitive intervention techniques, there was relatively little difference among their respective *ES*s, as shown in Table 11.1.

Analysis of variance indicated that the differences among the four major technique categories were statistically significant ($F = 2.78$; $p < .05$). Post hoc analysis using Tukey's HSD procedure indicated that the difference between the smallest (social-cognitive) and highest (operant) mean *ES* approached statistical significance ($p < .09$); the other differences between the means were not significant. (It is technically possible for an analysis of variance to yield significant results where post hoc analyses using relatively conservative procedures such as Tukey's do not; different mathematical procedures are involved in each of these analyses.) Therefore, the following conclusions should be interpreted with some caution.

As detailed in Table 11.1, the highest mean *ES*s were reported in studies where direct reinforcement of appropriate social behavior was the intervention procedure. The supplementary analyses indicated that social and material reinforcers were equally effective. In most of these studies, aggression or rate of social interaction was the outcome measure. Impressive results were obtained for either variable (for aggression: $M = .97$; $SE = .18$; $n = 6$; for rate of interaction: $M = .85$; $SE = .18$; $n = 4$). However, markedly poorer outcomes were reported for the three studies that explored the effects of reinforcement procedures on social-cognitive measures ($M = .40$; $SE = .11$).

Of the four major technique categories, the second highest mean *ES*s were reported for modeling studies. Further analysis of these results revealed that modeling has a very clear effect on measures of social interaction ($M = .97$;

$SE = .17$; $n = 17$). Modeling appears even more effective than direct reinforcement in achieving improvement on this variable. Modeling appears somewhat less effective in alleviating problems of aggression ($M = .70$; $SE = .06$; $n = 3$), and much less effective when social-cognition dependent variables are considered ($M = .49$; $SE = .13$; $n = 10$). While filmed or videotaped models appear to be superior to either live models or audiotapes, it should be recalled that many impressive studies in which training was conducted by live peer models were eliminated from the data pool because they involved small n, within-subject designs.

Coaching is less expensive in terms of materials than any of the other techniques studied. As indicated in Table 11.1, the global effects are but slightly smaller than those of modeling studies. Supplementary analysis did not indicate marked fluctuations among the coaching studies with respect to type of outcome variable.

The smallest ESs were reported for social-cognitive interventions. Curiously, these techniques appear to have less effect on social cognitive measures ($M = .48$; $SE = .09$; $n = 29$) than on aggression ($M = .65$; $SE = .05$; $n = 16$). This may indicate a need for a closer look at the social-cognitive instruments in terms of their sensitivity to change after treatment.

Outcome Measure

The effects of social skills training appear to vary as a function not only of the outcome variable used, but also of the way it is measured. There was considerable variety in the dependent variables of the 51 studies in our data pool; there were multiple outcome measures in most studies. We found that the most meaningful classification of the dependent measures involved two dimensions: variable (e.g., aggression, self-concept) and instrument (e.g., teacher rating scale, direct observation). The resulting cell sizes were often too small to permit statistical comparison of the ESs.

The largest ESs were from studies in which social interaction was the outcome variable ($M = .86$; $SE = .13$; $n = 25$). In most of these studies, social interaction was measured by direct observation or role play, approximately equal in mean ES. Status among peers was much less sensitive to change than observed social interaction ($M = .47$; $SE = .21$; this measure was used in only four studies).

Relatively large ESs were reported for aggressive behavior ($M = .75$; $SE = .11$; $n = 16$). Aggression was usually measured either by direct observation or teacher rating. In the case of aggression, teacher ratings were slightly more sensitive ($M = .95$; $SE = .24$; $n = 5$) to the interventions than observations ($M = .83$; $SE = .06$; $n = 6$). The teacher ratings are somewhat difficult to interpret because they are rarely "blind"—the teacher-rater is usually aware that the child has participated in SST. Our data pool contains only two studies in which the teacher ratings are described as "blind." Even when the research design appears to permit this, one wonders how "blind" the ratings really are. Is the children's casual classroom conversation entirely devoid of clues that indicate the type of training the child is receiving?

Self-report instruments were used as outcome measures in 7 studies. These included 3 studies that utilized self-concept scales ($M=.55$; $SE=.27$) and 4 that used locus of control scales ($M=54$; $SE=.19$); the ESs for both types of self-report measure were thus relatively small. The 23 studies in which social-cognitive tasks were the outcome measure reported average ESs of only .57 ($SE=.07$). Little difference was apparent between the various ways of assessing social cognition (e.g., hypothetical story, role-play, observation).

Increases in the amount of social interaction after training are most obvious when the behavior is observed directly. While reputation among peers and such constructs as self-concept do not display as much change immediately after training as aggression or rate of interaction, follow-up studies may document long-term gains in these areas. It is imperative that future researchers attempt to document these gains, because reputation among peers—not teacher ratings or direct observation of social behavior—has been shown to relate most clearly to adult mental health.

The reliability of the outcome measure was also related to ES. The ESs in studies in which interrater reliability greater than .90 was achieved for the dependent measure ($M=1.01$; $SE=.69$; $n=13$) were much larger than the corresponding ESs in studies where this degree of reliability was not attained ($M=.64$; $SE=.34$; $n=13$). This difference was statistically significant ($F=4.663$. $p<.05$) and appeared to be independent of the type of measure used.

Therapist Characteristics

Most of the interventions in the studies reviewed were conducted by either research staff trained in psychology or classroom teachers. The global mean ES for teachers ($M=.63$; $SE=.24$. $n=17$) was somewhat lower than that for research staff ($M=.80$; $SE=.54$; $n=33$; this difference achieved statistical significance: $F=3.75$; $p<.05$). While there was little difference between the two therapist categories for coaching or social-cognitive precedures, both modeling and operant interventions were more effective when conducted by research staff. This may indicate that research staff are at an advantage when background knowledge in learning theory is needed; teachers can be as effective when the intervention is similar in style to other classroom teaching activities.

Child Characteristics

Table 11.2 is a summary of the analyses for the effects of age, sex, and diagnostic category. The subjects' ages were divided into four blocks according to the mean age of the participants in each study. The differences among these four age blocks was statistically significant ($F=3.12$; $p<.05$). Tukey tests indicated that the mean ES for the 5 to 10-year-old block differed significantly from both the youngest age block and the oldest. Thus, there appears to be a "latency period" during the elementary school years during which social skills training appears to

TABLE 11.2. Means and standard errors of effect sizes by child characteristics.

Technique	M	SE	n of ESs
	Age		
3-4 years			
Modeling	1.10	.29	8
Operant	1.13	—	1
Coaching	1.13	.06	2
Self-cognitive	.51	.31	3
Total	.97	.18	14
5-10 years			
Modeling	.62	.11	4
Operant	1.20	.65	2
Coaching	.26	.03	3
Social-cognitive	.33	.04	8
Total	.49	.09	17
11-13 years			
Modeling	.47	.13	3
Operant	1.20	.66	2
Coaching	.26	.03	3
Social-cognitive	.33	.04	8
Total	.62	.10	16
14-19 years			
Modeling	1.00	.14	3
Operant	.49	.23	2
Coaching	1.00	.14	3
Social-cognitive	.85	.13	3
Total	.87	.09	11
	Sex		
All males			
Modeling	.60	.17	4
Operant	.44	.12	2
Coaching	.81	.25	3
Social-cognitive	.70	.12	7
Total	.65	.08	16
Males > Females			
Modeling	.95	.18	14
Operant	1.08	.28	4
Coaching	.66	.16	7
Social-cognitive	.57	.08	19
Total	.75	.08	44
Males ≅ Females			
Modeling	.80	.36	3
Operant	1.08	.28	4
Coaching	.66	.16	7
Social-cognitive	.57	.08	19
Total	1.01	.21	8

TABLE 11.2. (continued)

Technique	M	SE	n of ESs
	Population		
"Normal"			
Modeling	.55	.16	7
Operant	1.03	.11	2
Coaching	.56	.28	3
Social-cognitive	.42	.08	12
Total	.53	.08	24
Sociometrically assessed from regular schools			
Modeling	1.23	.33	3
Coaching	.72	.15	4
Social-cognitive	.69	—	1
Total	1.00	.14	8
Withdrawn			
Modeling	1.23	.25	8
Operant	.56	.05	2
Social-cognitive	.50	—	1
Total	1.04	.20	11
Aggressive			
Modeling	.57	.15	5
Operant	.79	.18	7
Coaching	.86	.16	4
Social-cognitive	.66	.05	21
Total	.69	.06	37
Learning disabled			
Coaching	1.18	—	1
Modeling	.87	.22	2
Total	.97	.17	3
Mentally retarded			
Modeling	.59	.04	2
Operant	1.75	—	1
Coaching	.54	—	1
Total	.86	.26	4

be less effective than during either preschool or adolescence. This pattern is most pronounced for coaching and modeling interventions, but does not apply to operant procedures. There may be differences in children's motivation to acquire new social skills at different ages. We might speculate that there is a decline during the elementary school years in children's intrinsic motivation to seek or accept adult direction with regard to peer relations, rekindled later on as adolescents become unsure of their social adequacy. It would be logical to expect the response to operant procedures not to follow suit because they probably depend less than the other techniques on intrinsic motivation. Another explanation, offered to us by a social skills therapist who is highly experienced with elementary-school-age children, is that many of the procedures used at this age involve more "talk" than children this age are prepared to follow. Perhaps intervention procedures have been properly adapted to the needs of the preschooler (e.g., by making use of puppets, concrete materials, etc.), but make unrealistic assumptions about the elementary school student's capacity for abstract conceptualization of social relations. This would also be less applicable to the operant procedures, which involve relatively little verbal explanation. It should be noted that the age analysis was complicated by the fact that there were many studies in which a very broad age range participated. In many of these, there was no supplementary analysis for age effects. Such failure to control for the developmental level of the child is not limited to SST research; it applies as well to research on child psychotherapy in general (see Barrett, Hampe, & Miller, 1978).

None of the studies was conducted exclusively with female subjects. However, as detailed in Table 11.2, the effectiveness of social skills training appears to increase with the proportion of female subjects, although this difference did not achieve statistical significance ($F=1.64$; $p > .10$). If confirmed by future research in which sex differences in responsiveness to social skills training are explored more directly and systematically, this trend may relate to more global findings that females are more likely than males to seek or accept help for personal problems (see Greenglass, 1982).

Several conventions were used in coding the diagnostic classifications summarized in Table 11.2. "Normal" was coded for subjects from regular classes unless they had been identified by a prescreening procedure as having any type of peer relations deficit or psychological exceptionality. Where candidates for social skills training were identified by sociometric or peer rating procedures conducted in regular school settings, the subjects were coded as "sociometrically assessed." Where the subject population was described as emotionally disturbed or receiving psychological treatment, the study was further scanned so that the participants might be classified as either aggressive or withdrawn. In a very few cases, this was impossible, and the study was eliminated from the analysis. The aggressive and withdrawn categories were also used when subjects were so identified by any screening procedure except for peer rating regardless of the nature of the child's class or school.

Analysis of variance was conducted in order to compare the differences among the six major population classifications, and indicated that the differences among their ESs were statistically significant ($F=3.02$; $p < .05$). Tukey tests indicated that only the difference between the first two classifications ("normal" vs. sociometrically assessed subjects from regular schools) achieved statistical significance. Since this particular distinction is of considerable theoretical and practical importance, it merits specific consideration. The finding that the ESs are smallest for the "normal" category may indicate merely that social skills training engenders little change when conducted with children who do not need it. An alternative explanation is an entirely statistical one—the "normal" subjects may simply have achieved high enough scores on the pretraining measures to make any improvement mathematically difficult to demonstrate. We should note that the number of studies in which subjects were screened by sociometric procedures was relatively small. This may be because adults in some settings find the idea of children rating each other's behavior somewhat difficult to accept.

It may nevertheless be profitable for practitioners to overcome these obstacles—perhaps by using sociometric procedures that consumers find less objectionable (see Asher, chapter 10 this volume)—because sociometric screening procedures seem to discriminate subjects that profit from social skills training. We should also note that these few studies involved a variety of sociometric techniques that are not readily comparable. Thus, our data are insufficient to answer such theoretically important questions as whether rejected children benefit as much from social skills training as their neglected counterparts (see Coie, Chapter 8 and Asher, Chapter 10 this volume).

Training was found to be more effective for withdrawn than for aggressive subjects. This difference is most pronounced in modeling studies. We might speculate that problems of withdrawal are more related to actual skill deficit, and are therefore alleviated by training appropriate skills using such techniques as modeling. Aggression may have more to do with the *application* of skills already acquired in troublesome situations. It is also quite possible that withdrawn children are more cooperative than aggressive children during the training sessions.

Duration of Intervention

The results of the analysis for duration of training are displayed in Table 11.3. In general, shorter interventions tended to have larger ESs, although the differences among the four major blocks are not statistically significant ($F=2.03$; $p>.10$). While we cannot, therefore, conclude that shorter interventions are more effective, neither can we make the facile assumption that longer is necessarily better. One limitation of our classification by duration of intervention is that the technique used is a confounding varible—certain types of intervention (e.g., modeling) are almost always briefer than others (e.g., social-cognitive). Therefore, it is perhaps more profitable to consider the data in Table 11.3 separately for each intervention procedure. It can be seen that the effect of length of treatment appears to be nonlinear within each major technique classification. Therefore, it would be important for future researchers to use repeated measures in order to determine the duration of treatment that is most efficient. It is possible that participants' interest declines during an extended intervention. Also, the complexity of the intervention procedure may be a mediating factor. Many of the longer interventions used multiple procedures. While therapist compliance with the procedure was systematically verified in very few studies, this may be a problem because the more complex, multifaceted interventions may require more extensive training. There may also be more of a tendency to "drift" from prescribed procedures when they are lengthy and complicated.

Limitations of This Study

The preceding conclusions should be interpreted with some caution because of several methodological limitations. While a thorough search of the published literature on social skills training was conducted, the final data pool is small

TABLE 11.3. Means and standard errors of effect sizes by duration of treatment.

Technique	M	SE	n of ESs
< 5 days			
Modeling	1.02	.23	10
Social-cognitive	.25	.08	2
Total	.89	.21	12
5-20 days			
Modeling	.81	.17	9
Operant	.98	.22	5
Coaching	.76	.16	8
Social-cognitive	.75	.11	11
Total	.80	.07	33
21-50 days			
Modeling	.43	.06	4
Operant	.64	.12	5
Coaching	.65	.23	2
Social-cognitive	.64	.06	17
Total	.60	.05	28
> 50 days			
Modeling	.75	.30	2
Operant	1.05	.56	2
Social-cognitive	.30	.02	5
Total	.59	.16	11

relative to meta-analyses in most other areas of inquiry. In some cases, we have made tentative, working conclusions based on a small number of very well-designed studies. The support for these conclusions would have been weakened considerably had we included additional studies that did not meet the design criteria. However, it would be most useful to repeat these analyses in the future as the relevant literature expands. Larger sample size could permit a number of additional analyses that might be quite revealing. For example, studies in which there was an attention control group might be compared with studies using no-treatment control only.

It should also be noted that, in order to facilitate comparison of the ESs, we have conducted analyses of variance. While this is not without precedent in meta-analysis (e.g., Carlberg & Kavale, 1980; Hansford & Hattie, 1982; Johnson, Johnson, & Maruyama, 1983; Kulik, Kulik, & Bangert, 1984 Steinkamp & Maehr, 1984; Willson & Putnam, 1982), it is somewhat controversial. Some statisticians contend that this entails too many violations of the assumptions underlying analysis of variance (Hedges & Olkin, 1985).

Future researchers conducting meta-analyses in this area may also wish to attempt to correct for several possible sources of bias in our data. Probably the most severe limitation of our data pool is the absence of small n, within-subjects studies. While current statistical techniques in meta-analysis cannot accommodate this type of data, this problem can surely be resolved. There are also several potentially fruitful sources of data that might be explored in the future. One of these is the British literature on children's social skills training; another important one is doctoral dissertations. Researchers in other areas have reported that the *ES*s in dissertations average .16 *SD* units smaller than those from journal articles (Cohen, Kulik, & Kulik, 1982; Kulik & Kulik, 1982; Smith, 1980).

Implications for Clinicians and Educators

Taken as a whole, the results just presented have a number of interesting implications for practitioners. First of all, it would appear both efficient and wise to opt for very well-defined interventions. The progress of the participants should be monitored continuously in an attempt to achieve an optimal duration of training. The age and sex differences found in responsiveness to SST should be considered in selecting subjects. These differences should also be considered carefully in designing training materials.

One should ensure that the participants in SST are in fact experiencing some verifiable social skills deficit. Particularly for certain types of intervention, therapists from an academic psychology background appear to be more effective than teachers. Psychology departments of school districts might consider conducting short-term social skills training programs as part of their services. Those developing SST packages for use by classroom teachers might consider expanding the training of the teachers involved. Perhaps the most important implication of this meta-analysis is that the success of SST varies considerably among subjects, settings, therapists, and techniques. Each intervention should therefore be carefully evaluated and revised as necessary.

Implications for SST Research

Our results have some important implications for the design of future research in the area. First of all, further exploration of age and gender differences in responsiveness to SST is needed in order to consolidate these findings. While our analysis is useful in comparing the results of different studies, none of the studies included focused specifically and systematically on subject characteristics. It would be very interesting, for example, to apply an intervention of the same basic technique and intensity to subjects sampled from the same population, but of various ages and both sexes. Those conducting studies involving both male and female participants, or a wide age range, should consider conducting and reporting supplementary analyses for age and sex differences in response to training. Possible differences between ethnic groups and socioeconomic levels in responsiveness to SST have not been widely assessed. In such studies, investigators may wish to compare the effectiveness of standard "packaged" SST programs with training procedures in which the skills have been adapted to reflect the social norms of the cultural group. While our data pool is too small to permit meaningful analysis of the interactive effects of the child characteristics (e.g., Age

× Sex, Age × Population), they do warrant further exploration. There may also be important interactive effects between these child characteristics and other effects reported (e.g., Sex × Technique, Age × Therapist, Age × Duration of Treatment).

As noted earlier, most interventions employ a combination of conceptually distinct training techniques. It would be helpful to establish the separate and combined impact of the various components of the more elaborate SST programs.

The combined results of the studies included in our analysis suggest that SST is at least as effective as most other forms of psychotherapy over short periods of time. However, the long-term effectiveness of SST, which has frequently been questioned in the literature (see Cartledge & Milburn, 1980), cannot be readily determined from the data we scanned in the initial stages of this work. It is imperative that the next generation of social skills training research focus adequately on the dimension of long-term change. It is quite conceivable that the variables associated with long-term improvements differ markedly from those reported earlier, which are based on immediate change after training.

The relation between the needs and deficits of the individual trainee and the content of training is receiving increased attention (see Coie, chapter 8 and Dodge, chapter 1 this volume; Schneider & Byrne, 1984). While the importance of tailoring the treatment to the child has been recognized, there is little data to demonstrate the value of the increased time investment involved. Indeed, most of the studies were designed with the assumption that the particular skill or skills trained are in some way lacking by the participants and needed by them. The need for the specific skill was not often established empirically either for the target population or child. While our data pool did permit us to compare the outcomes of various training *modalities* (e.g., modeling, problem solving), it would also be profitable in the future to focus more extensively on the *content* of training. For example, one might wish to establish whether withdrawn children profit most from training in appropriate entry to playgroups, self-expression, eye contact, conversational skill, delivery of reinforcement to peers, or other skills.

The experience of conducting this meta-analysis afforded us the opportunity of comparing notes with researchers who have completed meta-analyses of other psychological and educational interventions. These consultations with colleagues left us with the impression that the methodological standards for published literature in children's social skills training are about as high as for most other forms of treatment. The proportion of studies whose results are applicable to meta-analysis is, in any event, about the same. However, there is room for considerable refinement in the reporting of results. Researchers are, of course, under no obligation to produce results suitable for meta-analysis. However, many of the shortcomings that led to the elimination of studies from our data pool would also have precluded other researchers from replicating the research or making any meaningful use of the findings. Probably the two areas of greatest deficiency were the specification of the intervention procedure and the description of the participants.

Nevertheless, our concluding impression is that the science and art of children's social skills training have attained the degree of maturity that permits those interested to go beyond the global question of whether or not SST is effective to the more productive considerations of skill selection, subject selection, choice of technique, and cost-effectiveness.

References

Barrett, C. L., Hampe, I. E., & Miller, L. C. (1978). Research in child psychotherapy. In S. L. Garfield & A. E. Bergin (Eds.), *Handbook of psychotherapy and behavior change* (pp. 411-437). New York: Wiley.

Carlberg, C., & Kavale, K. (1980). The efficacy of special versus regular class placement for exceptional children: A meta-analysis. *Journal of Special Education, 14*, 295-307.

Cartledge, G., & Milburn, J. (Eds.). (1980). *Teaching social skills to children*. New York: Pergamon.

Cohen, P. A., Kulik, J. A., & Kulik, C. C. (1982). Effects of ability grouping on secondary school students: A meta-analysis of evaluation findings. *American Journal of Educational Research, 19*, 415-428.

Combs, M. L., & Slaby, D. A. (1977). Social skills training with children. In B. Lahey & A. Kazdin (Eds.), *Advances in clinical child psychology*. New York: Plenum.

Conger, J. C., & Keane, S. P. (1981). Social skills intervention in the treatment of isolated or withdrawn children. *Psychological Bulletin, 90*, 478-495.

Glass, G. V. (1976). Primary, secondary, and meta-analysis of research. *Educational Researcher, 5*, 3-8.

Glass, G. V., McGaw, B., & Smith, M. L. (1981). *Meta-analysis in social research*. Beverly Hills, CA: Sage.

Greenglass, E. R. (1982). *A world of difference: Gender roles in perspective*. Toronto: Wiley.

Gresham, F. M. (1981). Social skills training with handicapped children: A review. *Review of Educational Research, 51*, 139-176.

Hansford, B. C., & Hattie, J. A. (1982). The relationship between self and achievement/performance measures. *Review of Educational Research, 52*, 123-142.

Hedges, L. V., & Olkin, L. (1985). *Statistical methods in meta-analysis*. New York: Academic Press.

Johnson, D. W., Johnson, R. T., & Maruyama, G. (1983). Interdependence and interperson attraction among heterogeneous and homogeneous individuals: A theoretical formulation and a meta-analysis of research. *Review of Educational Research, 53*, 5-54.

Kulik, C. C., & Kulik, J. A. (1982). Effects of ability grouping on secondary school students: A meta-analysis of evaluation findings. *American Educational Research Journal, 19*, 415-428.

Kulik, J., Kulik, C., & Bangert, R. (1984). Effects of practice on aptitude and achievement test scores. *American Educational Research Journal, 21*, 435-447.

Schneider, B. H., & Byrne, B. M. (1984, November). *Individualized intervention for social competence*. Paper presented at the meeting of the Association for the Advancement of Behavior Therapy, Philadelphia, PA.

Smith, M. L. (1980). Publication bias and meta-analysis *Evaluation in Education, 4*, 22-24.

Steinkamp, M. W., & Maehr, M. L. (1984). Gender differences in motivational orientations toward achievement in school science: A quantitative synthesis. *American
Educational Research Journal, 21*, 39-59.
Urbain, E. S., & Kendell, P. C. (1980). Review of social-cognitive problem-solving interventions with children. *Psychological Bulletin, 88*, 109-143.
Willson, V. L., & Putnam, P. R. (1982). A meta-analysis of pretest sensitization effects
in experimental design. *American Educational Research Journal, 19*, 5-54.

Appendix: Final Data Pool

Amerikaner, M., & Summerlin, M. L. (1982). Group counseling with learning disabled
children: Effects of social skills and relaxation training on self-concept and classroom
behavior. *Journal of Learning Disabilities, 15*, 340-343.
Bolstad, O. D., & Johnson, S. M. (1972). Self-regulation in the modification of disruptive
classroom behavior. *Journal of Applied Behavior Analysis, 5*, 443-454.
Camp, B. W., Bloom, G. E., Hebert, F., & van Doorminck, W. J. (1977). "Think Aloud":
A program for developing self-control in young aggressive boys. *Journal of Abnormal
Child Psychology, 5*, 157-169.
Chandler, M. J. (1973). Egocentrism and antisocial behavior: The assessment and training
of social perspective-taking skills. *Journal of Developmental Psychology, 9*, 326-332.
Chandler, M. J., Greenspan, S., & Barenboim, C. (1974). Assessment and training of
role-taking and referential communication skills in institutionalized emotionally
disturbed children. *Developmental Psychology, 10*, 546-553.
Elardo, P. T., & Caldwell, B. M. (1979). The effects of an experimental social development program on children in the middle childhood period. *Psychology in the Schools,
16*, 93-100.
Evers, W. L., & Schwarz, J. C. (1973). Modifying social withdrawal in preschoolers: The
effects of filmed modeling and teacher praise. *Journal of Abnormal Child Psychology,
1*, 248-256.
Evers-Pasquale, W. L. (1978). The peer preference test as a measure of reward value: Item
analysis, cross-validation, concurrent validation, and replication. *Journal of Abnormal
Child Psychology, 6*, 175-188.
Evers-Pasquale, W. L., & Sherman, M. (1975). A variable influencing the efficacy of
filmed modeling in modifying social isolation in preschoolers. *Journal of Abnormal
Child Psychology, 3*, 179-189.
Factor, D. C., & Schilmoeller, G. L. (1983). Social skill training of preschool children.
Child Study Journal, 13, 41-56.
Fechter, Jr., J. V. (1971). Modeling and environmental generalization by mentally retard-
ed subjects of televised aggressive or friendly behavior. *American Journal of Mental
Deficiency, 6*, 266-267.
Filipczak, J., Archer, M., & Friedman, R. M. (1980). In-school social skills training: Use
with disruptive adolescents. *Behavioral Modification, 4*, 243-263.
Furman, W., Rahe, D. F., & Hartup, W. W. (1979). Rehabilitation of socially withdrawn
preschool children through mixed-age and same-age socialization. *Child Development,
50*, 915-922.
Geller, M. I., & Scheirer, C. J. (1978). The effect of filmed modeling on cooperative play
in disadvantaged preschoolers. *Journal of Abnormal Child Psychology, 6*, 71-87.

Gottman, J. (1977). The effects of a modeling film on social isolation in preschool children: A methodological investigation. *Journal of Abnormal Child Psychology, 5,* 69-78.

Gresham, F. M., & Nagle, R. J. (1980). Social skills training with children: Responsiveness to modeling and coaching as a function of peer orientation. *Journal of Consulting and Clinical Psychology, 48,* 718-729.

Houtz, J. C., & Feldhusen, J. F. (1976). The modification of fourth graders' problem solving abilities. *The Journal of Psychology, 93,* 229-237.

Iannotti, R. J. (1978). Effect of role-taking experiences on role taking, empathy, altruism, and aggression. *Developmental Psychology, 14,* 119-124.

Jakibchuk, Z., & Smeriglio, V. L. (1976). The influence of symbolic modeling on the social behavior of preschool children with low levels of social responsiveness. *Child Development, 47,* 838-841.

Kaufman, K. F., & O'Leary, K. D. (1972). Reward, cost, and self-evaluation procedures for disruptive adolescents in a psychiatric hospital school. *Journal of Applied Behavior Analysis, 5,* 293-309.

Keller, M. F., & Carlson, P. M. (1974). The use of symbolic modeling to promote social skills in preschool children with low levels of social responsiveness. *Child Development, 45,* 912-919.

Kendall, P. C., & Wilcox, L. E. (1980). Cognitive-behavioral treatment for impulsivity: Concrete versus conceptual training in non-self-controlled problem children. *Journal of Consulting and Clinical Psychology, 48,* 80-91.

Kirschenbaum, D. S. (1979). Social competence intervention and evaluation in the inner city: Cincinnati's social skills development program. *Journal of Consulting and Clinical Psychology, 47,* 778-780.

Ladd, G. W. (1981). Effectiveness of a social learning method for enhancing children's social interaction and peer acceptance. *Child Development, 52,* 171-178.

La Greca, A. M., & Santogrossi, D. A. (1980). Social skills training with elementary school students: A behavioral group approach. *Journal of Consulting and Clinical Psychology, 48,* 220-227.

Mannarino, A. P., Christy, M., Durlak, J. A., & Magnussen, M. G. (1982). Evaluation of social competence training in the schools. *Journal of School Psychology, 20,* 11-19.

Marburg, C. C., Houston, B. K., & Holmes, D. S. (1976). Influence of multiple models on the behavior of institutionalized retarded children: Increased generalization to other models and other behaviors. *Journal of Consulting and Clinical Psychology, 44,* 514-519.

Marsh, D. T., Serafica, F. C., & Barenboim, D. (1980). Effect of perspective-taking training on interpersonal problem solving. *Child Development, 51,* 140-145.

McClure, L. F., Chinsky, J. M., & Larcen, S. W. (1978). Enhancing social problem-solving performance in an elementary school setting. *Journal of Educational Psychology, 70,* 504-513.

O'Connor, M. (1977). The effect of role-taking training on role-taking and social behaviors in young children. *Social Behavior and Personality, 5,* 1-11.

O'Connor, R. D. (1969). Modification of social withdrawal through symbolic modeling. *Journal of Applied Behavior Analysis, 2,* 15-22.

O'Connor, R. D. (1972). Relative efficacy of modeling, shaping, and the combined procedures for modification of social withdrawal. *Journal of Abnormal Psychology, 79,* 327-334.

Oden, S., & Asher, S. R. (1977). Coaching children in social skills for friendship making. *Child Development*, *48*, 495-506.

Peterson, C., Peterson, J., & Scriven, G. (1977). Peer imitation by nonhandicapped and handicapped preschoolers. *Exceptional Children*, *43*, 223-224.

Rickel, A. U., Eshelman, A. K., and Loigman, G. A. (1983). Social problem solving training: A follow-up study of cognitive and behavioral effects. *Journal of Abnormal Child Psychology*, *11*, 15-28.

Robin, A., Schneider, M., & Dolnick, M. (1976). The turtle technique: An extended case study of self-control in the classroom. *Psychology in the Schools*, *13*, 449-453.

Sarason, I. G., & Ganzer, V. J. (1973). Modeling and group discussion in the rehabilitation of juvenile delinquents. *Journal of Counseling Psychology*, *20*, 442-449.

Schneider, B. H. (1984). *Individualized intervention for social competence* (Contract No. MA-512-02-491). Toronto: Ontario Ministry of Education.

Spence, A. J., & Spence, S. H. (1980). Cognitive changes associated with social skills training. *Behavior Research and Therapy*, *18*, 265-272.

Staub, E. (1971). The use of role playing and induction in children's learning of helping and sharing behavior. *Child Development*, *42*, 805-816.

Stone, G. L., Hinds, W. C., & Schmidt, G. W. (1975). Teaching mental health behaviors to elementary school children. *Professional Psychology*, *6*, 34-40.

Talkington, L. W., & Altman, R. (1973). Effects of film-mediated aggressive and affectual models on behavior. *American Journal of Mental Deficiency*, *77*, 420-425.

Turkewitz, H., O'Leary, K. D., & Ironsmith, M. (1975). Generalization and maintenance of appropriate behavior through self-control. *Journal of Consulting and Clinical Psychology*, *43*, 577-583.

Wanat, P. E. (1983). Social skills: An awareness program with learning disabled adolescents. *Journal of Learning Disabilities*, *16*, 35-38.

Weinrott, M. R., Corson, J. A., & Wilchesky, M. (1979). Teacher-mediated treatment of social withdrawal. *Behavior Therapy*, *10*, 281-294.

Yarrow, M. R., Scott, P. M., & Waxler, C. Z. (1973). Learning concern for others. *Developmental Psychology*, *8*, 240-260.

Zahavi, S., & Asher, S. R. (1978). The effect of verbal instructions on preschool children's aggressive behavior. *Journal of School Psychology*, *16*, 146-149.

CHAPTER 12

Programmatic Research on Peers as Intervention Agents for Socially Isolate Classmates

Phillip S. Strain

Over the last 8 years, my colleagues and I have been examining the influence of peer-mediated treatments on the social interactions of young children with significant social, communicative, and cognitive deficits. More specifically, we have devoted most of our efforts toward an examination of social initiations, or interaction bids, and the responses to these interaction bids among various clinical groups.

This line of inquiry has been guided by a specific process model for building social interaction interventions. The proposed process model is built upon four sequential steps or, if you will, research themes that sequentially: (a) address ethologically the significance of the content and style of an intervention; (b) assess the initial effects of intervention on target behaviors; (c) measure the generality of treatment effects; and (d) examine the practicality of intervention use within an ongoing service system. This process model, and its application to the peer social initiation intervention, form the principal themes of this chapter. Each of the four model steps will be described, along with a specific example of how the model steps were implemented with the peer initiation intervention.

Prior to describing the intervention development model, it is important to distinguish between the peer social initiation intervention and the typical social exchanges between preschool children. Two primary differences may be identified. First, the peer social initiation intervention involves a nonreciprocal pattern of interaction in which a child is trained to carry a disproportionate share of the responsibility for beginning (initiating) social interaction with a withdrawn child. In typical social encounters among preschool children, one sees an equal proportion of initiating behavior between peers (Greenwood, Walker, Todd, & Hops, 1981). Second, the peer social initiation intervention differs from typical social encounters in that peer therapists are taught to initiate toward target children using a restricted range of behaviors.

Step 1 of Intervention Development Model

The first step is *to establish the developmental relevance or the naturally occurring social processes upon which the intervention procedures themselves and the target skills are based*. One need not go beyond the fingers on a single hand to count the number of interventions in which the target skills have been derived empirically. By empirically derived, I refer to evidence indicating that individuals who engage in the designated skills have more positive social contacts, are more liked, have more friends, and so on, than persons who do not. For the most part, it is clear that the intervention techniques (e.g., reinforcement, modeling, coaching, group contingencies) most widely used to improve the peer social performance of young children have no conceptual or empirical link to the target behaviors. In fact, our most frequently used interventions bear little or no resemblance to the natural processes of peer influence.

Why should interventions mimic extant environmental supports for peer interaction? This question is fundamental, especially when we consider that our "artificial" interventions are spectacularly effective on occasion. The answers to the question lie in a careful and critical evaluation of intervention effectiveness and alternatives to current intervention modalities. Hops (1983) and Strain and Fox (1981) noted that social interaction treatments for disabled populations have yet to produce other than transient, setting-specific effects. On the other hand, there are repeated demonstrations of large behavioral changes (still limited over time and environments) in children who essentially started from "ground zero" in terms of positive peer interactions (e.g., Strain, Shores, & Kerr, 1976; Whitman, Mercurio, & Caponigri, 1970; Young & Kerr, 1979). On balance, we might conclude that available interventions for disabled populations often produce clear functional or statistically significant effects; however, the developmental relevance, social significance, and generalized effects of said interventions are questionable.

When we examine closely the nature of interventions used to date to improve the peer social skills of disabled children, our limited treament success seems more predictable than surprising. First, the brevity of interventions is most evident. For example, typical adult and peer interventions may be in effect for a 20-min period once each day for 20-40 days. Assuming the maximum strength dose, we have a 13½-hr treatment for a complex skill deficit that may have a multiple-year history! While the 20- to 40-day period may be sufficient to yield statistically significant effects, such a time frame is limited clinically.

We know that the procedural characteristics of many interventions produce less than favorable outcomes, along with obvious benefits. For example, the powerful reinforcing quality of an attentive adult can increase the frequency of a child's interactions but also yield too brief interaction episodes that are "interrupted" by reinforcement delivery (Greenwood, Walker, Todd, & Hops, 1981; Shores, Strain, & Hester, 1976). Also, persistent overtures to play directed by a teacher to a withdrawn child can increase the frequency of the target child's social responding but also limit the opportunities for reciprocal play initiations (Strain & Fox, 1981). We often find that the predictable, highly structured nature of most social skills interventions lead to rapid acquisition of new skills, but also to the display of these skills in similarly contrived settings only (Odom & Strain, in press). In summary, many of the most widely used social skill interventions that have *not* been derived empirically yield both positive and negative effects.

Assuming the accuracy of this intervention critique, how should we interpret our current body of outcome data and what procedural alternatives are evident? In answer to the first question, overwrought pessimism and fingerpointing seem very inappropriate. On the contrary, if episodic, occasionally counterproductive interventions can produce relatively clear effects on both functional and non-functional target behaviors, then we should be optimistic about the prospects for more carefully designed interventions and more carefully selected target skills. In answer to the second question, a return to the naturalistic study of peer social skills seems necessary. Via such naturalistic study we can identify functional skills and intervention procedures that minimize untoward effects.

In applying naturalistic methods to the building of our social initiation intervention, we began with a study of 60 normally developing 3-, 4-, and 5-year-olds. Through a series of direct observations in free-play settings, and subsequent sequential analysis of the obtained interaction data, several specific social initiations were identified as reliably setting the occasion for positive interaction with peers. These behaviors included: organizing play (e.g., "Let's play house," "You play Mommy, I'll be Daddy"), sharing toys or materials, physically assisting another with a task or apparatus, showing affection (e.g., pats, hugs), and rough-and-tumble play (see Hendrickson, Strain, Tremblay, & Shores, 1982, for a complete account).

The next task was to test the generality of these observational findings in classroom groups comprised of normally developing and disabled children. In a study involving 80 children (40 disabled) very similar interaction patterns were found. Additionally, the "effective" social initiations were found to be characteristic of disabled children who were more likely to be selected as friends by the normally developing children (see Strain, 1983, 1984). Based upon these naturalistic data, we were able to identify intervention procedures (specific social bids) and behavioral targets (specific social bids) that were likely to produce optimal results for young disabled children.

Step 2 of Intervention Development Model

The second step in the proposed intervention development model is *to establish the initial effectiveness of the empirically derived intervention on functional target behaviors*. There are many available research strategies by which to demonstrate the effects of social skill interventions on target behaviors. These strategies may be divided into two broad categories: (a) between-groups procedures; and, (b) within-subjects experimental techniques. While the choice of experimental procedure most often seems dictated by conceptual bias and matters of convenience, the major issues associated with this intervention development step may lead toward the within-subject option.

In the initial development phases of building an intervention technique, three issues should have major importance. First, we need to know if the intervention (independent variable in the experimental context) can be precisely defined, implemented, and measured. Operationalizing the intervention and carefully monitoring the fidelity of its implementation is an absolute prerequisite for accurate replications.

Second, we need to know *when* the intervention effect takes place. Do we need 3 hr or 3 months, on average, to see an effect? This timing issue is paramount with disabled children, who, by definition, require the optimally *efficient* treatment (see Deno & Mirkin, 1977, for a thorough discussion of intervention efficiency). Monitoring the timing of effects is also made essential by the probable nonlinearity of the intervention-social skill relationship. For example, more intervention may not be better. Optimal effects may occur relatively early and taper off as a function of boredom, satiation, and so on. The third issue of principal concern at this intervention step is to document, indeed to highlight, any subject-specific effects that may lead to further study regarding who is and who is not a good candidate for the intervention.

For each of these three issues—the precise description and monitoring of the independent variable, measurement of the timing of intervention effects, and the documentation of subject-specific effects—I suggest that the traditions and methods of single subject procedures make them the best design alternative.

In applying single subject designs to the building of our social initiation intervention we began a series of studies in which normally developing preschool children were taught to direct effective social initiations toward disabled peers with poorly developed social skills. Since our naturalistic data indicated that the normally developing children would typically (with normally developing peers) be met with a positive response when they engaged in the designated initiations, it was essential to develop a training strategy to guard against intervention agents terminating their initiations when responses from target children were not immediately forthcoming. Specifically, a role-play and rehearsal strategy was employed whereby intervention agents were trained to engage in desired initiations in a context that mimicked the social withdrawal of the target subjects. On alternate training trials the adult trainer engages in behavior typical of the target subjects (e.g., adult trainer might turn away, engage in some incompatible behavior). Then, the adult trainer explained that sometimes the target children would act this way, but that it was the intervention agent's job to keep trying to engage the target child in social play. Table 12.1 summarizes a typical training regimen. In addition to the role-play and rehearsal strategy, peer intervention agents have often been provided with some tangible consequences during the course of their involvement with target children. For example, peer intervention agents have earned hamburgers, trinkets, and access to favorite activities. These rewards have not been made contingent upon any criterion level of behavior, but rather have been given for participation only.

In regard to the precise description and monitoring of the independent variable, specific peer initiations as depicted in Table 12.1 were incorporated into observational protocols. As such, it has been possible to link individual social initiations with effectiveness data. As a result of the daily monitoring of specific initiations, we have been able to determine that: (a) motor-gestural initiations generally lead

TABLE 12.1. Training procedures employed during each of four peer instructional sessions.

Training procedures	Desired peer behavior	Consequences and schedule of delivery
Session 1		
The teacher instructs the peer that he is going to learn how to help the teacher by getting other children to play with him. The teacher indicates that asking children to play a particular game is what they will practice first. Teacher then models appropriate behavior and asks peer to try asking him to play (sequence has 10 repeats)	"Come play," "Let's play school," "Let's play ball," etc.	Teacher delivers social praise to peer on an FR 2 schedule Teacher ignores every other response, then says, "Many times children will not want to play at first, but you need to keep asking them to play"
The teacher instructs the peer that it is also important to give children toys to play with. The teacher models appropriate behavior and asks peer to try giving him something to play with when he invites him to play (sequence has 20 repeats)	Verbal behavior identical to that shown above plus handing a play object (ball, block, toy truck, etc.) to teacher	Teacher delivers social praise to confederate on a FR 2 schedule Teacher ignores every other response, then says, "Sometimes children won't play, even when you ask nicely and give them something to play with, but you will need to keep trying very hard to get them to play"
Sessions 2, 3, 4		
Repeat of Session 1	Same as Session 1	Same as Session 1

to greater responsiveness than verbal initiations with cognitively impaired subjects; (b) target children most often respond to initiations with topographically identical behaviors (e.g., share initiations are followed by share responses); and, (c) initiations of affection are generally more effective when directed toward girls rather than boys.

Concerning the timing of intervention effects, repeated social bids have been found to result in immediate and substantial behavior change (see, for example, Hendrickson, Strain, Tremblay, & Shores, 1982). While most subjects do show some gradual improvement throughout the peer-mediated intervention, the large fraction of the total behavior change is realized early on in treatment. Without a daily record of intervention effects, as single case designs demand, this timing effect would be lost.

In terms of subject-specific effects, one of the more interesting treatment relationships revealed in these single subject designs is the lack of predictive power of the baseline phase. That is, some of the most profound behavior changes can be found with children who essentially engage in no positive social interactions *for several days* prior to intervention—an important assessment and treatment implication being that level of social disability should not be used to rule out eligible children from peer-initiation treatment.

Step 3 of Intervention Development Model

The third step in the intervention development model is *to replicate treatment effects on diverse clinical groups*. At this stage of intervention development we are concerned with the generality of effects across potential clients and the modification of program components to meet the idiosyncratic needs of certain children.

To date, the peer-initiation treatment has been used successfully with the following groups: preschool-age disabled children with the following diagnoses—autism, mental retardation, conduct disorders (the original clinical group); elementary-age disabled children with the following diagnoses—mental retardation, autism, conduct disorders; adolescent autistic youth; visually impaired elementary-age children; and, geriatric mentally retarded persons.

To illustrate the range of procedural modifications necessary for the successful implementation of the peer-initiation treatment across diverse groups, intervention efforts with visually impaired elementary-age children and geriatric mentally retarded persons are highlighted in the following. In our treatment effort with visually impaired children, several procedural modifications were required (Sisson, Van Hasselt, Hersen, & Strain, in press). First, we are dealing with older peer trainers who we suspected had developed some ideas about disabled persons, what they were like, why they were different, and so on. Based upon prior work (Gottlieb, 1975), we also suspected that many of their ideas were likely to be perjorative. Thus, we began intervention agent training with a didactic-like experience in which the adult trainers described various handicapping conditions (e.g., blindness, learning problems, hearing loss, physical disability) and then elicited questions and comments from the peer trainers. To further assist the peer trainers in understanding disabilities, they were asked to wear blindfolds and earmuffs while they played with toys. This experience was followed by another round of questions and comments from peer trainers.

A second necessary modification to the original intervention package involved the alteration of specific peer initiations to match the subjects' visual disability. Recall that organizing play, sharing toys, providing physical assistance, showing affection, and rough-and-tumble play were the initiations originally used by peer trainers. These initiations were modified such that the peer trainers were taught to provide necessary tactile and physical cues to the subjects. For example, play initiations were often preceded or accompanied by attempts to physically guide the target children in the direction of the play apparatus (e.g., tapping child on shoulder before requesting to play, guiding child's hand to a ball). Interestingly, the procedural changes produced treatment effects that were fundamentally equivalent to those achieved earlier with sighted preschoolers.

Certainly, the most severe modification of the peer-initiation strategy has involved elderly mentally retarded peer trainers and target subjects (Dy, Strain, Fullerton, & Stowitschek, 1981). This study involved the training of two peer confederates who each worked with two target subjects. Because of the confederate's level of intellectual functioning, we developed an extensive scripted role-play procedure to teach social initiation skills. An example of a daily routine is provided in Table 12.2.

In addition to this extensive role-play procedure, we added a prompting procedure whereby an adult was available to prompt confederate initiations, if needed, during actual training sessions. During the course of treatment we were able to fade the intensity of rehearsals and prompts to minimal levels without detrimental effects.

Beyond these treatment procedure modifications, we significantly altered the topography of initiations to correspond with the subjects' interests, age, and intellectual functioning.

While countless replications with other clinical groups are possible, it seems relatively safe to assume that the peer-initiation strategy is sufficiently robust and malleable as to be effective across many disability and age groups.

Step 4 of Intervention Development Model

The final step in the intervention development model is *to integrate the circumscribed treatment into an ongoing clinical program*. Here, the basic questions are whether and how the intervention can be used on a more wide-scale basis. To date, our efforts at system-wide implementation have focused on the development of a preschool intervention model for the treatment of autistic-like children (Hoyson, Jamieson, & Strain, 1984; Strain, Hoyson, & Jamieson, in press).

In order to implement a system-wide peer-initiation treatment, ten nonhandicapped children were recruited on a first-come, first-served basis from a lower-middle-income community in Pittsburgh, Pennsylvania. Five male and five female children who began the program between the ages of 36 and 48 months participated. Each youngster's initial performance on developmental measures indicated functioning at or near expected age-levels.

Autistic-like children ($N=6$) who participated were recruited from the metropolitan Pittsburgh area. Each youngster met the following inclusionary criteria: (a) been diagnosed, using DSM-III criteria, by an independent agency as autistic or austistic-like; (b) been observed during a 1-week evaluation/screening period to engage in repeated episodes of self-stimulation; (c) been observed

TABLE 12.2. Format of the role play procedure.

Procedural description [experimenter (E); confederate (C); observer (O)]	Sample script
A. Experimenter demonstration (3-5 min): E initiated interaction with the observer (O) by emitting motor/gestural and vocal/verbal behaviors. O simulated the reactions of the real target subject. This allowed E to focus the confederate's (C) attention to the task related motor/gestural and vocal/verbal behaviors that were effective in getting the particular target subject to respond. During the first few sessions it was necessary for E to provide explanations between demonstrations. As C became more proficient (based on her performance with the actual target subject), the amount of explanation was decreased as was the length of demonstration time	E to C: "C, watch me get O to put together this puzzle with me. Let's pretend that O here is Lou (name of target)." O: talked non-stop to herself. E to O: "Lou, here's a puzzle piece," as E handed O a puzzle piece. O: continued talking and ignored E. E to C: "Lou has a hard time paying attention. You have to put the puzzle piece into her hand." E to O: "Here's a puzzle piece Lou," as E handed the puzzle piece to O. O: took the puzzle piece and attempted to place it but couldn't find the correct place. Still talking. E to O: "Put it here Lou" (while pointing) O: put the puzzle piece in correctly. E to O: "Good. Here's another Lou" as E handed a puzzle piece to O. O: took the puzzle piece and E helped O put in the piece correctly.
B. Confederate practice (5-7 min): E initially reviewed the desired motor/gestural and vocal/verbal behaviors with C. Then C proceeded to role play with O, who again simulated the target subject's behavior. E prompted C when C was not emitting the desired initiation behaviors or when the initiation was one which would be unlikely to be responded to by the particular target subject. Occasionally, explanations were given by E regarding the necessity of specific initiation behaviors although this was only given when absolutely needed (i.e., when C kept on repeating the same error or when such initiation may trigger violent reactions from the real target subject). Throughout the session, O reacted to C's initiations as the target subject would. E occasionally praised C for emitting the desired behaviors. The session always ended with a positive comment	E to C: "Let's go over how you should get Lou to put together the puzzle with you. First, you should remember to put the puzzle piece right into her hands, and remember say something like "Here's a puzzle." Also Lou would need your help putting together the puzzle. You think you can remember all that? How about practicing now." C to O: "We'll put together the puzzle Lou" as C hands a puzzle piece to Lou. O: continued talking and ignored C. E to C: "Put it right in her hand and say, 'Here's a puzzle piece.'" C to O: "Here Lou," as C tapped Lou's hand with the puzzle piece. O: took the puzzle piece and waved it around as she continued talking. E to C: "Look's like Lou needs some help." C: Hold's O's hand and guides her to put in the puzzle piece saying, "Right there." E to C: "That's right, good."

during a 1-week evaluation/screening period to engage in no or minimal functional speech; (d) been observed during a 1-week evaluation/screening period to engage in prolonged tantrums; (e) been observed during a 1-week evaluation/screening period to engage in no or minimal positive interaction with peers; and, (f) been observed to function in the mild to severe range of retardation based upon administration of the McCarthy Scales of Children's Abilities. The six children who participated ranged in age from 30 to 53 months at the beginning of treatment. Exclusionary criteria employed in the recruitment process included: (a) primary mental retardation syndrome (e.g., Down's Syndrome); (b) physical evidence of central nervous system dysfunction; and, (c) current utilization of psychotropic medications.

Over the course of a 2-year period, 10 normally developing children (no more than 6 at one time) and the 6 autistic-like children, were enrolled in a 3-h/day, 5 day/week, 11-month preschool program. The use of normally developing children as instructional resources took three forms: (a) peers as indirect mediators of behavior change; (b) peers as behavioral models; and, (c) peers as direct agents of training. Each of these procedures is described in the following.

As indirect mediators of behavior change, the normally functioning age-peers and handicapped children participated in an interdependent classroom-wide contingency. For example, during a 15-min group instructional period, each of the nonhandicapped children may have a behavioral goal of answering 100% of teacher questions correctly. During this same time period, one of the handicapped children may have the goal of remaining in the assigned seat for 80% of the time; another handicapped child may have the goal of looking at the teacher when spoken to on 80% of the opportunities; still another handicapped child may have the goal of not body-rocking more than 10% of the time interval. For any of the children to receive a positive consequence, each must meet their goal.

In their role as behavioral models, nonhandicapped children participated in a Peer Imitation Training (PIT) program as outlined by Peck, Appolloni, Cooke, and Raver (1978). Here, a handicapped and nonhandicapped child are paired together for training. The nonhandicapped child is trained initially to model specific appropriate behaviors by an accompanying teacher. The teacher then prompts the handicapped child to imitate the modeled behavior and subsequently reinforces correct responding. Daily PIT sessions typically include 20-30 opportunities for children to imitate appropriate behaviors. In addition to the PIT procedures, which are designed to develop basic prerequisite skills in order for these severely handicapped children to profit from exposure to appropriate behavioral models, all daily group activities (e.g., free play, worktable time, snack time) were structured so as to enhance the likelihood of positive, appropriate behaviors being imitated by target children.

Probably the most consistent finding regarding the clinical implementation of the observational learning paradigm is that the model child's behavior must be obviously consequated (reinforced) by events that are also reinforcing to handicapped children (Strain & Hill, 1978; Strain & Kerr, 1979). Accordingly, teachers implement the following instructional procedures: (a) provide direct verbal, and where necessary, physical prompts for handicapped children to observe their peers (in a worktable example, "Jonathan, watch Tim hammer"); (b) provide direct reinforcers (any which are effective with *both* children) to the nonhandicapped child while specifying the desired behavior(s) ("Tim, I like the way you hit the peg with the hammer, you earned a piece of pretzel"); (c) provide direct verbal and, where necessary, physical prompts to the handicapped child to initiate imitative behavior ("Jonathan, you use your hammer like Tim"); and, (d) provide direct positive consequences to the handicapped child for approximations toward accurate imitation.

As direct agents of training, the normally developing children were exposed to a regimen very much like that detailed in Table 12.1. Specifically, nonhandicapped children were given an explanation of the task, such as, "Try hard to get the others to play with you." "Training to expect rejection" was accomplished through a role play in which the adult ignored every other initiation by the peer helper, explained this behavior, and, finally, encouraged the peer helper: "Keep trying, even when children don't play at first" (Strain, Shores, & Timm, 1977). These training steps were repeated in 20-min daily sessions (usually four), until the peer helpers could reliably make social bids to the occasionally reluctant adult.

In order to assess the effects of this system-wide peer-initiation, a multiple baseline across play settings was employed to assess social behavior outcomes. The design and accompanying data are depicted in Figure 12.1.

Figure 12.1 presents multiple baseline across settings data averaged across the autistic-like participants. Baseline data demonstrated a low, stable frequency of positive social behaviors during each of the three 10-min play periods. A clear demonstration of experimental control is evident in that behavioral improvement was noted only when peer-mediated intervention was applied. The dashed lines in each panel represent the range of performance demonstrated by normally developing children in each of the play settings. Across each setting the autistic-like children's eventual treatment level of positive interaction fell within the range established by their nonhandicapped peers.

Conclusions and Future Directions

In order to evaluate the effectiveness of the peer social initiation strategy and the utility of the overall intervention development model, it is necessary to recount some of the more universally accepted facts about the *purposeful* development of exceptional children's social skills.

First, almost all exceptional children, regardless of their disability or the etiology of that disability, have significant social handicaps. Often, the specific handicap is in the form of skill deficits (e.g., lack of verbal skills, lack of knowledge about how to make friends). It is also true, however, that the *primary* social handicap of many exceptional children rests with negative and biased peer attitudes and behaviors. Of course, most often we are confronted with a situation in which skill deficits interact with negative peer attitudes and behaviors.

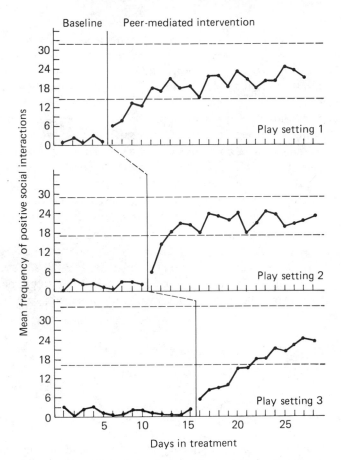

FIGURE 12.1. Autistic-like children's level of positive social behavior prior to and following peer-mediated instruction in each of three play settings.

Second, since the social behavior problems of exceptional chidlren often involve *both* skill deficits and negative peer perceptions and behaviors, skill training for exceptional children is a necessary but not sufficient tactic for maximizing pleasant, growth-enhancing social contacts for these youngsters. The social initiation tactic seems particularly efficient in that peers acquire skills that make them more successful in their efforts to interact with disabled classmates; and, of course, target children's behavior improves as well.

Third, the social skills and competencies of exceptional *and* normally developing children are stable behavior patterns. Put very strongly, when intervention is not available, no "spontaneous" improvement can be expected in this domain. Not only is there continuity across the childhood years in social competence, but there seems to be a strong relationship between early social isolation and maladjustment in adolescence and adulthood.

Fourth, while we know a great deal about tactics for producing changes in exceptional children's social behaviors, the *content* of instruction remains a major, unresolved issue. To date, most targets of instruction have been selected on the basis of professional judgment only. The initial ethological research step in the proposed intervention development model represents one attempt to rectify this problem.

Based upon our initial success with the peer initiation tactic, we are now pursuing the following: (a) an examination of cross-setting generalization; (b) a long-term study on outcomes for normally developing peer trainers; (c) a comparison of effects obtained by single versus multiple peer trainers; (d) a meta-analysis of outcomes produced by adult- versus peer-based interventions; and, (e) the development and field-testing of a curriculum package designed to train preschool personnel in the implementation of the system-wide peer-initiation model.

Acknowledgments. Preparation of this chapter was supported by NIMH Grant #37110-03 and Department of Education Contract #300-82-0368 to the University of Pittsburgh. However, the opinions expressed herein do not necessarily reflect the position or policy of either agency, and no official endorsement should be inferred.

References

Deno, S. L., & Mirkin, P. K. (1977). *Data-based program modification: A model.* Reston, VA: The Council for Exceptional Children.

Dy, E. B., Strain, P. S., Fullerton, A., & Stowitschek, J. (1981). Training institutionalized, elderly mentally retarded persons as intervention agents for socially isolate peers. *Analysis and Intervention in Developmental Disabilities*, *1*, 199-215.

Gottlieb, J. (1975). Public, peer, and professional attitudes toward mentally retarded persons. In M. Begab & S. Richardson (Eds.), *The mentally retarded and society*. Baltimore: University Park Press.

Greenwood, C. R., Walker, H. M., Todd, N. M., & Hops, H. (1981). Normative and descriptive analysis of preschool freeplay social interaction rates. *Journal of Pediatric Psychology*, *4*, 343-367.

Hendrickson, J. M., Strain, P. S., Tremblay, A., & Shores, R. E. (1982). Interactions of behaviorally handicapped children: Functional effects of peer social initations. *Behavior Modification*, *6*, 323-353.

Hops, H. (1983). Children's social competence and skills: Current research practices and future directions. *Behavior Therapy*, *14*, 3-18.

Hoyson, M. H., Jamieson, B., & Strain, P. S. (1984). Individualized group instruction of normally developing and autistic-like children. The LEAP curriculum model. *Journal of the Division for Early Childhood*, *8*, 157-172.

Odom, S. L., & Strain, P. S. (in press). Peer-mediated approaches for promoting children's social interaction: A review. *American Journal of Orthopsychiatry*.

Peck, C. A., Apolloni, T., Cooke, T. P., & Raver, S. (1978). Teaching retarded preschool children to imitate nonhandicapped peers: Training and generalized effects. *Journal of Special Education*, *12*, 195-207.

Shores, R. E., Strain, P. S., & Hester, P. (1976). The effects of amount and type of teacher-child interaction on child-child interaction during free-play. *Psychology in the Schools*, *3*, 171-175.

Sisson, L. A., Van Hasselt, V., Hersen, M., & Strain, P. S. (in press). Increasing social behaviors in multihandicapped children through peer intervention. *Behavior Modification*.

Strain, P. S. (1983). Identification of social skill curriculum targets for severely handicapped children in mainstreamed preschools. *Applied Research in Mental Retardation*, *4*, 369-382.

Strain, P. S. (1984). Social behavior patterns of nonhandicapped and developmentally disabled friend pairs in mainstream preschools. *Analysis and Intervention in Developmental Disabilities*, *4*, 15-28.

Strain, P. S., & Fox, J. J. (1981). Peer social initiations and the modification of social withdrawal: A review and future perspective. *Journal of Pediatric Psychology*, *6*, 417-433.

Strain, P. S., & Hill, A. D. (1981). Social interaction. In P. Wehman (Ed.), *Recreation programming for developmentally disabled persons*. Baltimore: University Park Press.

Strain, P. S., Hoyson, M., & Jamieson, B. (in press). Class deportment and social outcomes for normally developing and autistic-like children in an integrated preschool. *Journal of the Division of Early Childhood*.

Strain, P. S., & Kerr, M. M. (1979). Treatment issues in the remediation of preschool children's social isolation. *Education and Treatment of Children*, *2*, 197-208.

Strain, P. S., Shores, R. E., & Kerr, M. M. (1976). An experimental analysis of "spillover" effects on the social interaction of behaviorally handicapped preschool children. *Journal of Applied Behavior Analysis*, *9*, 31-40.

Strain, P. S., Shores, R. E., & Timm, M. A. (1977). Effects of peer initiations on the social behavior of withdrawn preschool children. *Journal of Applied Behavior Analysis*, *10*, 289-298.

Whitman, T. L., Mercurio, J. R., & Caponigri, V. (1970). Development of social responses in two severely retarded children. *Journal of Applied Behavior Analysis*, *3*, 133-138.

Young, C. C., & Kerr, M. M. (1979). The effect of a retarded child's initiations on the behavior of severely retarded school-aged peers. *Education and Treatment of the Mentally Retarded*, *14*, 185-190.

CHAPTER 13

Social Behavior Problems and Social Skills Training in Adolescence

Michael Argyle

Adolescence is a very interesting time of life for psychologists to study, but often very difficult for those involved: adolescents and their families. The difficulties lie mainly in the sphere of social behavior, and recent developments in the study of interaction have a lot to contribute here. The main practical application is in devising methods of social skills training for adolescents with social difficulties, and in advising parents and others who deal with them on the most effective ways of doing so.

Social Difficulties in Adolescence

Most adolescents find some social situations difficult. Bryant and Trower (1974) surveyed a 10% sample of Oxford undergraduates and found that a high proportion reported moderate or severe difficulty with common social situations, especially "approaching others" (36%), "going to dances/discotheques" (35%) and "going to parties" (26%). These were the figures for second-year students; first-year students reported much higher levels of difficulty. Nine percent of second-year students reported "moderate difficulty" or avoidance of 6 common situations out of 30 and were regarded as suffering from serious social problems. Zimbardo (1977) surveyed large samples of American and other students aged 18-21 and found that about 40% considered themselves to be "shy" now, while very few said that they had never been shy. Many adolescents feel lonely, 15%-20% feel "seriously lonely," 55%-65% "often feel lonely," girls more often than boys (Brennan, 1982).

Some situations are commonly found most difficult. Furnham and Argyle (1981) surveyed 143 adolescents and young adults, and found clusters of difficult situations (see Table 13.1). In my experience of social skills training, the most common difficulty for young neurotic outpatients is in making friends, or in making friends with the opposite sex. Social situations are found to be difficult when they involve the likelihood of conflict or rejection by others, intimacy, sexual or otherwise, public performances, or complex rules and rituals (Agryle, Furnham, & Graham, 1981).

Adolescents may also make life very difficult for others, as studies of their parents show. Marital happiness reaches its lowest period when the children are

TABLE 13.1. Difficult social situation clusters.
___

Assertiveness
  1. Complaining to a neighbor about noisy disturbance
  9. Taking an unsatisfactory article back to a shop

Intimacy
  2. Taking a person of the opposite sex out for the first time
  4. Visiting a doctor when unwell

Counseling
  6. Going around to cheer up a depressed friend
  5. Going to a close relative's funeral

Public performance
  8. Give short speech
  7. Being host at a large party
  3. Going for a job interview

Parties, and so on
  13. Going to a function with many people from a different culture
  14. Attending a wedding
___

adolescents (Walker, 1977). The standard social skills approach is to compare effective and ineffective performers of a skill, find where they differ, and teach the effective skills to others. Research of this kind has also shown the main areas of social competence—nonverbal communication, conversation, rewardingness, and so on, to which we now turn.

The Components of Social Competence

Competent social performance consists of a number of component skills, each of which is important, and some of which may go wrong in a number of different ways. If competent and incompetent performers are compared, for example popular and unpopular adolescents, they are found to differ on these components.

Nonverbal Communication

When successful and less successful performers of a skill are compared, nonverbal communication (NVC) is always found to be an important area of difference. Trower (1980) found that socially skilled patients looked, smiled, and gestured more than unskilled ones. Romano and Bellack (1980) found that ratings on assertiveness were predictable from smiling and vocal intonation. NVC consists of facial expression, tone of voice, gaze, gesture, postures, physical proximity, and appearance. NVC is important in the communication of emotions and attitudes to other people. A *sender* is in a certain state, or possesses some information; this is *encoded* into a message which is then *decoded* by a *receiver*.

We carried out some experiments comparing the impact of initially equated verbal and nonverbal signals, when combined, for friendly-hostile and superior-inferior. The nonverbal component had a far greater impact, and where the cues were conflicting the verbal was virtually ignored (Argyle, Salter, Nicholson, Williams, & Burgess, 1970).

More socially skilled people are better decoders of nonverbal signals. Anxious people overestimate signs of rejection; delinquents fail to see how much they are annoying others. Women are on average more accurate than men, despite a tendency to be more "polite" decoders, that is, they attend more to faces than to the leakier vocal and bodily channels, and therefore see what people want them to see (Hall, 1979).

Verbal Communication—Conversation

Socially inadequate people are usually very ineffective in the sphere of verbal communication, too. They often speak very little, fail to ask questions or to show an interest in others, and fail to produce the kinds of utterances that will be effective in particular situations or sustain conversations. They may be inadequate in the use of NYC to accompany speech. Trower (1980) found that the main difference in behavior between socially inadequate and other patients was that the latter talked more.

Conversational sequences are constructed partly out of certain basic building blocks, like the question-answer sequence, and repeated cycles characteristic of the situation. Socially inadequate people are usually very bad conversationalists and this appears to be due to a failure to master some of these basic sequences.

The social skill model described later generates a characteristic kind of four-step sequence (Figure 13.1). This is a case of asymmetrical interaction with A in charge. A's first move, A_1, produces an unsatisfactory result, B_1, so A modifies his behavior to A_2, which produces the desired B_2. Note the link A_1-A_2, representing the persistence of A's goal-directed behavior. The model can be extended to cases where both interactors are pursuing goals simultaneously, as in the following example, from a selection interview:

I_1: How well did you do at physics in school?

R_1: Not very well, I was better at chemistry.

I_2: What were your marks?

R_2: I got a C in physics, and an A in chemistry.

I_3: That's very good.

A valuable approach to conversational skills is through the formulation of maxims, of which those by Grice (1975) are the best known. He suggested maxims such as "be relevant to what has been said before," "be responsive to previous

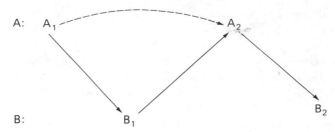

FIGURE 13.1.

speakers," "make your contribution no less and no more informative than is required." Other maxims that can be suggested are "hand over the conversation," "be polite," and "be friendly." Conversations can be regarded as competitive games, in which each person makes tactical moves, which are responsive to what has gone before and could lead to a possible successful outcome for the actor (Clarke, 1983). Politeness is also important—to avoid damaging others' self-esteem or constraining their autonomy (Brown & Levinson, 1978). Women have been found to be more polite, powerful people less so (Baxter, 1984). Humor is another conversational skill—it can avert conflict and soften criticism by discharging tension and redefining the situation as less serious or threatening.

Rewardingness

One effect of reinforcement is in the control of others' behavior. If A consistently gives small signs of approval immediately after B produces some form of behavior, the frequency of that behavior is rapidly increased (or decreased following disapproval). This is one of the main processes whereby people are able to modify each other's behavior in the desired direction. Clearly, if people do not give clear, immediate and consistent reinforcements, positive and negative, they will not be able to influence others in this way, and social encounters will be correspondingly more frustrating and difficult for them. This appears to be a common problem with many psychiatric patients who characteristically fail to control or try to overcontrol others.

Rewardingess also affects popularity. There are a number of different sources of popularity and unpopularity but there is little doubt that being a source of rewards is one of the most important (Rubin, 1973). A person may be rewarding because the interaction with him is enjoyable, for example making love, playing squash; he may be rewarding because he is kind, helpful, interesting, and so on; and some people are rewarding just by being attractive or of high status.

Taking the Role of the Other

There are individual differences in the ability to see another person's point of view, as measured by tests in which subjects are asked to describe situations as perceived by others. Those who are good at it have been found to do better at a number of social tasks (Feffer & Suchotliff, 1966) and to be more altruistic. Meldman (1967) found that psychiatric patients are more egocentric, that is, talk about themselves more than controls, and it has been our experience that socially unskilled patients have great difficulty in taking the role of the other. This appears to be a cognitive ability which develops with age (Flavell, 1968), but which may fail to develop properly.

Self-Presentation

When the self is activated, there is heightened physiological arousal, and greater concern with the impression made on others. This often results in some degree of "self-presentation," that is, sending information about the self. This is done partly to sustain self-esteem, and partly for professional purposes—teachers teach more effectively if their pupils think they are well informed, for example. If people tell others how good they are in words, this is regarded as a joke and disbelieved, at least in western cultures. Jones (1964) found that verbal ingratiation is done with subtlety—for example, drawing attention to assets in unimportant areas. Most self-presentation is done nonverbally: by clothes, hair style, accent, badges, and general style of behavior. Social class is very clearly signaled in these ways, as is membership of rebellious social groups (Argyle, 1975). Self-presentation is needed in all social skills, but especially in those that require performance in front of an audience, or where it is important to win the confidence of clients.

Physical attractiveness (PA) can be regarded as part of self-presentation, since it is partly, even mainly, under an individual's control. Attention to clothes, hair and skin, binding or padding, height of shoes or hat, diet and exercise, facial expression, and posture can do a great deal for PA. People who are attractive are believed, rightly or wrongly, to be superior in all sorts of ways, are liked more, and are treated better (Berscheid & Walster, 1974). The faces of mental patients were less attractive before they became patients and they became less attractive while being patients (Napoleon, Chassin, & Young, 1980).

A related area is *self-disclosure*. When getting to know someone it is important to keep to the rules—gradual disclosure, starting with safe topics, moving to more important ones, each reciprocating the other's disclosures. We shall see that one of the causes of loneliness is insufficient self-disclosure and intimacy of conversations. Females on average disclose more, and are disclosed to more, than males (Jourard, 1971).

A normally competent interactor sends mainly nonverbal signals to indicate his role, status, or other aspects of his identity. From these signals others know what to expect, including what rewards are likely to be forthcoming, and how to deal with him. Self-presentation can go wrong in a number of ways: (a) bogus claims which are unmasked; (b) being too "gray," that is, sending too little information; (c) sending too much, overdramatizing, as hysterical personalities sometimes do; (d) inappropriate self-presentation (a female research student who looks and sounds like a retired professor).

The Analysis of Social Situations

We saw earlier that certain situations are often found difficult (Table 13.1). Clients for social skills training (SST) usually report difficulty with particular social situations. The traditional trait model supposed that individuals possess a fixed degree of introversion, neuroticism, and so on, and that it is displayed consistently in different situations. This model has been abandoned by most psychologists because of an increased awareness of the great effect of the situation on behavior (e.g., people are more anxious when exposed to physical danger than when asleep in bed), and the amount of person-situation interaction (e.g., person A is more frightened by heights, person B by cows), resulting in low intersituational consistency (Mischel, 1968).

A number of studies have shown that patients are *less* variable in their behavior between situations, and that psychotics are less variable than neurotics (e.g., Moos, 1968). This means that the patients are failing to respond appropriately to the requirements of different situations. It suggests that training to deal with different situations may be useful. Furthermore, while some people are socially incompetent in many situations, others find only certain situations difficult. To carry out SST for such people it has been necessary to analyze the main features of situations, and to find out where these people are going wrong. Just as a newcomer might be baffled by, say, American football, so a newcomer might be baffled by certain social situations. What does he need to know to be able to perform competently? To understand a new game one needs to know such things as the goals (how to score and win), the moves allowed, the rules, the roles, and the physical setting and equipment. Similar information is needed for a social situation: the goals, rules, roles, physical setting, repertoire of moves, concepts used, and special skills.

We shall now examine some of the main features of situations that need to be taken into account.

Rules

Rules are one of the main features in our conceptual model of situations, and of relationships. By a rule we mean "behavior that members of a group believe should, or should not, be performed in some situation, or range of situations." This is based on the notion of appropriateness; when a person breaks a rule he has made a mistake.

We predicted that there would be universal rules that meet the common requirements of all social situations, such as preventing withdrawal and aggression, and making communication possible, and that there would be other rules that meet the requirements of particular kinds of situations—coordinating behavior so that goals may be attained, guarding against temptations, and helping with common difficulties.

Argyle, Graham, Campbell, and White (1979) carried out two studies using altogether 75 subjects, 25 situations, and 124 possible rules elicited in pilot interviews. The first prediction was that there would be universal rules. A cluster

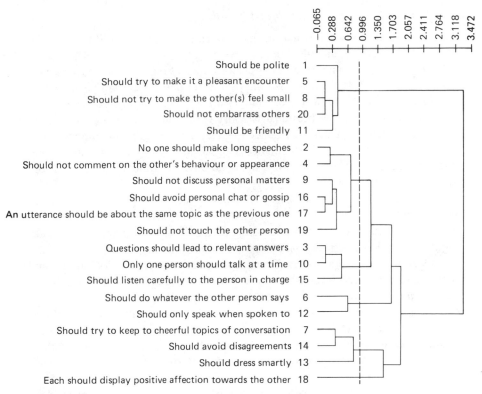

FIGURE 13.2. Cluster of rules. From "The Rules of Different Situations" by M. Argyle, J. A. Graham, A. Campbell, & P. White (1979), *New Zealand Journal of Psychology, 8,* p. 18. Reprinted by permission.

analysis produced a cluster which consisted of the rules applied to most situations (Figure 13.2, top cluster).

We also expected rules that would apply to groups of similar situations. The second cluster, for example, applied to formal situations. As expected, they were rules that guarded against common temptations ("on a first date, should not touch the other"), and avoided common difficulties ("at a pub, don't leave others to pay"), some of them specific to particular situations ("at a doctor's, make sure that you are clean, and tell him the truth").

Some apparently unruly situations among young people are also rule governed. Marsh, Harré, and Rosser (1978) interviewed football hooligans about how to "put the boot in" and allied matters. In these interviews a number of rules were stated more or less directly by informants, for example, it was not acceptable to injure members of the opposition though it was desirable to frighten them or make them look foolish.

Failures of social competence among young people are often due to ignorance of the rules of interviews, work situations, or other occasions.

Special Skills

The skills needed in social situations have much in common with those used for motor skills. The social skill model draws attention to a number of analogies between social performance, and the performance of motor skills like driving a car (see Figure 13.3). In each case the performer pursues certain goals, makes continuous response to feedback and emits hierarchically organized motor responses. This model has been heuristically very useful in drawing attention to the importance of feedback, and hence to gaze; it also suggests a number of different ways in which social performances can fail and the training procedures that may be effective, through analogy with motor skills training (Argyle, 1969; Argyle & Kendon, 1967).

The social skill model emphasizes feedback processes. A person driving a car sees at once when it is going in the wrong direction, and takes corrective action with the steering wheel. Social interactors do likewise; if another person is talking too much they interrupt, ask closed questions or no questions, and look less interested in what he has to say. Feedback requires perception, looking at, and listening to the other person. Skilled performance requires the ability to take the appropriate corrective action referred to as "translation" in the model—not everyone knows that open-ended questions make people talk more and closed questions make them talk less. It also depends on a number of two-step sequences of social behavior, whereby certain social acts have reliable effects on another. The social skills that are most effective vary with the situation, and also with culture and social class.

Shure (1981) describes how to train people in a problem-solving approach to difficult social situations, whereby they are encouraged to engage in "means-ends thinking." Maladjusted adolescents were less able than controls to formulate a step-by-step plan to deal with situations. In the selection interview various kinds of difficult candidates must be dealt with and interviewers can be taught the special skills needed for each. The "translation" part of the model often includes complex cognitive structures, including the rules and other features of

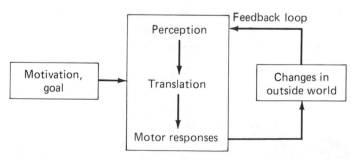

FIGURE 13.3. Motor skill model. From *Social Interaction* (p. 181) by M. Argyle, 1969, London: Methuen. Reprinted by permission .

the immediate situation and knowledge of social processes (Pendleton & Furn-ham, 1980).

Stressful and difficult social situations can be dealt with by mastering the appropriate skills. This will lead to successful performance, avoid rejection or other negative reactions from others, and this leads to reduced anxiety. It may, however, be necessary to control anxiety or other emotional responses, as in public speaking. Similar considerations apply to difficult or dangerous sports, like diving or ski jumping.

The Authenticity Problem

We have emphasized the importance of situations, and the variability of an individual's behavior between situations. A long series of studies (Endler & Magnusson, 1976) attempted to test trait theory and other models by finding the percentages of variance due to persons (P), situations (S), and P × S interaction. This was done with reported behavior (e.g., anxiety), and with observed behavior (e.g., talking, smiling). Typical results were:

Persons   15%-30%

Situations   20%-45%

P × S   30%-50%

However, many adolescents are not aware that situational variability is normal, and think that they or others are being insincere or inauthentic if they change their behavior to fit into a particular situation. They seem to be "P theorists," and think that traits rather than situations are the proper predictors of behavior. Snyder (1979) distinguished between high and low self-monitors. High self-monitors watch their behavior and effects on others carefully, and adjust more to the demands of different situations. Low self-monitors make a point of their genuineness and sincerity, and vary their behavior less. They are less socially skilled. Many adolescents seem to be low self-monitors. We will discuss now some of the relationship skills faced by adolescents.

Social Relationships in Adolescents

Most social behavior is not with strangers but with friends, siblings, parents, teachers, and so on—with whom there is a social relationship. Many problems of social behavior arise in connection with establishing or sustaining these relationships. Some of their properties are shown in a study by Wish, Deutsch, and Kaplan (1976) using multidimensional scaling on the judgments of students. Friends and siblings were seen as fairly close and equal, socioemotional and informal. Relations with parents are less close, unequal, and more intense.

We carried out a study of the sources of satisfaction and conflict in different relationships. For adult subjects, relations with adolescent children were seen as a major source of satisfaction, but also as a major source of conflict,

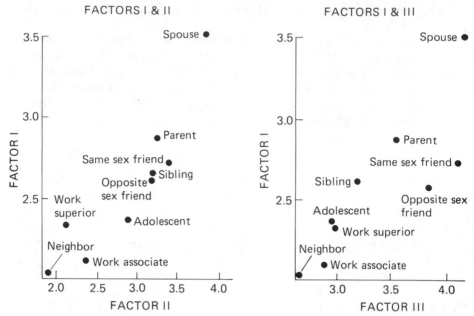

FIGURE 13.4. Relationships plotted on the satisfaction dimensions. From "Sources of Satisfaction and Conflict in Long-Term Relationships" by M. Argyle and A. Furnham, 1983, *Journal of Marriage and the Family*, 45, p. 486. Copyright 1983 by the National Council of Family Relations, 1910West County Road B, Suite 147, St. Paul, Minnesota 55113. Reprinted by permission.

especially conflict based on criticism (Figure 13.4). For the younger subjects, relationships with friends and siblings were intense, with high levels of satisfaction and conflict.

In another study, we investigated the most positive life events for young people. They were making new friends, seeing old friends, and falling in love (Henderson, Argyle, & Furnham, 1984).

Friends

During adolescence this is the most important relationship, and a great deal of time is spent with friends, often up to 3h/day, with more on the telephone. There are a few close friends, two to five, sometimes forming a gang or group, and a wider network with no boundaries.

From 12 onward, just before adolescence, children feel the need for a close friend, and are also prepared to allow the other some independence. They are moving toward a very important phase of friendship, where friends help them to become independent of parents, and to acquire further social skills. Friends now come in groups, or networks, and one of the main things they do is have fun (Fine, 1981).

This is the age at which same-sex friendship is most intense. During adolescence young people are becoming independent of their parents, undergoing physiological changes, and having to cope with sexual impulses. The main characteristics of adolescent friendships is their intensity. In fact they are so similar to love that some psychologists have thought that latent homosexuality is present. And when heterosexual relationships are taken up, the same-sex ones decline in intensity. At least we can say that they are a training or preparation for heterosexual intimacy (Kon, 1981).

Disturbed adolescents have difficulty in making or keeping friends. One reason is that they often have an inadequate idea of friendship. It does not only consist of receiving rewards from others—as younger children think; it involves loyalty, commitment, and concern for the other (La Gaipa & Wood, 1981). Adolescents choose as close friends people they admire, who they see as similar to their ideal self (the sort of person they would like to be), and they choose friends of the same age as themselves, who are facing similar problems. Great importance is attached to friends being trustworthy at 15-16, and friendships are very exclusive. There is a good deal of anxiety about jealousy and fear of losing friends at this age. Coleman (1974), in a study in London, using a sentence-completion method, found that 15-year-old girls would say, for example, "Often when three people are together . . . there is jealousy, I don't know why." Girls develop a need for a close friendships at an earlier age than boys, and move on to dating sooner. They have a few close friends, where boys have a group (or "gang"); and pairs of girls are more exclusive. Girls' friendships are like the romantic ideal of a tender relationship, while boys are companions in shared activities.

Friendship is not governed by legal or formal rules in the way that marriage is. But if you ask people what they think friends should or should not do in relation to each other there is a very high level of agreement. What they have in mind presumably is that if such rules are broken then a friendship is likely to break up.

We asked a sample of people to rate the importance of 40 possible rules for friendship; 27 were generally endorsed. These were checked further in other samples by finding which rules distinguished between current and lapsed friends, close and less close friends, and which rules, when broken, were blamed for the collapse of friendship. Using these different criteria, the rules for friendship given in Table 13.2 appeared to be most important.

There are two main kinds of rules here—rewardingness rules and third-party rules, that is handling the network skillfully. Loneliness is a common, and very distressing condition. Among adolescents and students it is quite widespread— 55% or more say that they often feel lonely. Those who feel lonely also feel depressed, anxious, bored, lacking in self-esteem, shy, self-conscious, and somewhat hostile to others (Peplau & Perlman, 1981). Some people are lonely because they are socially isolated, but it is possible to feel lonely when surrounded by friends and family if the relationships are felt to fall short of the quality desired. In some studies it has been found that lonely people have as many friends as the nonlonely, and are chosen as friends by others, but that there is a lower level of intimacy and self-disclosure (Williams & Solano, 1983). Lonely

TABLE 13.2. The rules of friendship.

Exchange
   17. Share the news of success with the other
   20. Show emotional support
   25. Volunteer help in time of need
   27. Strive to make him/her happy while in each other's company
   13. Repay debts and favors

Intimacy
   24. Trust and confide in the other

Third party
   11. Stand up for the other person in their absence
   23. Be tolerant of other friends
   10. Don't criticize in public
   12. Keep confidences
   26. Don't be jealous or critical of other relationships

Coordination
   21. Don't nag
   18. Respect privacy

Note. From "Rules of Friendship" by M. Argyle and M. Henderson, 1984, *Journal of Social and Personal Relationships*, *1*, (p. 234). Copyright 1984 by Sage Publications, London. Reprinted by permission.

people are aware of a discrepancy between their social attachments and what they would like; we now know that the problem is primarily that their friendships are not intimate enough.

A number of studies have documented the social skill differences that lead to loneliness, that is, not being able to establish friendships of the desired kind. The main findings are that the lonely engage in less self-disclosure, take less interest in other people, are less assertive, less rewarding, poor senders of friendly nonverbal signals, and have inadequate ideas of what friendship involves. This gives a guide to the most important friendships skills.

Heterosexual Relationships

Adolescence coincides with the onset of romantic and sexual relationships. There is a gradual shift from social life with mixed groups of friends to pairing off, and a shift to more intimate sexual activity. Some do this earlier, some later, others not at all.

In our Rules Study, we found a number of rules endorsed as the most important ones to apply to the opposite-sex partner in the dating relationship (Argyle & Henderson, 1985).

As a couple moves from casual to serious dating and to engagement, there is an increase in the level of love. There is also an increase in conflict and negativity from casual to serious dating, which levels off as the couple moves on to engagement (Braiker & Kelley, 1979). And with the increase in conflict which accompanies this change in the relationship, different rules emerge to help in regulating these potential conflict areas. In our study of dating girls, those involved in a single dating relationship thought that it was much more important to show the other partner unconditional positive regard, to look after him when ill, and to show an interest in his daily activities than did girls involved with more than one dating partner. The single partner daters also reported applying the rules differently in practice. They were more likely to be faithful, to ask for personal advice, to show distress or anxiety in front of the other person and to show interest in the partner's daily activities.

However the skills of courtship are not completely covered by rules. In order to attract members of the opposite sex, various strategies may be used—suggesting that one thinks highly of them, doing things for them, agreeing with them, and ascribing attractive characteristics to oneself, directly or indirectly—which can all be described as "ingratiation" (Jones & Wortman, 1973). One study compared men who were successful and unsuccessful in dating girls. The successful ones were more fluent at saying the right thing, and quickly, and they agreed more. Their nonverbal behavior was also different—they smiled and nodded more (Arkowitz, Lichtenstein, McGovern, & Hines, 1975). Nonverbal communication is one of the main ways of signaling sexual interest. Other nonverbal signals here include gaze, pupil dilation (though this is not under voluntary control), proximity and touch, and a state of bodily posture and alertness which signals a high level of arousal (Cook & McHenry, 1978). Attractive males have more dates and more social life, but this is mainly because they are also more assertive and socially competent. Attractive females are *not* more competent than other females: They do not need to be, since men take the initiatiave (Reis, Wheeler, Spiegel, Kermis, Nezlek, & Perri, 1982).

Relations with Parents

The relationship with children undergoes a major change, and sometimes a temporary breakdown, during adolescence. The child feels increasing urges to break out of a childish, dependent form of attachment to the parents, to one of greater independence and equality. This is less of a problem in primitive cultures where nothing changes very much, but more of a problem in our own where historical changes create a "generation gap" between the ideas and interests of parents and children.

We have seen that the period when the children are adolescents is a bad time for parents; it is often a bad time for the children, too: self-esteem is lower, and self-consciousness greater at 12 and 13 than either before or after. For most adolescents there is some degree of rebellion, if only to establish that they are separate individuals in their own right. For some there is a more serious rebellion, and rejection of the parents, though this is usually temporary. Rebellion is particularly acute among children who are socially mobile, or who have become attached to a deviate peer group; in developing countries adolescents often reject the traditional ways of their parents in favor of modern ideas.

Recent surveys suggest that there is a problem of communication or values for 25%-30% of adolescents and their parents, but that serious conflict is fairly rare. The nature of these conflicts was explored further by Coleman (1974) in a study in London, using a projective method, in which subjects completed sentences ("When a boy is with his parents . . .") and wrote stories about pictures. Negative themes were produced by over 90% of adolescents, on the subject of parents, but the contents were different for boys and girls. Boys reported feelings of frustration—"When a boy is with his parents . . . he is usually chained up." Girls on the other hand reported not feeling themselves when with their parents— "When a girl is with her parents . . . she is not herself . . . she has to behave differently . . . she becomes like them."

We studied sources of conflict in different relationships, and found that relationships with adolescent children were seen as high on a factor of conflict based on criticism, although they were quite low on the more important general factor (Argyle & Furnham, 1983). For boys the problem was frustration at restraints, demands for greater freedom. This is less important for most girls, because girls were socialized more strongly during childhood to be dependent and obedient, while boys were trained more to be independent. On the other hand, boys, as well as girls, have a lot of ambivalence during adolescence—while fighting for more independence they also need parental help and support, and may switch back suddenly into a more dependent relationship.

Social Skills Training for Adolescents

Social skills training is being widely used for all kinds of mental patients including adolescents, it is used in some schools and in many occupational training courses. It is less available to the general public, apart from assertiveness training for women, and heterosexual skills training on some campuses (Argyle, 1983).

The standard method is role playing, complete with modeling, videoplayback, and coaching (Argyle, 1983). A serious problem is how to achieve generalization to real-life situations. For those not inside institutions, "homework" is often used: trainees are asked to repeat the exercises (e.g., to make someone else talk more, or less) between sessions in real-life settings, and to report back. For those in hospital or prison, other staff members can continue the training between the formal sessions. And there can be "training for generalization," for example, teaching general principles and overlearning (Goldstein, 1979).

While this kind of training has been found to be quite successful, for adolescents and others, in numerous follow-up studies, it is now possible to augment it in several ways suggested by the research described previously.

Sending Nonverbal Signals. Facial expression can be trained using a mirror and later a videotape recorder, taking photographs as models (e.g., from Ekman & Friesen, 1975). Vocal expression can be trained using modeling and playback of audio taperecordings.

Perception of Nonverbal Signals. The Ekman and Friesen photographs can be used to train people to decode facial expression. Trainees can be taught to decode tones of voice by listening to taperecordings of neutral messages produced in different emotional states (Davitz, 1964). In each case it is easy to test the subject, for example by finding out the percentage of recordings they can decode correctly.

Conversational Sequences. Samples of the client's conversation are recorded and studied carefully. It is then possible to spot the particular errors being made, for example, failure to give a proactive utterance after answering a question, failure to initiate, lack of nonverbal responsiveness.

Taking the Role of the Other. Chandler (1973) succeeded in improving ability to see the other's point of view (and reducing delinquency) by means of exercises in which groups of five young delinquents developed and made videorecordings of skits about relevant real-life situations, in which each member of the group played a part.

Self-presentation. In addition to the usual role-playing exercises, trainees can be given advice about clothes, hair, and other aspects of appearance. Their voices can be trained to produce a more appropriate accent or tone of voice.

Focus on Situations. Social skills training can focus on the particular situations that are found difficult. A group of trainees works over the rules, difficulties, and other features of a situation, helped to decide on the best skills to use, and then practice these skills in role-playing. Situational analysis has been used in the treatment of obesity and alcoholism by discovering the situations in which overeating or drinking take place, and finding ways of coping with them.

Focus on Relationships. This can be done in several ways, for example, by (a) teaching trainees the appropriate set of rules; or (b) correcting misunderstandings about relationships (we showed that disturbed adolescents often have inadequate and immature concepts of friendship).

The methods of training for situations include a strong educational component. In the field of relationships, clients can be taught some of the facts of life, for example, that difficulties between adolescents and their parents are temporary and will be followed by a firm relationship, which lasts until the death of the parents; and that friendship involves a concern for the welfare of the other, and for the surrounding network of other friends.

It appears that males and females have rather different needs for SST. We have seen a number of areas in which women are usually more socially competent than men—they are better at sending and receiving NVC and are more rewarding and polite, they disclose more and form closer friendships, are better at reducing the loneliness of others. However, it is women who seek assertiveness training and their problems are more general than this. Many studies have shown how women like to form close friendships with equals but are less able or willing to cope with hierarchical, structured groups engaged in joint tasks, and rarely emerge as the leaders of such groups (Shaver & Buhrmeister, 1983).

Finally, I would like to criticize two approaches to SST that have become popular. One is the focus on assertiveness training. In my experience, relatively few clients require this, many more need to be able to make friends, which is an entirely different matter. The other approach is to conduct SST as a form of behavior therapy; bad conversationalists, for example, are reinforced for more frequent question-asking. I hope I have said enough ealier to show that conversation and other aspects of social performance are more complex than this, and require some understanding of these complexities.

References

Argyle, M. (1969). *Social interaction*. London: Methuen.

Argyle, M. (1975). *Bodily communication*. London: Methuen.

Argyle, M. (1983). *The psychology of interpersonal behavior* (4th ed.). Harmondsworth: Penguin Books.

Argyle, M., & Furnham, A. (1983). Sources of satisfaction and conflict in long-term relationships. *Journal of Marriage and the Family*, *45*, 481-493.

Argyle, M., Furnham, A., & Graham, J. A. (1981). *Social situations*. Cambridge: Cambridge University Press.

Argyle, M., Graham, J. A., Campbell, A., & White, P. (1979). The rules of different situations. *New Zealand Journal of Psychology*, *8*, 13-22.

Argyle, M., & Henderson, M. (1984). The rules of friendship. *Journal of Social and Personal Relationships*, *1*, 211-237.

Argyle, M., & Henderson, M. (1985). *The anatomy of relationships*. London: Heinemann.

Argyle, M., & Kendon, A. (1967). The experimental analysis of social performance. *Advances in Experimental Social Psychology*, *3*, 55-98.

Argyle, M., Salter, V., Nicholson, H., Williams, M., & Burgess, P. (1970). The communication of inferior and superior attitudes by verbal and non-verbal signals. *British Journal of Social and Clinical Psychology*, *9*, 221-231.

Arkowitz, H., Lichtenstein, E., McGovern, K., and Hines, P. (1975). The behavioral assessment of social competence in males. *Behavior Therapy*, *6*, 3-13.

Baxter, L. (1984). An investigation of compliance-gaining as politeness. *Human Communication Research*, *10*, 427-456.

Berscheid, E., & Walster, E. (1979). Physical attractiveness. *Advances in Experimental Social Psychology*, *7*, 158-215.

Braiker, H. B., & Kelley, H. H. (1979). Conflict in the development of close relationships. In R. L. Burgess & T. L. Huston (Eds.), *Social exchange in developing relationships*. New York: Academic Press.

Brennan, T. (1982). Loneliness at adolescence. In L. A. Peplau & D. Perlman (Eds.), *Loneliness*. New York: Wiley.

Brown, P., and Levinson, S. (1978). Universals in language: Politeness phenomena. In E. N. Goody (Ed.), *Questions and politeness: Strategies in social interaction* (Cambridge Papers in Anthropology, 8). Cambridge: Cambridge University Press.

Bryant, B., & Trower, P. (1974). Social difficulty in a student population. *British Journal of Educational Psychology, 44*, 13-21.

Chandler, M. J. (1973). Egocentrism and anti-social behavior: The assessment and training of social perspective-training skills. *Developmental Psychology, 9*, 326-332.

Clarke, D. D. (1983). *Language and action*. Oxford: Pergamon.

Coleman, J. (1974). *Relationships in adolescence*. London: Routledge and Kegan Paul.

Cook, M., & McHenry, R. (1978). *Sexual attraction*. Oxford: Pergamon.

Davitz, J. R. (1964). *The communication of emotional meaning*. New York: McGraw-Hill.

Ekman, P., & Friesen, W. V. (1975). *Unmasking the face*. Englewood Cliffs, NJ: Prentice-Hall.

Endler, N. S., & Magnusson, D. (Eds.). (1976). *Interactional psychology and personality*. Washington, DC: Hemisphere.

Feffer, M., & Suchotliff, L. (1966). Decentering implications of social interactions. *Journal of Personality and Social Psychology, 4*, 415-422.

Fine, G. A. (1981). Friends, impression management and preadolescent behaviour. In S. R. Asher & J. Gottman (Eds.), *The development of friendship*. Cambridge: Cambridge University Press.

Flavell, J. H. (1968). *The development of role-taking and communication skills in children*. New York: Wiley.

Furnham, A., & Argyle, M. (1981). Responses of four groups to difficult social situations. In M. Argyle, A. Furnham, & J. A. Graham (Eds.), *Social situations*. Cambridge: Cambridge University Press.

Goldstein, A. (1979). Social skills training. In A. Goldstein (Ed.), *In response to aggression*. New York: Pergamon.

Grice, H. P. (1975). Logic and conversation. In P. Cole & J. L. Morgan (Eds.), *Syntax and semantics: Vol. 3. Speech acts*. New York: Academic Press.

Hall, J. A. (1979). Gender, gender roles, and nonverbal communication skills. In R. Rosenthal (Ed.), *Skill in nonverbal communication*. Cambridge, MA: Oelgeschlager, Gunn ahd Hain.

Henderson, M., Argyle, M., & Furnham, A. (1984). *The assessment of positive social events*. Oxford University, Department of Experimental Psychology.

Jones, E. E. (1964). *Ingratiation: A social psychological analysis*. New York: Appleton-Century-Crofts.

Jones, E. E., & Wortman, C. (1973). *Ingratiation: An attributional approach*. Morristown, NJ: General Learning Press.

Jourard, S. M. (1971). *Self-disclosure*. New York: Wiley-Interscience.

Kon, I. S. (1981). Adolescent friendship: Some unanswered questions for future research. In S. Duck & R. Gilmour (Eds.), *Personal relationships 3: Personal relationships in disorder*. London: Academic Press.

La Gaipa, J. J., & Wood, H. D. (1981). Friendship in disturbed adolescents. In S. Duck & R. Gilmour (Eds.) *Personal relationships 3: Personal relationships in disorder*. London: Academic Press.

Marsh, P., Harré, R., & Rosser, E. (1978). *The rules of disorder*. London: Routledge and Kegan Paul.

Meldman, M. J. (1967). Verbal behavior analysis of self-hyperattentionism. *Disorders of the Nervous System, 28*, 469-473.

Mischel, W. (1968). *Personality and assessment*. New York: Wiley.

Moos, R. H. (1968). Situational analysis of a therapeutic community milieu. *Journal of Abnormal Psychology*, *73*, 49-61.

Napoleon, T., Chassin, L., & Young, R. D. (1980). A replication and extension of "Physical attractiveness and mental illness." *Journal of Abnormal Psychology*, *89*, 250-253.

Pendleton, D., & Furnham, A. (1980). Skills: A paradigm for applied social psychological research. In W. T. Singleton, P. Spurgeon, & R. B. Stammers (Eds.), *The analysis of social skill*. New York: Plenum.

Peplau, L. A., & Perlman, D. (1982). *Loneliness*. New York: Wiley.

Reis, H. T., Wheeler, V. A., Spiegel, N., Kermis, M. H., Nezlek, J., & Perri, M. (1982). Physical attractiveness in social interaction. II: Why does appearance affect social experience? *Journal of Personality and Social Psychology*, *43*, 979-996.

Romano, J. M., & Bellack, A. S. (1980). Social validation of a component model of assertive behaviour. *J. Consulting and Clinical Psychology*, *48*, 478-490.

Rubin, Z. (1973). *Liking and loving*. New York: Holt, Rinehart and Winston.

Shaver, P., & Buhrmeister, D. (1983). Loneliness, sex-role orientation and group life: A social needs perspective. In P. B. Paulus (Ed.), *Basic group processes*. New York: Springer-Verlag.

Shure, M. (1981). A social skills approach to child rearing. In M. Argyle (Ed.), *Social skills and health*. London: Methuen.

Snyder, M. (1979). Self-monitoring processes. *Advances in Experimental Social Psychology*, *12*, 85-128.

Trower, P. (1980). Situational analysis of the components and processes of social skilled and unskilled patients. *Journal of Consulting and Clinical Psychology*, *48*, 327-339.

Walker, C. (1977). Some variations in marital satisfaction. In R. Chester & J. Peel (Eds.), *Equalities and inequalities in family life*. London: Academic Press.

Williams, J. G., & Solano, C. H. (1983). The social reality of feeling lonely. *Personality and Social Behavior Bulletin*, *9*, 237-242.

Wish, M., Deutsch, M., & Kaplan, S. J. (1977). Toward an implicit theory of interpersonal communication. *Sociometry*, *40*, 234-246.

Zimbardo, P. G. (1977). *Shyness*. Reading, MA: Addison-Wesley.

CHAPTER 14

Designing Effective Social Problem-Solving Programs for the Classroom

Roger P. Weissberg

Several years ago I had a provocative lunch discussion with an argumentative, methodologically sophisticated colleague of mine. After we disagreed about the effects of Reaganomics on the poor, the value of the nuclear freeze, and whether Wayne Gretsky was an established hockey star,[1] he began talking about the many shortcomings of school-based social problem-solving (SPS) program evaluation research (!).

I asked him how he would design an SPS intervention outcome study.

First he commented, "The major purposes of SPS training are to improve children's problem-solving skills and social adjustment. Rather than dwelling on all the difficulties inherent in the use of hypothetical-reflective problem-solving measures (Krasnor & Rubin, 1981), let's talk about the best way to collect teacher ratings of adjustment."

"O.K.," I responded with hopeful interest.

"Adjustment ratings by teachers who conduct SPS lessons are biased and worthless," he said. "It's far more appropriate to collect data from teachers who have no knowledge of the treatment conditions of subjects."

Instead of disputing his first assumption—a topic for another chapter—I asked, "So how would you get blind ratings?"

"I would randomly assign subjects to an SPS intervention, an alternative treatment condition, an attention-placebo group, and a nontreatment control group. Each child would meet individually for six sessions with psychology graduate students outside the classroom," he said.

We debated about what nonsignificant multivariate analysis of covariance findings on postintervention teacher ratings of adjustment would mean. He argued, "Based on my rigorous design, nonsignificant results would suggest that the efficacy of SPS training was questionable." I countered, "The results would more likely reflect that your particular intervention (i.e., a six-session, individually oriented program conducted by graduate students) was ineffective, but would have few implications about the value of SPS training in general."

---

[1] Although we still disagree on the first two issues, my friend finally admits that Wayne Gretsky is a superstar.

At that point the focus of the conversation was about to shift again. I wanted to discuss clinical and educational considerations for designing effective SPS programs that promote children's problem-solving abilities and social adaptation. Unfortunately, we suddenly noticed the late hour and prematurely ended our conversation. We asked for separate checks, paid for lunch, and rushed back to the psychology department for a meeting.

This chapter presents some ideas and issues that I did not have time to express to my lunch partner about designing effective primary prevention, school-based SPS training interventions. Since 1977, my colleagues (from the University of Rochester and Yale University) and I have developed a variety of *classroom-based, teacher-taught* SPS programs for children from kindergarten (Winer, Hilpert, Gesten, Cowen, & Schubin, 1982) to eighth grade (Weissberg, Hawkins, & Krauss, 1985). The majority of our work has focused on interventions with suburban and urban second- to fourth-graders (e.g., Gesten, Flores de Apodaca, Rains, Weissberg, & Cowen, 1979; Gesten et al., 1982; Weissberg, Gesten, Carnrike, Toro, Rapkin, Davidson, & Cowen, 1981). In a recent review of our SPS classroom training efforts, Ellis Gesten and I reported that (a) trained children consistently improved on cognitive and behavioral problem-solving performance, but that (b) program impact on children's adjustment was mixed (Weissberg & Gesten, 1982). Interestingly, our pre- to postprogram adjustment outcome findings have become more positive with each successive intervention. One reasonable way to interpret this trend is to assume that we have conducted more powerful, beneficial programs as we have become more experienced with SPS-training design and implementation issues.

Although SPS training appears to be a sensible and attractive competence-building strategy in theory, developing SPS curricula and carrying out classroom interventions are complex undertakings. There are no clear formulas for how to teach children to be more effective interpersonal problem solvers. In fact, program content, structure, and teaching approaches should be varied to meet the instructional needs of different sociodemographic and clinical samples (Weissberg, Gesten, Rapkin, Cowen, Davidson, Flores de Apodaca, & McKim, 1981). It is important to point out that several veteran SPS researchers (e.g., Shure, Spivack, Elias, Elardo) failed to promote children's adjustment in their first program efforts but succeeded in later attempts. Perhaps it is overly optimistic to expect that a brand new competence training curriculum, taught for the first time by school teachers who are "trained" by consultants with little SPS background, will significantly improve children's social adaptation (Weissberg & Gesten, 1982). It seems reasonable to hypothesize that evaluators are more likely to find positive outcomes when programs that have been developed and refined over several years are implemented by well-trained knowledgeable teachers and consultants. It would be informative to test this hypothesis empirically using meta-analysis to compare the efficacy of programs implemented by SPS researchers with several years of program experience versus those conducted by first-time interveners.

Currently, SPS training is at a critical juncture because there is a controversial debate about its effectiveness. Since the 1970s there has been a dramatic increase in the number of SPS-related outcome studies. Recently, there have been at least six reviews describing research on more than 50 child-focused SPS programs (Durlak, 1983; Kirschenbaum & Ordman, 1984; Pellegrini & Urbain, in press; Rubin & Krasnor, in press; Spivack & Shure, 1982; Urbain & Kendall, 1980). Although certain reviewers suggest the results of school-based programs are exciting or encouraging (Prevention Task Panel Report, 1978; Spivack & Shure, 1982; Urbain & Kendall, 1980), others interpret findings as negative and discouraging (Durlak, 1983; Kirschenbaum & Ordman, 1984).

Pellegrini and Urbain (in press) expressed concern that interest in conducting preventive SPS interventions may diminish unless well-designed evaluations demonstrate the value of the approach. They and other reviewers have offered several important methodological recommendations to improve the interpretability of future SPS research such as (a) using alternative-treatment and attention-placebo comparison groups, (b) employing multimethod assessments of adjustment from multiple perspectives, and (c) evaluating long-term program outcomes to assess the durability of training effects. These suggestions are constructive and should be adopted in future SPS studies. Primary attention, however, must be devoted to making sure that the programs being assessed are effectively designed and executed. If an SPS intervention fails to enhance children's adjustment, possible shortcomings in curriculum content, instructional formats, program structure, and trainer competence must be considered before concluding that the training program has no beneficial effects—and yet they seldom are considered.

The rest of this chapter highlights critical issues involved in conceptualizing, designing, and implementing SPS training programs. Some of the comments are speculative and based on my reactions from conducting or observing interventions, rather than on research data. Several of the points to be made are those that first-time SPS interveners think about once they have completed a training program, that is, at a time when it is too late to benefit the children who were trained. Others reflect unresolved questions and dilemmas that must be answered through curriculum development and research efforts to improve the quality of future SPS interventions.

In a very important article, Ladd and Mize (1983) used cognitive-social learning principles to provide both an explanatory framework and a potential technology for conducting social skills training programs effectively. From their thoughtful and systematic conceptualization of training, it becomes clear that there may be some relatively good SPS intervention models, but there are no outstanding ones! One goal of this chapter is to express opinions that generate discussion and research to improve the technology of SPS training. The rest of this chapter is divided into four sections. First I will briefly describe the context from which my Rochester colleagues and I chose to develop classroom-based SPS interventions. This background presents a university-researcher/public-school collaboration model that may be useful and informative to academics who wish to see their social skills training packages effectively implemented in the schools. The next two sections focus, respectively, on (a) SPS curriculum content and direct instructional approaches that promote long-term skill acquisition and adjustment gains, and (b) developing program structures and teacher training procedures that conform to the ecological demands of school settings. The chapter concludes with a brief remark about ethical considerations for conducting SPS training research.

Deciding to Conduct SPS Research: The Rochester Context

Although book chapters rarely present the personal or environmental circumstances affecting one's choice to study a particular area, I will briefly present ours (i.e., The Rochester SPS Core Group—Gesten et al., 1979) because the Rochester situation is unique and has features worth emulating. In addition, the description (a) illustrates the value of effective, ongoing collaboration between university researchers and public school personnel, and (b) offers an introductory perspective of why elementary school teachers feel classroom SPS training is important.

In 1976, several faculty members and graduate students from the University of Rochester's clinical/community psychology program formed a team to conduct SPS research. At the time, all group members worked with Professor Emory Cowen. In many developmental-psychology and social-skills-training circles, Cowen is most frequently cited for his study relating children's negative peer ratings in third grade to their future tendencies to seek psychiatric treatment as young adults (Cowen, Pederson, Babigian, Izzo, & Trost, 1973). Among community and school psychologists he is better known for his 27-year involvement with the Primary Mental Health Project (PMHP) and other preventive mental health efforts.

The PMHP is a program for the early detection and prevention of school maladjustment that geometrically expands the amount of services elementary schools can provide to children with behavior problems (Cowen, Gesten, & Weissberg, 1980; Cowen et al., 1975). Its structural approach is based on four principal features: (a) focusing on young elementary school children who, with early intervention, can change significantly for the better before early behavioral warning signs become extended serious problems; (b) using active, systematic early detection and screening procedures to identify children experiencing problems (e.g., poor peer relations, frequent disruptiveness, lack of motivation) that interfere with effective learning; (c) bringing prompt, effective, preventively oriented help to large numbers of identified children, through the use of carefully selected, warm, caring, paraprofessional child-aides; and (d) modifying the roles of school mental health professionals from individual assessment and treatment of relatively few seriously troubled youngsters toward more training and supervision of child-aides and consultation with teachers so that more children receive effective help.

The PMHP began in one Rochester school in 1958, and now operates in more than 20 Rochester-area schools and several hundred schools nationwide

(Cowen, Spinell, Wright, & Weissberg, 1983). Its central staff is located at the University of Rochester's Center for Community Study and is comprised primarily of clinical/community psychology researchers with joint appointments in Rochester's psychology department, and mental health professionals who also work in local PHMP schools. Over the years, these schools and PMHP staff have developed a productive mutually beneficial collaborative relationship in which school service needs influence the direction of many evaluation and program development efforts, and research findings shape decisions about which services to provide and how to deliver them most effectively (Cowen et al., 1980).

Historically, the PMHP has been an early-secondary prevention program in which child-aides meet individually or with small groups of children, for one or two 30- to 45-min weekly sessions in a playroom setting. In addition to traditional supportive relational approaches, aides have been trained to provide a variety of innovative helping services such as crisis intervention to children of divorcing parents (Felner, Norton, Cowen, & Farber, 1981), Ginottian limit-setting approaches for acting-out children (Cowen, Orgel, Gesten, Wilson, 1979), and planned short-term intervention for youngsters with circumscribed social and behavioral problems (Winter, 1982). Many of these strategies were developed by PMHP staff in response to requests by school mental health professionals and child-aides, based on their observed clinical needs. PMHP researchers and program developers have collaborated successfully with school personnel because the latter group is interested, indeed eager, to pilot potentially effective, innovative intervention strategies.

In 1976 the PMHP, through the efforts of our SPS core group, began to collaborate with teachers to develop classroom-based primary prevention programs for all children, not just those experiencing adjustment difficulties. Until that time teachers played a very important but limited role in PMHP's service delivery system. Their major contributions involved (a) identifying appropriate referrals, (b) completing systematic problem and competence behavior scales, (c) offering inputs for establishing behavioral treatment goals, (d) helping the PMHP team to assess children's progress during follow-up conferences, and (e) trying occasional ad hoc strategies to enhance children's classroom functioning. The need to reconceptualize teachers roles in direct interventions was largely influenced by teacher comments during a series of feedback meetings with PMHP central staff. One eloquent teacher expressed the following recurrent theme:

I think PMHP is great. In fact, I wish every child in this school could have an aide! I also realize there are limitations to how much service you can provide in your playroom. How about doing something with teachers to promote the positive social development of all children in the classroom? I think it could benefit everyone, and maybe prevent a few kids from needing your specialized services.

Although we were conceptually committed to this viewpoint, we did not consider ourselves to be curriculum-development specialists, nor were we certain of what skills to teach to enhance social development. After reviewing the literature on social-skills, affective-education, and cognitive-behavioral interventions, we identified SPS training as a potentially beneficial primary prevention strategy. We were impressed by Spivack, Platt, and Shure's (1976) review of research with different age, socioeconomic, and clinical samples indicating that well-adjusted individuals do better than maladjusted peers on tests evaluating interpersonal cognitive problem-solving skills such as sensing problems, recognizing feelings, generating alternative solutions, anticipating consequences, and using means-end planning to reach specified goals. We also felt the mental health promotion and prevention possibilities of problem-solving training were highlighted by Spivack and Shure's (1974, 1982) intervention results in which teachers taught a 46-lesson program to low-income black inner-city preschoolers and kinder-garteners. They found that (a) trained children improved in alternative solution and consequential thinking (skill acquisition); (b) training improved the behavior of withdrawn and impulsive children (mental health promotion); (c) already adjusted children were less likely than comparable controls to develop behavioral problems (prevention); and (d) program gains remained stable 1 year after train-ing ended (generalization and maintenance).

Before attempting to pilot a problem-solving intervention we asked teachers for their reactions to the approach. One third-grade teacher, who became one of our first program trainers, became very interested. She commented,

During the last few years my students have been driving me crazy! When I work with small reading groups, children often interrupt and want me to solve their minor problems (e.g., "He took my pencil"; "She called me a name"). Sometimes I tell them to see me later, but they get frustrated and I feel guilty. If I quickly solve the problem so I can get back to my group, that reinforces them and they keep coming up. If this technique can help children resolve conflicts more independently and adaptively, I'd love to try it.

Importantly, we have found that SPS training strikes a responsive chord with most teachers. Of all the primary-prevention competence-training opportunities PMHP staff has offered to teachers, our SPS workshops have generated the most interest. Many teachers perceive it as a practical classroom management and social development approach that will benefit them and their students. As it turns out, teacher interest is a necessary but not sufficient factor in providing a pro-gram that promotes children's social adjustment. It has required several years of cooperative collaboration and battle-line program experience to develop an effective SPS training model. The next two sections present major program design and implementation issues.

Curriculum Content and Instructional Format Issues

There is considerable controversy about how to define SPS or what the essential components of SPS training should be. This lack of clarity is exemplified by the confusion about whether to call the approach SPS or interpersonal cognitive problem-solving (ICPS). Although many reviewers use SPS and ICPS inter-changeably, I think it is important to distinguish between the two terms. Spivack and Shure (1982) carefully label their training approach ICPS because they theorize that certain critical *cognitive* skills mediate the quality of one's social adjustment. They propose that the key goal of ICPS training is to promote adjustment by improving an individual's ability to think through and resolve interpersonal conflicts effectively, *not* by direct modification of behaviors. Spivack and Shure (1982) also comment:

Perhaps the most important underlying thread of all ICPS programs is that the learner is not told what solutions to problems are good ones or why, but instead is guided to develop the habit of generating multiple options, of evaluating these options, and when age appropriate, to plan the step-by-step means to reach a stated goal. The ICPS approach focuses upon *how* people think, *not* what they think so that those exposed to training can decide for themselves, what they might do and why. (p. 339)

In contrast, many researchers who call the approach SPS believe that successful problem-solving training promotes social adjustment through a complex interaction of cognitive, emotional, and behavioral factors (e.g., Elias, 1980; Krasnor, chapter 4 this volume; Rubin & Krasnor, in press). They have extended the seminal formulations of D'Zurilla and Goldfried (1971) and Spivack et al. (1976) by suggesting SPS includes the following sets of skills: (a) expectations that one can resolve most problematic situations and produce desirable outcomes; (b) the ability to recognize when problems exist as well the perspectives, motives, and feelings of involved participants; (c) the capacity to generate or access multiple alternative solutions to reach one's goals and to link them with realistic consequences; (d) the ability to select an adaptive strategy and develop an elaborated plan of implementation, including the flexibility to overcome potential obstacles; (e) carrying out that strategy with behavioral competence; and (f) the ability to self-monitor behavioral performance with the capacity to abandon ineffective solutions, implement back-up strategies, or reformulate goals as needed.

Translating such a model into a curriculum that teachers can use to train children to be adaptive problem solvers is difficult. The importance of these skills in mediating social adjustment varies for different ages (Spivack et al., 1976) and socioeconomic groups (McKim, Weissberg, Cowen, Gesten, & Rapkin, 1982). Furthermore, the most appropriate instructional methods for conveying social skills differ depending on the sociodemographic characteristics of the target group (Furman, 1980; Ladd & Mize, 1983). When we began our SPS program development efforts for suburban third graders in 1976, we had many questions about the most appropriate lesson content and which instructional formats to use. Key questions included: (a) Which skills are socially and developmentally appropriate to teach this group? (b) In what sequence should SPS skills be taught? (c) To what extent should training focus on cognitive versus behavioral skills? (d) What teaching methods (e.g., didactic lecture, modeling, coaching, role playing, self-instruction, positive reinforcement) are best for promoting skill concept acquisition, effective skill performance, and skill maintenance and generalization? and (e) What can trainers do, in addition to formal lessons, to encourage children's adaptive problem-solving in daily interactions?

Space limitations prevent me from detailing the many shortcomings of our first 17-lesson SPS pilot training program. Suffice it to say that we revised our program substantially during the next 4 years based on theoretical explanations of skill acquisition and behavior change (Bandura, 1977; Hawkins & Weis, in press; Ladd & Mize, 1983; Meichenbaum, 1977), exposure to the creative, thoughtful efforts of other SPS program developers (e.g., Allen, Chinsky, Larcen, Lochman, & Selinger, 1976; Bash & Camp, 1980; Elardo & Cooper, 1977; Spivack & Shure, 1974), our own clinical program experience and empirical data, and inputs by teachers and students. The rest of this section describes the current Rochester SPS curriculum for second- to fourth-grade teachers (Weissberg, Gesten, Leibenstein, Doherty-Schmid, & Hutton, 1980), and then (a) highlights a few key instructional choices we made in designing it, and (b) identifies several unresolved training issues that merit further consideration by SPS program developers and researchers.

Weissberg et al.'s (1980) teacher training manual presents 34 structured 20- to 30-min formal lessons, a variety of postprogram skill review and maintenance activities, and examples of problem-solving dialoguing approaches (see Spivack & Shure, 1982, pp. 362-368) used by teachers to help children develop their own solutions to interpersonal problems. The formal program had five units. *Recognizing Feelings in Ourselves and Others* (4 lessons) teaches youngsters ways to express a variety of emotions and to find out how others feel by looking, listening, and asking. Several games, pictures, stories, and role plays illustrate that all feelings, even upset feelings, are a normal part of life. *Problem Sensing and Identification* (5 lessons) teaches children that problems happen between people and cause upset feelings. After children name important commonly experienced classroom, playground, and home problems, they are told that the purpose of the program is to help them handle these interpersonal difficulties successfully by thinking of and trying their own solutions. *Generation of Alternative Solutions* (5 lessons) emphasizes that there are many different ways to solve problems. Thinking of lots of solutions increases the chances of trying effective options and having back-up strategies if a first solution fails. *Consideration of Consequences* (5 lessons) teaches children to anticipate and evaluate what might happen next before trying a solution and to try options likely to lead to positive outcomes. Considering realistic immediate and long-term outcomes, rather than merely brainstorming alternative consequences, is emphasized. During the first four units children learn a six-step process (a cognitive framework) for solving interpersonal problems:

Problem definition	(1) Say the *problem* and how you *feel*.
Goal statement	(2) Decide on your *goal*.
Impulse delay	(3) *Stop and think* before you act.
Generation of alternatives	(4) Think of as *many solutions* as you can.
Consideration of consequences	(5) *Think ahead to what might happen next.*
Implementation	(6) When you have a really good solution, *try it*!

After Step 6, children are encouraged to try other solutions if their first one fails, and are also told that changing one's initial goal is sometimes necessary. Once these core elements have been conveyed, *Integration of Problem-Solving Behavior* (15 lessons) teaches interpersonal strategies and behaviors (e.g., tone of voice, attention to another's mood, anticipating and overcoming obstacles) that help children implement solutions successfully. During several lessons children practice applying the entire problem-solving to real-life problems through role play and discussion.

Teachers also promote daily behavioral SPS use by (a) conducting group problem-solving meetings to address problems arising at school, (b) modeling the SPS process by demonstrating how they apply it to solve their problems, and (c) using SPS dialoguing when children request assistance in solving daily disputes with peers. For example, when asked by students to resolve a classroom conflict, teachers can respond by reflecting their feelings, asking what alternatives (besides telling the teacher) might be tried, and prompting the anticipation of realistic consequences for each. A child who has difficulty generating effective solutions is sometimes paired with another child for help. Finally, children are encouraged to implement the option they think is best and to inform the teacher about the outcome. Some reviewers suggest that SPS dialoguing is a critical training method for helping children both to integrate SPS concepts and to use them to resolve real-life conflicts (Spivack & Shure, 1982; Weissberg & Gesten, 1982).

After the formal 34-lesson program ends, teachers conduct at least one SPS encore meeting weekly for the rest of the school year. Typically they develop and lead activities such as presenting "Problem Solver of the Week" awards, conducting "Problem Solving Show-and-Tell" sessions, or discussing role-playing problems raised by students. The major goals of the 15 integration lessons and postprogram activities are to promote the maintenance and generalization of adaptive problem-solving behavior.

The preceding description briefly summarizes the general program content and teaching methods presented in Weissberg et al.'s (1980) 166-page curriculum guide. My retrospective evaluation of the manual (i.e., 5 years after its completion) is that although it has many positive clinical/educational features, it does not represent the only way—nor the absolute best way—to conduct SPS training. There remain, for example, unresolved controversies about the degree to which SPS programs should (a) employ directed self-instructional verus Piagetian discovery-oriented teaching approaches (Elias, 1980), (b) promote cognitive versus behavioral problem-solving skills (Michelson, Mannarino, Marchione, & Martin, 1982), (c) teach prosocial goals and behaviors or allow children to establish their own values, and (d) convey broadly applicable cognitive behavioral processes that are generalizable to many situations versus more discrete strategies for addressing specific tasks or problem areas (Durlak, 1983).

One unique training component of the Rochester program involves teaching children an explicit six-step cognitive framework for solving conflicts. At a fundamental level, one might question the desirability of training children to use a directed self-instructional approach for dealing with problems. Some beneficial interventions have adopted an alternative Piagetian-influenced discovery teaching strategy that encourages children to learn effective problem solving inductively through guided questioning, systematic exposure to a variety of problem situations, and discussing and practicing ways to handle those situations (e.g., Allen et al., 1976; Elardo & Cooper, 1977; Elias, 1980; Spivack & Shure, 1974). Research is needed to clarify the effects that directed self-instruction and discovery-oriented programs have on children with different sociodemographic, adjustive, and learner characteristics.

It is also important to examine the appropriateness of the six steps identified by the Rochester group. Are there too many steps? Are they presented in the proper order? Do they offer an optimal framework for solving problems? Winer's (1982) SPS program with suburban kindergarteners presents three steps: (a) say the problem, (b) think of lots of things to do, and (c) think of what might happen. Bash and Camp's (1980) intervention with elementary school children emphasizes four questions: (a) What is my problem? (b) How can I solve it? (c) Am I using the best plan? and (d) How did I do? Although most program children and teachers respond favorably to our basic six-step approach, more research is required to assess the comparative efficacy of competing self-instructional models.

Researchers should also evaluate the meaning and potential impact that each problem-solving step has on children's behavior. Illustratively, in our most recent SPS intervention, Weissberg et al. (1985) taught children to "think of lots of solutions" rather than to "think of as many solutions as you can." There are several reasons for the switch. Conceptually, one wonders whether generating too many solutions might lead occasionally to obsessionality and indecision rather than to selecting the best option. From a programmatic perspective, Weissberg, Gesten, Rapkin, Cowen, Davidson, Flores de Apodaca, & McKim (1981) found that prompting low-income inner-city children to keep on brainstorming solutions, without evaluating their effectiveness, sometimes resulted in a proliferation of maladaptive alternatives and disruptive behaviors. Based on that observation, they recommend that teachers (a) limit the number of aggressive solutions they allow children to offer, and (b) take a more active role in suggesting and modeling adaptive alternatives for children to consider. Finally, recent studies with older middle-income elementary school children suggest that solution effectiveness may play a more critical role than solution quantity in mediating social adjustment (Gesten et al., 1982; Hopper & Kirschenbaum, in press). Given that children tend to generate more adaptive strategies when they pair solutions with realistic consequences, one could reasonably argue that it is better to teach older children solution-consequence pairing from the start rather than teaching separate units on solution brainstorming and considering consequences. This, of course, can only be answered empirically.

SPS program developers also debate about whether training should be "value-free" or emphasize the importance of prosocial behavior. Spivack et al. (1976) suggest that research findings with inner-city preschoolers indicate "it is the ability to think of a wide range of solutions rather than specific content that most directly accompanies adjusted, adaptable behavior" (p. 26). Accordingly, they emphasize the importance of solution quantity over quality in their program. Children are taught to make their own judgments about which solutions are good by considering their consequences. This process is advanced outside of formal lessons when teachers dialogue with children to help them to consider the pros and cons of different options when conflicts occur during the day. In contrast, several SPS researchers who work with older children feel it is important to teach explicitly the importance of solution quantity *and* quality, focusing on social cognitive *and* behavioral skills. Illustratively, Bash and Camp (1980) train the selection of prosocial solutions by articulating four criteria for judging if a solution is a good one: (a) Is it safe? (b) Is it fair? (c) How does it make you and others feel? and (d) Does it solve the problem? Weissberg et al. (1985) accomplish a similar objective by suggesting that children's goals should be socially acceptable whenever possible. Michelson et al. (1982) do an exemplary job in teaching trainers and students to discuss, model, practice, and reinforce behavioral social skills that help people implement effective solutions to a range of problems. In one of the few comparative problem-solving intervention studies, they report that combined cognitive and behavioral problem-solving training benefitted children significantly more than separate cognitive or behavioral programs. Weissberg and Gesten (1982) also stress the importance of allowing children sufficient time to practice the behavioral integration of their newly acquired cognitive skills. They suggest that lengthening the Integration of Problem-Solving Behaviors unit from 4 lessons in their initial program to 15 in the current one played a critical role in helping children to consolidate their effective problem-solving behavior.

In conclusion, although several SPS classroom programs have enhanced the problem-solving skills and social adjustment of target children, there are still no outstanding SPS training models. Creative, persistent, and clinically sensitive program developers have designed relatively effective interventions, but SPS curriculum contents and instructional formats are still not sufficiently based on theory or research findings supporting their value. One danger of obtaining positive outcome findings is that curriculum developers often become content to replicate their results rather than continuing to improve their intervention procedures. This, unfortuntely, may lead to premature reification of a training effort that could benefit from further piloting and modification. Another related problem in the SPS literature is that most reviewers tend to group all interventions together without adequately emphasizing their varying contents and training methods. The major purpose of this section has been to highlight the importance of continuing to improve our efforts in these areas.

Structuring SPS Interventions to Succeed in the School Culture

Sarason (1982) brilliantly describes the complexity of entering the culture of schools as well as the difficulties inherent in introducing meaningful change in such settings. He makes it clear that there are many issues, beyond the curriculum content and instructional formats of training programs, that influence whether children benefit from an intervention. Questions identifying salient issues about successfully implementing a school-based SPS intervention may be grouped into two general categories: (a) structuring SPS programs to conform to the realities of the school setting, and (b) methods for instructing SPS trainers to teach lessons effectively.

Program Structure

Who should teach SPS programs? Should training be offered in or out of the classroom? What are the pros and cons of intervening with individuals, small groups, or classes? Empirical articles about interventions usually provide clear answers to the first two questions. Generally, however, the rationales underlying those decisions (i.e., the third question) are not expressed.

There are many valid reasons for choosing teachers to conduct classroom-based SPS programs. Rose (1982) suggests four: (a) interacting with a familiar adult and peers in a group setting is generally more attractive to children than meeting individually and infrequently with another adult; (b) because groups have a number and variety of children, there are multiple opportunities to observe the modeling of social skills as well as receive feedback, thus promoting effective social learning in a natural setting; (c) the group offers children the chance to teach one another skills, thus enhancing their own feelings of self-efficacy and social competence; and (d) given the high demand for services with limited mental health personnel, instructing teachers to offer yearly proactive social competence training may represent a beneficial cost-effective use of system resources. According to Hawkins and Weis (in press), classroom-based skills training has potential to be more powerful than individually oriented interventions because it maximizes opportunities for children to practice newly acquired abilities and receive consistent reinforcement for doing so.

Once one chooses to implement a school-based social-competence intervention there are several structural programmatic issues to consider: When in the school year should training begin? How long should each lesson last? How many formal lessons should there be per week and during the entire training experience? Is 1 year of training enough? How might other school personnel (e.g., non-program teachers, principals) support and enhance SPS training?

It is important to emphasize that it requires a significant amount of time for teachers and children to learn, integrate, and apply cognitive and behavioral problem-solving approaches adaptively. Training should start as early as possible in the school year. Interventions that begin in January or February may not allow sufficient time for children to practice and assimilate key concepts. Unfortunately, the educational and clinical quality of SPS training is sometimes sacrificed by the needs of researchers to (a) collect valid preprogram data (usually done from late September through mid-October), or (b) make final decisions about the assessment battery and intervention strategies to be used. The former delay is understandable and our clinical experience suggests that starting an intervention in late October allows sufficient training time so that the educational integrity of a program is not sacrificed. On the other hand, when program and evaluation planning are not completed until after winter recess, one might consider beginning the intervention during the subsequent school year rather than offering what may be too little training too late.

Successful SPS interventions with preschoolers and kindergarteners generally consist of 30 to 50 lessons presented during a 3- to 4-month period. Four to five 15- to 20-min lessons are taught weekly. With older elementary school children 20- to 30-min lessons are taught two or three times weekly. This frequency seems to meet the instructional needs of students and the preferences of teachers who require as much time as possible to teach traditional academic subjects. Weissberg and Gesten (1982) comment that programs that end shortly after the core SPS concepts have been conveyed often fail to produce maintenance and generalization of skill and adjustment improvements. They suggest that trainers should determine that children can transfer or adapt problem-solving strategies to a variety of situations before discontinuing formal training. There should also be ample opportunity to provide children with feedback and reinforcement when they attempt to solve problems independently. Consequently, a major portion of the formal curriculum should emphasize helping children master the application of skills once they have learned the entire problem-solving process. In general, the behavior of most program children starts to change, not while they are learning individual component skills, but rather once the overall cognitive strategies are learned and practiced. Thus, the final *Integration of Problem-Solving Behaviors* unit and postprogram activities appear critical to achieving long-term benefits.

Providing SPS training at the systems level is probably more beneficial and powerful than offering a one-time, single-setting classroom intervention. Accordingly, it is critical to develop low-cost methods to help other school personnel (e.g., principals, lunchroom monitors, other teachers) and parents support children's application of SPS learnings in other settings. Program teachers often express concern that some children's behavioral gains will be lost unless there is reinforcement for adaptive problem-solving behavior throughout the school and in next year's class. Some program evaluation findings suggest that 2 years of training may produce stronger positive effects than 1 (Spivack & Shure, 1982). However, conducting consecutive years of extensive formal training becomes extremely complex, especially since program activities must be varied to maintain children's motivation to learn. It may be more desirable to train entire school staffs both to offer brief booster review sessions and to use SPS dialoguing. In addition, parents may become informed training collaborators by (a) receiving occasional newsletters describing the content of lessons and informing them of ways to promote effective problem solving at home, (b) observing a class lesson toward the end of the program to see the entire process in action, or (c) attending parent workshops that both explain the rationale for SPS training and teach them to use dialoguing techniques.

Promoting SPS Trainer Competence: Instructional Issues

No matter how well-designed a training program and curriculum guide are, an SPS program will fail to improve children's social adjustment unless it is taught effectively by the trainer. Highly competent SPS instructors must master many diverse skills. At the most basic level, they should understand key program concepts and be able to convey them clearly to students. Learning to apply SPS strategies to resolve their own interpersonal problems often enhances teachers' motivation and ability to help their students do the same. Ideally, effective SPS trainers will also (a) be able to model adaptive problem-solving thinking and behavior, (b) use SPS dialoguing flexibly to support and reinforce each child's improved problem-solving behavior, (c) learn to distinguish when it is appropriate to employ dialoguing or another intervention approach to help children in need, and (d) be able to identify and remediate specific SPS deficits in children with varying skill levels or behavior problems. Realistically, it generally requires consultative support and teaching a program at least once before teachers become proficient in most of these areas.

There are several teacher-training or peer-group supervision procedures that can speed the development of instructional competence. Before formal classroom training begins, a few teacher meetings should be devoted to overviewing the entire training manual, learning key SPS concepts, and applying the SPS model to resolve a few commonly experienced teacher problems. The quality of actual classroom instruction appears to be better when teachers understand the entire SPS process from the start, rather than acquiring discrete concepts piecemeal. After the classroom program begins, it helps to have weekly group training/supervision meetings to discuss how previous lessons went and role play upcoming lessons. During these sessions, experienced teachers or consultants can (a) demonstrate how to dialogue with children, (b) discuss ways to evaluate students' skill acquisition levels (e.g., asking them to say out loud how they would solve a particular problem), and (c) consider situations where SPS approaches may be more or less appropriate to use than other management techniques. The opportunities to share reactions about the program, exchange suggestions about classroom management techniques, and watch each other teach have been characterized by teachers as valuable learning experiences. In addition, most teachers have welcomed the assistance of undergraduate aides in conducting lessons.

Although there has been little empirical research relating the instructional performance of SPS trainers to children's behavioral outcomes, it may be the case that training is most beneficial when teachers also model SPS behavior and dialogue with children outside of formal lessons. If this is true, identifying which SPS program elements mediate adjustive gains becomes more complex than initially proposed by Spivack and Shure (1974). Perhaps teacher instructional performance variables (e.g., fidelity to training procedures, use of dialoguing) and classroom social environment should be considered as potential adjustment mediators along with traditional factors such as cognitive and behavioral problem-solving skills and processes.

SPS program developers must also consider how to package interventions of documented effectiveness to increase their potential for widespread successful dissemination. Clearly, SPS curricula should have detailed lesson plans to increase the likelihood that problem-solving concepts are accurately conveyed. Treatment fidelity might also be promoted by including a series of video- or audiotapes demonstrating experienced trainers and coping models: (a) teaching key concepts, (b) modeling problem-solving thinking and behaviors, and (c) using SPS dialoguing with children (Kendall & Hollon, 1983). A tape showing a teacher training/supervision group with suggested guidelines for how teachers might set up their own local group might also be included.

It is also important to identify ways to minimize teacher-training and lesson-preparation time. Teacher workloads may be reduced by developing materials that present certain concepts and activities on films, tapes, or even computers. Finally, for SPS programs to become rooted in local schools, they must be supported by district administrators and Board of Education members. Although many teachers are eager to conduct SPS training for a variety of reasons (e.g., classroom management, creating a cooperative classroom learning environment, recognizing the importance of promoting positive social development), a reward or benefit structure should be established so that those who teach SPS programs are not doing so entirely through their own motivation and on their own time.

Concluding Comments

During the last decade there has been a dramatic increase in the number of SPS programs being implemented in elementary school classrooms. This proliferation has occurred in spite of mixed evaluation findings about the approach's efficacy. The major purpose of this chapter has been to identify issues that might help SPS program developers and researchers design and implement more effective classroom interventions. In that context I have suggested that there is considerable room for improvement in our training procedures.

During the Ottawa Conference (Research Strategies in Children's Social Skills Training, June 21-24), when I first presented the ideas in this paper, one of my esteemed colleagues asked, "Given our limited knowledge about fundamental relationships between SPS skills and adjustment, is it ethical to subject school children to SPS interventions?" Although we still have a lot ot learn, I think we know enough to pilot preliminary training projects. Furthermore, it is possible that we may learn more about SPS and adjustment linkage from the process of intervening than from basic research.

A variation on my colleague's question may be more important, heuristic, and challenging to answer: Under what conditions is it appropriate to intervene in the schools?

One prerequisite may be to develop a close ongoing collaborative relationship with school personnel in which the welfare of children is always paramount—that is, more important than the research study being conducted. It might be a more ethical practice to abandon rigorous experimental controls when implementing new interventions for the first time. Why not consider them pilot efforts that we are willing to modify as we go along based on the reactions of children, teachers, parents, and principals? Under those conditions we will achieve greater understanding about effective ecologically valid ways to conduct training programs. This approach, in combination with more basic research, will enable us ultimately to be more helpful to the children we are trying to serve.

Acknowledgments. My current social problem-solving research is funded by the William T. Grant Faculty Scholars Program in Mental Health of Children and by BRSG S07-PR07015, awarded by the Biomedical Research Support Grant Program, Division of Research Resources, National Institutes of Health. Much of the program development effort described in this chapter was supported by the New York State Department of Education.

I express my appreciation to Ellis L. Gesten, Emory L. Cowen, Gregory M. Herek, and SPS researchers and program participants from Rochester and Yale for their thoughtful contributions and supportive involvements in developing many of the ideas presented in this chapter.

References

Allen, G. J., Chinsky, J. M., Larcen, S. W., Lochman, J. E., & Selinger, H. V. (1976). *Community psychology and the schools: A behaviorally oriented multilevel preventive approach*. Hillsdale, NJ: Erlbaum.

Bandura, A. (1977). Self-efficacy: Toward a unifying theory of behavior change. *Psychological Review*, *84*, 191-215.

Bash, M. S., & Camp, B. W. (1980). Teacher training in the Think Aloud classroom program. In G. Cartledge & J. F. Milburn (Eds.), *Teaching social skills to children: Innovative approaches* (pp. 143-178). Elmsford, NY: Pergamon.

Cowen, E. L., Gesten, E. L., & Weissberg, R. P. (1980). An interrelated network of preventively oriented school-based mental health approaches. In R. H. Price & P. Politizer (Eds.), *Evaluation and action in the community context* (pp. 173-210). New York: Academic Press.

Cowen, E. L., Orgel, A. R., Gesten, E. L., & Wilson, A. B. (1979). The evaluation of an intervention program for young school children with acting-out problems. *Journal of Abnormal Child Psychology*, *7*, 381-396.

Cowen, E. L., Pedersen, A., Babigian, H., Izzo, L. D., & Trost, M. A. (1973). Long-term follow-up of early detected vulnerable children. *Journal of Consulting and Clinical Psychology*, *41*, 438-446.

Cowen, E. L., Spinell, A., Wright, S., & Weissberg, R. P. (1983). Continuing dissemination of a school-based mental health program. *Professional Psychology*, *13*, 118-127.

Cowen, E. L., Trost, M. A., Lorion, R. P., Dorry, D., Izzo, L. D., & Isaacson, R. V. (1975). *New ways in school mental health: Early detection and prevention of school maladaption*. New York: Human Sciences Press.

Durlak, J. A. (1983). Social problem-solving as a primary prevention strategy. In R. D. Felner, L. A. Jason, J. N. Moritsugu, & S. S. Farber (Eds.), *Preventive psychology* (pp. 31-48). New York: Pergamon Press.

D'Zurilla, T. J., & Goldfried, M. R. (1971). Problem-solving and behavior modification. *Journal of Abnormal Psychology*, *78*, 107-126.

Elardo, P. T., & Cooper, M. (1977). *Aware: Activities for social development*. Menlo Park, CA: Addison-Wesley.

Elias, M. J. (1980). *Developing instructional strategies for television-based preventive mental health curricula in elementary school settings*. Unpublished doctoral dissertation, University of Connecticut, Storrs, CT.

Felner, R. D., Norton, P. L., Cowen, E. L., & Farber, S. S. (1981). A prevention program for children experiencing life crisis. *Professional Psychology, 12*, 446-452.

Furman, W. (1980). Promoting social develoment: Developmental implications for treatment. In B. B. Lahey & A. E. Kazdin (Eds.), *Advances in clinical child psychology* (Vol. 3, pp. 1-40). New York: Plenum Press.

Gesten, E. L., Flores de Apodaca, R., Rains, M., Weissberg, R. P., & Cowen, E. L. (1979). Promoting peer related social competence in schools. In M. W. Kent & J. E. Rolf (Eds.), *Primary prevention of psychopathology: Vol. 3. Social competence in children* (pp. 220-247). Hanover, NH: University Press of New England.

Gesten, E. L., Rains, M., Rapkin, B. D., Weissberg, R. P., Flores de Apodaca, R., Cowen, E. L., & Bowen, R. (1982). Training children in social problem-solving skills: A competence building approach, first and second look. *American Journal of Community Psychology, 10*, 95-115.

Hawkins, J. D., & Weis, J. G. (in press). The social development model: An integrated approach to delinquency prevention. *Journal of Primary Prevention*.

Hopper, R., & Kirschenbaum, D. S. (in press). Social problem-solving and social competence in preadolescents: Is inconsistent problem solving problematic? *Developmental Psychology*.

Kendall, P. C., & Hollon, S. D. (1983). Calibrating the quality of therapy: Collaboratiave archiving of tape samples from therapy outcome trials. *Cognitive Therapy and Research, 7*, 199-204.

Kirschenbaum, D. S., & Ordman, A. M. (1984). Preventive interventions for children: Cognitive behavioral perspectives. In A. W. Meyers & W. E. Craighead (Eds), *Cognitive behavior therapy for children* (pp. 377-409). New York: Plenum Press.

Krasnor, L. R., & Rubin, K. (1981). Assessment of social problem solving in young children. In T. Merluzzi, C. Glass, & M. Genest (Eds.), *Cognitive assessment* (pp. 452-478). New York: Guilford Press.

Ladd, G. W., & Mize, J. (1983). A cognitive-social model of social-skill training. *Psychological Review, 90*, 127-157.

McKim, B. J., Weissberg, R. P., Cowen, E. L., Gesten, E. L., & Rapkin, B. D. (1982). A comparison of the problem-solving ability and adjustment of suburban and urban third-grade children. *American Journal of Community Psychology, 10*, 155-169.

Meichenbaum, D. (1977). *Cognitive-behavior modificaiton: An integrative approach*. New York: Plenum.

Michelson, L., Mannarino, A. P., Marchione, K., & Martin, P. (1982). *Relative and combined efficacy of behavioral and cognitive problem-solving programs with elementary-school children*. Unpublished manuscript, University of Pittsburgh, Pittsburgh, PA.

Pellegrini, D., & Urbain, E. S. (in press). An evaluation of interpersonal cognitive problem-solving training efforts with children. *Journal of Child Psychology and Psychiatry*.

Prevention Task Panel Report (1978). *Task panel reports submitted to the President's Commission on Mental Health* (Vol. 4). Washington, DC: U.S. Government Printing Office.

Rose, S. R. (1982). Promoting social competence in children: A classroom approach to social and cognitive skill training. *Child & Youth Services, 5*, 43-59.

Rubin, K., & Krasnor, L. R. (in press). Social cognitive and social behavioral perspectives in problem solving. In N. Perlmutter (Ed.), *The Minnesota Symposium on Child Psychology*. Hillsdale, NJ: Erlbaum.

Sarason, S. B. (1982). *The culture of the school and the problem of change* (Vol. 18, 2nd ed.). Boston: Allyn and Bacon.

Spivack, G., Platt, J. J., & Shure, M. B. (1976). *The problem-solving approach to adjustment*. San Francisco: Jossey-Bass.

Spivack, G., & Shure, M. B. (1974). *Social adjustment of young children*. San Francisco: Jossey-Bass.

Spivack, G., & Shure, M. B. (1982). The cognition of social adjustment: Interpersonal cognitive problem-solving thinking. In B. B. Lahey & A. E. Kazdin (Eds.), *Advances in child clinical psychology* (Vol. 5, pp. 323-372). New York: Plenum Press.

Urbain, E. S., & Kendall, P. C. (1980). Review of social-cognitive problem-solving interventions with children. *Psychological Bulletin, 8*, 109-143.

Weissberg, R. P., & Gesten, E. L. (1982). Considerations for developing effective school-based social problem-solving training programs. *School Psychology Review, 11*, 56-63.

Weissberg, R. P., Gesten, E. L., Carnrike, C. L., Toro, P. A., Rapkin, B. D., Davidson, E., & Cowen, E. L. (1981). Social problem-solving skills training: A competence building intervention with second to fourth-grade children. *American Journal of Community Psychology, 9*, 411-423.

Weissberg, R. P., Gesten, E. L., Liebenstein, N. L., Doherty-Schmid, K., & Hutton, H. (1980). *The Rochester social problem-solving (SPS) program: A training manual for teachers of 2nd-4th grade children*. Rochester, NY: University of Rochester.

Weissberg, R. P., Gestern, E. L., Rapkin, B. D., Cowen, E. L., Davidson, E., Flores de Apodaca, R., & McKim, B. J. (1981). The evaluation of a social problem-solving training program for suburban and inner-city third-grade children. *Journal of Consulting and Clinical Psychology, 49*, 251-261.

Weissberg, R. P., Hawkins, J. A., & Krauss, D. H. (1985). *The evaluation of a social problem-solving intervention with middle-school children*. Unpublished manuscript, Yale University, New Haven, CT.

Winer, J. I., Hilpert, P. L., Gesten, E. L., Cowen, E. L., & Schubin, W. E. (1982). The evaluation of a kindergarten social problem-solving program. *Journal of Primary Prevention, 2*, 205-216.

Winter, J. T. (1982). *An evalution of a planned short-term intervention approach for children with school adjustment problems*. Unpublished doctoral dissertation, University of Rochester, Rochester, NY.

CHAPTER 15

Documenting the Effects of Social Skill Training With Children: Process and Outcome Assessment

Gary W. Ladd

Although social scientists have long been interested in methods for guiding children's behavior and development, the use of skill training procedures as a means of influencing the course of children's peer interactions and relationships is a relatively recent undertaking. Concern for socially disadvantaged children has been a primary impetus for this work, and recent findings from research on the correlates and antecedents of peer status (see Ladd & Asher, 1985), as well as evidence linking childhood peer problems with later maladjustment (see Kohlberg, LaCrosse, & Ricks, 1972; Ladd & Asher, 1985) have intensified the search for effective interventions. At present, however, little is known about how skill-based interventions may affect children's social skills or lead to changes in their peer relations.

The purpose of this chapter is to examine some of the key assumptions that underlie current research on social skill training with children, and to explore the implications of these assumptions for future assessment practices. Assessment is regarded as an important, but often neglected area of social skill training research —one that requires further attention if both the broader outcomes of intervention (e.g., effect on peer relations) as well as the specific processes of behavior change are to be understood. Before turning to these issues, however, some of the trends and issues that have preceded and possibly influenced the assumptions that guide current research in this field are reviewed.

Considerable evolution has occurred in researcher's ideas about the factors responsible for children's difficulties in peer relations and the means by which these problems may be resolved. Early efforts to intervene on behalf of unpopular children were conducted amid speculation that children of low social status were either victims of the social structure of their peer groups or architects of their own difficulties. Moreno (1934) favored the view that low social status was a position that evolved from the structure or organization of the peer group and was, therefore, a condition imposed on the child. Other early researchers, such as Koch (1933, 1935) and Northway (1944), were more inclined to view low peer status as a consequence of the child's attributes and social behaviors. Given the type of intervention research conducted during this era (e.g., Chittenden, 1942; Koch,

1935), it seems clear that the latter perspective was dominant among the early researchers who sought to explore both the origins and treatment of children's peer difficulties.

During the 1950s and 1960s investigators began to refer to unpopular children as "social isolates" and, in their descriptions of these children, imply a lack of involvement and participation in the peer group. Accordingly, the aim of much of the intervention work conducted during this era was to increase the isolate's frequency of interaction (e.g., Allen, Hart, Buell, Harris, & Wolfe, 1964; O'Connor, 1969, 1972) or contact with higher status peers (see Bonney, 1971; Lilly, 1971). Although seldom explicitly stated as the justification for intervention research, this perspective appears to be consistent with the "contact hypothesis" advanced by Allport (1954) to explain the relationship between social experience (i.e., contact) and attitude formation (e.g., prejudice).

The next major change in the underlying assumptions guiding peer-oriented intervention research grew out of research with both adults and children and has come to be called the "skill deficit hypothesis" (Asher & Renshaw, 1981; Curran, 1979; Ladd & Mize, 1983). Included in the skill deficit hypothesis are the following key propositions: (a) many children experience difficulties in peer relations (i.e., peer neglect, rejection, friendlessness) because they lack basic interpersonal skills; (b) social skills can be learned, that is acquired by children from interventions designed to teach social skills; and (c) the social skills children acquire through training generalize to the peer group and are instrumental in resolving their peer difficulties.

Due to the prominence of these assumptions in current social skill training theory and research, each will be examined in greater detail in the following sections. In reviewing this material, attention will be focused on the extent to which these assumptions are grounded in empirical research, and on the implications of each proposition for assessment practices in social skill training.

Assumption 1: Children With Poor Peer Relations Lack Social Skills

The premise behind this assumption is that children vary in the degree to which they possess and utilize specific social abilities, and these differences are, in turn, responsible for their successes or failures in peer relations. The origins of these individual differences are not well-understood, but are generally attributed to a variety of psychosocial and environmental factors including developmental lags, aberrant socialization, learning disorders, and lack of experience with peers.

Approaches to Defining and Documenting Skill Deficits

While attractive in a global sense, the exact meaning of the skill deficit concept has been difficult for researchers to define (see Curran, 1979; Ladd, 1984). For some investigators (e.g., Curran, 1979), a skill deficit is synonymous with the absence of observable behaviors—especially those behaviors that serve important social functions (e.g., gaining entry to play activities). Rather than an absence of behavior, other investigators have interpreted the concept as referring to social abilities that may, relative to peers, be judged as less well developed, inappropriate, or inept. In contrast to the former view, this concept of a skill deficit is often broadly defined and may include cognitive and affective factors as well as overt behaviors (see Ladd & Mize, 1983).

Along with efforts to define skill deficits, researchers have been faced with the difficult task of demonstrating that children with problematic peer relations are, in fact, deficient in specific social skills. One approach to identifying children's skill deficits follows from the "absence of behavior" definition, and consists of observing the extent to which children fail to exhibit the target social skills in peer interaction (see Bierman & Furman, 1984; Ladd, 1981; Oden & Asher, 1977). Unfortunately, it cannot be assumed that low rates of occurrence are equivalent to the absence of a skill in the child's repertoire. Nonetheless, this approach does suggest chronic disuse or a lack of reliance on specific social skills.

A second type of evidence used to document skill deficits stems from the latter definition and is exemplified by investigator's efforts to compare the characteristics of socially successful and unsuccessful children. This approach differs from the former means of identifying skill deficits in that deficiencies are measured in relative rather than absolute terms (e.g., degree to which children's skills differ from a reference group of "competent" peers, rather than an arbitrary standard such as zero frequency). One potential problem with this approach is that most of the past research in this area is correlational in nature. Due to this design constraint, it is often unclear whether the characteristics that discriminate socially successful and unsuccessful children are consequences of their peer problems rather than causes. While this is an important distinction, it may be fallacious to argue that only the long-term antecedents of peer problems should be viewed and treated as skill deficits. For example, while a lack of self-confidence may be a result rather than a cause of a child's escalating interpersonal difficulties, its function thereafter may be to inhibit his or her social overtures and involvement with peers. Although not technically a cause of the peer problems, the low self-confidence may serve to maintain the difficulty, and thus may be viewed as a deficit in need of remediation.

In sum, there are a number of issues associated with the definition and documentation of social skill deficits that make it difficult to test adequately the assumption that poor peer relations can be a result of skill deficiencies. There is, however, a growing body of empirical evidence that may help to delineate potential areas of skill deficit and, by doing so, help to illuminate avenues for successful remediation. The section that follows is intended to provide a closer look at these findings and their potential implications for social skill training and assessment.

Types of Social Skill Deficits as Identified in Past Research

There has been a growing tendency to view children's interpersonal skillfulness as the ability to orchestrate a range of cognitive, motoric, and affective processes (see Asher & Renshaw, 1981; Ladd & Mize, 1983). Within each of these three domains, numerous factors have been identified as "components of skillfulness" and, therefore represent potential areas of skill deficit. Some of the factors that have become prominent in the literature on children's social skills are reviewed by domains in the sections that follow.

Social Cognitive/Knowledge Deficits

Only recently have investigators begun to explore the relationship between children's social cognitions and knowledge and their functioning in the peer group. Among the variables that have received the most research attention are children's goals in social situations, their knowledge of appropriate strategies for achieving social goals, and children's ability to comprehend and monitor social events accurately.

Research on children's interpersonal goals has its roots in the problem-solving literature and is guided by the hypothesis that the lack of structure afforded by most social situations (i.e., social situations are seen as inherently ambiguous or "weakly scripted") requires that children continuously devise a plan or purpose for their involvement (Renshaw & Asher, 1983). Because goals are thought to mediate behavior, it is also hypothesized that children who tend to construe goals that are situationally or socially inappropriate will experience difficulty in peer relations.

Recent research in this area has been conducted with both grade-school and preschool children, and has been designed to relate individual differences in children's goal orientation to their social status among peers. Using both a production and recognition task, Renshaw and Asher (1983) asked third- through fifth-graders to indicate their goals for each of four hypothetical peer situations (e.g., entering a group). Whereas well-accepted children were found to differ from low-accepted children in that their spontaneously produced goals were rated by judges as more positive and outgoing, differences due to peer status were absent on the goal-recognition task. These findings imply that, while unpopular children may be able to recognize "appropriate" social goals, they may lack the skills needed to produce them spontaneously in peer situations.

In a subsequent study, Taylor and Asher (1984) employed a questionnaire to elicit grade-schooler's goals for game situations with peers. Analyses revealed four distinct goal types (e.g., relationship, performance, avoidance goals) that were found to vary with age and peer status. Whereas relationship goals were found to be more predictive of peer popularity among third- and fourth-graders, performance-oriented goals were more associated with status differences among fifth- and sixth-graders. These findings suggest that low-status children may be less likely to view task situations in ways that allow them to seek affiliative ties or operate as competent "performers."

Although less research has been conducted on the goal orientations of pre-school children, observational approaches to assessment are suggested in at least two studies (Krasnor, 1982; Lubin & Forbes, 1981). Unfortunately, these investigators did not explore the relationship between children's social goals and their effectiveness with peers.

Researchers have also been intrigued by the possibility that socially disadvantaged children might differ from peers in their knowledge about how to achieve social goals. Consistent with the assumptions found in the problem-solving literature, it has been hypothesized that once children have chosen to pursue a social goal they must also formulate a means to that end (i.e., devise a strategy to achieve the goal).

Much of the research conducted with grade-school children has been designed to examine variations in the content or *quality* of children's interpersonal strategies for peer situations. Gottman, Gonso, and Rasmussen (1975) asked popular and unpopular children to role play friendship-making strategies with an adult. Consistent with a strategy-deficit interpretation, results showed that unpopular children knew less about friendship making then did popular children. Pursuing this line of research, Ladd and Oden (1979) asked grade-schoolers to suggest aid-giving strategies for hypothetical situations in which a peer was depicted in need of help, and found that unpopular children's strategies were unique (nonnormative) relative to same-sex classmates and often situationally inappropriate. Along with the data collected on children's goals, Renshaw and Asher (1983) examined the strategies suggested by popular and unpopular grade-schoolers for four hypothetical peer situations presented under two conditions: with or without an explicitly defined social goal. Although a wider range of strategies was obtained in the no-goal condition, those offered by popular children were rated as more positive and accommodating toward peers than those suggested by low-status children regardless of the goal condition. This seemingly consistent pattern of findings is contradicted by a study (Vosk, Forehand, Parker, & Rickard, 1982) in which a fixed-alternative format was used to elicit grade-school children's strategies. Results indicated no difference between popular and unpopular children in their strategy choices; a finding the authors attributed to lack of response variance.

Considerable research on children's strategy knowledge has also been conducted with preschool children. Using a hypothetical situations methodology, Asher and Renshaw (1981) found that, although the strategies suggested by unpopular preschoolers did not differ from those of popular peers in assertiveness, their ideas were more often rated as unfriendly or ineffective. Rubin and Daniels-Bierness (1983) found that the quality of young children's strategies bore a relationship to their peer status in both kindergarten and first grade. Similar relationships were also obtained by Rubin, Daniels-Beirness, and Hayvren (1982) with an additional sample of kindergarteners. In an investigation by Mize and Ladd (1984), preschoolers' strategies, when rated for friendliness, were found to correlate with measures of classroom behavior and peer status. By observing children's actual problem-solving strategies in the classroom, Sharp (1983) found that children who were classified by teachers as low in social competence tended to employ more nonverbal and antisocial strategies as means of coping with the classroom environment than did those rated as high in competence.

Beyond these qualitative distinctions, much of the problem-solving research with children has also been focused on the *quantity* of alternative strategies a child may possess for resolving social dilemmas. Presumably, measures of this type are important because they reflect the range of strategies available for the child to act upon in a given situation. While some researchers have found a relationship between this form of strategy knowledge and children's social adjustment (e.g., Spivack & Shure, 1974), others have not.

Ladd and Oden (1979) found that, beyond information about the normativeness of children's strategies, the range of grade-schooler's ideas about how to assist peers bore little relationship to their sociometric status. Weissberg et al. (1981), in a study with children from mixed socioeconomic backgrounds, also failed to detect a relationship between the range of strategies children suggested and their overall social adjustment.

Studies with preschoolers provide somewhat stronger evidence for a relationship between strategy alternatives and peer competence. Studies by Rubin and colleagues (Rubin, 1982; Rubin & Daniels-Beirness, 1983; Rubin, Daniels-Bierness, & Hayvren, 1982) revealed that young children who employ a wide range of alternative strategies on problem-solving tasks tend to play more constructively and are better liked by peers. Similarly, Olson, Johnson, Belleau, Parks, and Barrett (1983) found that the total number of strategies suggested by preschoolers on the PIPS predicted their classroom involvement and participation with peers. In contrast, however, Sharp (1981) found that preschoolers trained in problem-solving increased in their ability to generate alternative strategies but made no corresponding changes in their behavior toward peers.

Videotape methodology has been the dominant method for studying children's social perceptions. The small amount of empirical work conducted in this area is based on the hypothesis that, before children can formulate effective social goals, strategies, and so on, they must first be able to detect and interpret available interpersonal and contextual cues. Ince, Messe, Stollack, and Smith (1980) found that children who were rated by their teachers as socially competent were more accurate in their recall of interactions depicted on videotapes, and imputed more positive attributes to the interactants than did less-competent children. Putallaz (1983) created a measure of perceptual accuracy by asking pre-first-grade boys to watch and interpret videotapes of their attempts to join peer confederates in various group activities. Findings indicated that ratings of the content accuracy of children's reconstructions were, along with their ability to produce situationally relevant behaviors, predictive of their peer status in first grade.

There is also evidence to suggest that aggressive children, considered by many to be at risk for peer difficulties (see Dodge, 1983), are more likely to misinterpret situational and interpersonal cues. Dodge and colleagues (see Dodge, 1980; Dodge & Frame, 1982; Dodge & Newman, 1981) have found that in situations where a peer's intentions are ambiguous, aggressive children are more likely to misconstrue the peers' actions as hostile or threatening.

A relationship between children's other-oriented perceptual skills and their competence in peer relations has also been reported in studies with preschoolers. Peery (1979) found that, on a social comprehension measure designed to assess children's ability to identify others' affective states, popular preschoolers had significantly higher scores than their rejected classmates. Gouze, Gordon, and Rayias (1983) found that aggressive preschoolers, when compared to nonaggressive agemates, were more inclined to orient and attend to agonistic social encounters, as depicted in puppet show scenes.

In contrast to research with adults (e.g., Snyder, 1974), methodological and measurement constraints have interfered with researchers attempts to study self-monitoring deficits in children. One exception, however, is a recent study by Saarni (1984) in which children's tendencies to reveal negative expressive behaviors (disappointment over a less than desirable gift) were studied in relation to social situations where, by convention, positive expressive behaviors are expected (gratitude toward the giver). Results indicated that, whereas older children tended to maintain positive expressions after receiving an undesirable gift, younger children often failed to conceal their disappointment. One interpretation of these findings is that younger children are less aware of the social conventions governing such situations and/or are less able to monitor the degree to which their actions are consistent with these norms. Unfortunately, no effort was made to determine whether individual differences in this skill predict problems in peer relations.

Behavioral Deficits

Two sources of empirical information are often considered useful in defining potential deficits in behavioral skill, including: (a) studies on behavioral correlates and antecedents of peer status, and (b) investigations designed to test the effectiveness of behaviorally oriented interventions with unpopular children. From the former domain, there is growing evidence to suggest that unpopular children lack prosocial skills. Data on grade-school children suggest that low-status children are less able to cooperate with peers, engage in social conversation, communicate effectively, dispense positive reinforcement, cite social norms, and so on (e.g., Coie & Kupersmidt, 1983; Dodge, 1983; Gottman et al., 1975; Ladd, 1983). Similar findings have been reported with preschool samples (e.g., Hartup, Glazer, & Charlesworth, 1967; Moore & Upedegraff, 1964).

The use of aggressive behaviors also marks children who differ in peer status, as can be seen in a substantial number of studies conducted with both grade-school and preschool children (e.g., Coie & Kupersmidt, 1983; Dodge, 1983; Ladd, 1983; Rubin, 1982). However, these findings would seem to suggest a behavioral excess rather than deficit hypothesis and may, therefore, imply an approach to intervention that is focused on more than just the facilitation of prosocial skills.

Children with diminished peer popularity or sociability may also be deficient in their ability to engage in age-appropriate play styles. Rubin and colleagues

(Rubin, 1982; Rubin & Daniels-Beirness, 1983; Rubin et al., 1982) have found that popular preschoolers are more able to pursue constructive play activities and participate in group dramatic play and games with rules. Less-popular children, in contrast to agemates, were more likely to engage in more immature forms of play (e.g., rough and tumble, solitary functional, and dramatic play) and disruptive activities.

The behaviors children use as they attempt to integrate themselves into peer activities also appear to differentiate popular and unpopular children. Research conducted with both grade-school and preschool children (Dodge, Schlundt, Schocken, & Delugah, 1983; Putallaz, 1983; Putallaz & Gottman, 1981) suggests that, when popular children are in the role of "newcomer," they are more skilled at producing behaviors that complement peers' activities than are unpopular children. The tendency for unpopular children to employ more disruptive entry bids may be indicative of a deficiency in their ability to adopt the peers' frame of reference and produce situationally appropriate or relevant responses.

Socially successful children have also been found to direct their interactions to peers of similar status, respond more positively to peers' overtures (e.g., Dodge, 1983; Ladd, 1983; Putallaz & Gottman, 1981), and maintain interactions for longer durations (Dodge, 1983). Although far from conclusive, these findings suggest that deficits in children's responsiveness to peers may be related to problem in peer relations.

Finally, in several recent skill interventions that have produced improvements in children's peer relations (e.g., Bierman & Furman, 1984; Gresham & Nagle, 1980; Ladd, 1981; Oden & Asher, 1977), the training has been designed to enhance children's prosocial behaviors with peers. These data would seem to corroborate the data from correlational studies suggesting that deficits in prosocial behavior are partly responsible for children's peer difficulties.

Affective Deficits

It is also possible that children's ability to participate effectively in peer relations is influenced by their affective dispositions and states (see Ladd & Mize, 1983). Using a self-report measure, Wheeler and Ladd (1982) found a moderate but significant correlation between grade-school children's feelings of self-confidence toward performing specific social skills and their social status among peers. As part of a larger research program, Harter (1982) assessed children's views of their competence in peer relations and found it to be correlated with peer status. These findings seem to suggest that children who are experiencing peer difficulties are more likely to doubt their own abilities and perceive themselves as less able to form peer relationships.

Children who are less well-liked by peers may experience higher levels of anxiety. Wheeler and Ladd (1982) found an inverse relationship between measures of children's self-confidence and generalized anxiety. In developing a situation-specific anxiety measure called the Children's Concerns Inventory, Buhrmester (1982) found significant negative correlations between children's self-reported anxiety about peer acceptance and their peer and self-assessments of sociometric status.

Finally, the findings of Goetz and Dweck (1980) suggest that low- as opposed to well-accepted children are may be prone to interpret mild peer rejection as resulting from their own incompetence. These same children were also less likely to persist in efforts to gain inclusion into a peer activity and showed greater deterioration in their use of alternative behavioral strategies. While data from this study and the preceding investigations are suggestive of deficits in the affective dispositions of socially successful and unsuccessful children, considerable research is needed to clarify if and how these factors may serve to impede to maintain children's peer difficulties.

Implications for Social Skill Training and Assessment

Although not all the variables reviewed in the preceding section may prove to be deficiencies that contribute to children's peer difficulties, these factors can be seen as a list of suspected deficits that may warrant attention in skill-based interventions. Although firm conclusions about the range or type of skill deficits experienced by children within or across age levels must await further investigation, it may be useful to consider how the extant information may be used to shape the design and curriculum of contemporary social skill training interventions.

Skill Deficits as a Source of Training Objectives

Prior research on potential skill deficits may be classified into three broad domains, as patterned after a model proposed by Ladd and Mize (1983) and illustrated in Table 15.1. Within each of these domains, potential skill deficits may be identified along with existing measures and assessment methods.

Further examination of the existing data base reveals both similarities and differences by age levels (i.e., preschool vs. grade school) in the types of deficits studied and, consequently, the implications for intervention. Findings pertaining to children's social cognitions/knowledge would seem to provide support for the development of interventions designed to foster primarily strategy content (e.g., prosocial solutions to peer problems) as opposed to diversity, especially with older children. The recent research on children's social goals, which has been conducted primarily with grade-school children, suggests the additional objective of helping children to view peer activities as opportunities for developing and maintaining affiliative relationships, as opposed to contexts for maximizing self-gains or avoiding others. Among grade-school children, current findings raise the possibility that success in peer relations may also be enhanced by fostering their abilities to process and remember social events (Ince et al., 1983), draw accurate inferences about peers' motives (Dodge, 1980; Dodge & Frame, 1982), and monitor their own behaviors (Saarni, 1984). For preschoolers, the lower scores received by unpopular children on the social comprehension measures employed by Putallaz (1983) and Peery (1979) can be interpreted as a basis for

TABLE 15.1. A taxonomy of potential social skill deficits and corresponding assessment methods as identified in previous research with preschool and grade school children.

Domain/deficit type	Assessment method	Sample/exemplary studies
Social cognitive/ knowledge deficits		
Social goals	Hypothetical situations	
	Enactive interview	Preschool
		Mize & Ladd (1984)
	Verbal interview	Preschool
		Mize & Ladd (1984)
		Grade school
		Renshaw & Asher (1983)
	Written questionnaire	Grade school
		Taylor & Asher (1984)
	Classroom situations	
	Direct observations	Preschool
		Krasnor (1982)
Social strategies	Hypothetical situations	
	Enactive interview	Preschool
		Mize & Ladd (1984)
	Verbal interview	Preschool
		Asher & Renshaw (1981)
		Olson, Johnson, Belleau, Parks, & Barrett (1983)
		Mize & Ladd (1984)
		Rubin & Daniel-Bierness (1983)
		Rubin (1982)
		Sharp (1981)
		Spivack & Shure (1974)
		Grade school
		Ladd & Oden (1979)
		Renshaw & Asher (1983)
		Weissberg et al. (1981)
	Role playing	Grade school
		Gottman, Gonso, & Rasmussen (1975)
	Fixed alternatives	Grade school
		Vosk, Forehand, Parker, & Rickard, (1982)
	Classroom situations	
	Direct observations	Preschool
		Sharp (1983)
Social recall	Videotaped interactions	
	Stimulus recognition	Grade school
		Ince et al. (1980)
	Stimulus recall	Grade school
		Dodge & Frame (1982)
		Dodge & Newman (1981)

TABLE 15.1. (continued)

Domain/deficit type	Assessment method	Sample/exemplary studies
Perceptual accuracy	Videotaped entry situations Stimulus reconstruction	Preschool Putallaz (1983)
Cue interpretation/ social comprehension	Simulated situations Behavior observation	Grade school Dodge (1980)
	Vignettes Verbal report	Grade school Dodge & Frame (1982)
	Cue matching	Preschool Peery (1979)
Monitoring peer behavior	Puppet shows Direct observation	Preschool Gouze et al. (1983)
Self-monitoring	Simulated situations Direct observation	Grade school Saarni (1984)
Behavior deficits		
Prosocial behaviors	Classroom situations Direct observation	Preschool Hartup et al. (1967) Moore & Updegraff (1964) Grade school Gottman et al. (1975)
	Structured play groups Direct observation	Grade school Dodge (1983) Coie & Kupersmidt (1983)
	Playground situations Direct observation	Grade school Ladd (1983)
Play patterns/styles	Classrooms situations Direct observation	Preschool Rubin (1982) Rubin & Daniels-Bierness (1983) Rubin, Daniels-Bierness, & Hayvren (1982) Grade school Benson & Gottman (1975)
	Playground situations Direct observation	Grade school Ladd (1983)

TABLE 15.1. (continued)

Domain/deficit type	Assessment method	Sample/exemplary studies
Behavioral relevance	Simulated entry situations Direct observation	Preschool Putallaz (1983) Dodge et al. (1983) Grade school Pullataz & Gottman (1981)
	Unstructured play groups Direct observation	Grade school Dodge et al. (1983)
Responsiveness to peer's overtures	Classroom situations Direct observation	Grade school Benson & Gottman (1975) Dodge (1983) Gottman et al. (1975) Preschool Masters & Furman (1981)
Affective deficits		
Social self-efficacy	Paper and pencil scale Self-report	Grade school Wheeler & Ladd (1982)
Perceived social competence	Paper and pencil scale Self-report	Grade school Harter (1982)
Social anxiety	Paper and pencil scale Self-report	Grade school Buhrmester (1982)
Incompetence attributions	Vignettes Fixed alternatives	Grade school Goetz & Dweck (1980)

teaching children to interpret peers' actions and feeling states accurately. Given the exaggerated salience that aggressive acts appear to have for less-competent preschoolers (Gouze et al., 1983), it may be that redirecting their attention toward peers' prosocial behaviors would promote greater awareness and/or learning of socially adaptive responses.

Data from both correlational and experimental intervention studies suggest that children with peer problems may benefit from procedures designed to foster prosocial skills. However, the specific prosocial skills that are likely to lead to improved peer relations at various ages are not well-defined. Whereas skills such as communicating effectively and giving social reinforcement have been found to be related to peer competence both in preschool and grade school (e.g., Hartup et al., 1967; Rubin, 1982), research on other correlates such as norm setting and social conversations has been limited to older samples (e.g., Ladd, 1983; Putallaz & Gottman, 1981).

Existing research on the play patterns of socially successful and unsuccessful children suggests differing emphases in interventions for older and younger children. Whereas interventions with preschoolers might be focused on increasing their involvement in organized group and constructive solitary play activities (see Rubin, 1982), research on the play patterns of grade-school children (e.g., Ladd, 1983), suggests a need to re-engineer the social environment so as to provide greater access to activities with well liked peers (see Bierman & Furman, 1984).

Interventions aimed at remediating behavioral deficits may also take the form of teaching children how to integrate themselves into play groups by employing behaviors that complement rather than disrupt peers' activities. Moreover, because there is evidence linking deficits in behavioral relevance with peer difficulties, both for preschool and early grade-school children (e.g., Dodge et al., 1983; Putallaz, 1983), there is reason to anticipate that interventions of this type may benefit children at both age levels.

Procedures for modifying children's responsiveness to peers may also be warranted. For example, children may benefit by learning how to adopt reciprocal roles in play activities, reward peers' overtures, and maintain interactions. Moreover, research with both older (e.g., Benson & Gottman, 1975; Dodge, 1983) and younger children (Masters & Furman, 1981) supports this recommendation.

Potential affective deficits may also warrant attention in future intervention studies. Based on the findings of Goetz and Dweck (1980), it can be argued that less-competent children may benefit from learning to monitor and modify self-defeating attributions about their social abilities and relationships. Teaching children to attribute social difficulties to a lack of effort as opposed to personal incompetence may help to inoculate them against future helplessness and debilitating affective states. Alternatively, interventions may also be geared toward helping children see themselves as competent performers of specific social skills and desirable playmates. Although interpersonal anxiety may not represent a "deficit" as such, in an emotional sense it may represent the antithesis of self-confidence (see Wheeler & Ladd, 1982) and, thereby, justify the inclusion of methods for relieving these emotions during skill-training interventions.

Assessment of Skill Deficits in Social Skill Training

The literature on children's skill deficits also has important ramifications for assessment practices in social skill training. Until recently, it was often assumed that children who were experiencing peer difficulties would benefit from learning a prescribed set of social skills. Assessments designed to identify the specific skills that might be lacking or deficient in the child's repertoire and, potentially contributing to his or her peer difficulties, have seldom been employed.

A current trend is for investigators to supplement the criteria used to identify children with peer problems (e.g., sociometric indices) with measures of the specific skills targeted for remediation (see Bierman & Furman, 1984; Ladd,

1981). While an advance over earlier studies, the risk here is that many additional deficits, some of which may be of equal or greater importance than those stressed in the training curriculum, may go unnoticed and untreated.

Several compelling reasons suggest that a comprehensive program of diagnostic assessments should be employed. First, because a wide variety of skill deficits may contribute to children's peer difficulties, it is difficult for investigators to fully anticipate the various skills that should be included in a training curriculum. Second, interventions based on diagnostic information may be more efficient. Rather than attempting to teach children all possible skills, investigators may concentrate on children's individual deficits, eliminating the need for lengthy, "generic" interventions. Finally, as discussed in subsequent sections, comprehensive assessments of children's skill deficits pave the way for a more direct test of the skill deficit hypothesis.

Unfortunately, such an approach to deficit assessment is not without its shortcomings. It is likely that members of any given sample of socially disadvantaged children, even those with identical peer problems (e.g., peer neglect vs. rejection), will exhibit differing skill deficit profiles, and require individualized interventions. From an implementation standpoint, this may be both impractical and also limiting in the sense that the generalizability often achieved with group designs will be diminished. Potential solutions may include grouping children according to the types of initial deficits they display, or designing a training curriculum capable of addressing each child's deficits, even if some children are required to "learn" skills they already know.

In addition to delineating potential diagnostic criteria, the research on children's skill deficits may also begin to provide the necessary instrumentation for subject selection and evaluation in social skill training. For example, the diversity and/or quality of children's social goals and strategies can be assessed by eliciting verbal responses to hypothetical (picture) peer situations. While these measures may be useful with grade-school children, reliance on verbal self-reports may be less appropriate for preschoolers. To date, both recognition (fixed-alternative responses) and enactive assessments (having children act out their responses with puppets and props) have been developed as alternatives, and the latter method has been shown to produce responses that are stable and predictive of preschoolers' peer competence (Mize & Ladd, 1984). Whether any of these measures that present children with peer situations are sufficiently varied or ecologically valid remains debatable. For social skill investigators, it may be important to identify situations that are frequently encountered or pose adjustment problems for the child (see Dodge & McClaskey, 1984).

It may also be feasible to supplement information gained from hypothetical situations with observations of children's social goals and strategies in actual peer situations (e.g., Krasnor, 1982; Lubin & Forbes, 1981; Sharp, 1983). As Krasnor and Rubin (1981) have suggested, this methodology is less subject to repsonse biases, such as social desirability, and provides information about what children actually do as opposed to what they think or intend to do. On the other hand, data such as these are highly dependent on the observer's inferences about the types of strategies children employ and their corresponding intentions. Rather than advocate one form of assessment over the other, it may be that both yield valuable diagnostic information. Whereas information from hypothetical methods may tap children's understanding and awareness of potential goals and strategies, observational assessments may reflect their ability to produce and act on this knowledge in actual social situations.

Techniques such as asking children to recount events observed in videotaped situations can be used to assess children's ability to recall social information (e.g., Dodge & Frame, 1982; Ince et al., 1980). As Dodge and Frame (1982) have demonstrated, both the form of social information presented (e.g., hostile vs. benevolent behavior), and the method for obtaining children's responses (e.g., recognition vs. recall tasks), can be varied as a means of diagnosing perceptual deficits. Investigators may also find the videotape methodology employed by Putallaz (1983), which emphasizes the child's interpretation (reconstruction) of social events occurring in analog situations useful for diagnosing deficits in perceptual accuracy. Measures based the slow motion and still-frame analyses used by Saarni (1984) might also be developed to assess the extent to which children monitor and adjust their expressive behaviors to conform with specific social norms and conventions in peer situations.

Other instruments and media may provide alternative avenues for assessing children's perceptual skills. Peery (1979) employed short stories or vignettes to assess preschooler's ability to interpret affective cues in specific situations. Gouze et al. (1983) employed a series of rapidly displayed cartoons to assess preschoolers' recall of social information, and also observed children's attention patterns during a puppet show to study selective information gathering and recall.

To document children's behavior toward peers, investigators have employed either direct observation or videorecording, and have relied on one of three major sampling techniques (see Altmann, 1974) to compile the behavior record: point-time (e.g., Oden & Asher, 1977), focal individual (e.g., Dodge, 1983; Gottman et al., 1975; Rubin & Daniels-Beirness, 1983), or scan sampling (Ladd, 1981, 1983). The level of analysis and range of codes used to document children's prosocial behaviors vary widely over studies, and thus limit meaningful comparisons. Efforts to identify deficits in prosocial behaviors are probably best guided by the strength of the evidence linking specific behaviors to problems in peer relations. Some of the most convincing findings in this regard come from recent attempts to pinpoint the behavioral antecedents of peer status (see Coie & Kupersmidt, 1983; Dodge, 1983).

Observation may also provide a means for assessing variation in children's play patterns. As has been demonstrated with grade-schoolers (e.g., Ladd, 1983), measures of the percent of time children spend in various peer contexts (e.g., with low- as opposed to high-status peers, older vs. younger companions) may provide information about the nature of children's current relationships, and the supportiveness of the contexts in which they are likely to implement new skills. Additional observational measures, such as those developed by Rubin and colleagues for preschool children (e.g., Rubin, 1982; Rubin & Daniels-Beirness, 1983), provide a method for assessing both the cognitive sophistication (e.g., functional, constructive) and social orientation (e.g., solitary, group) of children's play. This combination of codes has proven to be effective for discriminating (both concurrently and predictively) between popular and unpopular children and, therefore, may be of considerable diagnostic value with this age group.

The relevance of children's behavior, as they attempt to integrate themselves into ongoing peer activities, has been assessed primarily with observational methods. With grade-school children (Putallaz & Gottman, 1981), assessments have been conducted by videotaping children's attempts to join a simulated peer activity, and then coding their verbalizations into specific entry tactics (e.g., Dodge et al., 1983; Putallaz, 1983). A similar methodology has been employed with younger children, except that Putallaz (1983) also had adult judges rate the quality of their entry behaviors. Dodge et al. (1983) videorecorded entry strategies in both analog and free-play situations, and had adult coders note both the types of bids and the sequence of children's tactics. The value of the latter approach is underscored by the fact that Dodge et al. (1983) found some entry *sequences* to be more successful than others. It is conceivable that a similar methodology could be used to detect deficits in children's tactics for a variety of other peer situations.

Most of the research on children's responsiveness to peers has been designed to examine the relationships (e.g., reciprocity) between the types of behaviors children initiate and receive from peers (e.g., Benson & Gottman, 1975; Gottman et al., 1975; Masters & Furman, 1981). While these methods provide information about deficits in the frequency, symmetry, and source of children's social interactions, they are of less value for evaluating differences in children's *responsiveness* to peers' overtures. A measure implemented by Dodge (1983) with grade-school boys may be more useful for this purpose. From videorecordings of children's interactions, coders recorded both the subjects' roles (i.e., initiator or recipient) and durations of their interactions with peers. The results suggested that popular children more often "rewarded" peers' initiations by responding with positive behaviors and prolonging the length of the interaction.

Research suggesting methods for assessing children's affective deficits has been conducted largely with grade-school samples and, with one exception, focuses on self-report, paper-and-pencil measures. If it is the case that self-doubt or diminished confidence inhibits children's involvement with peers, or reduces their efforts to persist at solving social difficulties, then measures of these constructs such as the social subscale of the Perceived Competence Scale for Children (Harter, 1982) and the Children's Self-Efficacy Scale (Wheeler & Ladd, 1982), may be of considerable diagnostic value to social skill training investigators. Similarly, the peer acceptance subscale of the Children's Concerns Inventory (Buhrmester, 1982), which is comprised of questions about children's concerns related to making and keeping friends, may provide investigators with a useful diagnostic tool for assessing children's social anxiety. Finally, it may be advantageous to determine children's attributional dispositions concerning peer rejection prior to social skill training. Toward this end, Goetz and Dweck (1980) developed a questionnaire comprised of four vignettes, each of which requires that children articulate the likely reasons for potential rejection by peers. Causal attributions implied by the subject's responses are coded into mutually exclusive categories (e.g., subjects' incompetence, rejector's traits, chance event, etc.). Identification of the subjects' attributional style may help to identify those children who are vulnerable to "learned helplessness" in peer situations.

Assumption 2: Children Learn Social Skills From Social Skill Training

A second major premise in this field is that the skills needed for satisfactory peer relations can be learned, and that social skill training programs serve this function with socially disadvantaged children. Several issues are pertinent to investigators' efforts to test this assumption and, thus, will be considered prior to an examination of relevant empirical evidence.

Presumably, the purpose of social skill training is to teach children social skills that will, in turn, lead to improved peer relations. Skill learning them, can be seen as the primary objective of social skill training—an effect that must be achieved before secondary outcomes such as improved peer relations can be achieved. Measures designed to reflect progress in skill learning can be seen as process assessments since they are designed to provide evidence about factors that presumably mediate secondary outcomes.

The concept of skill learning has seldom been discussed in the literature, possibly because it has been viewed by researchers as intuitively obvious. Yet closer inspection of this concept suggests two possible meanings that may, in turn, imply differing approaches to assessment. First, skill learning can be defined as the acquisition of novel behaviors. This view would seem to follow from models of social skill training in which deficits are viewed as "absent behaviors." Secondly skill learning can be defined as changes in the sophistication or quality of children's existing behaviors, relative to some criterion or standard (e.g., competent peers). Such a definition follows from approaches to social skill training in which deficits are seen as "lags" in the child's competence or skill proficiency. Equipped with a definition of skill learning, investigators may proceed to the task of selecting measures that are capable of detecting the anticipated behavioral changes.

Documenting Skill Learning in Social Skill Training Research

Most investigators have relied on measures of behavior frequency or rate as a means of assessing children's skill learning in social skill interventions (see Table 15.2). The dominance of this approach suggests that most investigators tend to define children's skill deficits as behaviors that are absent or seldom used in peer

TABLE 15.2. Process assessment: Measures used to document skill learning in previous social skill training studies.

Implied definition of skill learning	Timing/type of assessments	Sample/exemplary studies
Skill acquisition	Pre-post, rate of peer interaction	Withdrawn preschoolers Gottman (1977) Keller & Carlson (1974) O'Connor (1969, 1972)
	Pre-post, frequency or percent of time spent in targeted behaviors	Withdrawn preschoolers Keller & Carlson (1974) Aggressive preschoolers Chittenden (1942) Zahavi & Asher (1978) Low-accepted grade-schoolers Gresham and Nagle (1980) LaGreca & Santogrossi (1980) Low-accepted, skill deficient grade-schoolers Ladd (1981) Low-accepted, skill deficient preadolescents Bierman & Furman (1984)
	Ongoing, rate of peer interaction	Adult-oriented preschoolers Allen et al. (1964)
	Ongoing frequency or percent of time spent in targeted behaviors	Withdrawn, aggressive preschoolers Hart et al. (1968) Low-accepted grade-schoolers Oden & Asher (1977) Low-accepted, skill-deficient preadolescents Bireman & Furman (1984) Handicapped preschoolers Strain, Shores & Kerr (1976) Handicapped grade-schoolers Cooke & Apolloni (1976)
Skill proficiency	Pre-post, level of friendship-making skill	Low-accepted grade-schoolers LaGreca & Santogrossi (1980)
	Post-test, level of skill knowledge	Low-accepted grade-schoolers LaGreca & Santogrossi (1980)
	Pre-post, level of self-efficacy, perceived social competence	Low-accepted, skill deficient preadolescents Bierman & Furman (1984)
	Ongoing level of behavioral assertiveness	Nonassertive grade-schoolers Bornstien, Bellack, & Hersen (1977)

interactions, and view skill acquisition as the goal of social skill training. The pervasiveness of this view is further evidenced by the fact that this approach to documenting skill learning cuts across both training paradigms and subject populations. For example, preschooler's interaction rates and/or behavior frequencies served as pretest and outcome measures in a series of interventions in which subjects watched films of peer models demonstrating various social behaviors (e.g., Gottman, 1977; Keller & Carlson, 1974; O'Connor, 1969, 1972). With the exception of the Gottman (1977) study, significant increments were found in children's interaction rates and use of trained behaviors with peers.

Change in behavior frequency or rate has also been the hallmark of skill learning in many operant-based skill training programs with both normal and handicapped children. For example, investigators who have designed programs based on contingent teacher attention (e.g., Allen et al., 1964; Hart, Reynolds, Baer, Brawley, & Harris, 1968), and adult prompts and reinforcement (e.g., Cooke & Apolloni, 1976; Strain, Shores, & Kerr, 1976), have employed measures of children's rates of peer interaction or frequencies of trained behaviors as outcome criteria, and often report substantial gains on these measures.

Gains in the frequency of specific behaviors have also been sought by investigators employing cognitive-social learning methods with preschool, grade-school, and preadolescent children. Two investigators found that training increased the frequency of targeted skills (Bierman & Furman, 1984; Ladd, 1981), and two others reported a significant decline in negative behaviors (Chittenden, 1942; Gresham & Nagle, 1980). La Greca and Santogrossi (1980), in contrast, found increased rates of peer interaction following training, but no change in the class of behaviors trained (prosocial skills). Compared to its counterparts, the Bierman and Furman (1984) study was unique in that a multimethod approach was used to assess the trained skills, including observations of the frequency with which children used specific conversational skills in both a natural context (the lunchroom), and semistructured task situations (e.g., talk sessions, dyadic interview).

Assessments designed to measure change in skill proficiency are far less common in the social skill training literature, but perhaps no less important for understanding an intervention's effects on children's skill training. Bornstein, Bellack, and Hersen (1977) implemented an intervention aimed at skills judged to be deficient in the subjects' repertoires, and terminated the program only after the children demonstrated a pre-established level of skill proficiency. Blind ratings by judges were also used to assess the level of skill mastery achieved by subjects as demonstrated in role-play situations. Using proficiency-related measures to document children's skill learning, LaGreca and Santogrossi (1980) found that trained subjects, as compared to controls, demonstrated greater skill knowledge on a video recognition task, and were rated as more competent on a make-a-friend role-play measure. Similarly, Bierman and Furman (1984) employed two measures designed to assess posttraining changes in the quality of children's perceived social competence.

Efforts to document skill learning have been restricted not only by a narrow definition of skill learning, but also by the limited number of skill domains within which investigators have looked for behavior change. With the exception of the skill knowledge and perception measures used in recent studies (Bierman & Furman, 1984; LaGreca & Santogrossi, 1980), nearly all of the process assessments used in past interventions have been designed to reflect change in children's overt behaviors toward peers.

Assuming that interpersonal skillfulness is multifaceted, as has been suggested in recent models of social skill training (e.g., Ladd & Mize, 1983), it would seem necessary to assess children's progress in each of the domains that underlie competence in peer relations. Unfortunately, pinpointing skill domains for training and asssessment is a difficult task since research on the type of skills children need to successfully negotiate and maintain peer relationships is far from complete. One solution to this dilemma is for researchers to rely on theoretical models that explicate the requisite skills for peer competence as a basis for their training curricula and evaluations. Both diagnostic (deficit) and process (skill learning) assessments as well as skill training can then be geared toward specific skill domains. For example, Ladd and Mize (1983) proposed a model of skill training in which children's skill knowledge, their ability to translate skill knowledge into competent performance, and their proclivity to monitor, adjust, and generalize skill knowledge and performance, are seen as essential to developing and maintaining positive peer relationships. Were such a model to be used as the basis of a social skill training program, many of the measures found in Table 15.2 might be considered both as potential diagnostic tools for identifying skill deficits, and as process assessments for documenting skill learning in these respective domains (e.g., deficits and corresponding gains in skill knowledge might be assessed with measures of children's goals and strategies for peer situations).

A final issue to be considered in relation to process assessment is the timing of these evaluations. In addition to assessing behavior change at the conclusion of skill training, as has typically been the case in past research, it may be beneficial to conduct process assessments during the course of the intervention as well. Such assessments have the advantage of increasing the temporal proximity between the training manipulations and assessments and, thus, provide the most direct evidence concerning the impact of training on behavior. This may be especially helpful for understanding the effects of specific procedures, especially when the intervention consists of multiple manipulations or components. Moreover, assessments conducted in this manner might enable investigators to monitor subjects' rate of change in specific domains or progress relative to training partners.

Although commonly employed in small *n* studies, investigators using group designs have seldom conducted process assessments during the course of intervention, and those who have report mixed findings. Oden and Asher (1977) monitored changes in children's prosocial behaviors during training, but did not find differences between the trained children and their counterparts in a peer pairing condition. Data from ongoing process assessments implemented during a recent intervention by Bierman and Furman (1984) were separately analyzed and reported by Bierman (in press). In this case, children in a conversational skills training condition were assessed at two points during the intervention (i.e., in sixth and tenth sessions), and compared to peers in a control group. Results indicated that while the trained children increased significantly over sessions in their use of trained conversational skills, their counterparts in a control group did not change.

Assumption 3: The Skill Learning that Occurs in Social Skill Training Leads to Improved Peer Relations

Until recently, measures of children's social behavior (e.g., rate of interaction) often served as both an index of peer disorders (e.g., social isolation) and the criteria for evaluating the effects of intervention. The trend in contemporary social skill training research, however, has been to supplement behavioral indices with measures that reflect the quality of children's peer relations. Sociometric assessment, typically measures of peer acceptance and friendship, have been increasingly used both as criteria for subject selection and evaluation.

There are at least two advantages to incorporating measures of peer status into skill-based interventions. First, when used in conjunction with skill assessments, these measures may be used to identify children who are both in need of assistance with peer relations, and lacking in the requisite social skills (see Ladd, 1984). Second, and perhaps more relevant to the issue at hand, is the advantage of employing sociometric measures as outcome criteria in social skill interventions. In addition to documenting change in children's social skills (process assessment), efforts to assess the effects of intervention on children's peer relations (outcome assessment) promise to shed light on the hypothesis that skill learning leads to improvements in peer relations.

Progress in Peer Relations as a Function of Skill Learning

Interventions that include assessments of children's skill learning and peer relations are few in number, and evidence bearing on the relationship between these variables is mixed. Some confusion concerning this issue arises from seemingly nebulous findings concerning the impact of social skill training on skill learning. For example, a skill training intervention conducted by Oden and Asher (1977) failed to yield evidence of behavior change even though subjects showed significant short- and long-term gains in peer status. Although changes in children's behavior and peer status were reported for a similar intervention conducted by Gresham and Nagle (1980), the training, which was designed to foster prosocial behaviors, had as much of an impact on children's negative as positive interactions. In another study, LaGreca and Santogrossi (1980) found that training in prosocial skills increased children's rate of interaction but had little effect on their positive behaviors with peers. Similarly, Siperstein and Gale (1983) provided learning-disabled children with training in prosocial skills and found significant gains in "independent" behaviors rather than positive peer interactions.

Subjects did, however, evidence gains on a friendship measure. Findings such as these make it difficult for investigators to demonstrate a correspondence between skill training and skill learning, and this, in turn, limits potential inferences concerning the relationship between skill learning and the quality of children's peer relations.

Further uncertainty is created by results indicating that behavioral changes are not always accompanied by improvements in peer relations. Change in peer status was not observed in the LaGreca and Santogrossi (1980) investigation, perhaps because the training increased children's rate of interaction rather than their expertise at prosocial relationship-enhancing behaviors. However, the same explanation does not adequately account for the findings of Bierman and Furman (1984). These investigators found that, although training in conversational skills did result in the anticipated behavioral gains, these increments did not lead to lasting changes in children's peer relations. When comparing findings, however, it is important to note that Bierman and Furman's subjects were somewhat older (preadolescents) than those found in the majority of social skill training studies.

The preceding social skill training procedures can be distinguished from those that produce change in relevant social skills as well as children's peer relations. Ladd (1981) found that, compared to controls, children trained in three prosocial communication skills utilized two of the three skills more often in their interactions with peers. Furthermore, these behavioral gains were accompanied by significantly higher levels of peer acceptance at posttest and follow-up. Lasting gains in skill learning and peer acceptance were also reported by Bierman and Furman (1984) for a program that combined training in conversational skills with cooperatively structured experiences with peers. These findings led Bierman and Furman to conclude that, without a receptive and facilitative peer environment, skill learning alone may not lead to improved peer relations.

As Bierman (1984) recently observed, variations in the design and methods of past social skill training studies may account for some of the aforementioned inconsistencies. Several factors may account for the inability, on the part of some researchers, to demonstrate a correspondence between their training curriculum and its effects on children's social behaviors. In the majority of studies where investigators have failed to find behavioral change, or have found gains in seemingly irrelevant behaviors, sociometric criteria have been used as the sole criteria for subject selection. Because behavioral assessments have rarely been used for subject selection purposes, it is possible that the subjects participating in these interventions were not deficient in the trained skills and, therefore, not likely to benefit from training in these behaviors. Alternatively, in the Ladd (1981) and Bierman and Furman (1984) studies, both of which provide evidence of gains in the trained behaviors and peer status, only those children who received low scores on both behavioral and sociometric measures were selected for training.

Other factors, such as the types of skills trained and the measures used to document behavior change, may also account for the inconsistent findings. In general, evidence suggesting a link between gains in skill learning and peer relations has been lacking in studies where the skills trained are numerous and diverse, as opposed to few in number and homogeneous in content. For example, Oden and Asher (1977) taught children several concepts that exemplified a range of specific prosocial behaviors (e.g., cooperation). Gresham and Nagle (1980) expanded this curriculum to include a variety of other friendship-making and prosocial behaviors. The content and range of skills taught by LaGreca and Santogrossi (1980) were equally broad and numerous. In contrast, data that do suggest a relationship between gains in skill learning and peer relations tend to come from studies where investigators have trained a small number of verbal communication skills, such as asking questions and offering suggestions (Ladd, 1981), or self-expression and leadership skills (Bierman & Furman, 1984).

Perhaps another reason why the latter studies have provided more convincing evidence of behavior change is that the process assessments used in these investigations corresponded closely to the trained skills. In many studies (e.g., Gresham & Nagle, 1980, LaGreca & Santogrossi, 1980; Oden & Asher, 1977), investigators relied on rather global assessments of behavior change as a means of documenting change in skill learning (e.g., "positive" social behaviors) and, consequently may have failed to detect actual training effects.

Also pertinent to this assumption is the possibility that differences in training methods account for variation in children's skill learning and success in peer relations. Moreover, some of the skills children have been taught may not be conducive to progress in peer relations. Because these factors and their potential relationship to training outcomes received considerable attention in recent literature (e.g., Ladd, 1984; Ladd & Asher, 1985; Ladd & Mize, 1983), further consideration will not be devoted to this topic.

Perhaps the most direct and convincing evidence of the effects of social skill training on children's social skills and peer relations comes from an expanded analysis of the Bierman and Furman (1984) data, as reported by Bierman (1984). Unlike most investigators who have mapped children's progress in terms of post-training differences in peer behavior and relationships, Bierman looked for improvements in children's conversational skills during the course of training, and explored the relationship between these process assessments and children's performance on several outcome measures, including classroom peer status. These analyses revealed that, unlike children in a peer experience condition, subjects who received both skill training and peer experience made significant gains in conversational skills. Moreover, significant partial correlations, adjusted for pretest, were found between the trained children's gains on this process measure and their scores on various outcome criteria, including peer status.

To conclude, recent innovations in assessment promise to yield further insights into the effects of social skill training with children. In particular, efforts to assure that children who receive social skill training do, in fact, lack the skills targeted for change, may help to clarify whether skill learning occurs and is of benefit to the subject. Perhaps the most convincing evidence of this effect can be obtained by implementing process assessments throughout the intervention, and by determining whether the findings are suggestive of increments in skill acquisition or proficiency.

Once investigators can demonstrate that social skill training leads to behavior change, they may begin to explore the relationship between skill learning and children's status in peer relations. Ultimately, data such as these may begin to expand our understanding of the potential or likely benefits that social skill training may provide for children with problematic peer relations.

References

Allen, K. E., Hart, B., Buell, J. S., Harris, F. R., & Wolfe, M. A. (1964). Effects of social reinforcement on isolate behavior of a nursery school child. *Child Development, 35*, 511-518.

Allport, G. W. (1954). *The nature of prejudice*. Cambridge, MA: Addison-Wesley.

Altman, J. (1974). Observational study of behavior: Sampling methods. *Behavior, 49*, 227-267.

Asher, S. R., & Renshaw, P. D. (1981). Children without friends: Social knowledge and social skill training. In S. R. Asher & J. M. Gottman (Eds.), *The development of children's friendships* (pp. 273-296). New York: Cambridge University Press.

Benson, C. S., & Gottman, J. M. (1975). *Children's popularity and peer social interaction*. Unpublished manuscript, Indiana University, Bloomington, IN.

Bierman, K. L. (in press). Process of change during social skills training with preadolescents and its relationship to treatment outcome. *Child Development*.

Bierman, K. L., & Furman, W. (1984). The effects of social skills training and peer involvement on the social adjustment of preadolescents. *Child Development, 55*, 151-162.

Bonney, M. E. (1971). Assessment of efforts to aid socially isolated elementary school pupils. *Journal of Educational Research, 64*, 359-364.

Bornstein, M. R., Bellack, A. S., & Hersen, M. (1977). Social skills training for unassertive children: A multiple baseline analysis. *Journal of Applied Behavior Analysis, 10*, 183-195.

Buhrmester, D. (1982). *Children's concerns inventory manual*. (Available from Duane Buhrmester, Department of Psychology, UCLA, Los Angeles, CA)

Chittenden, M. F. (1942). An experimental study in measuring and modifying assertive behavior in young children. *Monographs of the Society for Research in Child Development, 7*, No. 1 (Serial No. 31).

Coie, J. D., & Kupersmidt, J. B. (1983). A behavioral analysis of emerging social status in boys' groups. *Child Development, 54*, 1400-1416.

Cooke, T. P., & Apolloni, T. (1976). Developing positive social-emotional behaviors: A study of training and generalization effects. *Journal of Applied Behavior Analysis, 9*, 64-78.

Curran, J. P. (1979). Social skills: Methodological issues and future directions. In S. S. Bellack & M. Hersen (Eds.), *Research and practice in social skills training*. New York: Plenum Press.

Dodge, K. A. (1980). Social cognition and children's aggressive behavior. *Child Development, 51*, 162-170.

Dodge, K. A. (1983). Behavioral antecedents of peer social status. *Child Development, 54*, 1386-1399.

Dodge, K. A., & Frame, C. L. (1982). Social cognitive biases and deficits in aggressive boys. *Child Development, 53*, 620-635.

Dodge, K. A., & McClaskey, C. L. (1984, April). A situational approach to the assessment of social competence in children. In G. W. Ladd (Chair), *From preschool to high school: Are children's interpersonal goals and strategies predictive of their social competence?* Symposium conducted at the annual convention of the American Educational Research Association, New Orleans, LA.

Dodge, K. A., & Newman, J. P. (1981). Biased decision-making processes in aggressive boys. *Journal of Abnormal Psychology, 90,* 375-379.

Dodge, K. A., Schlundt, D. C., Schocken, I., & Delugah, J. D. (1983). Social competence and children's sociometric status: The role of peer group entry strategies. *Merrill-Palmer Quarterly, 29,* 309-336.

Goetz, T. E., & Dweck, C. S. (1980). Learned helplessness in social situations. *Journal of Personality and Social Psychology, 39,* 246-255.

Gottman, J. M. (1977). The effects of a modeling film on social isolation in preschool children.: A methodological investigation. *Journal of Abnormal Child Psychology, 5,* 69-78.

Gottman, J. M., Gonso, J., & Rasmussen, B. (1975). Social interaction, social competence, and friendship in children. *Child Development, 46,* 709-718.

Gouze, K., Gordon, L., & Rayias, M. (1983, April). *Information processing correlates of aggression: A look at attention and memory.* Paper presented at the biennial meeting of the Society for Research in Child Development, Detroit, MI.

Gresham, F. M., & Nagle, R. J. (1980). Social skills training with children: Responsiveness to modeling and coaching as a function of peer orientation. *Journal of Consulting and Clinical Psychology, 18,* 718-729.

Hart, B. M., Reynolds, N. J., Baer, D. M., Brawley, E. R., & Harris, F. R. (1968). Effect of contingent and non-contingent social reinforcement on the cooperative play of a preschool child. *Journal of Applied Behavior Analysis, 1,* 73-76.

Harter, S. (1982). The perceived competence scale for children. *Child Development, 53,* 87-97.

Hartup, W. W., Glazer, J. A., & Charlesworth, R. (1967). Peer reinforcement and sociometric status. *Child Development, 38,* 1017-1024.

Ince, R., Meese, L. A., Stollack, G. E., & Smith, H. C. (1980, September). *Person perception and psychosocial competence in children.* Paper presented at the annual meeting of the American Psychological Association, Montreal, Canada.

Keller, M. F., & Carlson, P. M. (1974). The use of symbolic modeling to promote social skills in preschool children with low levels of social responsiveness. *Child Development, 45,* 912-919.

Koch, H. L. (1933). Popularity among preschool children: Some related factors and a technique for its measurement. *Child Development, 4,* 164-175.

Koch, H. L. (1935). The modification of unsocialness in preschool children. *Psychology Bulletin, 32,* 700-701.

Kohlberg, L., LaCrosse, J., & Ricks, D. (1972). The predictability of adult mental health from childhood behavior. In B. Wolman (Ed.), *Manual of child psychopathology* (pp. 1217-1283). New York: McGraw-Hill.

Krasnor, L. R. (1982). An observational study of social problem solving in young children. In K. H. Rubin & H. S. Ross (Eds.), *Peer relationships and social skills in childhood* (pp. 113-132). New York: Springer-Verlag.

Krasnor, L. S., & Rubin, K. H. (1981). The assessment of social problem solving skills in young children. In T. Merluzzi, C. Glass, & M. Genest (Eds.), *Cognitive Assessment* (pp. 452-476). New York: Guilford Press.

Ladd, G. (1983). Social networks of popular, average, and rejected children in school settings. *Merrill-Palmer Quarterly, 29,* 283-307.

Ladd, G. (1984). Social skill training with children: Issues in research and practice. *Clinical Psychology Review, 4,* 317-337.

Ladd, G. W. (1981). Effectiveness of a social learning method for enhancing children's social interaction and peer acceptance. *Child Development, 52,* 171-178.

Ladd, G. W., & Asher, S. R. (1985). Social skill training and children's peer relations. In L. L'Abate & M. Milan (Eds.), *Handbook of Social Skills Training and Research* (pp. 219-244). New York: Wiley.

Ladd, G. W., & Mize, J. (1983). A cognitive-social learning model of social skill training. *Psychological Review, 90,* 127-157.

Ladd, G. W., & Oden, S. (1979). The relationship between peer acceptance and children's ideas about helpfulness. *Child Development, 50,* 402-408.

LaGreca, A. M., & Santogrossi, D. A. (1980). Social skills training with elementary school students: A behavioral group approach. *Journal of Consulting and Clinical Psychology, 48,* 220-227.

Lilly, M. S. (1971). Improving social acceptance of low sociometric status, low achieving students. *Exceptional Children, 37,* 341-347.

Lubin, D., & Forbes, D. (1981, April). *The development of applied strategies in children's peer interactions.* Paper presented at the biennial meeting of the Society for Research in Child Development, Boston, MA.

Masters, J. C., & Furman, W. (1981). Popularity, individual friendship selection, and specific peer interaction among children. *Developmental Psychology, 17,* 344-350.

Mize, J., & Ladd, G. W. (1984, April). Preschool children's goal and strategy knowledge: A comparison of picture-story and enactive assessment. In G. W. Ladd (Chair), *From preschool to high school: Are children's interpersonal goals and strategies predictive of their social competence?* Symposium conducted at the annual meeting of the American Educational Research Association, New Orleans, LA.

Moore, S. G., & Updegraff, R. (1964). Sociometric status of preschool children as related to age, sex, nurturance-giving, and dependence. *Child Development, 35,* 519-524.

Moreno, J. L. (1934). *Who shall survive?: A new approach to the problem of human inter-relations.* Washington, DC: Nervous and Mental Disease Publishing.

Northway, M. L. (1944). Outsiders: A study of the personality patterns of children least acceptable to their agemates. *Sociometry, 7,* 10-25.

O'Connor, R. D. (1969). Modification of social withdrawal through symbolic modeling. *Journal of Applied Behavior Analysis, 2,* 15-22.

O'Connor, R. D. (1972). Relative efficacy of modeling, shaping, and the combined procedures for modification of social withdrawal. *Journal of Abnormal Psychology, 79,* 327-334.

Oden, S. L., & Asher, S. R. (1977). Coaching children in social skills for friendship making. *Child Development, 48,* 495-506.

Olson, S. L., Johnson, J., Belleau, K., Parks, J., & Barrett, E. (1983, April). *Social competence in preschool children: Interrelations with sociometric status, social problem solving, and impulsivity.* Paper presented at the biennial meeting of the Society for Research in Child Development, Detroit, MI.

Peery, J. C. (1979). Popular, amiable, isolated, rejected: A reconceptualization of sociometric status in preschool children. *Child Development, 50,* 1231-1234.

Putallaz, M. (1983). Predicting children's sociometric status from their behavior. *Child Development, 54,* 1417-1426.

Putallaz, M., & Gottman, J. M. (1981). An interactional model of children's entry into peer groups. *Child Development, 52*, 986-994.

Renshaw, P. D., & Asher, S. R. (1983). Children's goals and strategies for social interaction. *Merrill-Palmer Quarterly, 29*, 353-374.

Rubin, K. H. (1982). Non-social play in preschoolers: Necessarily evil? *Child Development, 53*, 651-657.

Rubin, K. H., & Daniels-Beirness, T. (1983). Concurrent and predictive correlates of sociometric status in kindergarten and grade one children. *Merrill-Palmer Quarterly, 29*, 337-352.

Rubin, K. H., Daniels-Beirness, T., & Hayvren, M. (1982). Social and social-cognitive correlates of sociometric status in preschool and kindergarten children. *Canadian Journal of Behavioral Science, 14*, 338-349.

Saarni, C. (1984). An observational study of children's attempts to monitor their expressive behavior. *Child Development, 55*, 1504-1513.

Sharp, K. C. (1981). Impact of interpersonal problem-solving training on preschooler's social competency. *Journal of Applied Developmental Psychology, 2*, 129-143.

Sharp, K. C. (1983, April). *Quantity or quality of strategies: Which indicates competency in social problem solving?* Paper presented at the biennial meeting of the Society for Research in Child Development, Detroit, MI.

Siperstein, G. N., & Gale, M. E. (1983, April). *Improving peer relationships of rejected children.* Paper presented at the biennial meeting of the Society for Research in Child Development, Detroit, MI.

Snyder, M. (1974). Self-monitoring of expressive behavior. *Journal of Personality and Social Psychology, 30*, 526-537.

Spivack, G., & Shure, M. B. (1974). *Social adjustment of young children: A cognitive approach to solving real-life problems.* San Francisco: Jossey-Bass.

Strain, P. S., Shores, R. E., & Kerr, M. M. (1976). An experimental analysis of "spillover" effects on the social interaction of behaviorally handicapped preschool children. *Journal of Applied Behavior Analysis, 9*, 31-40.

Taylor, A. R., & Asher, S. R. (1984, April). Children's interpersonal goals in game situations. In G. W. Ladd (Chair), *From preschool to high school: Are children's interpersonal goals and strategies predictive of their social competence?* Symposium conducted at the annual meeting of the American Educational Research Association, New Orleans, LA.

Vosk, B., Forehand, R., Parker, J. B., & Rickard, K. (1982). A multimethod comparison of popular and unpopular children. *Developmental Psychology, 18*, 571-575.

Weissberg, R. P., Gesten, E. L., Rapkin, B. D., Cowen, E. L., Davidson, E., Flores de Apodaca, R., & McKim, B. J. (1981). Evaluation of a social-problem-solving training program for suburban and inner-city third grade children. *Journal of Consulting and Clinical Psychology, 49*, 251-261.

Wheeler, V. A., & Ladd, G. W. (1982). Assessment of children's self-efficacy for social interactions with peers. *Developmental Psychology, 18*, 795-805.

Zahavi, S., & Asher, S. R. (1978). The effect of verbal instructions on preschool children's aggressive behavior. *Journal of School Psychology, 16*, 146-153.

Author Index

Subject Index